The History of BBC Broadcasting in Scotland, 1923–1983

BBC Broadcasting House, Glasgow. Copyright © BBC (courtesy of BBC Scotland)

The History of BBC Broadcasting in Scotland, 1923–1983

W.H. McDOWELL

EDINBURGH UNIVERSITY PRESS

Edinburgh University Press
22 George Square, Edinburgh

Typeset in Linotron Ehrhardt
by Nene Phototypesetters Ltd,
Northampton, and
printed in Great Britain by
The University Press, Cambridge

A CIP record for this book is
available from the British Library.

ISBN 0 7486 0376 X

The publisher acknowledges
subsidy from the Scottish Arts
Council towards the publication
of this book.

Contents

List of Figures and Tables

Preface

This study is an institutional history of the BBC which focuses primarily on the history and development of BBC public service broadcasting in Scotland. It covers the period from the founding of the British Broadcasting Company in 1922 and the establishment of the first local stations in Scotland in the early 1920s, through to the early 1980s when the BBC provided two network television channels with Scottish opt-out programmes, and a national radio channel for Scotland, supplemented by area and community radio stations as well as network radio services. Scottish developments in broadcasting have been placed within the wider UK context because of the interrelationship between both, particularly as Scotland represents only one of the BBC's Regions, albeit defined as a 'national Region'. This perspective is used in order to highlight how BBC Scottish broadcasting has evolved during this period as part of an essentially centralised broadcasting organisation.

This history of Scottish broadcasting is also a history of BBC Regional broadcasting, not least because many of the issues of concern to Scottish broadcasting were also of concern to other BBC Regions. Moreover, it is also concerned with the relationship between London and the Regions. The approach adopted in this study is chronological: an attempt has been made to subdivide the period into distinct phases to coincide with significant events in the history of broadcasting, while not neglecting key themes such as growth, centralisation and competition which persist over longish periods of time. The present study covers both programme policy and programme content, although these are not regarded as two distinct aspects of broadcasting because the nature of an organisation and the policies which it pursues obviously influence in varying degrees the programme output. With such a large volume of programme output, reference to individual programmes has had to be selective and has tended to focus on those which were landmarks in the development of ideas or in the treatment of issues. Although Scotland benefited from access to network programmes, the strength of BBC programme output did owe much to the input of ideas from the Regions. In examining Scottish broadcasting, several points need to be borne in mind. For example, what makes a programme item recognisably Scottish? Will an item be recognisably Scottish if it focuses on events in a Scottish location or context, or is treatment of an issue the determining factor as to what can be regarded as essentially Scottish? This history also covers the work of policy-makers in the BBC, and, in this, the chronology of developments is given due emphasis because office-holders inherit situations which are governed by decisions taken by their predecessors. Also, this chronological account helps to emphasise how various issues in broadcasting can both gain and lose importance over time.

This historical account of BBC broadcasting in Scotland seeks to analyse, among other things, the interaction between organisational structure, policy-making, programme output and the wider institutional constraints. It focuses on the institutional links between BBC Scotland and the BBC centrally; the implications of financial policy for the provision of BBC programme services in Scotland; the various technical, financial and social aspects governing the geographical extension of BBC broadcasting services in Scotland; and the varied competitive pressures which have affected radio and television programme services in Scotland.

With very little published material on broadcasting in Scotland, and with no standard work on the BBC in Scotland to provide a regional counterpart to Asa Briggs' work on the history of BBC UK broadcasting, the historical research which culminated in the present study was a venture into largely uncharted territory. The present study is an extension and further development of work on postwar Scottish broadcasting which had previously been submitted for a research degree at the University of Edinburgh. The present history covers the earlier period in more detail and brings the historical account forward into the 1980s when interesting developments were taking place in anticipation of a significant expansion in the number of programme services available to the audience in Scotland. It is much more difficult to cover more recent broadcasting history without access to the relevant unpublished material and also because problems can occur in trying to provide a proper perspective on more recent events. The research draws upon a wide range of source material including BBC written archival material, other unpublished papers, taped interviews, official publications, BBC reference source material, books, pamphlets, and journal and newspaper articles.

Among the numerous individuals consulted and organisations contacted since 1985 in connection with my original research project on the postwar history of the BBC in Scotland, a project which has provided a useful basis for the present study, I wish to thank once again the following individuals in particular for their advice on various aspects of the research: Lord Briggs (the BBC's official historian); John Gray (Chief Assistant, Radio, at BBC Scotland until 1978); Professor Alastair Hetherington (Controller of BBC Scotland, 1976 to 1978); David Pat Walker (Assistant Controller of BBC Scotland until 1984); Dr George Bruce (BBC Arts Producer in Scotland, 1956 to 1970); Andrew Stewart (Controller of BBC Scotland, 1957 to 1967); Professor Alan Thompson (BBC National Governor for Scotland and member of the BBC Board of Governors, 1976 to 1979); Jacqueline Kavanagh (Written Archives Officer) and her staff at the BBC's Written Archives Centre; Miss Pat Spencer (BBC History of Broadcasting Unit); Douglas Stewart (BBC Information Officer for Scotland, 1954 to 1972); Dr Robert McIntyre (President of the Scottish National Party, 1958 to 1980); David Hutchison (Senior Lecturer in Communication Studies at Glasgow College of Technology, now known as Glasgow Polytechnic); John McCormick (former Secretary and Head of Information at BBC Scotland, former Secretary to the BBC, and currently Controller of BBC Scotland); Ian Phillips (BBC Director of Finance); and Roger Baxter (BBC Head of Central Finance Services). Finally, I must again thank John Simpson and David McCrone of the University of Edinburgh who supervised the doctoral thesis on which this present study was to some extent based.

W.H. McDOWELL
Edinburgh, October 1991

Foreword

This is the first published history of broadcasting in Scotland and it is based on an immense amount of painstaking work inside and outside BBC archives. It tells a story that deserves to be told. It also deals with basic underlying issues, some of which have not changed, however great the changes in technology and in the structures of public service broadcasting. It is a contribution to the history of Scotland as well as to the history of the BBC.

Unfortunately the author has not had full access to BBC archives, and the archives themselves are not in place or catalogued for the last years in his volume – some of the most interesting and important years in the story. Oral interviews are indispensable, and the author has made the most of them. So, too, are the programmes themselves, when they have survived in recorded form. They are, after all, the *rationale* of broadcasting. Yet neither kind of evidence is a substitute for documents; and it is a matter of public importance that the BBC, hard-pressed financially, shall maintain, extend and catalogue its unique collection of documentary archives. It is equally a matter of public importance that scholars shall have access to them.

A standard narrative history like this should encourage research and writing by other historians and, what is equally valuable, by people who have participated directly in broadcasting. There is an increasing interest in the history of the media, which plays such a central part in our lives; and this history, among the other purposes that it will fulfil, will provide a long needed framework within which others can pursue more detailed studies. There are different possible approaches. That is one of the many fascinations of broadcasting history.

I am glad to write this foreword. I was one of the examiners of the university thesis on which it was based. I told the author then that I hoped that his work would be published as soon as possible. He has achieved this in record time, an achievement in itself.

Asa Briggs

Acknowledgements

The author would like to thank the following for their kind permission to reproduce illustrations and extracts from copyright material: BBC Engineering Information Department for the reproduction of maps in figures A4.1 to A4.7; BBC Scotland for the reproduction of an illustration of Broadcasting House, Glasgow; BBC Written Archives Centre for extracts from BBC unpublished papers, BBC *Handbooks*, *Radio Times* and *The Listener*; the *Herald* for the cover illustration; the Church of Scotland for an extract from the submission of the Church and Nation Committee to the Annan Committee on Broadcasting; HarperCollins for an extract from *A Seamless Robe: Broadcasting – Philosophy and Practice* by Charles Curran; the Macmillan Press for an extract from *The BBC: Public Institution and Private World* by Tom Burns; extracts from *The History of Broadcasting in the United Kingdom*, vol. 4: *Sound and Vision* (1979) by Asa Briggs by permission of Oxford University Press; Peters, Fraser and Dunlop for material from *Into the Wind* by J.C.W. Reith; the Saltire Society for an extract from the pamphlet *Broadcasting: Recommendations of the Saltire Society's Broadcasting Committee*; and the Scottish Arts Council for an extract from the Council's submission to the Annan Committee on Broadcasting.

Abbreviations

ABC	Associated Broadcasting Company
ABS	Association of Broadcasting Staff
AM	Amplitude modulation
AR	Audience research
ATV	Associated Television
BBC	British Broadcasting Corporation
BCS	Broadcasting Council for Scotland
BH	Broadcasting House
BREMA	British Radio Equipment Manufacturers' Association
DBS	Direct Broadcasting by Satellite
EBU	European Broadcasting Union
FM	Frequency modulation
GAC	General Advisory Council
GFP	General Forces Programme
HDTV	High-definition television
HF	High frequency
HIDB	Highlands and Islands Development Board
IBA	Independent Broadcasting Authority
ILR	Independent Local Radio
IPPA	Independent Programme Producers' Association
ITA	Independent Television Authority
ITV	Independent Television
Kw	Kilowatts
LBA	Local Broadcasting Authority
LF	Low frequency
MF	Medium frequency
NTC	National Television Council
NTSC	National Television System Committee
OB	Outside broadcast
OBA	Open Broadcasting Authority
PAL	Phase Alternation Line
PCM	Pulse code modulation
PMG	Postmaster-General

PTA	Popular Television Association
SAC	Scottish Advisory Council
SB	Simultaneous broadcast
SBCS	School Broadcasting Council for Scotland
SECAM	Séquentiel Couleur à Mémoire
SHF	Super-high frequency
SHS	Scottish Home Service
SNP	Scottish National Party
SRO	Scottish Record Office
SSO	Scottish Symphony Orchestra
STUC	Scottish Trades Union Congress
STV	Scottish Television
TAC	Television Advisory Committee
TAM	Television Audience Measurement
TV-am	ITV contractor for breakfast television
UHF	Ultra high frequency
VCR	Video cassette recorder
VHF	Very high frequency
WAC	Written Archives Centre

Part One

The formative years of broadcasting, 1922–45

The BBC's early history and constitutional position, 1922–6

Wireless enthusiasts knew a significant amount about the principles of radio telephony prior to the founding of the BBC in 1922. Publications such as *Popular Wireless* helped disseminate knowledge, and the First World War assisted these amateurs, who built their own receivers, by promoting technical work connected with wireless communications, not least the design and manufacture of the thermionic valve which had first been patented in 1904 by Professor J.A. Fleming. With wireless societies anxious to hear the transmission of speech and music, this was a technical advance which offered a convergence of scientific and commercial possibilities. However, the Post Office favoured research into wireless transmissions for scientific purposes rather than as a means of distributing public entertainment. Post Office control over broadcasting derived from the 1869 Telegraph Act which conferred power over telegraphs, and from the Wireless Telegraphy Act of 1904 which extended controls to cover wireless telephony.

In 1919 the Marconi Company began to test the reception of speech over long distances. This was followed on 23 February 1920 by experiments in radio telephony, designed to ascertain public interest in wireless, and begun by the Marconi Company at its Chelmsford station for a limited period. In January 1922 the Post Office allowed Marconi to transmit speech and music for a duration of thirty minutes each week from the station at Writtle, near Chelmsford. On 14 February, regular transmissions began from station 2MT which was located in a hut at the Marconi field station at Writtle. These transmissions, which served to increase demand for a regular broadcasting service, continued until January 1923. This chapter traces the early history of the BBC from its founding as a company in 1922, up until the dissolution of that company on 31 December 1926, and its reconstitution as a public corporation on 1 January 1927. These years demonstrated that wireless (i.e. telephony without wires) could be transformed from a technical invention of interest to enthusiastic amateurs, into a workable broadcasting system operated by the BBC.

It was on 4 May 1922 that Mr F.G. Kellaway, the Postmaster-General (PMG), announced in the House of Commons that, after having received several proposals for permission to open transmitting stations, he had decided, on the advice of the Wireless sub-committee of the Imperial Communications Committee, to permit the establishment of a few broadcasting stations.[1] For this purpose, the country would be divided into areas which would include Glasgow or Edinburgh, and Aberdeen. Permission to open these stations was only to be granted to British firms who were genuine manufacturers of wireless apparatus. The PMG said that he had asked all the firms who had applied to open stations to come together at the Post Office to cooperate so that 'an efficient service may be rendered and that there may be no danger of monopoly and that each service shall not be interfering with the efficient working of the other'.[2] A committee of manufacturers was appointed after a conference attended by representatives of twenty-four manufacturers of wireless equipment had been held on 18 May to agree on an acceptable scheme. At that time, there was no public demand for broadcasting. Nevertheless, six of the principal British manufacturers of wireless apparatus, who were fascinated by the popularity of broadcasting in the United States where there were over 200 radio stations by 1922, decided to approach the Post Office to seek permission to operate a broadcasting service in Britain, as they were confident that it was a course of action worth pursuing. Amateur experimenters were also, it must be said, in favour of the introduction of a broadcasting service. The six manufacturers were: Marconi Wireless Telegraph Company; Metropolitan-Vickers; Radio Communication Company; British Thomson-Houston; General Electric; and Western Electric. These British manufacturers, in effect the early broadcasters, were therefore engineers and their aims were commercial (i.e. to extend the market for wireless receivers). Five of these manufacturers had a financial interest in the production of valves. At the time, there was little evidence of the informational, educational or entertainment potential of broadcasting. The wireless manufacturers were prepared to provide the necessary capital and operate the service at no cost to the taxpayer. Their profits were to depend upon the sale of wireless receivers, and so naturally they had a financial interest in stimulating demand for receivers by providing a broadcasting service of programmes which would be acceptable to the public. What they probably underestimated was the fierce competition to sell both complete sets and components for sets, a factor which reduced their potential profits.

In August 1922 the wireless manufacturers agreed, partly as a means of preventing competition, to form a company: the British Broadcasting Company (BBC). This was to be a monopoly for which the manufacturers were to provide the capital to establish and operate eight broadcasting stations, and to transmit programmes under the general control and supervision of the PMG. Some form of supervision was necessary if only to prevent interference between broadcasting stations, to monitor programme output, to control broadcasting hours and to avoid an American-style unregulated free-for-all in broadcasting. In America, where broadcasting was regarded as a mass medium, no licences were required to operate receiving sets, and it was relatively easy to obtain transmitting licences, hence the proliferation of radio stations causing interference. The government did not want wireless to interfere with vital communications, a distinct possibility given Britain's smaller land mass. Stations were therefore to be limited to a power of 1½ kilowatts and were allocated wavelengths which would not interfere with other services or with each other. Moreover, in Britain, where radio had the potential to reach a mass audience, it was perceived by the Post Office that there was a need for control to be exercised by a public authority.

After the BBC was formed on 18 October 1922 at a meeting held at the Institution of Electrical Engineers, British manufacturers of wireless equipment were deemed to be eligible for membership of the company if they acquired one or more £1 shares. In order to exclude foreign receivers and components, they agreed to sell only wireless receivers manufactured in Britain of a type approved by the PMG, and also to pay the BBC a royalty on receivers sold bearing the BBC mark. This mark consisted of the letters 'BBC' within a circle and bearing the words 'type approved by the Postmaster General'. Most of the £100,000 capital was contributed by the six leading wireless manufacturers. These six manufacturers had agreed to take up 60,000 of the £1 shares, thus leaving the remaining 40,000 shares to the smaller firms. Lord Gainford, a former PMG, was chairman of the company, and the other directors comprised the appointed representatives of the six principal wireless manufacturers and two independent members elected by the other shareholders. The PMG issued the broadcast receiving licences at ten shillings per annum to fund the broadcasting service, and paid half of the proceeds from the licences to the BBC. The BBC's income, therefore, consisted of royalties on receivers together with the proceeds from the licence fee. The Licence and Agreement between the PMG and the BBC took effect from 18 January 1923, but the company was granted permission to commence broadcasts two months earlier on 14 November 1922 from the Marconi Company's London station (call sign 2LO) using a 1kw transmitter.[3] The transmission of news bulletins and weather reports on that day signalled the official start of broadcasting in Britain.

Under the terms of the licence, the BBC was permitted to establish eight stations and to select sites for approval by the PMG, and was required to pay a royalty of £50 per annum to the PMG in respect of each station operated by the company. The sites chosen were as follows: Aberdeen, Glasgow, Manchester, Cardiff, Birmingham, London, Newcastle and Plymouth. Bournemouth was later substituted for Plymouth, and Belfast was added to the list. Relay stations were later opened between November 1923 and December 1924, two of them in Scotland at Edinburgh and Dundee, in order to extend the service to other major populated areas. The British Broadcasting Company was registered on 15 December 1922, and the first meeting of the Board of Directors was held on 21 December at Magnet House in London, during which matters such as the registration of the company and the appointment of John Reith as General Manager were dealt with.[4]

This scheme was acceptable at the time because in this wholly new venture it was the manufacturers, not the taxpayers, who took a risk in introducing a broadcasting service. It would have been unfair if taxpayers had been required to pay for a service which only those in possession of wireless receivers could enjoy – a principle endorsed by the Sykes Committee on Broadcasting in 1923. There was governmental control over the profits generated by the company which were limited to a fixed dividend of $7\frac{1}{2}$ per cent per annum, and the Post Office ensured that only half the proceeds of the licences were to be paid over to the company. There was, however, no state control over broadcasting in the sense that no government department selected programme material. The wireless manufacturers had access to the best technicians available, and so there was a reasonable expectation that in technical terms safeguards would operate. Also, it was administratively more convenient for the Post Office to license one company as a monopoly supplier of broadcast material than to license individual manufacturers and thus be accused of favouring some at the expense of others. The Post Office was free to license other companies, as reaffirmed in the supplementary licence of 1923, but chose not to do so.[5] The Directors of the BBC believed that they had been granted an exclusive licence to broadcast, but there was no legal manufacturing monopoly. It was easier to opt for a monopoly given the need for radio manufacturers to reach an agreement on the question of patents in order to start a broadcasting service and thereby generate interest in the sale of wireless receivers. It was difficult to envisage how another broadcasting company could broadcast without the use of patents controlled by members of the BBC.

Initially the licence to broadcast was limited to two years (i.e. to 31 December 1924). Nevertheless, by agreeing to accept the financial risks involved, the manufacturers were able to attain some degree of protection against imported wireless apparatus. They could claim that it was entirely through their efforts that a demand had been created for wireless receivers. They were cautious of the possibility that an excess number of receivers from the American market might be shipped to Britain, thus threatening the production of British receivers and thereby undermining the manufacturers' income. Much more likely was the possibility – which did materialise – that some individuals would build their own receivers using foreign components, which would be less expensive than purchasing a receiver from a British trader which would include the BBC royalty payment. The latter problem, as will be later noted, caused concern and forced the government to appoint a committee to examine the issue.

It was John Reith who converted the commercially-founded British Broadcasting Company into what was to become a renowned and established British institution which not only began to reflect historical events but itself became a subject of historical interest. John Reith was born in Stonehaven in Scotland on 20 July 1889. He was the youngest son of a Free Church of Scotland Minister in Glasgow, the Very Rev. Dr George Reith.[6] John Reith had a somewhat austere upbringing, and his father exerted a significant moral influence during his childhood years. Reith entered Glasgow Academy in 1896 and went eight years later to boarding school in England. After leaving boarding school in 1906, he attended Glasgow technical college for two years and subsequently served a five-year engineering apprenticeship in locomotive shops in Glasgow. In 1913 he travelled to London to seek employment and joined the firm S. Pearson and Son Ltd. In the following year he joined the forces and went to war. John Reith developed leadership skills during this period, and these were put to use when he later joined the BBC. After being wounded in October 1915, he spent the remainder of the war years first in charge of a rifle factory near Philadelphia and later in engineering work at Southwick in Sussex. After the war, Reith returned to Glasgow in 1920 to become General Manager of the engineering firm William Beardmore and Company of Coatbridge, but he resigned from this company in March 1922. On 13 October 1922 he scanned the advertisements for public appointments in a newspaper and noticed one which invited applications for officers, including General Manager, of the British Broadcasting Company. At that time Reith had no knowledge of broadcasting, whether in technical, programme or organisational matters. He nevertheless applied for the post of General Manager and was interviewed on 13 December. On the following day he received a telephone call from Sir William Noble, Chairman of the Broadcasting Committee, informing him that he had been offered the appointment. Thus began an influential partnership between Reith and the BBC which profoundly influenced the purpose and direction of British broadcasting for many years. A year later, on 14 November 1923, John Reith was appointed Managing Director of the Company.

Broadcasting began on 14 November 1922, and at that time Reith knew little about its potential. There was a conflict between his presbyterian background and his ambitions which influenced his temperament. According to Malcolm Muggeridge, who took part in televised conversations with him in 1967, Reith may have experienced a sense of Calvinist predestination – a belief that God had predestined him to take charge of this new medium of communication. Years after he left the BBC in June 1938 to become Chairman of Imperial Airways, he was to regret that decision to leave the BBC because he believed that the programme standards which he had sought to maintain were sliding into oblivion.[7] However, many of the assumptions on which the BBC was founded were altering even before Reith left the Corporation. He would have experienced difficulty in coping with the BBC after the Second World War, particularly the expansion of television. His philosophy perhaps served the BBC best in the early years when it was seeking to become an accepted and established institution; in the postwar years his philosophy was subject to increasing strain. As Asa Briggs pointed out, Reith held firmly to his moral beliefs, and this placed him at odds with broadcasters in the postwar years.[8] Reith was both paternalistic and authoritarian, and had great strength of character. Moreover, unlike subsequent BBC Governors, he was a permanent official, and this strengthened his position when dealing with other people. In the postwar period, no-one was ever again able to exert an influence comparable to that which he had exerted during the formative years of broadcasting.

John Reith wanted broadcasting to be funded from public rather than private sources, and to operate under unified control as a national institution. Central control was deemed to be efficient, economical and likely to maintain high programme standards. The BBC represented a mixture of private enterprise and public control. Reith, however, was aware that central control could constrain local initiatives in broadcasting. In his book *Broadcast over Britain*, published in 1924 before the BBC became a public corporation, Reith stated: 'With all the central control and the central management affairs, there still remains ample scope for the exercise of the ingenuity and enterprise of the local staff, assisted by their local advisory committees. The stations should be centres of real interest and influence in their areas.'[9] Unified control also involved the provision of a public service which could be extended to all parts of the country. It necessitated the need to sever the link with the radio trade. The radio industry would nevertheless benefit, according to Reith, by the provision of a public broadcasting service which was regarded as satisfactory by the public which it served. A purely commercial system might have been expected to concentrate only on providing a broadcasting service in the large cities rather than in rural and sparsely populated areas; it might also have focused more extensively on programmes geared to popular tastes, thus narrowing the range of programme output. Likewise, Reith did not want broadcasting to be subject to excessive government control. His definition of serving the national interest involved transmitting the best material available to the BBC throughout most parts of the country within the resources available. Reith thought it did not involve pandering to popular taste; it did involve investing radio with a social purpose. Reith wanted broadcasting to widen the personal experience of the audience which it served. Given that he had grown up in an age devoid of broadcasting, it was perhaps natural that he would be more in awe of its possibilities and less likely to take it for granted than subsequent generations.

One of the factors which Reith and the BBC had to take account of was the appointment by successive governments of committees of inquiry to examine the broadcasting services. In the period 1922–6, before the reconstitution of the BBC as a public corporation, there were two such committees of inquiry: the Sykes Committee in 1923, and the Crawford Committee in 1925. The problem referred to earlier, whereby some people built their own receivers using foreign components rather than purchase the more expensive British-built receivers, highlighted the need to clarify the conditions under which licences were to be issued. Furthermore, the BBC believed that experimental licences were being issued to more people than were genuine experimenters. Thus, on 24 April 1923, the government appointed a committee chaired by Sir Frederick Sykes to consider the options available. It seemed unfair that users of ready-made sets had to pay the BBC a royalty to meet the cost of broadcasting while users of home-assembled sets escaped paying such a royalty. The Sykes Committee, whose report was published on 23 August 1923, favoured the issue of a single annual receiving licence (value 10s) of which 7s 6d should be paid to the BBC; it wanted the royalties system to cease – in effect a withdrawal of the conditions about British origin and the marking of receivers with the BBC emblem; and finally it proposed that the BBC's licence should be extended for a further two years until 31 December 1926. Despite the proposed increase in the BBC's share of the licence income and the two-year extension of the licence, this did not persuade the BBC to waive its rights against the use of foreign components and receivers.

A compromise solution was reached on 1 October 1923 which can be noted as follows: (1) the BBC's licence was extended until 31 December 1926;[10] (2) up to 31 December 1924, two types of licences would be issued – the 10s licence, of which 7s 6d would be paid to the BBC covering receivers with the BBC mark, and a separate constructors' licence (value 15s) of which 12s 6d was to be paid to the BBC on sets constructed using British-made components; (3) the BBC royalty payment from its members was to be reduced; and (4) from 1 January 1925 only the single 10s licence would be issued, involving the cessation of the royalty system, the BBC marking and protection from foreign apparatus. There was also a provision for adjustments to be made in the proportion of the licence which the Post Office paid to the BBC. The growth in the number of licences which were purchased enabled the constructors' licence to be dropped and the standard 10s licence to be introduced earlier than planned (i.e. on 1 July 1924). Only the restriction on the use of foreign apparatus was continued until 31 December 1924. Thereafter, a single 10s licence covered the use of apparatus for experiments and for broadcasting.

Between the years 1922 and 1926, the number of licence-holders increased from 35,000 to over two million. The geographical extension of broadcasting beyond the then existing main and relay stations was facilitated by plans, first initiated in August 1924, for the construction of a permanent high-power station. These plans came to fruition with the opening on 27 July 1925 of the long-wave 25kw station (5XX) at Daventry in Northamptonshire. This station, opened by the PMG Sir William Mitchell-Thomson with Reith and Lord Gainford in attendance, was built on high ground 650 feet above sea level. Programmes were reeived at Daventry by land line from London. With its 600-foot aerial, it was anticipated that reception would be possible on crystal receivers within a radius of 100 miles of the transmitter. It therefore ended the prospect of the continuation in the foreseeable future of local stations. An article in *The Times* vividly described the opening of the station with characteristic wonderment:

> From the outside the building has a purely utilitarian appearance. Within is an amazing collection of instruments and machinery which make possible this new high-power broadcasting. There are big valves of an unimagined incandescence – the older air-cooled type – and others ten times as big as the valve of a receiving set, but glowing

faintly and actually cooled by a set of water jets. Some of these valves are modulators to rectify the current coming from the microphone; others are amplifiers, but the whole, arranged on panels in one big instrument room, makes a scene in which one feels that wonders may easily be worked.[11]

The Sykes Committee in 1923 reaffirmed the belief that broadcasting should become neither an unrestricted commercial monopoly nor a financial burden on the taxpayer.[12] The government had since then taken note of the expansion of broadcasting, and so in the summer of 1925 it appointed a committee under the chairmanship of the Earl of Crawford to advise on the scope of the broadcasting service and its management, control and financial aspects after the expiry of the BBC's licence on 31 December 1926. The Committee's report, published on 5 March 1926, outlined its recommendations for changes which were to lead to a transition in the status of the BBC from company to public corporation. The report said:

> Broadcasting has become so widespread, concerns so many people, and is fraught with such far-reaching possibilities, that the organisation laid down for the British Broadcasting Company no longer corresponds to national requirements or responsibility. Notwithstanding the progress which we readily acknowledge, and to the credit of which the Company is largely entitled, we are impelled to the conclusion that no company or body constituted on trade lines for the profit, direct or indirect, of those composing it can be regarded as adequate in view of the broader considerations now beginning to emerge.[13]

Broadcasting was expected to remain a monopoly, the BBC was to become a public corporation, and the PMG remained the parliamentary spokesman on broad questions of policy affecting the broadcasting service. The BBC's status and duties were now clearly expected to correspond with those of a public service. The Crawford Committee proposed that the new licence should operate for ten years, but also mentioned that the government should be free at a later date, should circumstances change, to supplant or modify the BBC. There was thus a qualifying clause about the BBC's monopoly, although the Committee did not elaborate upon what it regarded as constituting such a change in circumstances. It had the foresight to recognise that future circumstances might render the monopoly obsolete. The BBC was regarded now as a public utility whose resources had to be efficiently developed in the national interest. In September 1926, Reith sent a memo to all Station Directors asking them to review the usefulness and efficiency of existing staff with a view to transferring them to the Corporation at the end of the year. At midnight on 31 December 1926, the BBC was transformed from a limited company in the private sector into a corporation in the public sector.

On 1 January 1927, the British Broadcasting Company became the British Broadcasting Corporation. With the transition from company to corporation, the staff of over 700, together with all fixed assets, including twenty low-power transmitters and one high-power long-wave station, passed to the new corporation. Reith became Director-General, and a Board of Governors with the Earl of Clarendon as Chairman replaced the Board of Directors. In the *Radio Times*, a message from the Earl of Clarendon was printed, part of which read as follows:

> The progress that has been achieved by the British Broadcasting Company, and the nature and importance of its contribution to the well-being of the community, are known to us all. Innumerable and serious difficulties have been overcome, and the far-sighted policy pursued has embraced developments of the service far beyond what has yet been achieved. It will be our constant aim to carry out to the best of our ability the plans which are already in train for the completion of these developments.[14]

Reith wanted the company to become a corporation because of the emphasis on public service. Indeed Asa Briggs stated: 'Without the initiative of business enterprise there would have been no BBC: without a concept of public service there would have been no Corporation. Reith saw the Corporation as the logical successor to the Company.'[15] Reith wanted the BBC to be a public service both in its constitutional structure and in its programme output. It was to become a public service in which wireless manufacturers had no direct control.

When the BBC became a public corporation, what was significant was that the new authority was established under Royal Charter, granted on 20 December 1926, and headed by a Board of Governors. The granting of a Royal Charter was a development which was not repeated in the establishment of the nationalised industries after 1945, or indeed with the Independent Television Authority (ITA) which was established by Act of Parliament in 1954. This appeared to give the BBC a degree of status unlike that of other public corporations, although the BBC and nationalised industries both exercised control over their day-to-day administration. Nevertheless, nationalised industries were expected to conduct their operations with due regard to the issue of profitability, whereas if this same principle had been strictly applied to the BBC then no transmitters would ever have been planned and built to bring broadcasting to remote areas, such as in the north of Scotland and in the Islands, since it would not have been profitable to do so. Furthermore, the Charter also divorced the establishment of the BBC from any political decision (i.e. by indicating that the BBC was not created by the government). The Charter gave the BBC a greater degree of independence than it would have experienced if it had been established by statute. For example, the issue of impartiality, which was a statutory obligation for Independent Television (ITV), was not so for the BBC, where it was merely embodied in a code of practice. Likewise, the ITA had to ensure that programmes maintained a proper balance in their subject matter, whereas the BBC's Charter made no reference to the question of balanced programme output. The appointments to the BBC Board of Governors were made by the King in Council (in effect the Prime Minister) and not by a departmental minister. There was governmental control over broadcasting to ensure public accountability, but no detailed ministerial intervention. Indeed the Corporation was given independence in its daily programming and administration, thus leaving the government to exercise control over general policy affecting the conduct of the broadcasting service. The PMG continued to exercise control over the technical aspects of broadcasting, such as frequencies and the power and type of modulation used for each transmitting station. So despite the status, authority and independence conferred by the Charter, the BBC had only relative autonomy from the government, which determined the level of the licence fee and allocated wavelengths. The Post Office could scrutinise BBC estimates, and the Public Accounts Committee could scrutinise BBC accounts, although the latter were audited by a firm of chartered account- ants and not by the Comptroller and Auditor General. Parliament had to approve the level of revenue granted to the BBC each year and could also debate general broadcasting issues, but excluding matters relating to programme content or staffing. Furthermore, successive governments had the power to appoint and to remove Governors, to control the level of the BBC's capital expenditure, to decide not to renew the Licence, to establish additional broad- casting stations, to prescribe the hours of broadcasting, to veto broadcasts, or to appoint committees of inquiry to examine the conduct of BBC services. In short, governmental powers over the BBC were considerable, although it was recognised that freedom of broadcasting could not be reconciled with very close governmental and parliamentary control over the BBC.

The Royal Charter set the objects for which the BBC was incorporated and outlined its powers and organisation, whereas the Licence and Agreement authorised the BBC to use stations and equipment for broadcasting and specified the technical conditions for the operation of these stations. The Postmaster-General was the sole Minister responsible for broadcasting, hence he had control over the social and technical aspects of broadcasting. If there had been a Minister specifically responsible for the social aspects of broadcast- ing, then it was possible that this might have lessened the BBC's independence of government. The PMG was primarily concerned with the technical aspects, thus the social aspects of broadcasting derived incidentally from the PMG's responsibilities for technical aspects. The role of the PMG tended to be regulatory rather than overtly interventionist. A further point worth noting is that, with public corporations, a distinction can be drawn between general (long-term) policy for which there was accountability to Parliament, and daily administration where greater autonomy was permitted. Interestingly, in the BBC it was the daily activities which were of most concern to the public and which were likely to form the basis of parliamentary questions, yet it was only with BBC general policy that the Corporation was responsible to the public through Parliament. The BBC furnished annual reports to the PMG for presentation to Parliament, but unlike other public corporations there was a greater identification of general policy with daily activities in the BBC. Although successive governments disliked intervening directly in broadcasting for fear of being accused of imposing a form of censorship, the newly-created Corporation for its part recognised that it could never be totally independent of the government and Parliament, nor more autonomous than other public corporations. These constitutional matters were of crucial importance to the type of broadcasting service which the BBC was able to deliver to its listeners, but listeners were understandably more concerned with programmes than with the details of BBC organisation and constitution. It is therefore necessary to focus on the local stations and their subsequent replacement by regional broadcasting in order to assess the development of the broadcasting service in Scotland from 1923, when the first BBC local station was opened in Scotland, up until 1932, when listeners first had access to alternative programmes under the Regional Scheme.

BBC *local stations in Scotland and the advent of the Regional Scheme, 1923–32*

During the interwar years, radio increasingly filled the leisure hours of many people, particularly those living in remote areas. The price of wireless receivers fell, giving an increasing number of people access to radio. In December 1923, there were almost 600,000 licences in force in the United Kingdom, but this figure had risen to almost five million by 1932, with 302,313 of these licences current in Scotland as at the end of August 1932 shortly before the start of the dual programme service from the Scottish Regional transmitter at Westerglen. These figures increased as broadcasting services were extended throughout the country. Broadcasting created radio personalities and also exposed listeners to metropolitan culture and national news. It soon became one of the most important social and cultural influences on society, no longer existing solely as a hobby for amateur wireless experimenters and enthusiasts. Programmes which were broadcast at regular times helped to provide a structure to daily life. In contrast to the potential for programme diversity, there was the counterbalancing element of standardisation – of views, of news, of accents, of culture. Through radio, listeners were exposed to the same music and the same forms of entertainment. Throughout this period, local and regional culture tended to be diminished at the expense of metropolitan culture.

Broadcasting initially began on a local basis in 1922 with the opening of station 2LO in London. Up until May 1923, the local stations were self-contained and not linked with one another to provide simultaneous broadcasts. When communications links were provided by the Post Office, thus enabling programmes to be relayed to all stations, programme schedules had to be planned more carefully to take account of the material available from other stations. Transmissions were sufficiently strong to permit reception within a twenty- to twenty-five-mile radius of main cities for listening using a crystal receiver. Valve sets were needed for reception at longer distances. With crystal sets, the signal which reached the aerial set off a current which was detected by the crystal and then sent to the headphones. For several years, there was little technical improvement in receivers, but there were changes in their design. The popularity of self-constructed sets reduced the incentive for manufacturers to make technical progress. Indeed there were reasonable profits to be made from marketing components in comparison with complete receivers. These crystal sets, which did not require a power supply and were suitable for reception of programmes close to the local stations, were relatively easy to construct using diagrams in wireless magazines such as *Wireless World*. It was only from about 1933 that valve receivers, battery- or mains-powered to enable the valve to amplify the incoming signals, were purchased in greater numbers than crystal sets. This change took place not merely because of the falling real cost of valve sets, but also because crystal sets had poor selectivity and thus were not capable of providing adequate reception of the national and regional programmes which were then broadcast under the Regional Scheme which became fully operational in Scotland in 1932.

Prior to the advent of the Regional Scheme, the BBC opened four local stations in Scotland located in Glasgow, Aberdeen, Edinburgh and Dundee. These stations relied upon local talent to provide localised topical interest programmes. The BBC opened its first Scottish station (call sign 5SC), located at 202 Bath Street, Glasgow, on 6 March 1923. The BBC chose Glasgow as the site for the first station in Scotland because a large percentage of the population of Scotland lived in or near Glasgow. The programmes from the Glasgow station were broadcast from a 1½kw transmitter installed in a tower room of the Port Dundas power station of the Glasgow Corporation Electricity Department. This was regarded as an ideal site because the aerial on the chimney was situated on high ground and power supplies were readily available. The Glasgow studio was connected by a half-mile cable to the transmitter. A land line provided the link between London and Glasgow which, because of its distance, was at times subject to interference from telephone and telegraph lines. Arthur Burrows (Assistant Controller and Director of Programmes in London) vividly described, in a book published in 1924, his visit to the Glasgow transmitting station at Port Dundas: 'The final approach is by a spiral staircase of iron, and the hum of the transformers and the weird glow which is thrown over everything by the lemon-yellow lights from the valves, make a fitting climax to the little adventure which the visit to the station entails.'[1] Glasgow was designated as a main station because it used what was then regarded as a high-power transmitter. On the opening night, speeches were given at a special ceremony by Sir Thomas Paxton (Lord Provost of Glasgow) and Lord Gainford (Chairman of the BBC Board of Directors). John Reith, who was then General Manager of the BBC, was also present at the opening ceremony. Herbert Carruthers, an organist and music conductor, was appointed as Station Director. In common with other Station Directors, he was in charge of the organisation and programme output of the station, subject to general control from London. Several thousand licences were issued within the first few months of opening of the station. Programmes normally began at 3.30pm, with closedown varying between 10.30pm and midnight. Regular programmes included local news, talks by academics, topics for women, and a children's hour. National news was taken on a simultaneous broadcast (SB) from London. Initially, listeners appeared to be more concerned about the quality of reception than about the content of the programmes broadcast. This was not surprising given the limitations of the crystal receivers, the strength of the signals, the limited range of programme material, the reluctance of artists to agree to take part in broadcasts, and the sheer novelty of a broadcasting service.

A year after the opening of the Glasgow station, the *Glasgow Herald* stated that not only had critics been wrong to state that the novelty of wireless would wear off, but also 'broadcasting has become a definite part of the fabric of our social life'.[2] During these early years, stations sought to be the first to take part in specific types of broadcasts, which in itself gave an indication of the novelty of the medium. For example, in August 1923, *Rob Roy* was the first play to be broadcast. It was later given a repeat transmission on simultaneous broadcast to other stations, notable because it was the first SB from a local station. Station Directors kept in constant liaison with headquarters in London over the use of London programmes, their replacement by local programmes, and offers of local programmes for SB to London or to other stations. In February 1924, almost a year after the opening of the Glasgow station, Mr D. Millar Craig was appointed as Assistant Controller, Scotland. He was based in Glasgow and was given control over all the Scottish stations and the Belfast station. His primary function was to interpret BBC policy in the light of Scottish needs. He was one of only a few Assistant Controllers; those senior to him in the organisational hierarchy included the Controller and Reith as Managing Director. The post of Assistant Controller (Scotland) was later replaced by that of Northern Area Director. The BBC's studio premises in Glasgow underwent several shifts in location from 1924 through to the 1930s. On 7 November 1924, staff moved to 21 Blythswood Square and remained there until 1930 when a further move took place to 268 West George Street. On 14 July 1930, most Glasgow staff moved over to the new Scottish headquarters in Edinburgh. The Station Representative and some engineers remained at the Glasgow station. In April 1936, Queen Margaret College was purchased by the BBC from Glasgow University for adaptation as a broadcasting centre. In 1938 the BBC moved again, this time to the new premises at Hamilton Drive. The BBC's local station in Glasgow was followed by the opening of local stations in other major Scottish cities. The second local station to be opened in Scotland was located at Aberdeen. The main station at Glasgow closed on 12 June 1932 when Regional broadcasting superseded the local stations.

Aberdeen was the BBC's most northerly station and was opened as a main station (call sign 2BD) on 10 October 1923. The opening ceremony took place in the studio at 17 Belmont Street on premises which belonged to the Aberdeen Electrical Engineering Company. Among those present at the opening ceremony were the Lord Provost of Aberdeen, John Reith, Sir William Noble (a Director of the BBC) and Captain P.P. Eckersley (the BBC's Chief Engineer). The opening address at 9.00pm which was relayed to Glasgow was followed by music from the pipers and military band of the 2nd Gordon Highlanders. According to newspaper reports at the time, large crowds gathered outside the premises of wireless retailers in the city where demonstrations with loud-speakers were being given. Mr R.E. Jeffrey, who had been involved in the drama production of *Rob Roy* at the Glasgow station, had been appointed a few weeks earlier as Aberdeen Station Director. He was supported by two assistants and three engineers. Jeffrey served as Station Director until 29 July 1924, when he was succeeded by Neil McLean. It was perhaps unfortunate that the site for the Aberdeen station was chosen so close to nearby electrical generators, be-cause this tended to interfere with the clarity of transmissions. Also, on several occasions, severe weather brought down the telephone lines to Aberdeen which carried the programmes from Daventry. The transmitter was housed in the Aberdeen steam laundry company premises; the aerial was slung between two tall Marconi masts. In May 1925 the studio premises were extended, and, with a separate entrance to the premises made, the address was altered to 15 Belmont Street. Programmes from Aberdeen normally began at 3.30pm with closedown occurring between 10.30pm and midnight. Typical programmes broadcast included a regular children's hour, a women's half-hour, local news, national news on simultaneous broadcast from London, community singing concerts, weather forecasts for farmers, Gaelic concerts, and charity events to raise funds for local causes such as the installation of wireless sets in hospitals. Listeners to the Aberdeen station, unlike those who listened to the Edinburgh station which was opened in 1924, were reported to be less inclined to accept simultaneous broadcasts from London.[3] Instead they preferred a greater volume of locally-originated programme material. In addition to light music and comedy, local news bulletins were also especially popular during the period of the General Strike in 1926, factors which helped to increase demand for wireless sets. During 1924, a station orchestra was formed, but this was reduced to an octet in December 1926 as a stage in the process of centralisation which was affecting the BBC as a whole and which in Scotland involved the pooling of resources with the other local stations. During 1928, with the introduction of the Regional Scheme, some staff were transferred to London. However, because of Aberdeen's position as the only station in the north of Scotland, together with the presence of fierce criticism of any attempt to reduce the station's programme activities, the station was permitted to continue broadcasting its own programmes on a separate wavelength. It continued to do so until 9 September 1938, but its status during this period was downgraded from main to relay station. Nevertheless, Aberdeen was, for example, permitted to continue producing a separate *Children's Hour* whereas the Edinburgh and Dundee relay stations were forced to drop theirs and instead take the Regional *Children's Hour* from Glasgow as from 1 November 1928. On 1 October 1929, the Regional Scheme came into operation, and this resulted in the disbanding of the Aberdeen octet and the transfer of further staff. Neil McLean, who remained at the station, was now designated Aberdeen Representative. He was replaced on 29 September 1930 by Ian Whyte, but on a part-time basis. The Scottish Regional Director believed that for policy and programme reasons it was better to have at least a part-time representative at Aberdeen than no representative at all. Ian Whyte also acted as a musical adviser to the Scottish Region because of his musical knowledge. But, with a heavy workload, Whyte was provided with support from a full-time junior assistant as from April 1931. On 31 October 1931, Ian Whyte was transferred to Edinburgh as musical adviser, to be succeeded at Aberdeen by Moultrie Kelsall.

On 1 May 1924, the BBC opened a relay station at Edinburgh, the third to be opened in Britain. It was designated as a relay station because it had a more limited transmitter range than the Glasgow or Aberdeen stations. The transmitter had a power of only 200 watts in comparison with the 1½kw (i.e. 1,500 watts) for the main stations. In common with the other relay stations opened throughout the country, the BBC planned these stations as a means of extending broadcasting coverage beyond what was possible with the existing main stations. All stations, both main and relay, were sited in urban areas, and so rural and isolated areas were either poorly served if close to a major city, or in most cases not served at all. On the opening day of the Edinburgh station (call sign 2EH), a concert was broadcast from the Usher Hall. Programmes that evening began at 7.30pm, and the opening speeches which were simultaneously broadcast to all stations began at 9.00pm. National and local news were broadcast half an hour later, and the service closed down at 10.15pm.[4] Those present at the opening ceremony included John Reith (Managing Director of the BBC) and the Lord Provost of Edinburgh. George Marshall was appointed as Station Director; he was later transferred to Glasgow in March 1926 and succeeded by Mr J.C.S. MacGregor who had been one of the two station assistants. The transmitter at Edinburgh was installed in a wooden hut in the quadrangle of Edinburgh University's Old College. The aerial, which was suspended from the university chimney, gave poor reception but it remained there until 26 April 1931 when it was moved to St Cuthbert's Cooperative Society in Fountain Hill Road. Interestingly, the historic rivalry between Edinburgh and Glasgow resulted in a decision to receive most programmes from London rather than from Glasgow. Indeed, a glance through the *Radio Times* confirms that many programmes were taken on SB from London. Many relay stations throughout Britain did in fact prefer to take the London programme rather than programmes from the nearest main station.

Programmes from Edinburgh tended to begin at 5.00pm with closedown between 11.00pm and midnight. Edinburgh had its own children's hour programmes which were broadcast regularly. National news and weather forecasts were taken on SB from London. The first BBC offices in Edinburgh were located in the city centre in a music shop, Townsend and Thomson's, at 79 George Street; new premises at 87 George Street were officially opened on 31 July 1925 by Captain P.P. Eckersley, the BBC's Chief Engineer. In common with the other Scottish local stations, the Edinburgh station's programme activities were scaled down from January 1928 in preparation for the Regional Scheme, e.g. from 1 November 1928, Edinburgh was obliged to take the

Regional *Children's Hour* programme from Glasgow. Unlike in Aberdeen, there was little outcry over this, probably because, as a capital city, Edinburgh could be expected to be called upon to supply a reasonable number of Regional programmes. Under the process of centralisation, the Station Director was replaced by a Station Representative. On 30 September 1928, Mr Cleghorn Thomson became Scottish Regional Director under the Regional Scheme. This replaced the previous post of Northern Area Director. At this time, a decision was taken to base a press representative, Mr Kennedy Stewart, in Edinburgh to serve the Scottish Region. When the BBC's Station Representative was transferred to London on 1 October 1929, Mr Stewart had to fulfil the dual function of press and Station Representative. At a meeting of the Board of Governors on 16 October 1929, approval was given for the transfer of the Scottish HQ from Glasgow to Edinburgh.[5] Reith had no strong views about which site should be chosen for the Scottish headquarters. With the reception of programmes spreading to more remote areas and not confined to main population centres such as Glasgow, it perhaps appeared more natural for the capital city to be regarded as the new home for the Scottish headquarters, especially since under the Regional Scheme it was expected to administer Scotland as a national unit. On 29 May 1930, staff moved out of the George Street premises and into new premises nearby at 5 Queen Street. Many Glasgow staff moved over to Edinburgh on 14 July. The new Scottish headquarters at Broadcasting House, Edinburgh, was opened on 29 November 1930 by William Adamson, Secretary of State for Scotland. The Lord Provost of Edinburgh, Sir John Reith (BBC Director-General) and Mrs Snowden (a member of the Board of Governors) were among those present at the opening ceremony. The BBC's Edinburgh premises did however lack sufficient space, and so, during the second half of the 1930s, additional premises were rented at York Place and at 42 Queen Street. The difficulty in obtaining suitable compact premises was one of the reasons which persuaded the BBC to transfer its headquarters back to Glasgow during the war years. On 12 June 1932, the Edinburgh local transmitter closed down when the Scottish Regional transmitter at Westerglen came into service.

The last of the four local BBC stations in Scotland was located in Dundee, which was the ninth relay station opened by the BBC. In February 1924, Dundee Town Council indicated that it wanted a main or at least a relay station for the city. Mr D. Millar Craig (BBC Assistant Controller, Scotland) promised Dundee a relay station, and one was eventually opened on 12 November 1924. The station (call sign 2DE) was opened by the Lord Provost at a ceremony at the Caird Hall attended by Rear Admiral C.D. Carpendale (BBC Controller), the Principal of St Andrews University, and the BBC's Assistant Controller for Scotland. The evening programmes on the opening night lasted from 7.30 to 9.55pm, and the opening speeches were simultaneously broadcast to all stations. The BBC's offices and studio in Dundee were located at 1 Lochee Road. The transmitter was housed at Caldrum Jute works in St Salvador Street and the aerial was attached to a pole from the highest chimney stack in the city. Mr E. Heddle, a lecturer at the Royal Technical College in Glasgow, was appointed as Station Director and remained so throughout the entire period of the existence of the station. Dundee preferred to take most of its programmes from London rather than from Glasgow. The station provided its own local interest programmes and, in common with the other Scottish local stations, began by broadcasting its own *Children's Hour* programmes. During 1928, preparations began in Dundee, as in other stations, for the introduction of the Regional Scheme. In January 1928, the assistant to the Station Director was transferred to Glasgow and his post was not filled. On 1 November 1928, the *Children's Hour* programme from Dundee ceased and in its place the Regional equivalent was taken from Glasgow. Under the policy of centralisation, the Dundee studio closed on 1 October 1929, leaving only the transmitter operational. The Station Director, whose services were no longer required, then left the BBC. The transmitter at Dundee closed down on 12 June 1932 when the Scottish Regional transmitter at Westerglen was opened. Thereafter, Dundee had no BBC presence, and so only outside broadcasts were taken from the city.

For almost a decade, programmes in Scotland were broadcast mainly during the evenings from these local stations, each with their own wavelengths and local programmes. They could contribute programme material to other stations and did take a varying number of programme items on simultaneous broadcast from London. Not all locally-originated programmes were on purely Scottish subjects, and no attempt was made to create a single Scottish service. Moreover, not all programmes maintained high standards. Indeed, at times the BBC's head office in London was concerned about the poor quality of material provided by local artists in the provinces, not just in Scotland. In March 1925, Arthur Burrows, Director of Programmes, commented in a paper on programme expenditure, that given the poor quality of local material, any increase in the programme allowance for provincial stations would be wasted.[6] London scrutinised broadcasts from provincial stations after instances of what were regarded as poor-quality programmes, such as the Burns' Night programme from Edinburgh on 25 January 1926. These instances provided ample justification in London for a policy of centralisation in which the location of any production was dependent upon where programmes could be produced economically and to the highest standards; that location invariably turned out to be London. However, there was a limit to what the local stations could achieve in technical and artistic terms given the limitations on manpower and on technical and financial resources as well as the restricted pool of available local talent. The BBC simply regarded it as more sensible to centralise resources in order to improve the range and quality of programmes rather than dilute resources by channelling even more resources to each of the local stations. As regards the type and volume of programme output, the Glasgow and Aberdeen stations supplied more original material than the Edinburgh and Dundee relay stations. Many of the variety programmes were built around the stars of the music hall and theatre, although there was often some reluctance by theatre managers to agree to artists taking part in such broadcasts. Many artists in any case lacked knowledge of broadcast techniques. Initially, the BBC made use of amateur and semi-professional singers until satisfactory agreements could be reached to use professional artists. Most local stations had their own orchestras and so music became a staple diet of programme output. There were also local news items supplied by local press correspondents, as well as special fishing and farming bulletins, appeals for good causes, plays by local authors, religious programmes, special programmes for Scottish anniversaries such as St Andrew's Day and Burns' Night, and talks given by local academics. Scripted shows did not become more commonplace until during and after the war, when the BBC sought to widen the range of programme output. Listeners in the remoter parts of Scotland did not have access to local programmes. It was only with the advent of the Regional Scheme, when the four low-power local stations were replaced by two high-power transmitters, that it was possible to extend broadcasting coverage. This scheme offered a choice of programme (national or regional), better reception and better-quality programmes, and also brought all Regions into greater contact with national events. It did so at the expense of localised services. Thereafter, broadcasting in Scotland was viewed as a national service within a much larger United Kingdom broadcasting service.[7]

To extend broadcasting coverage, it was not possible to open more relay stations in Scotland, firstly because they were only suitable for extending coverage to small, densely-populated urban areas rather than large, sparsely-populated rural areas, and secondly because there was a limit to the number of wavelengths which could be used without giving rise to mutual interference between stations. The introduction of the long-wave, high-power 25kw station at Daventry in 1925 brought about eighty per cent of people in the UK within the reception area of a programme service by giving a signal up to about 200 miles. Long waves gave rise to less attenuation of the signal than medium waves over long distances, but were subject to greater electrical interference in populated industrial areas. It therefore appeared that although the Daventry station was a pointer to the direction of regional broadcasting, medium rather than long waves would have to be used to extend coverage within the Regions. The BBC's Regional Scheme which replaced the local stations was due to the desire, with a limited number of wavelengths, to give listeners in all parts of the country, including many rural areas, access to radio programmes, and was a means of providing a choice of programmes for those people already able to receive the broadcasting service. Local stations were unable to achieve either of these aims. Given the restrictions on wavelengths and power of stations, it appeared that what was required was a small number of high-power stations situated in rural areas but near to major cities in order to serve the maximum number of people in the Regions, not the cities. By spreading the field strength more evenly, this would minimise interference between stations. Moreover, because of the limited number of wavelengths available, transmitters had to be synchronised to enable several stations throughout the country to transmit the same programme on the same wavelength without causing mutual interference. From November 1926, the BBC therefore planned to build five high-power, medium-wave stations to replace the existing main and relay stations. One of these stations was expected to be based in Scotland. Each station would be provided with twin transmitters in order to radiate two programmes, namely a national programme from London, and a Regional programme which would exist as an alternative to the London Programme. The use of medium waves reduced the geographical coverage area by one third in comparison with the Daventry long-wave station. In other words, this would restrict the service area to a radius of about seventy to eighty miles from the transmitter. However, it was expected that the Scottish station would be sited in the central belt and thus serve the majority of the population of Scotland. But this did mean that the high-power, medium-wave station would be unable to extend transmissions to the Highlands and hilly areas to the north, no matter how powerful the transmitter. All BBC Regional stations were to be provided with the facility for simultaneous broadcasts because of the economies achieved by linking stations in this manner.

The BBC Regions were based primarily on technical considerations in order speedily to extend broadcasting throughout the country, but the arguments in favour of greater centralisation of output were not wholly technical. There were also financial considerations to be taken into account. It was intended that all material, except Regional programmes, should originate in London on the grounds that the best artistic talent and facilities could be found there. This general policy was accepted at a meeting of the Control Board (composed of Reith and his senior officials) on 10 November 1926. The Control Board minutes for 17 November elaborated on this and noted: 'The point is that we should give the listener the best, and the best can be only given where the funds available are spent upon a few good programmes sent S.B. to many centres rather than diluted to make every centre an origination [sic] of two programmes each.'[8] Details of the Regional Scheme were prepared by Peter Eckersley, the BBC's Chief Engineer, and contained in a lengthy report prepared in June 1927.[9] The BBC preferred to meet the costs out of current income rather than borrow to finance the Regional Scheme. The extension of the broadcasting service under the Scheme would in any case increase the number of licences purchased and thereby increase the BBC's income. In deciding as to how a contrast in programme material between the National Programme and the Regional Programme could be achieved, it was decided that items would be classified as either universal or speciality. The former comprised programmes, mainly music, which required little mental effort to enjoy and were suitable for broadcasting on the National Programme. Speciality programmes, such as drama or talks, which required more effort to enjoy, were deemed to be suitable for either the National or the Regional Programme. The Scottish Regional

Programme schedule was therefore to consist of speciality items originating from London or Scotland. A balance of programme material was expected to be offered on both the National and Regional Programmes.

On 21 August 1927, an experimental 30kw transmitting station (5GB) came into service at Daventry in order to assess the reception area of a high-power medium-wave transmitter for broadcasting the National Programme and as a model for the design of further Regional stations. In practical terms, the trend towards centralisation of output did not diminish appreciably until the arrival of very high frequency (VHF) broadcasting on low power in the 1950s offered opportunities for the planning of genuine local radio stations. The first step towards the full implementation of the Regional Scheme, which had an impact within Scotland, took place on 1 November 1928 when Edinburgh and Dundee ceased to be regarded as stations but retained their studios and transmitters. The Station Directors at Glasgow, Edinburgh and Dundee disappeared with the curtailment of local activities; Aberdeen retained its Station Director. It had been decided at a meeting of the Control Board in July 1928 to leave a representative at each of the relay stations even though these stations would for practical purposes cease work under the Regional Scheme.[10] These changes were also accompanied by changes in titles: transmitters were now to be referred to as transmitters and not as stations, studios were to be referred to as offices, local programmes were to be known as Regional programmes, and the Northern Area Director (David Cleghorn Thomson) was to be known as the Scottish Regional Director. On 16 October 1928, the Northern Area Director prepared a detailed allocation of duties for the Regional staff. There was little doubt that the National Programme was expected to be the senior of the two programme services. Indeed, under the system of simultaneous broadcasting where the same programme was simultaneously broadcast from a number of transmitters, the principle adopted was that so-called 'provincial' programmes should concentrate on purely local matters, thus in practice eliminating those provincial programmes which were of a similar character to those available from London and broadcast at the same time.[11] London had access to the best talent and facilities, and so the BBC in Scotland tended to focus on more traditional programme material and items not covered in the National Programme. Aware of the justifiable concern of Regional Directors as to the local programming implications of the policy of centralisation, Reith stated the following year that 'The local cultural loss should be, to a considerable extent, offset by the quality of the London programmes, and to a further extent by the activities still open to Regional Directors'.[12] Reith promised Regional Directors that there would be greater cooperation and consultation between the Regions and Head Office over policy and programming matters. He also added that Regional Directors should seek to ascertain which staff would be required in the future and who would be made redundant. There were undoubtedly arguments for and against centralising resources. Indeed, even in the mid-1970s, Lord Hill (then BBC Chairman) stated that although bigness in any organisation had its dangers, this was a poor argument for throwing away the economies of scale and quality of output which the concentration of talent and resources in large centres permitted.[13]

The Regional Scheme enabled those listeners who wished to receive the National Programme from London to be able to do so without being interrupted by any Scottish programme transmitted on a separate wavelength. Likewise, those who preferred to listen to mainly Scottish programmes were able to do so without being deprived of access to the National Programme. These changes gave greater freedom to Scottish-based producers to build up a diet of Scottish programmes within available resources without having to deny listeners in Scotland any item in the National Programme each time that a Scottish item was broadcast. During these interwar years, the BBC did not strictly address a national community because there were Regional services and in any case not all parts of the country could receive radio broadcasts. Not all isolated areas were brought into close touch with much larger centres of population. Scotland was more homogeneous than other BBC regions, but there were social, economic and cultural differences between the Highlands and the Lowlands and between major cities such as Glasgow and Edinburgh. With the prospect of Regional broadcasting, listeners in the north of Scotland did not wish to miss out on the expected improvements in the quality of reception. In April 1928, the PMG was asked in the House of Commons whether he was aware of dissatisfaction in the north of Scotland because of the poor reception of programmes caused by interference from ships and coastal stations, and therefore when it was intended to provide a high-power station in Scotland.[14] In the following year, the BBC confirmed that one of the Regional stations was to be sited in Scotland. The Regional Scheme came into force on 1 October 1929, and Scotland was the first Region to reorganise staff in preparation for the Scheme. A week later, on 8 October, the Scottish Regional Director gave a talk, broadcast from all Scottish stations, to outline the new programme policy in Scotland. There were to be fewer programmes broadcast from Scottish studios because Scotland was not expected to duplicate programmes which could be produced better in London. The Scottish Regional Director also remarked that many of the programmes which were broadcast in Scotland did not have any distinctive national character and that these were the type of programmes which on artistic and economic grounds might not be justified in being produced in Scotland. It can also be noted that listeners were becoming accustomed to the high quality of London programme items through the use of simultaneous broadcasts and so unfavourable comparisons were sometimes drawn between Scottish and London-originated programme material. These programme factors therefore increased the justification for a policy of centralisation. There was a reduction in the opportunities available for Regional programmes in the period before Scotland was provided with the technical means for transmitting a separate programme from that of the National Programme. Reith believed that the disquiet of Regional Directors at the loss of their orchestras was primarily because of two factors: concern that London would be unable to handle the increased volume of programme work, and because it might lead to an overbearing metropolitan outlook. Greater contact between Regional Directors and Head Office was thus deemed to be necessary, not least to keep the Regions fully informed about forthcoming developments under the Regional Scheme.

During 1929, several areas were considered near Falkirk to find a suitable site for the Scottish Regional station. A portable transmitter was used in order to calculate field strengths. In the following year, construction work began at Westerglen. This site was considered ideal because it was 500 feet above sea level and approximately midway between Glasgow and Edinburgh and so able to serve eighty per cent of the population of Scotland. There were also telephone line and power facilities available at Westerglen. The Scottish Regional station, with its twin 500-feet masts, 50kw power and range of about seventy miles, was opened on 12 June 1932. Westerglen was the BBC's third twin-wave transmitting station. The Scottish transmitter was synchronised with the transmitters at Brookman's Park in London and at Moorside Edge in Huddersfield because of the scarcity of wavelengths. Synchronisation, which involved the operation of transmitters on the same wavelength, enabled many more areas of the country to be covered than would have been possible otherwise. BBC staff in Scotland hoped that the creation of a separate Scottish service would enable more music and talks programmes and outside broadcasts to be made as well as strengthening output in other subject areas. In practice, most of the programmes on both the National and Regional wavelengths were to emanate from London. The opening of the Scottish Regional station resulted in the closure on 12 June of the Glasgow, Edinburgh and Dundee local transmitters, and the conversion of Aberdeen into a local station, the term 'relay station' no longer being used. Partly due to the difficulty of receiving other stations, Aberdeen retained a separate wavelength and programme centre for relay and local purposes. This also reduced the potential for centralisation of programme activities within Scotland. However, with Aberdeen now operating as a low-power station, this caused some reception problems for listeners in the scattered communities in the Highlands.

The transmitter for broadcasting the National Programme from Westerglen began tests on 22 August 1932, followed by a month later on 25 September by the full dual programme service (i.e. Regional and National Programmes). Listeners could now choose between alternative programmes transmitted on separate wavelengths. These changes gave a boost to the use of valve sets because these receivers possessed good selectivity (i.e. the ability to separate transmissions of broadly equal strength even when wavelengths did not vary significantly). Good selectivity was needed to enable listeners to obtain clear reception of both the National and the Scottish Regional Programme. By this time, wireless sets were becoming less of a novelty and more a part of the household. Battery-powered valve sets gave way to mains-powered sets, except in those parts of Scotland which were devoid of an electricity power supply and instead relied upon gas lighting. Valve sets were more expensive than the simple crystal sets which were widely used during the previous decade, and so ownership of them took time to spread through all social classes. Competition and mass production of valve receivers during the 1930s assisted in lowering their cost and so making them more widely available in Scotland. Scottish programme staff were mindful of the need to provide 'a distinctive contrast to the more highly developed and standardised Metropolitan programmes transmitted as "National" '.[15] So there were programmes specifically for the Scottish audience including local news, music concerts, religious services, dance music, vaudeville, drama and schools programmes. Not all this material found favour with the discerning Scottish audience, but equally not all subject material, such as vaudeville, was suitable for a wider audience through the medium of radio. Outwith Scotland, the four other Regional services covered the Midlands, the north of England, the west of England and Wales, and Northern Ireland. With the opening of Westerglen and these other stations, broadcasting services were extended beyond populous areas to cover more rural areas, although the problem remained of encouraging more people in Scotland to listen to radio.

3

The development of national and Scottish regional broadcasting, 1932–9

Even before the British Broadcasting Company became a public corporation in 1927, the potential of broadcasting was recognised. In an article in the monthly journal *Nature*, it was stated that broadcasting not only involved an amalgam of scientific and technical factors but also encompassed a variety of influences on a whole range of human activities – political, commercial, educational, recreational and social.[1] Radio permitted the broadcaster's voice to reach innumerable homes, particularly with the extension of broadcasting during this period. Broadcasting both reflected society and was influenced by society. Newspapers and periodicals began to take greater interest in commenting on programmes and on the philosophy of broadcasting. It created radio personalities and broadened cultural and intellectual interests, although it increasingly tended to project national events with greater frequency than regional or local matters of interest. Throughout this period, listeners in Scotland could tune in to two alternative programme services: the National Programme from London, and the Scottish Regional Programme. The latter Programme broadcast both Scottish and non-Scottish programme material. There were also pioneering developments in television broadcasting during these years, accompanied by institutional growth, increases in the size of the audience and growth in the geographical extension of programme services. It was the social purposes offered by the technical possibilities of the medium of radio which Reith wished to develop, and this provides an appropriate starting point at which to examine how National and Scottish Regional broadcasting developed from 1932, when the Regional Scheme took full effect in Scotland, through to September 1939, when Regional services were suspended because of the outbreak of war in Europe.

There were limitations on the extent to which broadcasting could bridge the gap between regional cultures, different cultural tastes (i.e. highbrow, middlebrow, and lowbrow) and different social classes. However, listeners were undoubtedly exposed to a selection of the best of the various arts, and all within the comfort of the family home. Writing in *The Listener* in 1932, ten years after the start of broadcasting, Sir Oliver Lodge noted his impressions of broadcasting:

> In music we are given the best of the old masters and of the new. We are privileged to hear the great conductors of the age without a special

journey to London. We can listen comfortably from our easy chairs
to our great teachers in philosophy and science, in literature, and
theology. We are not given partisan politics, but we have an opportunity of listening to every party.[2]

The question was really the extent to which such appreciation extended
throughout the social spectrum, and throughout all parts of the country. A book
published in 1933 referred to broadcasting as 'a means of enlarging the
frontiers of human interest and consciousness, of widening personal experience, of shrinking the earth's surface'.[3] But not everyone was enthusiastic about
radio. Newspaper proprietors, news agencies, theatre managers, publishers,
recording companies and recording artists were concerned about the spread of
radio for fear that it might undermine their vested interests. Equally, not all
people were enthusiastic about metropolitan news and culture. Also, not
everyone was willing to purchase a wireless receiver. Many people still
continued to buy books, read newspapers and go to the cinema. Listening to a
play on the wireless was qualitatively different in terms of atmosphere in
comparison with sitting among a selected audience in a theatre. Indeed, in
1926, the Crawford Committee on Broadcasting did not think that broadcasting
would pose a threat to other means of communication. In the pre-television era,
radio made its own stars rather than relying on those who had achieved fame in
other media. Radio offered the broadcaster a direct and intimate contact with
his audience, yet at the same time it offered him an audience which could be
counted in millions. This potential power of broadcasting was partly responsible for the attempt to invest it with a social purpose as embodied in the
Reithian public service ideals.

The origins of the Reithian public service ethos and the constituent elements
of this ethos need to be considered. The history of broadcasting was for over
thirty years the history of one institution, namely the BBC, which enjoyed a
monopoly of broadcasting until the advent of commercial television in 1954.
The monopoly assisted the practical operation of the Reithian ideal of public
service as reflected in the provision of programmes which satisfied the three
criteria of information, education and entertainment. The proportion of each of
these three elements was never defined. Sir John Reith used his influence to
ensure that the BBC took a lead in cultural taste rather than merely following
existing cultural trends. Although the British Broadcasting Company was born
of a merger of commercial interests when wireless manufacturers decided to
merge into a single cartel, Reith was anxious for the broadcasting service to
operate as a public service. The freedom of the BBC from both commercial
pressure and direct government control assisted Reith in putting his public
service ideals into practice. He wanted the BBC to be a public service not only
in performance (i.e. standards and range of programme output) but also in
constitutional terms. He envisaged that each aspect would interact with the
other. For example, the Board of Governors was regarded as the most
appropriate mechanism for ensuring that the BBC carried out its public service

duties to inform, educate and entertain the audience and to maintain uniformly high programme standards in this process. Reith wished to secure as much independence as possible for the BBC within the technical, financial and political structure in which the Corporation operated. Also, during this period, announcers were carefully selected in order to project the public image of the BBC. This was possible because the BBC began as a small organisation in which Reith was able to know most of his staff personally; it proved less easy in later years due to the growth of the BBC. Reith's cultural mission appeared to give the BBC too much influence as an arbiter of public tastes and as a definer of standards. However, Reith often argued that the public did not know what material it wanted, thus it was left to the BBC to provide the necessary cultural enlightenment and cultivate a more informed democracy. He believed that culture could be communicated successfully to a mass audience rather than remaining the privilege of a few. In this he was later proved to be overoptimistic in his estimation of public taste.

John Reith believed that the BBC had both an ethical and an intellectual responsibility towards the audience which it served. In his autobiography he stated: 'It was, in fact, the combination of public service motive, sense of moral obligation, assured finance, and the brute force of monopoly which enabled the BBC to make of broadcasting what no other country in the world has made of it – these four fundamentals.'[4] To use broadcasting primarily as a means of entertainment was to Reith a waste of precious resources. He wanted to invest broadcasting with a richer social purpose. In the introduction to the first issue of the annual *BBC Handbook*, he accepted that radio had a positive role to play in offering a means of relaxation, but also drew attention to its educational potential by stating that 'The mere fact that such a medium is there – able to override distance, to overcome inequalities of teaching ability, to broadcast seed on a wind that will take it to every fertile corner – imposes the duty of taking advantage of it'.[5] The absence of regular scheduling and continuity announcers was a sign that the BBC expected listeners to choose their programmes intelligently to enable them to enlarge their range of interests and to expand their knowledge. It was therefore regarded as foolish for listeners simply to turn on the wireless and expect automatically to find programme material which would be of interest to them. Reith summed up BBC policy in these early years in the following terms:

> So the responsibility as at the outset conceived, and despite all discouragements pursued, was to carry into the greatest number of homes everything that was best in every department of human knowledge, endeavour and achievement; and to avoid whatever was or might be hurtful. In earliest years accused of setting out to give the public not what it wanted but what the BBC thought it should have, the answer was that few knew what they wanted, fewer what they needed. In any event, it was better to overestimate than to underestimate.[6]

BBC policy was aimed at bringing to the microphone the best exponents available on different topics. This met with mixed results because, in a field such as light entertainment, variety artists in Scotland and indeed throughout the country feared that on radio they would quickly exhaust their material. The justification for the Reithian ethos was also linked to the BBC's conception of the audience which it served. The BBC tended to address the audience as a collection of individuals, often within families, rather than as a mass audience. Indeed, in a speech which Lord Reith delivered in March 1963 to mark the fortieth anniversary of broadcasting in Scotland, he stated that the pioneers of broadcasting spoke in terms of public service, not mass communication – individuals counted far more than masses.[7] This was a point emphasised by the BBC in the immediate postwar period when, in seeking to outline the dangers of introducing a commercial broadcasting system, it argued that such a system would only provide programmes geared to a mass audience. The BBC preferred to think of the audience in terms of majorities and minorities – all listeners would at different times fall into both categories depending upon their tastes and interests. The Reithian ethos tended to atomise the audience rather than view it in unitary terms. The BBC's conception of its audience was reflected in the use of mixed programming, whereby in any given day a diversity of interests would be catered for on one channel. The audience was expected to listen to the radio selectively and intelligently. In contrast with postwar broadcasting, there were few fixed time-slots, hence in theory listeners would be exposed to a wider range of programme material by virtue of being unable on many occasions to ignore certain programmes and opt mainly for either lighter or more highbrow programme items. A further point is that not only did the BBC think of its audience as composed of individuals; the BBC was thought of by the listeners as one individual with many voices but only one mouth. In one sense, it meant that the BBC was regarded as a body greater than the sum of its parts.[8] In another sense, this was true because all announcers tended to sound alike.

The issue of the accents used by announcers was at times a particularly sensitive one between Scotland and the other Regions, and London. It was closely linked with Reith's conception of the BBC as a public-service broadcasting organisation. In 1924, referring to the pronunciation of words on radio, Reith stated that 'We have made a special effort to secure in our various stations men who, in the presentation of programme items, the reading of news bulletins and so on, can be relied upon to employ the correct pronunciation of the English tongue'.[9] During 1926, Reith established an advisory committee on Spoken English, replaced in 1939 by a Pronunciation Unit. He sought to avoid bringing local accents and dialects to the microphone, partly because he wanted announcers to sound intelligible in all parts of the country and not irritate anyone; and partly because the standard BBC accent reinforced the authority of the BBC. For example, in 1927, reference to the need for a first-class announcer for the proposed Scottish Regional station was explicitly taken to mean one with a perfect English manner of speech.[10] However, there was, strictly speaking, nothing resembling 'BBC English' because the BBC never imposed its own pronunciations on English words. The problem was that the particular accent which the BBC opted for (i.e. an educated southern English voice known as received pronunciation) tended to identify the BBC with a particular section of society – southern English, middle- and upper-middle-class, and public-school-educated. This irritated some Scottish listeners. During a period in which radio was the dominant medium, accents were more noticeable than they would have been if they had been accompanied by visual images as in the postwar television era. It is also interesting to note that, unlike America, there was no individualised announcing and so the personality of the announcer was subservient to the corporate image of the BBC. Furthermore, it appeared that there was a class barrier which was being erected between the BBC and some members of the audience which it served, although this was less evident in Scotland. This may have been due to the alleged greater professionalism of announcers in London in comparison with their counterparts in the Regions. [11] Nevertheless, accents delivered by announcers of Scottish birth tended to emanate from educated Scots who had lost their broad Scottish accent. Only from the 1960s was a wider range of regional accents heard on the BBC, thus giving the impression that the BBC was less distant socially from the audience which it served. This process continued to such an extent that, during the 1980s, popular network programmes, such as the Scottish production *Tutti Frutti* with its strong Scottish accents, must have been barely understandable to many English viewers.

The BBC was able to pursue a Reithian policy of public service because, during these interwar years and in the immediate postwar period, it could take its audiences for granted given the absence of any national competitive broadcasting system. The BBC could provide a variety of services because radio was a less expensive medium than television and, most importantly, because income was guaranteed via the licence fee regardless of the popularity of individual programmes.[12] Reith's strength of character as Director-General was also a significant factor. Unfortunately, the Reithan ethos tended to become associated with metropolitan rather than local or regional culture. This reflected a narrowness in Reith's outlook. He combined his high-minded policy with a degree of caution in not wishing to offend either the government or important individuals in society. Yet in a sense it was almost impossible to pursue fully the Reithian idea of informing the public without offending somebody, since news which was reliable and impartial might also be controversial. Nonetheless, the Reithian ethos enveloped programme staff because they believed that they belonged to a closed community. Conflicts among staff over the direction of BBC policy were in most cases internalised rather than made public. It was only with the growth and complexity of the BBC, especially during the war years, the departure of Reith in June 1938, and the experience of wartime broadcasting, that the Reithian ideals began to come under greater pressure. The physical growth of the BBC, with a staff of almost 4,000 by the time Reith left in 1938, made it increasingly difficult for him to stamp on it his public service ideals. In particular, Reith disliked the use of listener research and the development of television, both of which from his perspective were viewed as threats to his public service philosophy because they would pander to popular rather than 'serious' cultural tastes. Reith never really accepted the development of television, firstly because he had a greater affinity with, and acquaintance of, sound rather than television broadcasting; and secondly because television threatened to impose far more pressures on the Reithian public service ethos than sound broadcasting had ever done. He consequently wished to constrain its autonomy. Yet it was initially within sound broadcasting during the war years that the challenge to the Reithian ideals first became most evident. The Forces Programme which was created to cater for more popular tastes and maintain the nation's morale, paved the way for a more far-reaching departure from Reith's public service ideals which came to fruition during the postwar reorganisation of the broadcasting services.

The BBC Regions were too large to represent communities with a common sense of social and cultural identity. Scotland was a nation of regions and so could not easily be treated as a single region as the BBC sought to do. In Scotland, the BBC was given the status of 'National Region'. It was regarded as a Region because Scotland represented only one part of a unitary BBC covering the whole of the United Kingdom; it was regarded as a National Region because it served a nation, thus distinguishing it from one of the BBC's English Regions. According to the BBC, Scotland was in broadcasting terms both a nation and a region. The Corporation regarded the words 'Region' and 'Regional' as a convenience for denoting broadcasting outwith the London area. In 1938, in a letter to the Scottish National Party about broadcasting in Scotland, the BBC's Controller (Public Relations) offered the following comments on the use of the term 'Region' in BBC terminology:

> May I explain that we regard the term 'Region' as one of administra-
> tive convenience, and we do not think that listeners generally share
> your view that it carries a deprecatory connotation, or that the use of it
> by the BBC implies a failure to recognise the special claims of Scotland
> as a nation.[13]

Listeners in Scotland and BBC staff in Scotland experienced a greater sense of separate identity from London than did listeners and staff in the English Regions. Friction between London and the Regions was not uncommon. For example, as early as 1930, Regional Directors had disliked the practice whereby officials at Head Office negotiated with outside bodies and individuals in their Regions without informing them, thus undercutting their authority.[14] There is also evidence that the BBC's staff in Scotland were concerned that the Corporation was regarded as a wholly English institution, thus undermining its status in Scottish society. In 1936, the Scottish Regional Director sent a memorandum to the Director-General regarding the need for the BBC to avoid the use of the term 'English' when 'British' was meant.[15] It appears that

Scottish sensitivity on this subject was not wholly catered for, because, just over four years later, another memorandum stated that a reminder was to be issued to programme staff on the same issue.[16]

Broadcasting in Scotland was not regarded as so popular a pastime as it was in other parts of the country, thus prompting Melville Dinwiddie, the incoming Scottish Regional Director, to agree with Reith that there was a need in Scotland to popularise broadcasting and increase the number of licence-holders in proportion to the population.[17] Scotland was a poorer country than England and this, together with the cautious nature of Scots, helps to explain why fewer people possessed receiving sets. Also, there were many crystal sets still in use in the large cities and this may have dissuaded individuals from discarding them in favour of a valve set. In rural areas which did not have a mains electricity supply, listeners with valve sets had to rely upon battery models. A few months after taking up his appointment as Scottish Regional Director, Dinwiddie sent a report on broadcasting in Scotland to Reith and commented: 'The task in Scotland, therefore, is one of providing programmes for listeners, many of whom cannot afford proper receiving sets, and of breaking down the national reserve which is very apparent in many country districts. What is required, therefore, is a campaign of intensive propaganda and increased programme efficiency.'[18] Moreover, it was noted that Scottish newspapers were not always anxious to publicise or to comment upon radio programmes, but they did publish a daily list of programmes. Dinwiddie regarded publicity for Scottish programmes and the maintenance of good contacts with newspapers as important, as well as the need to raise the prestige of the BBC in various cities, notably Dundee (where there was no local station) and Aberdeen. Most daytime programme items were taken from London and the other Regions, whereas during the evenings Scottish items, such as broadcasts by the BBC Scottish Orchestra, were fitted into the programme schedule. Dinwiddie particularly disliked the use of the term 'Scottish national transmitter' since this implied a programme of peculiar interest to Scottish people. Sometimes Scottish material was taken by the other Regions, and occasionally material which was broadcast in the National Programme might be repeated at a later date on the Scottish Regional Programme, a process referred to by the BBC as diagonalisation. The output of the Scottish station was designed to cater for the whole of Scotland, not local areas, and this resulted in some degree of submerging of cultural diversity within Scotland. Some attempt was however made, such as in the programme *Frae A' The Airts*, to gather material from a number of different rural localities as a means of recording the life and traditions of the people. There were also outside broadcasts, but in the case of concerts the promoters were perhaps understandably more concerned about these than about studio performances by artists, and so the BBC did not entirely have a free hand. In cultural terms, broadcasting provided an outlet for new artists and composers, whereas established artists were more cautious about radio. The Scottish *Children's Hour* continued to be a popular regular feature, but in general the BBC did not escape criticism in the press about the lack of Scottish items which were broadcast.

The Scottish Regional Director, whose powers did not extend to technical matters, was given a weekly programme allowance which was assessed quarterly. The amount could be exceeded in any given week provided that the excess was saved within the quarterly period. Scotland was entitled to notify Head Office of future programme developments which might necessitate an increase in the programme allowance for the subsequent quarterly period. The Scottish Region could also apply for a special grant to cover any specifically expensive programme. The Scottish Regional Director, who was responsible to the Controller (Programmes) in London with regard to programme policy, had to decide on the balance between the transmission of London material, English Regional material and Scottish-originated material. But financial considerations constrained this decision-making process, as Asa Briggs noted: 'There were few outside programmes which they were bound to take, but their ability to produce local programmes was limited not only by human resources but by programme finance.'[19] The Scottish Region, in common with the other BBC Regions, was at a disadvantage compared to London because it did not have the staff, training or material resources (studios and equipment) to specialise in the type of output which was of a sufficiently high standard to be confidently recommended for national broadcasting to any great extent.[20] Regions wanted to be in a position whereby they could contribute more items to the National Programme. Also, if many programmes from London were strongly recommended for inclusion in the Regional Programme, then this left less room to include Regional material. Although expenditure could be shared on programmes contributed to the National Programme, in general Regional programmes were expected to contrast with the National Programme and this therefore placed further constraints on the ability of Scotland to produce programmes which were likely to have a national appeal. In theory it should have been possible to treat subjects of national interest from a regional perspective, but Regions did not always find items from other Regions acceptable.

The introduction of the Regional Scheme thus brought about advantages and disadvantages. It provided better reception for listeners and alternative programme services, but it was, as indicated, accompanied by a degree of centralised control.[21] There was consultation between Scotland and London which took place via the exchange of memoranda and at the meetings of the Regional Director and Regional Programme heads. By the early 1930s, the centralised nature of broadcasting was being commented upon. For example, an article in *The Listener* in 1934 on the constitutional position of the BBC stated that 'The British system, though it has a number of regional stations both in its northern and southern areas, is largely centralised on a national basis in London, and pivoted on Broadcasting House'.[22] It is not simply the case that it was more cost-effective to centralise production; there was an implicit assumption that culture emanating from local areas was in some sense inferior to metropolitan culture. Central control from London was viewed by Reith and the BBC as consistent with the Corporation's monopoly position, the efficient use of resources to expand broadcasting, and the maintenance of public service ideals (i.e. uniformity in both policy and standards). BBC Regions such as Scotland were not, except in exceptional cases, expected to embark on any project if such work could be performed equally well or at higher standards and more economically by London. Yet local items were expected to be of a reasonable standard that might merit their inclusion in the London Programme. At a meeting of Regional Programme Directors held in January 1934, the Controller (Programmes) emphasised that there should be no competition between London and the Regions in programming matters and that Regional material had always to be subject to justification on artistic and economic grounds.[23] This often resulted in Regions producing programmes which London could not supply. Perhaps it did seem that broadcasting which began on a local basis because of technical factors (i.e. the absence of high-power transmitters) had been replaced by a more authoritative and paternal approach to broadcasting in which the professionals replaced the amateurs.[24]

The relationship between London and the Regions had been of concern to Regional Directors for some time. They were not always willing to accept the overriding character of national policy. At a Control Board meeting in February 1933, it was noted that Regional Directors wished to be informed of important policy changes affecting them through their meetings at Head Office rather than having final decisions conveyed to them by memoranda. They wanted more frequent meetings with Head Office staff and more frequent interchange of specialists between London and the Regions. In 1935, the BBC undertook a survey of the Regions. Visits were made to interview staff, inspect premises, and to monitor Regional programmes and the reactions of listeners to them. The overall aim was to gain a greater understanding of Regional needs and problems. The Report on the Regions by Charles Siepmann, the recently-appointed Director of Regional Relations, was compiled in January 1936. This report drew attention to the dangers resulting from centralisation in London. Siepmann argued in the report that the Regions were being deprived of opportunities for self expression because of lack of resources. He commented:

> Centralization represents a short-sighted policy. The provinces are the seedground of talent and the ultimate source of our supply for London programmes. The existence and development of our Regional work provides an effective insurance policy against the drying up of resources of supply for our programmes.[25]

Siepmann drew attention to the power of broadcasting to create standardisation in tastes, standards and values in line with the wishes of London. This was contrasted with enthusiasm among listeners in the Regions for local broadcasts. Siepmann argued that the case for Regional broadcasting should not be measured by the single yardstick of artistic achievement, but must take account of the patronage of local arts and coverage of local life and local interests. He noted that Regional Directors were critical of the fact that Regional needs were not being given fair consideration by Head Office. There was found to be a need for more staff to assist in widening the range of Regional material. Regional staff tended to be 'jacks of all trades' who often thereby had to work much harder than their London colleagues. It was also noted that they were spending too much time on administrative rather than programme work and thereby finding it more difficult to bring their standards up to those of Head Office, as well as to cast their net much wider geographically within the Regions to enable them to draw upon artistic talent from a much wider area. Taking all these factors into account, Siepmann therefore argued for a number of changes: a greater delegation of responsibility to Regional Directors; better working conditions and training to provide the opportunities for Regional staff to raise their professional standards; better studio facilities and equipment to help improve programme quality and thereby enrich provincial life; more Regional listener research to help shape programme policy; the use of publicity, such as through exhibitions and lectures, to explain BBC policy in the Regions; and more regular contacts between London and the Regions for all grades of staff in order to avoid misunderstandings between them. Siepmann wanted heads of departments in London to become more aware of Regional programme output. For example, visits by senior staff in London could assist in assuring the provincial press and listeners in the Regions that Head Office was taking an interest in their programme needs and activities. Furthermore, the report by Siepmann stated that the policy whereby Regions were not to embark on projects which could be produced better in London had impoverished Regional programme initiatives. It was also thought to be desirable for a greater proportion of Regional material to be included in the London Programme. In Scotland, Siepmann specifically argued in favour of an extension of facilities for talks, outside broadcasts and feature programmes; in all Regions he pointed to the need for Regional services to be more evenly equated with Regional needs and resources.

The mere fact that the BBC decided to initiate a survey on the Regions appeared to indicate at least some concern about the degree of centralisation which had taken place since 1929. In commenting upon the Siepmann Report, the BBC's Controller of Programmes agreed that more Regional material should be broadcast nationally if standards were acceptable, but added that there was no desire to establish autonomous programme centres which would merely replace London centralisation with local centralisation. There was agreement on the need to strengthen programme staffing in Scotland and improve studio facilities, assuming that there was adequate material available to build upon, and that high standards could be attained. It was generally accepted that Regions were understaffed and that there was a need for regular exchanges of staff between London and the Regions. The BBC was not alone in looking at Regional broadcasting because a government Committee of Inquiry was at this time also examining the various broadcasting services.

On 17 April 1935, the government had appointed a committee chaired by Viscount Ullswater to consider the constitution, control and finance of the broadcasting service, and to advise on the conditions under which the service was to be conducted after 31 December 1936 when the Charter and Licence would expire. The Ullswater Report was published on 16 March 1936. On constitutional matters, the committee recommended that the BBC's Charter should be extended for ten years from 1 January 1937 and that the number of Governors, who were incidentally not expected to be specialists or representatives of any localities, should be increased from five to seven. The licence fee was to remain at ten shillings and the ban on advertising was to continue. But it was suggested that a serving minister should be responsible for broadcasting, thus leaving technical matters to the PMG. In referring to the size of the BBC Regions, the committee stated that it was undesirable that large populations which differed widely in their character and culture should be combined within a single Region.[26] Furthermore, it recognised that Regions were subject to financial constraints since they were expected on most occasions to operate within the limits of their weekly programme allowance and had to consult with London if they wished to pay higher fees to artists. The Ullswater Committee believed that there was a need for a satisfactory proportion of Regional material to be included in programmes and that therefore the BBC should seek to increase the volume of programme items originating within the Regions, as well as to continue with the policy of decentralisation as indicated in the Corporation's report on the Regions. It was also suggested that there needed to be some review of the BBC's advisory structure. In particular, the committee believed that although the BBC's General Advisory Council should continue in operation, there should be a similar type of committee for each Region which Regional Directors could consult as required. Moreover, it was argued that specialised committees should also be established in each Region. However, although the Ullswater Committee suggested that the membership of these advisory committees should be 'comprehensive', especially in order to include younger people, it was prepared to allow the BBC to make appointments to these committees. At that time, Scotland was already served by advisory committees covering religion, music and appeals as well as a sub-council of the Central Council for School Broadcasting.

The government published its recommendations (Cmd 5207) on the Ullswater Report in June 1936. It accepted that the Charter should be extended for ten years and that the number of Governors should be increased to seven. The ban on advertising was to remain, but the government did not accept that responsibility for broadcasting should be divided between the PMG and a senior minister. The PMG was to continue to be responsible for all aspects of broadcasting policy. The government accepted that the BBC should continue a policy of decentralisation and thus include a higher proportion of Regional material in programme output. It also suggested that there should be a General

Advisory Committee in each Region in addition to the Regional specialist advisory committees. In July, just after the publication of the government's memorandum on the Ullswater Report, the BBC outlined its decisions on the report by the Director of Regional Relations. The Corporation accepted that broadcasting had to reflect the life of the whole country, not merely that of the metropolis, but it was again confirmed that there was no desire to replace metropolitan by Regional centralisation. It was recognised that Regional programmes contrasted with metropolitan output and needed to be included in both the National and London Regional programmes as well as to cater for local interests. The BBC went on to state that 'There is thus considerable and definite justification, not only for the existence of the Regional organisations, but also for the development of their activities'.[27] In its annual report for 1936, the BBC again emphasised that there remained ample scope for Regional programme diversity. However, the BBC added a cautionary note about the limitations on the autonomy of the Regions consistent with the need to ensure uniformity of policy in some areas such as staffing, finance and programme standards. Greater provision was later made for the representation of Regional views in London and for more specialised staff in the Regions, but central control over the number of staff employed in the Regions continued to be exercised. This placed continuing constraints on Regional programme activity because Regions were asked to tailor their programme commitments to the number of staff available. One area where improvements did take place after 1936 was in the introduction of a systematic procedure for ascertaining the views of listeners throughout the country on the content of programmes in order to assist in the planning of programmes geared as closely as possible to the interests of listeners in the various Regions.

The BBC, as already noted, had a series of advisory committees, but these had inherent limitations in their ability to keep the BBC in touch with public opinion. These committees tended in any case to be composed of subject specialists rather than ordinary listeners. Regional Programme Directors recommended at a meeting held in 1934 that the BBC should begin a systematic survey of listeners' habits and that a statistical department should be established for this purpose. Just over two years later, on 1 October 1936, the BBC eventually established a Listener Research Department. It was an attempt to introduce a systematic study of audience reaction to programme material, a reaction which could not be gauged accurately via letters from listeners since these tended to come from middle-class listeners and were not necessarily representative of public opinion. Indeed it can also be said that those people who were either very enthusiastic or very critical of programmes were more likely to send letters than those who mildly praised BBC output. So although the BBC never regarded itself as out of touch with public opinion due to the large correspondence which it received from listeners, the Corporation was anxious to determine the number of listeners who tuned in to its broadcasts as well as the reaction of listeners to these broadcasts. Licence figures only indicated ownership of receivers, and, because there was only one licence per household, there were obviously more listeners than licences. Also, unlike the theatre and the cinema, there were no box-office receipts or applause from the audience. The collection of data on listening habits was regarded as a means of assisting programme planning and demonstrating that the BBC did take account of the preferences of listeners. It was not regarded as a means whereby the public would be able to dictate programme content.

The BBC appointed Robert Silvey of the London Press Exchange as its Listening Research Officer. Reith disliked the whole philosophy behind audience research because he was suspicious that public opinion would in time be allowed to influence or even dictate programme content. If so, then this would circumvent the Reithian belief that the BBC should provide those programmes which it (the BBC) thought was in the best interests of the public which it served. Reith suspected that audience research would become the master rather than the servant of programme planners. He may also have suspected, and quite rightly, that given a free choice the public would prefer more popular to more serious programme material. Moreover, the concept of audience research had undesirable associations with market research, and Reith did not regard the audience as a market. Nevertheless the BBC went ahead and used two methods to ascertain listener preferences: daily interviews in each Region to determine which programmes the public listened to on the previous day; and listening panels to gauge audience reaction to programmes. Listeners who completed a log of which programmes they had listened to over a period of time were used to compile the listening barometer. The social survey of listening was later expanded in 1948 to encompass the viewing of television programmes in the London area. The survey undoubtedly became more complex when programme output and services were expanded after the war. The use of audience research in Scotland did enable the BBC to gauge the reaction of listeners in Scotland to the choice between the National Programme and the Scottish Regional Programme, but ultimately it was the BBC who decided on the use to which the results obtained were put in determining programme policy. In general, audience research statistics provided a valuable guide to the reaction of listeners to programmes, but they could not act as a substitute for the judgement of individual producers.

This discussion of broadcasting during the interwar years has concentrated primarily on sound broadcasting, and naturally so, because for the bulk of the audience during this period BBC broadcasting was in effect radio broadcasting. However, although the growth of television broadcasting, its eclipse of radio broadcasting and its extension to the Regions such as Scotland did not occur until the 1950s, the origins of television broadcasting can be traced to the interwar years. By the early 1930s, many of the basic ideas about the operational characteristics of television had been formulated. In the autumn of 1929, the BBC gave the Baird Company facilities for experimental transmissions which began on 30 September using low-definition television (thirty lines per picture), but this system produced little picture detail. These transmissions continued during the following year with sound signals added. In August 1932, the BBC arranged with Baird Television public experimental transmissions from the Corporation's London station at Brookman's Park. A studio was made available at Broadcasting House and the first television programme was transmitted on 22 August. The drawback with this system was that because it operated at only thirty lines per picture, little detail could be produced. Also, in the Baird system, each picture was repeated $12\frac{1}{2}$ times per second and so irritating flicker was visible. A suitable system had to be one which would provide better picture definition (i.e. more lines per picture) and less flicker (i.e. more pictures per second). With the need to determine which system might be technically satisfactory in the long term for public transmission, the government decided to appoint a committee to look into the matter.

On 14 May 1934, the government appointed a committee under the chairmanship of Lord Selsdon to consider the development of television, to advise the PMG on the relative merits of the various television systems, and to examine the conditions under which any public service of television should be provided. The report of the Television Committee was published in January 1935.[28] Given the inherent limitations of low-definition television, the Selsdon Committee sensibly rejected its use in any public television service. The committee instead recommended that any system adopted had to produce at least 240 lines per picture and a minimum picture frequency of twenty-five per second. High-definition television thus required the use of very high frequencies which had a shorter range than the medium waves which were used for radio broadcasting. The committee wanted Baird and Marconi-EMI to be allowed to demonstrate their systems in a service operating from London. Thereafter, a network of stations could be built to serve the rest of the country. The government subsequently accepted the committee's recommendations. Sir H. Kingsley Wood (the PMG) indicated in the House of Commons in January 1935 that because of the close relationship between sound and television broadcasting, the BBC would be entrusted with the conduct of the television service. In the light of experience gained from the London television station, the PMG said that consideration would be given to the establishment of additional stations in other parts of the country. The PMG went on to state: 'I wish to emphasise that, whilst high-definition television has now reached such a stage of development as to justify these first steps being taken towards the establishment of a public television service, many difficulties will have to be overcome before a service can be provided on a national scale.'[29] This ruled out the prospect of the early extension of television to Scotland.

In the absence of any separate television licence, the initial system had to be funded from the ten-shilling sound licence. The Selsdon Committee had recommended that the BBC should be entrusted with control over television, and so on 2 November 1936 it was the BBC which introduced the first regular, public, high-definition, VHF television service in the world. The BBC did not wish to lose its monopoly or for television to be developed on a commercial basis by private enterprise. Under its Director of Television, Gerald Cock, the service began on an experimental basis by broadcasting for one hour each evening from two small stations at Alexandra Palace, London. The site was 300 feet above sea level and so the 300-foot aerial was able to reach to 600 feet above sea level. The Baird (240-line) and Marconi-EMI (405-line) systems were used alternately each week until 8 February 1937, when the latter system was officially adopted. The high costs of initiating and sustaining a television service prevented television from eclipsing sound broadcasting. In those pioneering days, few people possessed television receivers (which only had eight-inch by six-inch picture tubes), because they were expensive since unlike the early wireless receivers they were not assembled by amateur enthusiasts, yet neither were they mass-produced. At any rate, there were few programmes because of restrictive practices by theatrical and musical interests, and because broadcasting hours were limited to about two hours daily and transmissions were confined to the London area. There was some pressure on behalf of traders to get television extended to Scotland and other BBC Regions. Indeed, in June 1939, a deputation which included representatives from the Scottish Radio Retailers' Association urged the PMG to support the speedy geographical extension of television. The government was however unwilling to sanction the cost of the extension of television to the Regions. The slow expansion of television to the Regions made the Scottish Regional Programme Director's comments in 1937 appear in retrospect premature when he wondered whether arrangements would be made for training Regional sound producers in television production. Reith had misgivings about the potential impact of television, fearing that it would encourage passive viewing among the audience. Others believed that television would make casual listening impossible because of the presence of the visual element. The BBC Annual for 1936 indicated that television would have a more profound effect than radio on communications.[30] But it was not to do so for some time because on 1 September 1939, the television service closed down because of the Second World War. By that time, about 23,000 receivers were in use and programme output had increased to three-and-a-half hours each evening. In radio, Regional broadcasting was also suspended and was replaced by a single national Home Service Programme, supplemented in January 1940 by a Forces Programme. Full Regional broadcasting services did not resume until after the war.

Broadcasting during the war years, 1939–45

With the outbreak of war in 1939, the BBC's Scottish Region, in common with other Regional services, was merged into a single Home Service programme which was planned in London and broadcast from 7.00am to midnight. The change to a single Home Service was initiated for security reasons. The synchronising of transmitters throughout the country, so that each would transmit the same programme, was aimed at avoiding giving navigational assistance to enemy aircraft. By grouping transmitters on one wavelength, enemy aircraft were thus unable accurately to locate any individual transmitter from a distance of over twenty-five miles. When these aircraft entered an area of approximately fifty miles in diameter around any transmitter, the BBC was ordered to close the transmitter to prevent aircraft from receiving any navigational bearing. However, listeners often continued to receive a signal, albeit sometimes weak, from other transmitters which were in any case transmitting the same programme. Wavelengths released through the synchronising of transmitters were thus used for broadcasting to European countries. Under these unusual conditions there was uncertainty as to when Regional services would resume, and, if so, whether they would operate on the same lines as the prewar service. A greater focus on Regional broadcasting had taken place after the BBC's review of Regional services during 1935 and 1936. The onset of war in Europe now thwarted attempts at developing these programme services. The single Home Service was unable to cater fully for the interests of listeners in Scotland, but it was in fact the paucity of Scottish items broadcast during the war years which gave added impetus to the need to plan for a new and expanded Scottish Regional service for the postwar period. Crucial decisions were to be taken from 1942 to 1944 which were significant in determining the structure which Regional programme services were to assume in the postwar period.

During the war, BBC staff and studios were dispersed both within London and to the Regions as a precaution against attack by enemy aircraft. In Scotland, broadcasting administration was transferred from Edinburgh to Glasgow for fear that the Edinburgh premises would be bombed. The war years also resulted in a rapid expansion of BBC staff throughout the UK from over 4,000 to almost 12,000. This was mainly attributable to the expansion of the overseas broadcasting services. The BBC also lost many of its existing staff. In Scotland, some key staff left to join the Forces, and this was also a factor in lessening programme activity. The Corporation compensated for the loss of staff and the need to recruit many new staff by employing women. The growth in staff numbers and the loss of many of the prewar members of staff both served to undermine the unity of the staff. Yet one of the most striking facts about these years was the popularity of broadcasting among listeners. Perhaps this was not unexpected given paper shortages, which reduced the size of newspapers, magazines and journals, as well as the closure of theatres and cinemas. Radio therefore assumed greater importance as a source of news and entertainment. With the advent of war, listeners wished to hear news and not specifically Scottish programmes. In broadcasting terms, the war was – as indicated in the title of the third volume of Asa Briggs' *History of Broadcasting* – a 'war of words', not of visual images, because of the importance of radio as a source of news and entertainment in the absence of television.[1] At the end of September 1939, there were just over nine million licences held in the UK, of which 783,883 were current in Scotland; by 1945 this figure had increased slowly to 9.7 million. During the war years there was a significant reduction in the production of receivers. The practical effect of this was that a significant number of small manufacturers ceased to produce receiving sets, thereby leaving a much smaller number of major manufacturers to dominate the market. But in these conditions of restricted competition, it was possible for manufacturers to devote more research into technical improvements which were ultimately beneficial to listeners.

Wartime conditions also brought about changes in the method of funding the BBC's services and in governmenal control over the Corporation. Most of the non-technical powers of the PMG were now transferred to the Minister of Information. The Minister had the right to prescribe broadcasting hours and to veto any broadcast. The government had an obvious interest in exercising greater – but not absolute – control over the BBC during this period, particularly on matters directly related to the war effort. As regards the funding of programme services, the BBC now derived its income from an annual Grant-in-Aid.[2] This gave additional leverage to the government over the BBC as a safeguard that programmes would not be detrimental to the conduct of the war effort. The BBC was, for example, not permitted to include in its news bulletins any commentary which was not approved by the government. There was constant liaison between the BBC and the government during the war years. There was censorship to the extent that unscripted programme material was not permitted to be broadcast 'live' for fear of providing information to the enemy. However, the BBC did not use radio as an instrument of propaganda. The Corporation was therefore able to enhance its reputation during the war years, both at home and abroad. This reputation was enhanced with its unemotional style in delivering news bulletins. Overall, the BBC thus retained a degree of independence from the government because it was never subject to absolute control by the Ministry of Information, but equally it never had complete freedom of action.

There was little Scottish material broadcast during the first few weeks of the war. Those programmes which were broadcast were confined to items such as music from the BBC Scottish Orchestra or religious services of the Church of Scotland. On 27 September 1939, Regional programme policy was discussed at a meeting of the Control Board and the following two points were agreed upon: peacetime Regional policy had to disappear and so Regional output would be subject to the needs of the whole country, but nevertheless some programmes would be drawn from the Regions; and the number of Regional contributions would decline as increasing demand was made on engineering staff.[3] What this implied within the constraints of a single Home Service was the introduction of centralised programme planning with programmes expected to have general rather than Regional appeal. It also meant a significant reduction in the number of programmes which were taken from the Regions. These were the criteria which were outlined at a further meeting two days later.[4] Within these constraints, it took time for more Scottish material to be slotted into the programme schedule. In November 1939, a Gaelic news summary and a weekly Gaelic programme were introduced. On 4 December, daily morning programmes of physical and mental exercises were included in the Home Service and continued to be broadcast throughout the war years. A war news section and a Scottish Recording Unit were established to gather items for both the Home and Overseas services. Scottish news stories were provided not merely for listeners at home but were also included in the Forces Programme (introduced in January 1940) and the General Forces Programme (introduced in February 1944) for the benefit of Scots serving abroad in the armed forces. Nevertheless, before the end of the year, Regional Directors were asking for a greater employment of Regional artists and inclusion of Regional programme items in the Home Service.[5] This was agreed in principle. By this time, Scotland no longer had the services of its advisory committees because meetings of these committees had been suspended in September 1939. The changeover to a single Home Service had also prompted members of the Saltire Society to write to the BBC's Director-General to protest at the virtual cessation of Scottish programmes. But the prospect of the introduction of a special programme for the Forces appeared in theory to offer a brighter prospect that more Scottish programme items might be heard by a wider audience.

It was agreed in principle at a meeting of the Control Board on 29 November 1939 that plans should be prepared for a special service for the fighting forces.[6] These plans came to fruition on 7 January 1940 when the BBC introduced an alternative programme on an experimental basis to provide lighter programme material (i.e. dance and jazz music, variety, sports items and news) for the troops serving in the British Expeditionary Force. Based on the evidence of listener research, the BBC did not believe that the troops were likely to want talks or drama. It was hoped that this programme would also be of interest to listeners at home. Indeed, the alternative programme was not specifically regarded by the BBC as a programme purely for the Forces. The

Radio Times commented upon the introduction of the new programme service:
> We hope that these new programmes will be welcomed by the men
> for whom they are meant. But we should explain that this week's
> special programmes are only a beginning. This is an experiment. If
> it succeeds, the BBC hopes to provide a much more complete pro-
> gramme for the Forces before very long.[7]

The alternative programme included Home Service items. It continued to
broadcast on an experimental basis until 17 February. On the following day, an
extended programme was provided from 11.00am to 11.00pm. This Forces
Programme included more items of interest to listeners in the Forces stationed
at home and abroad. It included regular broadcasts of records, association
football and variety concerts interspersed with programme material taken from
the Home Service. The Home Service broadcast trailers for items in the Forces
Programme. The BBC hoped that the new service would boost the morale of the
troops, many of whom listened using portable receivers. Apart from the need to
sustain the morale of troops serving overseas or in isolated camps in Britain far
from their families and friends, the BBC was also anxious not to lose this
audience to overseas stations, and so this provided additional justification for
the introduction of the Forces Programme. The new service was also of interest
to many listeners at home, and indeed attracted a larger audience than the
Home Service. From July 1940, the Home and Forces Programmes were
planned as contrasting services. Civilian listeners took some comfort from the
fact that they were sharing listening of the Forces Programme with their friends
and relatives who were serving in the fighting forces.

Radio thus helped to compensate for the geographical distance between
them. But the introduction of the new service did not lead to any significant
increase in the number of Scottish items broadcast. Indeed, on a visit to
Scotland during 1940, the BBC Chairman and Director-General were reported
to have found a widespread feeling that Scotland was under-represented in
programme output.[8] It was noted that efforts would be made to remedy the
situation. One week later, approval was given for a weekly *Scottish Half-Hour*
and also for the fortnightly talk to be broadcast weekly.[9] More Scottish items
were broadcast in the overseas services than in the domestic services, and so
there was no comprehensive and varied service which could reflect the culture
and life of Scotland. The situation could not be rectified until Scotland was
provided with a separate wavelength, but this was not to occur until after the
war. There were also problems in receiving the services which were available.
In November 1940, the Minister of Information, Alfred Duff Cooper, was asked
whether he was aware that the Forces Programme was inaudible over wide
areas in Scotland.[10] A low-power transmitter was opened in Aberdeen, one of
several transmitters built during the war years. With high-power transmitters
being closed down during air raids, these low-power transmitters were built in
order to compensate for the loss of service when the main transmitters were
closed. The low-power transmitters did not have to close down until enemy

aircraft were within a few miles of the transmitter, and so programmes could still be heard during the early stages of an air-raid. One further matter which was of concern to listeners in Scotland, and which gave rise to some irritation, was the inclusion of announcements on the radio without any indication given as to whether or not they applied to Scotland. These incidents, which gave rise to some confusion and inconvenience, were brought to the attention of the Minister of Information to enable him to convey details to other government departments.

Towards the end of 1941, the BBC began to consider changes to its organisational structure to take account of changes which had been brought about because of the peculiar needs of wartime broadcasting. By October 1941, the BBC had come to the conclusion that it would be beneficial to appoint a businessman of wide experience to oversee organisational and financial matters. With this in mind, there was a proposal to approach Robert Foot, who was General Manager of the Gas, Light and Coke Company. At a special board meeting on 28 October, the BBC Chairman was authorised to invite Mr Foot to join the staff of the Corporation.[11] It was not until a meeting of the Board of Governors on 21 January 1942 that it was decided that executive control of the BBC under wartime conditions, involving a growth in the number and variety of staff and financial problems, called for different qualities and experience from those suited for peacetime control. The Governors therefore wanted a change in the Director-Generalship. Accordingly, Frederick Ogilvie, a former Vice-Chancellor of Queen's University Belfast who had succeeded Reith in 1938, was now asked to relinquish his post as Director-General. Ogilvie left the BBC a few days later and was replaced by two Directors-General, namely Robert Foot and Sir Cecil Graves (formerly Deputy Director-General). Foot was expected to deal mainly with administrative matters, and Graves was to take overall responsibility for programme output. These changes were relevant to broadcasting in Scotland because Foot was in favour of giving more autonomy to the Regions. Under his reorganisation, centralisation was to be replaced by a greater degree of decentralisation.

Robert Foot altered the centralised decision-making structure which had survived for many years under Reith's control. Reorganisation was prompted by the need to secure better administrative and financial control. The financial costs of broadcasting had risen significantly because of wartime needs. It therefore became increasingly important to gain greater information and hence greater control over how financial resources were being used. In administrative terms, the plan was to review Reith's centralised structure. Foot abolished the central administrative division and instead left each division to be responsible for its own administrative operations. This served to reduce rivalry between programme and administrative staff which had resulted from Reith's reorganisation of 1933 in which these two functions were separated organisationally. Foot was anxious to give more autonomy to Regional Directors especially in view of the restrictions on their activities since the start of the war. At a meeting of Regional Directors held on 22 April 1942, Foot outlined the proposed arrangements for increased administrative control in the Regions by Regional Directors and for stricter financial control generally within the BBC.[12] There was a proposal that output Controllers should be responsible financially and functionally for programme expenditure in the Regions; the status of Regional Directors was to remain unchanged, although Regional Directors viewed the changes as resulting in a transfer of their powers to the output Controllers. What was agreed was that although Regional programme staff should be both financially and functionally responsible to output Controllers for programme expenditure, Regional Directors would be responsible both politically and operationally for the conduct of the service in their Regions. Regional Directors were also to be invited to monthly meetings in London with the Controllers and were permitted to have better access to the Director-General.

By this time, programme staff in Scotland were producing a more varied range of items for listeners within wartime constraints. These programme items included concerts given by the BBC Scottish Orchestra under its conductor Ian Whyte, a series entitled *Roads in Scotland* about the Scottish countryside, *Scottish Portraits* on the work of famous Scotsmen, variety in the weekly *Scottish Half-Hour*, a *Children's Hour*, Scottish news, some Gaelic broadcasts, contributions to schools programmes, Sunday religious broadcasts, drama, and coverage of anniversaries such as the St Andrew's day broadcasts. Scotland had a news unit which contributed items to a magazine programme. This was part of a general expansion of news-gathering services during the war years. The Scottish Recording Unit travelled throughout the country to gather suitable items for broadcasting. Under wartime conditions, and because of the need to expand the output in the overseas services, the BBC made greater use of recorded items. This was particularly important, given that programmes which were broadcast overseas had to be repeated at different times of the day to suit the various local listening hours in different countries. This Scottish programme output was only part of a much larger programme schedule, but at least during 1942 staff were aware that Regional broadcasting would be given special attention in any postwar reorganisation. A year earlier, a book written by Peter Eckersley, the BBC's first Chief Engineer, had been published in which criticism was directed at the scale of prewar Regional broadcasting. Eckersley looked back upon the Regional Scheme and remarked that it had failed to live up to expectations. He complained that although the Scheme was designed to represent a technical means to provide alternative outlets for alternative programmes, it was used as a double outlet for virtually the same material.[13] Regions, such as Scotland, were never able to provide a complete service devoid of sustaining material from London or the other Regions. Indeed, the Regional Scheme as such did not provide listeners throughout the country with a choice of contrasting programmes at all times of the day. Given these reflections on Regional broadcasting midway through the war years, the question was to what extent a postwar service could be planned differently to avoid the deficiences which had accompanied the prewar service and to compensate for the absence of a separate Scottish service during the war years.

During 1943, proposals began to emerge concerning the possible structure of postwar services. Up until then, improvements in the Regional content of the programme schedules had been piecemeal. For example, in May 1943 the Board of Governors believed that it would be a good idea if opportunities could be taken where possible to include in the news bulletins items of public interest affecting the Regions. What appeared to be required at this time was a more thorough review of the needs of the Regions. In the absence of separate Regional services because of wartime requirements, such a review in effect meant a review of the options available for the postwar period. During the 1930s, there had been a centralising of production departments in London, a process which had been intensified during the war years for manpower, technical and military reasons, thus resulting in reductions in both Regional staff and Regional programme output. The expansion in programme output in the war years was a product primarily of the central and overseas production departments. So, during 1943, Regional Directors believed that it was necessary to map out the contours of the reversal of this trend as it might apply in the postwar period.[14] They advocated the need for an equalising of competition between London and the Regions and also between the Regions themselves. Attention was drawn to the fact that the central production departments were using their powers to ensure a regular transfer of the best talent from the Regions to London, thereby further depleting Regional output. What was desired was a revival of territorial broadcasting in order to provide sufficient coverage of local affairs to counterbalance the existing preoccupation of broadcasting and the national press with national and international affairs; and a greater use of external sources of programme material, mainly from the Regions for general, as opposed to territorial, broadcasting.

In December 1943, at a luncheon given in London by the BBC Governors to mark the Corporation's twenty-first anniversary, Mr Brendon Bracken (Minister of Information) praised the BBC's part in the war effort and went on to say that the reduction in Regional broadcasting during the war years had created the impression that the BBC was too London-minded. The Minister hoped that when the war was over, Regional broadcasting would flourish again. He remarked that a measure of home rule in broadcasting might be given to some BBC Regions and hoped that this might lessen the impact of the monopoly, especially if Regions competed against each other as suppliers of programme material. The questions which had to be considered were, first, whether there were sufficient resources to restore a credible Scottish service after the war; and second, whether Scotland would be given greater autonomy to reverse the centralising trend which had become evident from 1928 when Scottish staff and programmes were reduced and made subject to greater central control. There was also the question as to whether there would be scope for competition between London and the Regions, and even between the BBC Regions. In the

Yearbook for 1944, the BBC's Director-General, Robert Foot, commented upon the future pattern of postwar broadcasting services and stated that 'Plans for the postwar period will be based on a determination to restore programme services rapidly to the highest possible level of technical and artistic quality. This will be no scheme based on a metropolitan concentration of resources in London.'[15] He went on to argue that these plans would give more emphasis to Regional resources, combined with more responsibilities being allocated to Regional programme staff. However, listeners in Scotland were not looking purely for Scottish programmes in any future reorganised service. They were just as interested in non-Scottish programmes such as *Brains Trust*, ITMA and *Music while you Work*. Any postwar Scottish Regional service would have to be planned to take account of these considerations.

At the beginning of 1944, there was a readjustment in the programme services which were available to listeners at home and overseas. On 27 February 1944, the BBC introduced the General Forces Programme which was aimed at both home and overseas listeners. It superseded the Forces Programme and the General Overseas Service. The latter had relayed programmes to more distant countries where Forces were stationed, such as the Far East and the South-West Pacific. Part of this programme now became available to listeners in Britain under the new arrangements. Scottish-originated programmes such as the *Scottish Half-Hour* were now broadcast in the General Forces Programme. The change resulted in listeners both at home and abroad now hearing the same programme at the same time. The BBC argued that this was what the Forces wanted (i.e. the ability to listen to the same programme that their families were listening to at the same time). The cover page of the *Radio Times* offered the following comments which summed up the philosophy governing the introduction of the GFP:

> Now, for old and young, rich and poor, at home and scattered of necessity over the earth's surface, the wireless set will, we hope, become a symbol of the hearth, a gathering place for affectionate reunion. Those drawn round it, though divided in space, will be united in mood. To be sharing the same news, the same tunes, the same jokes, the same prayers and hymns, will, we believe, quicken the feeling of nearness and of kinship.[16]

The BBC also hoped that the GFP would lessen demand for commercial broadcasting after the war. This concern for the postwar pattern of broadcasting also embraced plans for the resumption of television. These plans were debated during 1944.

In January 1944, Gerald Cock prepared a memorandum for the Director-General on the conditions which would govern the operation of a postwar television service.[17] He hoped that lack of experience and the financial stringency which had accompanied the planning and operation of the prewar television service would not be repeated. Cock believed that one of the many problems which was likely to confront a postwar service would be opposition from vested theatrical, film and sporting interests, and so he suggested various possibilities for overcoming these potential obstacles. On technical matters, Cock recommended a change to a much higher line standard (i.e. 567 lines in comparison with the prewar 405-line standard), and also indicated that the possibility of colour television should not be ignored. With regard to the geographical coverage of the television service, he argued that a system of priority should be determined which would include the nature of the distribution system and plans for the siting of main and relay transmitters. He also indicated that new studio plant should be designed for television and that adaptation of existing but unsuitable premises should be avoided. Moreover, Cock believed that television studios should be located close to central London to avoid the necessity for lengthy journeys by important artists. Not surprisingly, although he recognised the necessity for covering Regional activities, he emphasised that television could be operated more economically in centralised studio plant in London. This argument sounded familiar because it had also been expounded during the 1920s as justification for a policy of centralisation in sound broadcasting. It seemed that in Scotland, as in the other Regions, outside television broadcasts would be more feasible because they would not require expensive and sophisticated studio plant.

On the issue of staff organisation, Gerald Cock stated that television should be given the status of a division instead of a department in order to reflect the special skills of staff involved in television production, some of whom would have to be specially retrained. Towards the end of the war, the Minister of Information was asked whether he would press the BBC to provide in their postwar reorganised programme an extension of the television service to include the north of England, Scotland and Wales and thereby provide an additional amenity for residents in these areas as well as creating a more equitable distribution of retail trade between London and the rest of the country.[18] The Minister indicated in his reply that the BBC Governors would give favourable consideration to the extension of television outwith London when the outcome of the forthcoming Hankey Committee's report on television was known, a committee set up in 1943 to consider aspects of the operation of a television service after the war. The war delayed research work on television broadcasting because members of the BBC's research department either joined the armed forces or were seconded to government scientific establishments to assist in the war effort. Some engineering staff also helped to sustain the expansion of overseas sound broadcasting during the war years. The question was whether television would have to be developed after the war solely by the BBC, given that commercial interests would be unlikely to want to fund television development until there was evidence of a large potential audience. There was uncertainty when television would resume after the war, whereas with sound broadcasting a restructured service was likely to be introduced much sooner. It was both the structure and the philosophy governing postwar sound broadcasting which were of more immediate concern to the BBC and which were therefore examined in some detail during 1944 and the first few months of 1945.

In 1940, Regional Directors had agreed to recommend strongly that in any postwar reorganisation of the BBC services, Regional broadcasting should be given greater scope. What was envisaged were separate services for Scotland, Wales and Northern Ireland to complement the national service. The use of a large number of low-power stations to transmit material of local interest was also advocated.[19] By 1945, the BBC sought to make provision for separate Regional services in its reorganisation of sound broadcasting. Early in 1945, the Director-General told Regional Directors that the Corporation wished to restart Regional broadcasting on a strong footing, to encourage competition within the BBC to produce the best programmes consistent with the most efficient allocation of resources and manpower, to strengthen Regional output and to lessen antagonism between the Regions and London.[20] The Director-General also proposed that Regional Directors should take turns on a monthly rota basis to attend meetings in London, thus enabling them to gain a clearer view of overall policy and to assist in keeping the Regional perspective in mind when forming policy. This was in fact agreed. This concern about the structure of postwar broadcasting had been given added impetus after William Haley, formerly BBC Editor-in-Chief, replaced Robert Foot as Director-General on 31 March 1944. In November of that year, the Minister of Information had been asked in the House of Commons when a Scottish Regional station would reopen, given dissatisfaction in Scotland with existing programmes. There was therefore some pressure to outline what services were planned. Regional broadcasting represented one element in a projected restructuring of the format of the radio services.

The different programme services which were envisaged were initially referred to by the BBC in the planning stage as Programmes A, B and C. Programme A was intended to be a Regionalised programme of the same cultural standard as the Home Service, with a balanced programme output, and aimed at the middlebrow audience; Programme B was expected to be a popular programme presenting lighter material, not aimed at a mass audience, but nevertheless contrasting with Programme A; and Programme C was to be aimed at a high cultural level focusing on the arts and serious discussion, to be experimental in nature, and to provide an intelligent alternative during peak listening hours to Programme A. The Board of Governors approved in principle the latter recommendation of the Director-General.[21] The Regional components of Programme A were to be allowed to make contributions to Programmes B and C. In April 1945, Basil Nicolls (Senior Controller) prepared a revised outline of the structure of the postwar sound services.[22] In it, the title suggested for Programme A was the National Programme, with the components supplied by the Regions to be named geographically, such as the Scottish Programme, the Midland Programme, and so on. Possible titles for Programme B which were suggested included the National Alternative

Programme, BBC Popular Programme, or BBC Light Entertainment Programme; the title proposed for Programme C was the BBC Arts Programme. No simultaneous broadcasting was to be allowed between any two of the three programmes, except that Regions contributing to Programme C could take their programmes on SB in their Regional programme. Regional programmes were expected to be contrasted with Programme B. There was to be no charge for any programmes taken on SB because the originating service would cover such costs. Programmes A, B and C eventually became known as the Home, Light and Third Programmes. The Scottish Regional Programme, which was suspended during the war years, was superseded in July 1945 by the Scottish Home Service with its separate wavelength. In the postwar period, Scottish broadcasting was in a better position adequately to reflect the life, culture and interests of the people of Scotland.

Part Two

The reorganisation of broadcasting services and the end of the monopoly, 1945–54

The postwar reorganisation and development of BBC broadcasting, 1945–9

A new phase in the development of broadcasting, both in Scotland and throughout the country, began in 1945 with the reorganisation of the BBC's sound broadcasting services and the particular programme policies associated with each of those radio networks which were introduced between July 1945 and September 1946. A new sound broadcasting structure therefore emerged within a year of the resumption of postwar broadcasting. The introduction of the BBC Scottish Home Service in July 1945 marked the resumption of Scottish Regional broadcasting after a break of almost six years because of the war. The relationship between the Scottish Home Service and the other sound networks, and an account of why the period from 1947 to the mid-1950s has been regarded as a 'golden age' in Scottish radio broadcasting, form an essential part of the history of broadcasting from 1945 when Regional services resumed, until 1949 when the first major postwar inquiry into broadcasting under the chairmanship of Lord Beveridge began its work. During this period, television was also restarted, and, just over three years later in December 1949, it began to be extended to the Regions; it did not, however, reach Scotland until March 1952. The immediate postwar years also led to constitutional and organisational changes in BBC broadcasting. In January 1947, a Scottish Advisory Council was formed, one of a number of Regional Advisory Councils additional to the existing advisory committees, and charged with the responsibility of providing advice on Regional programme policy. This constitutional change was followed in December 1947 by an organisational change when the BBC's administrative reorganisation led to the creation of a Board of Management, with the administration of Regions such as Scotland then placed under the supervision of a Controller. Melville Dinwiddie, who was the BBC's Scottish Director, consequently became known as Controller, Scotland. By 1949, when the Beveridge Committee on Broadcasting was appointed and began its detailed examination of the BBC, the Corporation had four years' experience of operating an extended range of programme services, both national and Regional. It had done much in a very short space of time, but there were aspects of Regional broadcasting which troubled the Beveridge Committee and which were to lead to proposals for greater devolution beyond what the BBC had so far thought appropriate or been prepared to concede.

On the outbreak of war in 1939, Regional broadcasting was discontinued and a single Home Service was broadcast, supplemented in January 1940 by a Forces Programme operating initially on an experimental basis and from February 1940 as a complete alternative programme to that of the Home Service. Before the end of the war, the BBC had begun the process of analysing what kind of programme services should be offered to the public when the war was over. The Forces Programme contained much lighter programme material (i.e. dance music, variety, sport) than the Home Service and represented the first real attempt by the BBC to cater for a particular category of listener. The popularity of this programme, which helped to maintain the morale of listeners at home and those in the Forces both at home and abroad, gave an indication that perhaps provision should be made for such a programme service after the war. The Home Service, however, was not aimed at one definable group and could neither compete with the more popular items on the Forces Programme nor adequately cater for minority audiences. This indicated the need for a separate network catering for more specialised interests. The upshot was the BBC's plan to introduce three radio services: the traditional Home Service (the middle strand in BBC broadcasting which was not expected to operate as a national network programme because it had a Regional element); a Light Programme (to replace the Forces Programme and compete with Radio Luxembourg by providing entertainment programmes); and an arts programme, later renamed the Third Programme (to cater primarily for minority and specialised interests). This was a recognition by the BBC that its audience was not homogeneous and therefore wanted separate programme services, each of a recognisably different character. It was expected that there would be some degree of interchangeability of programme items between the Home Service and Third Programme and the Home Service and Light Programme, but less so between the Light and Third Programmes.

After the demise of the Scottish local stations in the 1920s, there were, prior to 1939, basically two BBC radio services: the National Programme which was broadcast throughout the UK, and the Scottish Regional Programme established under the Regional Scheme. The latter programme provided near-national coverage within Scotland, in contrast to the four local Scottish stations which had failed to cover coastal or mountainous areas. On the outbreak of war in September 1939, the Scottish Regional service was merged with the UK Home Service which consequently contained little Scottish material. Preparations were later made for the type of Scottish radio service which could be developed after the war. Towards the end of 1943, the Saltire Society decided to ascertain the views of its members on the BBC's Scottish programme output. A questionnaire was issued in May 1944 asking about the quality and timing of programmes, hours of output, and so on. The results, plus comments, were published in a pamphlet later that year.[1] It was argued that there was a need to stimulate Scottish output and for programmes not to be confined to dealing with purely Scottish subjects. The BBC was criticised for relegating Scots to a parochial role within the UK. Members of the Society wanted the BBC to provide a Scottish perspective on national and international events. The publication of the Society's pamphlet was noted in the monthly report for September 1944 by the BBC's Scottish Regional Director, Melville Dinwiddie. The introduction of the postwar Scottish Home Service provided the opportunity for increasing the volume of Scottish programmes.

On 29 July 1945, the Home Service was restored on a Regional basis and the Light Programme was introduced. The basic Home Service covering London and the Home Counties was supplemented by six Regional services which included the Scottish Home Service (SHS). Both these programmes were supplemented by the Third Programme on 29 September 1946. The General Forces Programme reverted from medium-wave to short-wave radiation and therefore now served only Forces listeners overseas. These changes were a recognition that the BBC was no longer addressing one great audience but rather a variety of audiences with their own interests. The changes also signalled a break from prewar Reithian paternalism to the extent that there was no longer any identifiable balance of light and serious material on any channel. With the reintroduction of Regional broadcasting, listeners in Scotland therefore had a choice between the Scottish Home Service and the more popular programme material which was broadcast on the Light Programme. Sir William Haley, BBC Director-General, commented on the front cover of the *Radio Times* about the return to Regional broadcasting:

> It will be the BBC's aim to make its six regionalised Home Services alert, living things; steadily developing in strength and character, drawing on their native resources and taking the best from elsewhere. The regions will seek the widest development of technique and talent. Their existence should lead to rivalry both of creativeness and of craft, and to the fostering of those national and local cultures which are an enduring part of our heritage and which broadcasting can encourage more powerfully than any other medium.[2]

In planning the three sound services, it was decided that each should come under the supervision of a Controller. These Controllers were to be allowed to decide which programme material to accept from the supply departments. Indeed, under the system of competition, programme planners were to have the right to specify and insist on their exact requirements from producers in the supply departments. Artistic policy was, however, to remain the prerogative of the supply departments; the planners were to be given responsibility for programme and public policy. These arrangements were regarded by the BBC as putting devolution into practice, because the determination of programme output was not decided by a single central authority, and competition was expected to prevail between each of the three programme services. In Scotland, as in the other Regions, the absence of separate planning and supply departments meant that Regional policy consisted only of programme and public policy, thus leaving London with ultimate control over artistic policy.

Also, Regions were to have virtual autonomy with respect to the planning of the Home Service in determining their programme schedules. Programme assistants in the Regions were ultimately responsible to the head of the appropriate London department for artistic standards.

Shortly after the introduction of the Scottish Home Service on 29 July 1945, Melville Dinwiddie (Scottish Regional Director) noted in his monthly report the following comments on the new service:

> The first reactions of listeners in Scotland have been of general satisfaction. No special reception difficulties have been reported, and in one or two areas improvements on wartime reception have been noted. Listeners have appreciated the increase of Scottish items, and, although the press have given the programmes a mixed reception, and the Saltire Society have indicated that we are on trial and unlikely to meet their demands, the opinions expressed in listeners' letters and reports from reliable sources have been encouraging.[3]

The Scottish programme output ranged from news, talks and music (serious and light) through to features and drama, children's, schools' and religious programmes. Scottish news bulletins were broadcast five days a week, and news in Gaelic was transmitted once a week. Concerts were given on radio by the BBC Scottish Orchestra and Scottish Variety Orchestra, and there were outside broadcasts of football and rugby, plays by past and current Scottish playwrights, Scottish dance music, coverage of the General Assembly of the Church of Scotland, and broadcasts on Scottish anniversaries such as St Andrew's Day and Burns' Night. Programmes produced in Scotland worth noting included *Arts Review* (covering dramatic, literary and film criticism), *The McFlannels* (a very popular variety serial), *Sportsreel* (commentaries on sporting events on Saturday evenings), *Scottish Digest* (a monthly review of Scottish newspapers, both daily and weekly), *On the Record* (recordings made around the country using a mobile recording unit), *Seen from Scotland* (a weekly series of talks about Scotland), and *Scottish Opinion* (a monthly coverage of current affairs), as well as a number of other programmes such as *Scotland in Parliament, Farm Forum, Country Magazine* and *Children's Hour*. Scotland had the opportunity to cover local material and to promote indigenous talent, although it was not necessarily the case that the most successful Regional programmes were the most local in content. Programme items could be chosen because of their Scottish content, but equally it was important to cover items which, although not necessarily Scottish, nevertheless could benefit from a Scottish treatment by introducing a Scottish viewpoint on them. This could therefore widen the range of topics which could be covered by producers in Scotland, such as in the programme *Arts Review*. Scottish-originated programme output was expected to cater mainly for Scottish interests, but there was always the danger that an excessive or distorted image of Scotland could lead to criticism that Scottish output was too parochial and not related to events in the world beyond the Scottish border. The Scottish Home Service was integrated with the basic Home

Service and planned as an alternative to the Light and Third Programmes.

The justification for Regional services was that there was a recognisable need for the BBC to be seen to be catering for local life, culture and artistic talent, and that this could not be performed by one basic Home Service. In the preface to a pamphlet which was published shortly after the inauguration of the Scottish Home Service, Melville Dinwiddie stated that the service would draw upon new talent and seek to reflect the life and character of Scotland.[4] The introduction of the SHS was accompanied by greater, and often critical, interest by the press in radio programmes, and this took the form of regular radio columns. The BBC in Scotland supplied the press with news about programmes. According to the BBC, the critical attitude of the press was deemed to be representative of a Scottish attitude to a British organisation which had in turn resulted in lower listening figures and lower sales of the *Radio Times* in comparison with other parts of the country. There may have been some irritation in the use by the BBC of the term 'Region' to describe broadcasting in Scotland. On 13 July 1946, the Saltire Society published a pamphlet in which it was stated that the BBC was treating Scotland as a provincial centre and added:

> The term 'Regional' should be dropped entirely so far as Scotland is concerned. Strictly speaking it should only apply to the English provinces. Scotland is a nation containing at least five 'Regions' in the proper sense of the term, and its use to describe the whole of Scotland causes both annoyance and confusion.[5]

In its Annual Reports, the BBC argued that the normal use of the term 'Region' was not strictly applicable to the Regions of national status (i.e. Scotland, Wales and Northern Ireland), and that programmes were referred to as being 'Scottish' rather than 'Scottish Regional'. This failed consistently to allay such criticism.

The basic Home Service from London was broadcast to the London Region and for a significant proportion of the day to the six Regions, which included Scotland. Most Scottish programme material was broadcast during the evenings. The SHS had the option not to take the London programme and therefore substitute its own programmes whenever it wished to do so. There were few exceptions to this rule, such as the news, the transmission of party political broadcasts, and ministerial statements. In practice, the ability to opt out to transmit Scottish material depended upon the resources available (i.e. staff, finance and equipment) and the use to which they were put. In the postwar reorganisation, the Scottish Controller was given complete control over the annual programme allowance for Scotland, but the programme allowance of the basic Home Service was far in excess of that of the Scottish Home Service, or indeed of any of the large English Regions. Also, the spending of additional allowances by Scotland on importing popular London artists was, for example, unlikely to benefit the production of local programmes. In January 1947, the Scottish programme allowance was £1,750 gross per week, equivalent to that of the Midlands and North Regions, but greater than that received by Wales, West

Region and Northern Ireland. Variety programmes were popular with the audience although often subject to the greatest amount of criticism in the Scottish press. The dependence upon using stars of the theatre and the music hall in the early days of broadcasting in Scotland had given away to scripted shows specifically designed for radio, the most popular being *The McFlannels*. In general, radio sought to create its own stars and programme items rather than be too dependent upon existing artists and their variety material. The SHS incorporated some programme material from the Light and Third Programmes, and so its composition differed from the London Home Service where there was a more rigid separation of material. It also contributed some programmes to the Home Service, such as the radio adaptation of Lewis Grassic Gibbon's *Sunset Song*. Unlike England, broadcasters in Scotland were deemed to be less inclined to assume that the minority and majority audiences constituted separate publics; the Scottish audience was regarded as being more willing to accept a wide choice of programmes. There was also, according to George Bruce (BBC Arts Producer, 1956–70), less of a social distance in Scotland between the broadcasters and the public which they served.[6] Apart from the return of Regional programmes and the introduction of the Light Programme as a natural successor to the Forces Programme, the BBC was also engaged in the planning for the introduction of the Third Programme.

Prior to the introduction of the Third Programme, the BBC considered the nature of this new network and the general programme structure of each of the radio services. In a paper prepared in July 1946, it was stated that the Light and Third Programmes were expected to flank the Home Service on either side, the former carrying popular material and the latter covering more serious and cultural material. All three programmes, despite having their individual character, were designed to shade into each other rather than be rigidly stratified (i.e. there were to be differences in approach and treatment of subject matter rather than in range of content). Competition between them rather than central coordination was sought, especially as programme teams were obliged to contrast programmes and avoid clashes of similar material. With the imminent arrival of the Third Programme, the Director-General commented in this paper on the home programme policy of the BBC that 'We hope it will come not only to be a programme of great significance in the life of the country but also one that will give pleasure to a widening audience of all classes and ages to whom the riches it has to offer would otherwise be permanently denied'.[7]

On 29 September 1946, the Third Programme was introduced. This network was expected to cater for the best in the arts, literature, drama, classical music, opera and talks. It was a highbrow service designed to stimulate thought and meet cultural and intellectual needs. To do so, it needed to attract the interest of composers, writers, performers, playwrights, critics and poets. The rigid programme structure of the Home Service, utilising fixed time-slots, was replaced in the Third Programme by a more flexible arrangement, thus allowing programmes to be as long or as short as necessary depending upon the treatment required of different types of subject matter. Listeners were expected to be selective in their choice of programmes on the new network. The Third Programme gave broadcasters greater room for experimentation with different projects, but it could be criticised for creating, as Reith feared, a cultural ghetto because of its concentration on the more demanding programmes in terms of subject matter. Also, the coverage of the new service was uneven and poor throughout the UK, particularly in Scotland where coverage was confined to the main cities. The Third Programme had to assume a high level of education in its listeners, otherwise it would have duplicated the efforts of the other two networks.[8] It was also questionable whether the Third Programme could be expected to be of interest to the most intelligent people of all social classes or help to widen the cultural horizons of all age groups. The policy of associative planning, whereby material from the various arts and sciences would be placed together to deepen each listener's understanding of any given subject, reinforced the rather elitist character of the network. In Scotland, the percentage of people who listened to the Third Programme was above the UK average but less than the number who listened to the Scottish Home Service. There was also the occasional criticism that the Third Programme did not contain a sufficient volume of Scottish programme items. This situation did improve, and, together with an increasing number of high-quality programmes being produced in Scotland, led to a golden age in Scottish radio broadcasting which lasted until the mid-1950s when competition from television for staff, resources and audiences became more significant.

The reorganisation of the sound broadcasting services and the return of Regional radio programmes represents an important stage in the history of broadcasting in the immediate postwar years. So also does the return of television after the limited service which was available after November 1936 had been closed down on 1 September 1939 because of the onset of war. The BBC's television service restarted after the war, on 7 June 1946 in the London area. The service was extended throughout the country initially by using high-power transmitters. The television service was first extended to the Regions with the opening of the Sutton Coldfield station at Birmingham on 17 December 1949; television reached Scotland on 14 March 1952 when the Kirk O'Shotts station in central Scotland was opened. The postwar development of television not only led to the growth of the BBC in size and complexity, but also affected the status of television within the BBC in relation to the sound broadcasting services.

On 9 October 1945, the government announced that it had accepted the report of Lord Hankey's Committee on Television which was published in March 1945. This committee had originally been appointed in September 1943 to examine the development of a postwar television service. The Television Committee stated that the BBC's television service should restart on the prewar line standard because any change would have caused a two-year delay in resuming the service, would have failed to stem the dispersal of specialised staff engaged on war work who had been employed on television by the BBC before the war, and would have rendered prewar receivers obsolete. Also, the early resumption of television gave the BBC an opportunity to deepen its experience in using the 405-line VHF system before opting for a new line standard or method of transmission. The BBC was relieved that it would not have to face competition in television from a commercial competitor; but equally it needed sufficient financial and technical resources and skilled staff to resume a credible television service. In December 1945, the Minister of Information was asked in the House of Commons what his plans were for making television available in Scotland at the same time that it was introduced in England. The Minister merely stated that plans for the extension of television to the Regions would be considered by the Television Advisory Committee.[9] In June of the following year, the television service restarted on the prewar line standard but was confined to London, hence the service appeared to be experimental. There was pressure to extend television to the Regions, and there were practical reasons for conceding to this demand, as the Hankey Committee stated: 'it should be borne in mind that it is only by extension to the main centres of population in this country that the public will be convinced that Television has passed the experimental stage'.[10] The extension of television would permit the mass production of receivers, lower their costs and therefore make them more widely available to the public. It was thus not surprising that the Radio Industry Council hoped, for commercial reasons, for a rapid extension of television to the Regions.

The Hankey Committee wanted television to be extended to six of the most populous areas of the country. To extend coverage, the BBC planned to build five high-power and five medium-power transmitters. The former would serve about seventy-eight per cent of the population, the latter about ten per cent. The sites of the high-power transmitters were as follows: Alexandra Palace (London), Holme Moss (north of England), Sutton Coldfield (Midlands), Kirk O'Shotts (central Scotland) and Wenvoe (South Wales and west of England). One of the medium-power stations was to be located at Aberdeen. The location of transmitters was designed to take television to as many people as possible within given resources. Television was to be transformed from being regarded as merely an extension of sound broadcasting into a full service in its own right with its own characteristics and possibilities. In the immediate postwar years, television was not accorded a high priority in terms of capital resources because of the need to channel funds into postwar reconstruction. After the advent of the limited television service in November 1936, the ten-shilling sound licence was retained until June 1946 when it was increased to £1 (sound only), and a separate combined licence of £2 covering both radio and television was introduced.[11] However, this new combined licence was unlikely to cover the cost of television development because so few people had access to television, and so there was an expectation that some of the proceeds from sound-only licences would have to be used for this purpose. Those individuals who worked in sound broadcasting regarded themselves as working for the main broadcasting service and so resented the growth of the television service. They recognised that, in time, television would compete strongly with radio for a share of the audience, and that at some stage the number of television licences might exceed sound licences, thereby dispelling the belief that television was a luxury service aimed at a minority audience.

Initially, television resources were concentrated in central London and not regionalised, and so television was for many years regarded as a purely London service. In the 1944 report on conditions for a postwar television service, it was stated that 'Regional activities must play a part in Television, but clearly such activities could economically be produced only in the centralised London studio plant'.[12] Television was not extended to the Regions until 1949, and so contributions of programme material to London were initially confined to outside broadcasts. In an article in the Autumn 1949 issue of *BBC Quarterly*, Sir William Haley (BBC Director-General) stated that television, a more expensive medium than radio, was merely an extension of broadcasting – closer to the world of radio than to the world of films.[13] The centre of power therefore remained in Broadcasting House and not in the emerging television service. The delay until July 1954 in getting news bulletins on television was symptomatic of the attitude of radio staff to the medium of television, as was the decision to print television programmes at the back of the *Radio Times* rather than next to the radio programmes. Television was merely regarded as radiovision (i.e. the addition of visual images to sound programmes). In December 1949, listener research was extended to cover television. From June 1950, it became known under the umbrella term 'audience research'. In that same year, the BBC appointed a Director of Television, George Barnes, with a seat on the Board of Management.

With the growth of television, younger staff working in the television service wanted their special skills to be recognised in terms of status and remuneration. They wanted television to be recognised as a service in its own right rather than merely as a department; this change did not take place until October 1950. The extension of television coverage and broadcasting output resulted in television claiming an increasing share of resources. This was accompanied by the growth of the television audience – as television viewing spread downwards through the social class pyramid – and an increase in the number of combined (i.e. television and radio) licences purchased. It also led to the appearance in newspapers of columns specifically devoted to comments on the television programmes. Radio, however, remained the premier service, and so support for the proper development of television only materialised at the highest levels within the Corporation when Sir Ian Jacob succeeded Sir William Haley as Director-General in December 1952, ironically the same year that the government indicated that competition in television was in principle to be permitted. Indeed, one of the memoranda that the BBC was to submit to the Beveridge Committee on Broadcasting reflected Haley's view that television, despite its special production and engineering requirements, was basically an extension of sound broadcasting. He may also have believed that television would turn the public into passive viewers and thus undermine the BBC's high moral purpose which he regarded as being admirably fulfilled by radio. It was Sir Ian Jacob who recognised that television would become the dominant medium, and he remained at the BBC to witness the ascendancy of television over sound broadcasting.[14] Television did remain at a disadvantage in comparison with sound broadcasting because radio could broadcast for longer hours, it could provide a wider range of programme material, and it was less of a drain on material and manpower resources. Television had to begin to provide a more complete service, particularly for those people who no longer listened to radio during the evenings. It had to create its own stars rather than merely depend upon those artists who had achieved fame through sound broadcasting. The television service was extended outside London by the provision of high-power stations which were connected with Alexandra Palace in London to provide a network. The plan for five medium-power stations at Newcastle, Southampton, Belfast, Aberdeen and Plymouth was to be deferred in March 1951 by government restrictions on BBC capital development because of the needs of rearmament; these restrictions were withdrawn on 2 July 1953. A proper account of the development of television in Scotland falls outwith the period covered in this chapter because, although the BBC received permission from the government in 1949 to build high- and medium-power stations to extend television to the Regions, television did not arrive in Scotland until 1952. However, constitutional changes were introduced which did directly influence Scottish broadcasting during this period. These changes took the form of the establishment of a Scottish Advisory Council, one of a number of Regional Advisory Councils set up under the Charter of 1947, and given responsibility to advise the BBC on Regional programme policy. The Scottish Advisory Council was a forerunner to the formation of the Broadcasting Council for Scotland which exists to the present day.

The government White Paper of July 1946 stated that, in order to ensure that the BBC's Regional Directorates were kept in close touch with movements of thought and opinion in their Regions, there should be established in each Region a Regional Advisory Council to advise the Corporation on all matters affecting Regional programme policy.[15] This was duly incorporated in the new Charter which took effect from 1 January 1947 and was to remain in force for five years.[16] Scotland was therefore provided with a Scottish Advisory Council (SAC). It is interesting to note that these Councils were expected to offer advice to the Corporation and not to Regional Directors. The Board of Governors would receive this advice by obtaining the minutes of the meetings of these Councils. It certainly fell far short of the Saltire Society's desire for a Scottish Board of Governors. Appointments to these Regional Advisory Councils were to be made by the BBC, although the Corporation was prepared to consider consultation with the government to ensure that the Councils were of the type envisaged by the government in its White Paper.[17] By agreeing to the establishment of Regional Advisory Councils, the Governors of the BBC could be seen to be providing a measure of home rule to the Regions despite the considerable limitations to the powers of the Councils. The Councils met infrequently, they received little information on staffing and financial matters, and they did not exercise control over Regional policy. Their members were also appointed without consulting Regional organisations. Despite these limitations, the formation of the Councils was a recognition of the need for the BBC to keep more fully in touch with both the needs and interests of the Regions.

Prior to the formation of the Scottish Advisory Council, Melville Dinwiddie (Scottish Director) consulted with his senior staff and sent to the Director-General a list of twenty names of individuals who might be invited to become members of the Council. The BBC did not consult organisations for names of potential members, or invite members of the public to sit on the Council. The SAC was therefore not representative of any broadly-based public control of broadcasting in Scotland. Members were not expected to be chosen to represent particular organisations or interests;[18] they were expected to be capable of providing informed advice on broadcasting. Dinwiddie's first preference for Chairman of the SAC was Sir Hector Hetherington, Principal and Vice-Chancellor of Glasgow University, and one of the few individuals who had been considered in 1938 as a successor to Reith as Director-General. On 11 December 1946, Sir William Haley (BBC Director-General) wrote to Sir Hector Hetherington inviting him to become the first Chairman of the SAC. He agreed to act as Chairman of the Council, and so became *ex officio* a member of the BBC's General Advisory Council. The list of names of potential members of the Council was intended to reflect a broad range of interests, age groups and geographical areas within Scotland. Dinwiddie stated that 'It is hoped that the membership of the Committee will be so balanced as to benefit by their constructive contribution, without being unduly influenced by their extreme viewpoint'.[19] About twenty-four members sat on the Council, and the number varied little thereafter. This included the Chairmen of the existing Scottish Advisory Committees covering Religion, Agriculture and Appeals, as well as the Council for School Broadcasting and the Council for Group Listening. The term of office for members was staggered and it was expected that the SAC would hold three meetings a year. The BBC Governors wanted all Regional Directors to keep a continuous watch for future likely nominees for membership of these Regional Advisory Councils. A few days before the Scottish Council met, the Director-General mentioned that it was likely that the Scottish and Welsh Advisory Councils would raise the question of the allocation of revenue to Scotland and Wales in relation to the number of licence-holders in those countries. Although the Board of Governors viewed the issue as outside the terms of reference of the Advisory Councils, it was sufficiently concerned to ask the Director-General to prepare a statement on the allocation of expenditure just in case the topic was raised by the Councils.[20]

The first meeting of the Scottish Advisory Council was held on 27 January 1947 at Broadcasting House, Edinburgh. For this meeting, notes were prepared on the range of output of the Scottish Home Service. The meeting began with the Chairman introducing Sir William Haley, BBC Director-General, who then proceeded to describe the work of the BBC with particular reference to wartime broadcasting and to the reorganisation of the sound services in 1945. There were also some comments made on television progress, the Third Programme and the problems of broadcasting coverage. Melville Dinwiddie followed this with a short statement on BBC programme policy in Scotland. Members asked a number of questions ranging from the Scottish news service and the development of rural talent to the problems of provinciality and the need for a studio centre in Dundee. It was agreed that the agenda for future meetings should be compiled from items suggested by BBC staff and by members of the Council. The Chairman later prepared a paper outlining the functions of the Council for discussion at the second meeting. In that paper, Sir Hector Hetherington outlined what he took to be the two principal functions of the SAC: to review past and present radio programme output from the point of view of both policy and performance; and to suggest possible developments as a result of this continual process of review. The BBC had no desire for the Council to become too active and interventionist with regard to policy matters, as confirmed by the written comments of Sir William Haley (Director-General) at the foot of Sir Hector Hetherington's paper: 'I think this is all right so long as it doesn't get out of bounds'.[21]

The SAC dealt with a number of topics over the few years of its existence. A sample of these included the following: the desire for the Light Programme to incorporate more Scottish items; the need to augment studios, staff and equipment in Scotland; concern that the Scottish Football League refused to give permission for 'live' commentaries on important games; the desire for more variety items on the Scottish Home Service; the desirability of more Scottish talks being included in *The Listener*, although the Director-General believed that Scottish items should only be included on their merit, and likewise he was not in favour of a Scottish edition of *The Listener*; the BBC's relations with the press; the desirability of pre-election talks on Scottish subjects; the question of Regional devolution in broadcasting; suggestions for Gaelic lessons and the inclusion of more plays by Scottish writers in the Third Programme; the need to improve the reception of the Third Programme in Scotland; and the need for more Scottish items to be publicised on the front page of the *Radio Times*. Criticism was also directed at the national news because it was deemed to be compiled purely from the London point of view. London news bulletins were regarded as having ignored Scotland's interest in countries such as Canada. The desirability of more Scottish news being compiled in Scotland by Scottish editors prompted the request for a weekend Scottish news bulletin to supplement the weekday bulletins.[22] There was occasional criticism that too many London items were being included in the programme schedules and an insufficient number of Regional items, but the BBC argued that it took the best-quality items from wherever they were available. The Scottish Advisory Council continued to meet regularly until 25 November 1952. From January 1953, this purely advisory body was superseded by the Broadcasting Council for Scotland, which had more substantive (i.e. executive) powers over radio broadcasting in Scotland.

These constitutional changes in broadcasting which took effect in January 1947 were followed later that year by organisational changes. On 1 December 1947, the BBC's administrative reorganisation resulted in the appointment of five Directors, forming a Board of Management under the Chairmanship of Sir William Haley the Director-General; the first meeting of this Board was held on 5 January 1948. The Board of Management was in overall control of decision-making on a daily basis. It was, however, ultimately accountable to the Board of Governors for its actions. In addition to the Director-General, this Board comprised the following members: Sir Noel Ashbridge (Director of Technical Services); Basil Nicolls (Director of Home Broadcasting); Sir Ian Jacob (Director of Overseas Services); Sir Norman Bottomley (Director of Administration); and George Barnes (Director of the Spoken Word).[23] Under the previous arrangement, Ashbridge had been Deputy Director-General, Nicolls was Senior Controller, and Jacob and Barnes were Controllers of European Services and the Third Programme respectively. Below these five Directors in the organisational hierarchy, there were eleven Controllers, including, for example, Melville Dinwiddie (Scotland), Harman Grisewood (Third Programme), Norman Collins (Television) and R.E.L. Wellington (Home Service). Below these Controllers, home broadcasting was also served by fourteen professional heads, such as Cecil McGivern (Head of Television Programmes) and Robert Silvey (Head of Audience Research). The Board of Management was also in contact with other senior staff such as Harold Bishop (Chief Engineer) and the Heads of the various engineering departments. The Controller (Scotland) was directly responsible to the Director of Home Sound Broadcasting. Dinwiddie as Scottish Controller was assisted in non-programme matters by P.F. Dunbar (Scottish Executive) and an Assistant Publicity Officer (Scotland). Programme Services were under the control of Gordon Gildard who was Head of Scottish Programmes. Below him in the Scottish organisational hierarchy at Glasgow, there were a number of key staff who included H.H.E. Wiseman (Head of Scottish Music), Ian Whyte (Conductor of the BBC Scottish Orchestra), J. Crampsey (Drama Producer), A.P. Lee (Features Producer), Hugh MacPhee (Gaelic Producer), H.M. Lockhart (Variety Producer), Kathleen Garscadden (Children's Hour Organiser), G.D. Runcie (Talks Producer) and the Rev. Ronnie Falconer (Religious Broadcasting Organiser). There were also a Scottish Programme Executive, Music Assistants, a Gaelic Assistant, a News Editor, News Assistants, a Conductor (Light Entertainment) and Recorded Programmes Assistants. The Engineering Division was headed by F.W. Endicott (Engineer-in-Charge), and he was assisted by a number of staff such as the Senior Programme Engineer, Senior Recording Engineer-in-Charge and Senior Lines Engineer. BBC staff in Scotland were also based in Edinburgh and Aberdeen. In Edinburgh, Programme Services were under the control of the Assistant Head of Scottish Programmes. Other programme staff at Edinburgh included a Features Producer, Outside Broadcasting Producers, the Children's Hour Assistant, a Talks Producer, Schools Assistants and an announcer. The Secretary of the School Broadcasting Council for Scotland and Head of Scottish School Broadcasting was also based in Edinburgh, together with the Publicity Officer (Scotland) and engineering staff grouped in an Engineering Division. The staff complement at Aberdeen was much smaller than at Glasgow or Edinburgh. The Aberdeen Representative, A.H.S. Paterson, was one of a small number of staff which included George Bruce as one of the Programme Assistants, together with clerical staff and an Engineer-in-Charge who supervised the Engineering Division. There were announcers at Glasgow and Edinburgh but not in Aberdeen, and similarly for the Education Officers of the School Broadcasting Council. All the staff mentioned were in those posts in October 1948, just after the retitling of some key posts within Scotland. [24] This organisational structure did not remain static. It was subject to change as a result of the expansion of programme services, particularly the introduction of television in 1952 and the establishment of community and area radio stations from the mid-1970s. Changes took several forms as follows: the renaming of titles of posts; the introduction of new posts and the demise of others; the reorganisation of programme services into various departments; and finally the reallocation of staff not only within programme departments, but also between the various studio centres in Scotland. As will be noted in later chapters, there was a growth both in the number of staff and in the complexity of the BBC's organisational structure in Scotland in the subsequent decades because of the expansion of programme activity.

During 1949, the BBC began to assess its radio and television broadcasting services in order to gather information for the Beveridge Committee on Broadcasting which was appointed in the summer of that year. In a period in which television broadcasting was growing in importance to become within a few years the primary medium of communication, the question as to whether the BBC should retain control of this medium was highlighted at the time when the committee began its examination of broadcasting.[25] The question of the monopoly was a prominent issue in many of the submissions of evidence to this committee. Unlike previous committees of inquiry into broadcasting, the Beveridge Committee would not be able to take the monopoly for granted so easily. The issue of Regional devolution was also a key theme, and the proposals of the committee in this area were to lead to constitutional changes which for the first time resulted in the establishment of a body which was entrusted with control over both the policy and content of Scottish radio broadcasting.

6

The Beveridge Report on Broadcasting: submissions, recommendations and responses, 1949–51

The Beveridge Committee of Inquiry was appointed in 1949 to consider the constitution, control, finance and other general aspects of the domestic broadcasting services and to advise upon the conditions under which these services should be conducted after 31 December 1951. The Beveridge Committee on Broadcasting was the first large-scale independent inquiry since the war into the working of a public corporation. Initially, Sir Cyril (later Lord) Radcliffe was announced as Chairman of the committee, but he was unable to take up his duties because of his appointment as a Lord of Appeal on 27 May 1949. The task therefore fell to Lord Beveridge, author of the widely-known Social Security Report of December 1942. The appointment of Lord Beveridge to chair the committee was announced in the House of Commons on 21 June 1949. The first meeting of the committee was held on 24 June, and a press notice was issued inviting submissions from all persons interested in broadcasting to be sent to the committee by 1 October. The Chairman and Director-General of the BBC had an interview with Lord Beveridge in which procedural matters were dealt with. In particular, Lord Beveridge asked for all the BBC evidence already prepared, as well as for various additional memoranda.[1] In total, the committee received 223 memoranda, and this together with other papers brought the figure up to 368. The range and volume of evidence was much greater than that received by any previous Committee of Inquiry. Sixty-two full meetings were held, and these were supplemented by enquiries conducted by sub-committees. One of these sub-committees visited Scotland on 21 and 22 March 1950. Melville Dinwiddie (BBC Scottish Controller) did, however, feel that the discussion was rather diffuse and did not progress much beyond the routine of day-to-day working.[2] All the meetings of the Beveridge Committee were held in private in order to permit greater freedom of discussion and a franker expression of opinions. A substantial number of memoranda were published in a separate volume to the main report in order to represent the wide spectrum of views offered. It is useful to consider an examination of the Broadcasting Committee's report in terms of the submissions of evidence to the committee, its main recommendations and the responses to the publication of the report.

The BBC submitted a memorandum to the committee in September 1949 on the place of Scotland, Wales and Northern Ireland in the broadcasting system. Within the BBC's Regional operation, these three countries were all designated national Regions. With the need to maintain common programme standards, the BBC stated that the quality of Regional programmes had, subject to available resources, to approximate to those of national programmes. Uniformity in both technical standards and pay and conditions of service throughout the UK had to be maintained. However, the BBC stated that it was its policy to devolve a large measure of responsibility to the Regions to the extent that the Regions were responsible both for the choice of material to be included in their own programme schedules, and for the allocation of expenditure within their programme funds.[3] The BBC recognised the additional programme responsibilities of staff in Scotland in comparison with those in the English Regions. The Corporation stated that its policy of devolution provided reasonable scope for the exploitation of the services to meet the special needs of the national Regions. In the area of staffing, the BBC stated that although most senior appointments were made from the nationals of each country, it was not the policy of the Regions to follow a narrow nationalistic policy in programme terms, given that the aim was to provide the best informative, educational and entertainment programme material regardless of its country of origin. This policy was deemed to be necessary for both practical and programme policy reasons as follows:

> It must again be emphasised that no single Region could be regarded
> as an effective self-contained broadcasting organisation. All the
> Regions for the purposes of their own Regional programmes draw
> fully and gratuitously on material included in the programmes
> organised in London and on those organised in other Regions. This
> must remain so if listeners are to be given the best programmes.[4]

The point which the BBC wished to emphasise was that Scotland, in common with the other Regions, could all draw upon a fund of common services (i.e. engineering, administration, finance and programmes) far in excess of what they could command on an independent basis. In a submission to the committee, the Labour Party stated that it wished to see the encouragement of more competition between the BBC Regions. It favoured the improvement of Regional resources to enable the Regions to produce more of their own programmes and thereby displace more of the network output. It believed that greater decentralisation of responsibilities to the Regions would introduce a more welcome and beneficial competitive element into the BBC's services, and so stated that 'To this end the regions must have a wider measure of control over their own affairs, the right to choose their own staff, a bigger share of their licence income, more studio space of their own, more and better equipment, and a greater sense of independence'.[5]

On 21 October 1949, the Saltire Society submitted a paper to the Broadcasting Committee. The Society stated that broadcasting could influence public taste and opinion and that it therefore had the potential to assist the Scottish people to retain and develop their own distinctive culture. To achieve this, the Society argued that radio broadcasting should come under effective Scottish control, given what it regarded as the inadequacy of the BBC's Scottish Advisory Council with regard to Scottish programmes. So the Saltire Society proposed that a Board of Scottish Governors should be appointed and that it should be given executive powers over Scottish broadcasting.[6] It was believed that an autonomous Scottish broadcasting system would be capable of improving programme quality, stimulating technical advance and increasing staff and accommodation. As regards the function of the proposed Scottish Governors, the Saltire Society stated that they should be resident in Scotland, be appointed by a panel representative of Scottish interests with the Secretary of State for Scotland as Chairman, and have the power to initiate and control broadcasting policy in Scotland and to appoint staff. The Society also recommended that one Scottish Governor should have the right to sit on the Board of Governors in London, and that one member of the Board of Governors should be permitted to sit on the Board of Scottish Governors. These views were in agreement with those of many Labour MPs in Scotland, who believed that more autonomy and control over Scottish services should be vested in a separate broadcasting body in Scotland.

On 29 September 1949, the Scottish National Party (SNP) also submitted evidence to the committee on the conduct of BBC radio broadcasting in Scotland. In its memorandum to the committee, the SNP stated categorically at the outset that is wished to see the establishment of a separate broadcasting system for Scotland: a system which originated in Scotland, was controlled in Scotland, and which was funded from within Scotland. The SNP argued that the BBC was treating Scotland literally as a region rather than as a nation with its own distinctive culture and institutions.[7] Furthermore, the SNP referred to the inability of BBC announcers to discriminate between England and Britain when they were talking about the 'north'. The SNP regarded the BBC as principally English in outlook, London-controlled, and offering little opportunity for Scottish views to be heard about events in Scotland, or on topics in countries with which Scotland had trading, cultural or friendship links. The SNP wanted more resources to be made available to develop fully Scottish broadcasting, and there was criticism that news about other countries had to be channelled through London, thus providing information through a metropolitan prism. The SNP was critical of both the quality and quantity of radio programmes originating in Scotland. In particular, it was argued that quality could be improved if the BBC paid better fees to attract improved material from Scottish contributors. The poor broadcasting coverage of the BBC's Third Programme in Scotland, which was only available to listeners near to the local transmitters in Edinburgh, Glasgow, Aberdeen and Dundee, was also criticised, although the SNP added that this network was English in outlook because it contained little Scottish material. Overall, the SNP wanted the BBC to give more attention to Scottish interests in both the Third and Light Programmes. As regards the issue of political broadcasting, the SNP wanted equality on the air in Scotland with other major political parties. Also, the style of announcers was regarded as a contentious issue because it contributed to the view that the BBC was essentially English in outlook. The SNP wanted Scottish announcers to be allowed to speak in their own accents rather than have to modify these to fit in with what it regarded as BBC preconceptions. Finally, the SNP was anxious to see the publication of a Scottish edition of *The Listener* which would thereby provide more opportunities to publish Scottish talks and so be of some benefit to those listeners who missed the original broadcasts.

The BBC's Scottish Advisory Council forwarded its views on broadcasting in Scotland in a memorandum in November 1949. These views were initially channelled through the BBC to ensure that they were consistent with the policy of the Corporation. The Scottish Advisory Council first noted that any review of broadcasting in relation to Scotland had to take account of the resurgence of Scottish national consciousness. On technical matters, the Council recognised the constraining factors which prevented 100 per cent coverage of all radio programme services in Scotland, thus preventing many listeners in Scotland from having the choice of three radio services. The Scottish Home Service provided the best coverage by reaching ninety-five per cent of the population in Scotland; the Light and Third Programmes reached a smaller percentage of the population. The SAC therefore wanted the development of the highest power available under international agreements on medium wavelengths in order to improve broadcasting coverage.[8] The Council also pressed for more manpower and equipment for Scotland. In common with the SNP, the Council drew attention to the poor coverage of Scottish talks in *The Listener* and so proposed the introduction of a Scottish edition of the paper, although it must be noted that talks which sounded well when broadcast did not necessarily read as well when appearing in print. The Scottish Radio Retailers' Association, in its submission of 10 November 1949, highlighted the problems in areas which did not receive good reception of BBC programmes. The Association stated that listeners living in areas which could not receive all BBC services should be charged a smaller licence fee. However, given the changing nature of broad-casting coverage over time, such a scheme would have been administratively too complex and too costly to operate. With regard to the conduct and quality of broadcasting output, the Association reflected the views expressed in several other submissions to the committee, namely that broadcasting in Scotland should be controlled from Scotland rather than London and thus permit full use to be made of artistic talent within Scotland. On 21 June 1950, Lord Reith submitted a memorandum to the Broadcasting Committee in which he criticised the BBC policy of introducing the Third Programme because he was opposed to the segregation of cultural items on one radio service. As regards Regional output he stated:

> The Regions have a contribution to make; they should have adequate
> opportunity to make it. But the criterion should be interest and merit,

> not vague assessments of what, in quantity, should be justifiable.
> There is too much regional material at present; the cause of
> regionalism would positively gain from its reduction.[9]

This view ran totally counter to that of, for example, the Fabian Research Group, which wanted VHF to be used to develop local broadcasting to enable more local material to be produced, particularly as the Regional Scheme which was introduced in the 1930s had since then stifled genuine local programme output.

The Beveridge Committee received several submissions which argued that the BBC had been slow to develop Regional broadcasting or to extend the geographical coverage of television throughout the country. Scotland did not receive a television service until over a year after the Beveridge Report was published, and thus, understandably, most of the written submissions of evidence to the committee on Scottish broadcasting matters covered radio rather than television broadcasting. However, some submissions, such as that prepared by the SNP, commented upon the delay in providing Scotland with a television service. The SNP stated:

> We find it difficult to write with restraint on television. This is the invention of a Scot, it has become a BBC monopoly, and the BBC have denied it to Scotland. London and other parts of England have enjoyed the service for many years to the pleasure of the public and the profit of the supplying industry. If and when the service comes to Scotland, it must serve the entire country – Scotland is more than Edinburgh and Glasgow, just as England is more than London and Birmingham. The programmes must be Scottish. The present assumption of the BBC is that programmes must originate in London and filter out to the 'provinces'.[10]

However, when television did arrive in Scotland, it did not provide blanket geographical coverage, and neither was there a significant volume of Scottish material because of the absence of television studio facilities. The Scottish Radio Retailers' Association also noted with disapproval the absence of a television service in Scotland and, in common with the SNP, stated that private enterprise could have provided such a service in a shorter period of time. Another key theme on which the committee was to receive evidence was the BBC's monopoly of broadcasting. The BBC sought to defend its monopoly, whereas other opinions offered to the committee were to cover both the positive and the negative aspects of the monopoly.

In April 1950, the BBC submitted a memorandum to the committee in which it argued that it was in the public interest that the monopoly should be retained. The BBC referred to its impartiality, its attempt to preserve programme standards, to cater for minorities and raise public taste, and finally to the financial drawbacks of competition in broadcasting. The BBC stated that in a competitive situation it believed that the good programmes would be driven out by the bad, thereby resulting in fewer programmes for minorities. It also rejected the belief that the establishment of any independent corporations in the BBC Regions, such as Scotland, would bring about genuine competition, or that a commercial system would be able to cater adequately for the needs of rural areas.[11] The BBC sought to emphasise that the dangers of monopoly were kept under constant review by Parliament, the press and the BBC's own advisory structure, simply because the BBC did operate as a monopoly. It was argued that under a diversified and competitive system, external checks would be more difficult to operate effectively than under the existing BBC monopoly. The Corporation was also able to argue that there were governmental controls over the BBC's funding and transmitter development. The BBC rejected the idea that there was any tight internal central control exercised in the decision-making process. Indeed, it argued that under sponsored broadcasting (which was not adopted), responsibility for programmes would pass out of the hands of the broadcasting service and into those of the advertising agent. Lord Reith was opposed to any attempt to end the BBC's monopoly, which he believed was in the public interest. In his memorandum of 21 June 1950, he stated:

> It was the brute force of monopoly that enabled the BBC to become what it did; and to do what it did; that made it possible for a policy of moral responsibility to be followed. If there is to be competition it will be of cheapness not of goodness.[12]

The language which Reith used to justify the monopoly made its continuation much less attractive to, for example, the Scottish Radio Retailers' Association and British Actors' Equity Association. The Labour Party, however, wished to maintain the monopoly, partly because of fear that competition between the BBC and a commercial system would debase the BBC's high standards. This was based on the assumption that a commercial system could not provide high-quality programmes because it was not free from commercial profit-making pressures. The Fabian Research Group took a different view because, although it accepted that broadcasting should remain a public service financed by licence fees, it did not believe that the BBC should enjoy a cultural monopoly (i.e. the power to decide which programme material the audience should receive). There was criticism that the BBC had been slow to develop television because its main experience was with sound broadcasting. This was one of the reasons sometimes cited as justification as to why a commercially-based system would be able to extend television to Scotland in a shorter period of time than the BBC had done. Having considered the large volume of written and oral evidence given by many individuals and organisations, the Beveridge Committee now had to outline its recommendations on the future direction of broadcasting.

The Report of the Broadcasting Committee under the Chairmanship of Lord Beveridge was published on 18 January 1951. One of the subjects which the committee considered was the issue of devolution of responsibilities to the Regions. The report stated that there was found to be a greater degree of closeness among staff and less red tape in the Regions because of their smaller organisational structure in comparison with London. Moreover, there was a recognition that several submissions of evidence to the committee had asked for greater autonomy for Scotland and Wales. The report noted the BBC's view that the national Regions were subsidised because revenue reveived was less than expenditure incurred, and that therefore these Regions could not provide a complete programme service comparable to that available from the three radio networks. However, all BBC Regions contributed to the cost of shared services, such as the Light and Third Programmes, without regard to the extent to which they received good reception of these services or to the number or proportion of listeners. These factors would have reduced the Scottish deficit. Nevertheless, in the absence of an autonomous Scottish broadcasting system, the issue focused on how to ensure that the BBC paid full regard to the interests of the national Regions. The committee therefore recommended the creation of Broadcasting Commissions for the national Regions, each of which would have the power to initiate and decide on a Home Service programme in its Region, and that they should have powers in relation to financial matters, accommodation and staff.[13] Although the committee accepted that the BBC should have overall responsibility for finance, it was recommended that there should be an increasing allocation of block grants to these commissions; the BBC would, however, remain ultimately responsible for capital developments. The chairman of each of these commissions was expected to sit on the Board of Governors in London and so, in the case of Scotland, bring Scottish problems directly to the highest decision-making level within the BBC. The Broadcasting Committee referred to the proposed change from the limited scope and advisory nature of the Regional Advisory Councils in the national Regions to the executive powers of the proposed commissions as an attempt to substitute federal harmony for centralising unity in London. No similar changes were proposed for England, but the committee did state that there was a need to make the programme autonomy of the Regional Controllers more substantial and to bolster both the independence and activity of the English Regional Advisory Councils.

There were several other matters impinging on Regional sound broadcasting which the committee commented upon. On financial matters, the committee stated that the BBC had told Parliament and the public very little about its financial operations. The report stated that the BBC accounts gave little more information than the legal minimum required by the Companies Act of 1948. The committee therefore wished to see the breakdown of total expenditure by Regions or by services. The latter would be required in order to examine an issue such as Regional devolution, given that the BBC consistently argued that separate broadcasting corporations for Scotland and for Wales were not financially viable.[14] The committee also wanted the results of audience research to be more widely available, such as to Regional Advisory Councils, to enable judgements to be made as to whether the BBC was providing a responsible public service. Furthermore, the committee wanted the BBC to develop VHF broadcasting to improve coverage of existing services and so leave open the possibility of local radio stations using VHF on low power. The committee was also in favour of the BBC being authorised with the consent of the PMG to borrow up to £10 million for capital expenditure, and for the Corporation to consider the possibility of printing special editions of *The Listener* for Scotland and Wales.

Regional television development was an area which the Broadcasting Committee also considered in its examination of the BBC's programme services. Mindful of the fact that television studio facilities were concentrated in London, the report stated:

> We recommend that the Governors of the broadcasting authority should take into immediate and serious consideration the possibility of establishing supplementary studios outside London, and that till this can be done they should adopt special measures to correct the weighting of studio television by London. All that is said elsewhere as to the need for regional programme autonomy applies to television as to sound broadcasting. The more important that television becomes in relation to sound broadcasting, the greater the need to prevent it from becoming a source of uniform ideas.[15]

The committee accepted the BBC argument that control over sound and television should remain under the same authority, but nevertheless stated that the differences between the two media, in terms of both production and transmission, was greater than that recognised in the BBC's evidence to the committee, or in its present organisation. Basically, the committee did not want television development to be hampered by traditions inherited from sound broadcasting. Recalling Sir William Haley's view that television was an extension of sound broadcasting, the committee stated that this may be so with regard to the reception but not to the transmission of programmes, since television productions differed from radio productions in terms of staffing, costs, equipment and skills. The report stated that television should enjoy greater autonomy within the BBC, and that the Corporation should be prepared to borrow to finance capital expenditure on television. This would accelerate the extension of television to Scotland and the other BBC Regions and so counterbalance the metropolitan influence in television.

The committee had to address the fundamental issue of the BBC's monopoly in broadcasting, not least because this was referred to in many of the submissions of evidence to the committee. On this important issue, the committee stated that it had found a substantial body of opinion which challenged the monopoly. It did, however, state that if broadcasting was to have a social purpose then competition should not be allowed to become competition for audience size:

> We regret as a guiding principle in broadcasting competition for numbers of listeners. But we do not accept the assumption underlying the BBC Memorandum that the only alternative to monopoly is degrading competition for listeners, and that in broadcasting a monopoly alone can have high standards and social purpose.[16]

The committee was also unable to accept the supplementary argument in the BBC's memorandum that the past achievements of the Corporation justified its continuing to operate on the same lines without looking more seriously at an issue such as Regional devolution to Scotland and Wales. The committee endorsed the monopoly but wanted the BBC to take action in decentralising responsibilities. Selwyn Lloyd, the Conservative MP, however submitted a minority report objecting to the monopoly. He wanted the monopoly to be broken while television was still relatively young, and emphasised what he regarded as the potential dangers of monopoly: size; centralised control; growth of bureaucracy; Londonisation and metropolitanism; secretiveness; lack of technical innovation; a failure fully to develop television broadcasting; and a lack of alternative employment for both staff and performers. Selwyn Lloyd objected to the use of the 'brute force of monopoly' to raise standards; he wanted to raise standards by choice and not by compulsion. The committee was concerned about the power of monopoly, but most members did not believe that the solution was to bring in market competition via a commercial system for fear that this would lead to competition for viewers rather than healthy competition to raise programme standards. Sponsoring of programmes was rejected, but three members of the committee did not object to the use of spot advertising; only Selwyn Lloyd favoured a more overt commercial service. Overall, the committee proposed safeguards against the dangers of monopoly rather than the cessation of the monopoly.

In seeking to synthesise the various issues involved, the Beveridge Committee posed what it regarded as seven fundamental questions about broadcasting, and it attempted to answer them. The conclusions which it reached are noted as follows:

(1) the BBC Charter should not be renewed until account was taken of the potential dangers of monopoly;

(2) broadcasting should be continued as a monopoly, and, although there should not be separate corporations for Scotland and Wales, these countries should be given greater autonomy;

(3) broadcasting should continue to be financed via the licence fee, there should be no sponsored television, but spot advertising was not entirely rejected;

(4) the BBC should provide more information to Parliament and to the public on how it allocated financial resources (such as to the Regions), and should consult more often with its advisory bodies;

(5) the BBC should expand upon the information contained in its Annual Report and Accounts;

(6) to mitigate the effects of monopoly, the functions of the Governors should be extended to enable them to be more actively concerned with the formulation and execution of policy, there should be a Public Representation Service providing a channel for the public to influence the BBC, and that there should be quinquennial reviews of BBC activities;

(7) to ensure that the Governors brought outside opinion to bear on BBC activities, they should have the right to interfere with executive decisions if necessary.

Some of the points mentioned were implemented, such as greater devolution to Scotland and Wales, the maintenance of the licence fee system and the fuller breakdown of expenditure in the BBC Annual Accounts to indicate the breakdown of operating and capital expenditure in Scotland and in the other Regions. Other aspects which were not implemented included issues such as the retention of the monopoly, or the proposal to introduce a Public Representation Service and quinquennial reviews.

Various responses to the recommendations contained in the committee's report began to emerge. Preliminary consideration was given to these recommendations by the BBC Board of Management at a special meeting on 19 January 1951 and at the usual Board meeting on 22 January. The Corporation expected to formulate its observations on the Report within six weeks and submit these to the government.[17] In January 1951, the Labour Government promised that there would be a full parliamentary discussion before final decisions were taken on the recommendations contained in the Report.[18] On 13 February, the Scottish Advisory Council discussed the Report in relation to its effects on broadcasting in Scotland. The Council made four recommendations:[19]

(1) the degree of autonomy exercised by the Regional Controller was deemed to be satisfactory to the extent that any change would result in a less efficient service;

(2) the proposed commission for Scotland should be delayed until more wavelengths, materials and money were available for extending services;

(3) no programme alterations should take place that would prevent listeners in Scotland from receiving the basic Home Service as included in the Scottish programme;

(4) a Scotsman resident in Scotland who had a connection with the BBC in Scotland should sit on the Board of Governors.

Other points discussed related to the selection of members of the proposed commission, its constitutional position and its powers. There was some concern that the appointment of a commission might lead to the production of too many Scottish programmes, thereby inducing parochialism. The committee's report had sought to aim for the fullest degree of devolution consistent with the preservation of the unity of the BBC. However, Sir John Falconer (Chairman of the SAC) stated that he found the General Advisory Council to be concerned about the effect of the Beveridge recommendations on the unity of the BBC.[20] The next stage was the publication of a government White Paper in response to the committee's report.

On 10 July 1951, the government published its White Paper on broadcasting. The government began by accepting the majority view within the Beveridge Committee that the monopoly should remain: 'The Government agree with the majority of the Committee that the best interests of British broadcasting require the continuance of the Corporation on substantially the present basis.'[21] The White Paper stated that the new Charter would require the BBC to delegate to Scotland, Wales, Northern Ireland and the English Regions such powers as were necessary to secure a reasonable measure of independence and greater variety in programme-making. The government broadly accepted the views of the Beveridge Committee on the issue of devolution of responsibilities. The White Paper stated that 'The Government attach great importance to the maximum devolution to all areas on programme policy and otherwise, and they agree with the Broadcasting Committee that the existing arrangements are inadequate'.[22] However, although the government accepted the desirability of establishing Broadcasting Councils whose chairmen would be represented on the BBC Board of Governors, it agreed that overall responsibility for finance and for capital development had to be reserved for the Corporation. In the latter areas, the functions of the Councils would be merely advisory. So there were to be limitations on the operation of the Broadcasting Council for Scotland. The government noted that it was the policy of the BBC Governors to develop administrative devolution to the maximum possible extent, and this included the delegation of more power to the English Regional Advisory Councils. The proposal to introduce quinquennial reviews was rejected, but otherwise little else was to change: the PMG was to continue to remain responsible for broadcasting, and the BBC was to continue to be funded from licence revenue and to submit annual reports to Parliament (which would now incorporate the reports of the Broadcasting Councils for Scotland and Wales). The need to improve broadcasting coverage was recognised, and, although major developments were to continue to be constrained by restrictions on capital development, the government accepted that the Corporation should be authorised with the consent of the PMG to borrow up to £10 million for capital expenditure.

There were parliamentary debates on the government's memorandum and on the committee's report. In the House of Commons, Mr Patrick Gordon-Walker, Secretary of State for Commonwealth Relations, began the debate by stating that to speed up the extension of television broadcasting it was important that television should be centralised, not regionalised.[23] He added that Selwyn Lloyd's arguments in the minority report sprang from an objection to monopoly rather than from a positive desire for commercial programmes. Lady Megan Lloyd George said that most members of the Beveridge Committee favoured the retention of the BBC's monopoly not so much because the case for monopoly had been made, but rather because the case for commercial broadcasting or for alternative corporations had not been outlined to the satisfaction of the committee.[24] As regards the lack of television facilities in Scotland and Wales, Mr Charles Ian Orr-Ewing (Hendon North) stated:

> We have heard a great deal this afternoon about devolution and about
> the desirability of having something for Wales and something for
> Scotland. Surely they ought to have television studios in which to

create their own programmes from their own regions and not have something imposed on them from London and merely relayed in their vicinity.[25]

No studios were provided in Scotland prior to the launch of television there in March of the following year. The BBC believed that it was better to concentrate production resources in London and give priority to the geographical extension of television. On this basis, studios could be provided at a later stage.

The BBC's monopoly would have survived a little longer but for the election of a Conservative Government on 25 October 1951. In order to give full consideration to the many issues raised by the Beveridge Committee, the new government extended the BBC Charter for only six months from 31 December 1951. In May 1952, the Conservative Government published a White Paper (Cmd 8550) in which it indicated that some form of competition would be permitted. It also made provision for devolution to the Regions. The Scottish Advisory Council, at a meeting on 3 June 1952, discussed those aspects of the White Paper which affected Scotland. The Council agreed that some form of devolution for Scotland was necessary, although there was some uncertainty about the powers of the proposed Broadcasting Council in relation to the Scottish Controller.[26] A new Charter was published on 1 July 1952 and continued in force for ten years. Lord Reith, who had used his efforts to defend the monopoly, had mixed feelings towards the BBC. On 29 October 1952, he lunched with George barnes, BBC Director of Television, and later noted in his diary the attitude of Barnes towards the prospect of commercial television. Reith stated: 'He is sure commercial television is coming, does not think the BBC can possibly hold its prewar attitude and wants to lower standards still further to compete with commercial television. Miserable attitude.'[27] The BBC could not, however, maintain a fixed set of standards. The monopoly did not survive, thus prompting Lord Beveridge to state that the government was proposing to put television in the wrong hands. Beveridge later remarked in an article published in *Political Quarterly* that 'In a television corporation financed wholly by advertising revenue the tune will be called by the advertisers, and the programmes will be designed to get the maximum of popular appeal, irrespective of standards of taste'.[28] Beveridge now had to witness government policy forging a new direction for broadcasting. In purely Scottish terms, the most significant immediate developments were the arrival of BBC television in Scotland, the signs that there would be a diminished role for radio broadcasting because of future competition from television, and finally the formation of the Broadcasting Council for Scotland which superseded the BBC's Scottish Advisory Council. Possible competition from commercial television was a more distant prospect, and one which was not to affect the BBC in Scotland until 1957 when the first commercial television station began transmitting programmes in Scotland.

The arrival of BBC television in Scotland, radio developments, and constitutional changes, 1952–4

One of the most signficant long-term developments which had an impact on sound broadcasting, both in Scotland and throughout the rest of the country, was the arrival of television. The prewar television service was confined to London, but the postwar service was gradually extended to the Regions, reaching Scotland in March 1952. Its immediate impact in Scotland was muted. Most of the public did not possess television receivers and so there was no appreciable adverse influence on listening figures for the Scottish Home Service or the Light and Third Programmes. But the public was curious about television, if a little hesitant to invest money in purchasing or renting a television receiver. In the longer term, television did have an impact on the 'golden age' of radio broadcasting in Scotland, which came to an end in the mid-1950s. However, sound broadcasting was never totally eclipsed by television. Programme policy was altered to cater for competition from television. Also, technical developments, most notably VHF radio, offered the prospect both of better geographical coverage of radio services in Scotland and of reintroducing more localised services by using low-power transmitters. However, programme and technical changes do not by themselves provide a full account of the history of broadcasting in Scotland during the early 1950s. Constitutional change must also be considered. For the first time, a Broadcasting Council was to be established with executive control over the policy and content of sound broadcasting in Scotland. The background to its formation, the extent of its powers and the work of the Council reveal much about the BBC's attitude to broadcasting in Scotland and of the ability of the Corporation to adequately reflect Scottish life, culture and interests. These are the topics and themes which are worth exploring.

In March 1948, Sir William Haley, BBC Director-General, stated that television would be extended to Scotland when labour and materials became available. The Scottish Advisory Council certainly hoped that when television arrived in Scotland, facilities would also exist to contribute programme items to London. On 9 February 1949, the Postmaster-General announced a development plan for bringing the main centres of population within the range of television via five transmitting stations which would cover eighty per cent of the population of the UK. In May, the apparent lack of progress in extending television to Scotland was mentioned by some MPs in the House of Commons.[1] Restrictions on capital expenditure were blamed for the delay. At the time, the BBC was spending £1 of each £2 combined licence and up to one fifth of revenue from sound-only licences on television development. In July, it was remarked in the House of Commons that in delaying the extension of television, Scotland was being denied the fruits of one of its inventors, John Logie Baird. But the Assistant PMG, Charles Hobson, refuted any suggestion that Scotland was receiving unfair treatment: 'There is no question of being hard on Scotland or unjust to Scotland. None whatever. I think one thing we can say in the Post Office is that the needs of Scotland are consistently being attended to.'[2] This answer did not however appear to satisfy Scottish MPs. Later in 1949, the BBC received permission from the government to build five high-power and five medium-power stations, although work on the medium-power stations was later postponed in March 1951. It seemed that at last television would be extended to Scotland.

The BBC began test transmissions in order to determine a suitable site in Scotland for one of the high-power stations. Several sites were investigated using a mobile transmitter which radiated test signals from an aerial suspended about 600 feet above ground by a balloon.[3] The strength of the signal was recorded by a van which travelled around the countryside. After field strengths were examined and field strength contour maps prepared to illustrate the probable service area, a site at Kirk O'Shotts, almost midway between Glasgow and Edinburgh, was chosen for the high-power station. The PMG was then approached to obtain approval for the use of the site which would serve the populous central belt of Scotland. In January 1950, the BBC announced that orders had been placed for the supply of a 50kw vision transmitter designed and manufactured by EMI and then the most powerful television transmitter in the world, and a 12kw sound transmitter designed and manufactured by Standard Telephones and Cables. The aerial was designed by Marconi's Wireless Telegraphy Company. Plans for the building of the station were passed on 10 May 1950 and work on the site commenced on 20 June. Low-power sound and television transmitters were to be installed on a reserve basis in case a fault developed in the high-power main transmitters. Kirk O'Shotts was the third high-power station to be built under the BBC's plan to expand television coverage, and covered an area of twenty-five acres. In September 1950, work began on the construction of a two-way microwave radio relay link between Manchester and Kirk O'Shotts. It was the opinion of the Television Advisory Committee that a radio link was preferable to the use of cable.[4] Programmes were carried from London to Manchester via Birmingham by coaxial cable. The radio link from Manchester to Kirk O'Shotts was carried by a series of seven hilltop beacons, each thirty miles apart and operated on an unattended basis.

Bad weather and shortages of labour and materials contributed to the delay in bringing television to Scotland, and these delays prompted more questions in the House of Commons.[5] In January 1952, Noel Ashbridge (BBC Director of Technical Services) indicated that the Post Office had told the BBC that the earliest firm date they could give for providing a daily service from Kirk O'Shotts was 15 March 1952.[6] The Board of Management, however, wanted the two-way radio link between Manchester and Kirk O'Shotts to become operational on 14 March. It was hoped that, if programme arrangements were completed, then the Scotland-England rugby match at Murrayfield on 15 March could be broadcast using the Kirk O'Shotts transmitter. The first official test transmissions took place on 15 January 1952. Kirk O'Shotts was purely a transmitting station, and there was no provision of any television studio facilities in Scotland. Since Scotland was expected to broadcast the same programme as London, the televising of Scottish-originated material on the network was to depend upon the use of an outside broadcast unit initially used on a share basis with the north of England, but mainly based in Scotland. The BBC did not intend to build television studios outside London until after 1954, much to the disadvantage of Scottish artists who either did not wish or were unable to travel to London to take part in broadcasts. The BBC recognised that most of the programme material which would be taken from Regional centres would consist of sporting events through outside broadcasts, assuming that sporting promoters would not impose restrictions out of fear that televised broadcasts might decrease attendances. The BBC recognised the desire for Regions to have their own studio facilities, but argued that the concentration of production facilities in London would enable all viewers to benefit from the high standards and techniques used. It was not certain, however, to what extent London programmes would interest people in Scotland.

The BBC's television service in Scotland began on 14 March 1952. The service was opened using the low-power vision and sound transmitters. The Board of Management believed that the Kirk O'Shotts television station should be opened using the low-power transmitter because towards the end of the previous year it was impossible to foresee when the high-power transmitter would be ready. The Scottish Advisory Council and the Board of Governors agreed, and the Board decided that the Secretary of State for Scotland should be invited to perform the opening ceremony.[7] This ceremony was held in Studio One in Broadcasting House, Edinburgh. Lord Tedder (Vice-Chairman of the BBC Board of Governors) invited the Rt Hon. James Stuart (Secretary of State for Scotland) to declare the station open. Also present at the thirty-minute opening ceremony, which began at 7.30pm, were Sir William Haley (BBC Director-General), four of the six BBC Governors, Melville Dinwiddie (the BBC's Scottish Controller) and the Rt Hon. James Miller (Lord Provost of Edinburgh). The opening speeches were followed by Scottish country dancing. Concern over the implications of the arrival of television in Scotland prompted Melville Dinwiddie to make the following remarks in the *Radio Times* for that week:

At the start, viewing will take up much time because of its novelty, but

> discrimination is essential so that not every evening is spent in a
> darkened room, the chores of the house and other occupations
> neglected. We can get too much even of a good thing. Television is
> one of those luxuries that will soon become a necessity of modern life,
> but we need to treat it with discretion.[8]

On the day when transmissions began, the *Glasgow Herald* looked forward to the
evening's opening ceremony but made a cautionary note about the type of
television service which was to commence – not primarily a Scottish television
service but rather the arrival of television from England to Scotland:

> It should be clearly understood that the occasion heralds television in
> Scotland, not Scottish television. For an indefinite time, most of the
> programmes viewed in Scotland will come from the south, though
> Scotland in one way or another will contribute to the national service.
> It is the declared policy of the BBC to provide as wide a national
> television coverage as possible before considering the development of
> regional programmes.[9]

The BBC believed that the extension of the transmitter network merited a higher
priority than the provision of studio facilities outside London. In its Annual
Report published in September 1952, the BBC, in commenting upon the arrival
of television in Scotland, stated that 'The Scottish Press and public greeted the
arrival of television with enthusiasm and, although there has been some
disappointment at the lack of Scottish studio facilities and the consequent
paucity of Scottish items in television programmes, first reactions to the new
medium have been very favourable'.[10]

With the arrival of television in Scotland, many people watched the service
from outside shop windows. There was great curiosity but no sudden rush to
purchase or rent a television receiver. The impact of television on sales of
twelve-inch television receivers in Scotland was in fact initially disappointing.
By March 1952 when transmissions began, only 30,000 television sets had been
sold. This figure exceeded the number of television licences by almost 20,000,
hence a considerable number of sets were unlicensed. In March 1952, figures
available from the Post Office indicated that only 12,560 television licences
had been issued in Scotland, mainly to those people living in Edinburgh and
Glasgow where reception of programmes was expected to be satisfactory. Many
Scots were not prepared to buy a licence until they could fully estimate the
value of the new service or indeed the reliability of the television receivers. The
Scottish Advisory Council, however, sounded a more optimistic note by
remarking that 'Although present indications are that television has been
accepted more cautiously in Scotland than elsewhere in Britain, the number of
viewers will rapidly increase and the demand for more Scottish items will
become clamant'.[11] Sales of receivers were reported as being much lower in
Scotland than in other parts of Britain, according to figures for 1952 issued by
the Radio and Television Retailers' Association.[12] Demand for sets did,
however, increase just prior to the Coronation in June 1953, and sales were also

assisted by the reduction in purchase tax in the Budget. Radio remained the dominant medium, and there is little doubt that many people in Scotland were still interested in their favourite radio programmes for some time after the introduction of television.[13] This was understandable given the limitations on broadcasting hours, the narrower range of programme output compared to radio, and the fact that for some time Scotland was unable to transmit opt-outs (i.e. separate programmes from the network) because production staff and engineering facilities were committed to network requirements. Nevertheless, the arrival of television resulted in some alterations in the timings of the more popular items on the Scottish Home Service six months before the television service opened, so that most of the programmes which had a wide appeal could be heard outside the normal hours of television transmissions. More fundamentally, in the longer term, radio no longer had a captive audience, and programme planners now always had to take this factor into account in preparing the programme schedules.

The arrival of television in Scotland advanced the goal of the BBC to bring television services to eighty per cent of the population of the UK. The high-power transmitter at Kirk O'Shotts came into operation on 17 August 1952, thereby extending the service to a potential four million people, including those who lived in the hilly country to the north of the station. This was possible because the station was situated on high ground 900 feet above sea level, and the mast which carried the transmitting aerial towered 750 feet. The high-power transmitter operated at ten times the power of the low-power transmitter, thus making it the most powerful television transmitter in the world. Given that much of the service area to the north was hilly, some reception problems were anticipated. The aerial at Kirk O'Shotts had built-in heaters to prevent the surface from being covered by ice. The low-power transmitters were held in reserve in case serious faults developed in the high-power transmitters. It took many years and the provision of several smaller transmitters before the BBC could deliver a television service to most of the remaining twenty per cent of the population of Scotland. Until the provision of studios was complete, programmes from Scotland consisted of outside broadcasts which covered subjects such as the Edinburgh International Festival, football, a visit to the Forth Railway Bridge, rugby from Murrayfield, the opening of the General Assembly of the Church of Scotland, a visit to Edinburgh Castle, and the installation of the Duke of Edinburgh as Chancellor of Edinburgh University. With the growing interest in television, newspapers began to devote more space to listing and to reviewing television programmes. Within the BBC in Scotland, some staff who had worked in radio now moved over into television production. With the arrival of television in Scotland, the BBC staff complement was modestly increased, most notably with the appointment of a Television Organiser, an Outside Broadcast Producer (Television), a Stage Manager (Television), and later a Television Production Assistant and Television News Assistant. In April 1952, 144 programme staff (radio and television) were based in Glasgow, supplemented by 87 staff in the Engineering Division.[14] In the late 1950s, the number and type of television posts increased appreciably. The post of Television Organiser (Scotland) subsequently lapsed and was replaced by an Assistant Head of Scottish Programmes (Television) in charge of staff such as television Outside Broadcast Producers, Stage Managers, and Production Assistants as well as Film Editors, Film Cameramen, a Film Sound Recordist, a Designer, Make-up Supervisor, Wardrobe Supervisor, and a Floor Manager. The BBC in Scotland also later began to appoint television producers covering subject areas such as sports, current affairs and light entertainment. With the arrival of television, the Regional Studio Engineer for Scotland based at Glasgow was now provided with the services of two Assistant Engineers-in-Charge, one for radio and one for television, the latter being a newly-created post. In the mid-1950s, the Regional Studio Engineer became known as the Scottish Engineer; only in the mid-1960s was the post retitled Head of Engineering (Scotland). Most programme and engineering staff involved in television were based in Glasgow.

For many years, the lack of a television studio in Edinburgh, after Glasgow had been provided with television facilities, caused problems because visitors to the city could not always allocate time to travel to Glasgow for a televised interview. Facilities and equipment were however gradually improved over the years. With television, there was a need to concentrate production resources at one centre rather than have it spread over several sites in Scotland, since this would obviate the need to transport equipment between sites. Nevertheless, the BBC did later acquire premises at 4 Queen Street in Edinburgh for adaptation for television productions. But in the early 1950s, the BBC had been subject to restrictions on capital development and pressure to extend television to the Regions, and so the provision of television programmes from outwith Scotland was regarded as a higher priority than the provision of television studio facilities within Scotland. By March 1952, net licence income in the UK from sound-only licences was £9,742,610, almost four times the figure for combined (i.e. television and radio) licences.[15] The ratio of radio to television operating expenditure, consisting mainly of artists' costs and production and engineering staff costs, was roughly of the same order.[16] However, television development began to absorb a greater volume of capital expenditure than radio development as television was extended to the Regions. This gap widened in subsequent years, and during 1958–9 television operating expenditure also exceeded radio expenditure. But in the early 1950s, the impact of television on radio in Scotland was only marginal.

The years 1947–55 have sometimes been referred to by broadcasters as the 'golden age' of Scottish radio broadcasting. It was a period during which radio broadcasting in Scotland developed to provide a fuller reflection of Scottish life and contributed some high-quality programmes to the other radio networks, but was not yet subject to intense competition from television broadcasting for audiences and for resources. Scottish-originated programme material was broadcast on the Third Programme based on the criterion of quality and not on any attempt to achieve a balance in the proportion of material originating from the national Regions. Many Scottish-produced programmes were intended primarily for listeners in Scotland and thus represented genuine alternatives to programmes available on the other networks. Typical programmes broadcast included *Arts Review, Scottish Life and Letters* produced by George Bruce in Aberdeen, *Scotland in Parliament* which was a monthly programme where Scottish MPs described Scottish affairs in the House of Commons, *Sportsreel* covering sports on Saturday evenings, *The McFlannels*, schools' programmes, *Scottish News, A Matter of Opinion* which was a discussion programme covering current affairs topics, *Farm Forum* and *Children's Hour*. There were also outside broadcasts from the national Mod of An Comunn, the Royal Highland Show, and the Edinburgh International Festival. The magazine programme *Capital Letter* covered events at the Edinburgh Festival. Orchestral music was provided by the BBC Scottish Orchestra and the Scottish Variety Orchestra. Orchestral music was provided for the basic Home Service Programme, and the Scottish Variety Orchestra contributed items to the Light Programme.

Some of the drama output from Scotland, such as Stevenson's *Weir of Hermiston*, was taken by all BBC Regions. But it was the variety programmes which appeared to attract the largest audiences. The popular programme *The McFlannels*, which was a serial based on a working-class Glasgow family, was later replaced by *The Bardowies*. There was also the weekly scripted variety programme *It's All Yours*, although in general there was in Scotland, and also in London, a lack of variety material and scriptwriters. With variety serials, the BBC probably benefited by using experienced broadcast artists rather than relying on professional comedians, not all of whom acquired a suitable microphone manner. In drama, the BBC also encountered some problems in adapting plays for radio. With news, the problem seemed to be an inability to increase the number of Scottish bulletins because of financial constraints. In general, the BBC appeared to be anxious to promote closer harmony between itself and theatre and film interests in Scotland in order to overcome constraints of a non-financial nature. Some degree of pattern was built into the programme schedules to the extent that sports programmes would normally be broadcast on Saturdays, religious programmes on Sundays, classical music on Wednesdays, and so on. There was some degree of sensitivity by the BBC in Scotland about the use of the term 'opt-out' to describe programme items such as these which were aimed specifically at listeners in Scotland. The use of this term might imply that Scottish items were too parochial or second-rate and only designed for transmission when nothing suitable was available from the other sound networks. There was therefore some resistance in Scotland to the use of the word 'opt-out' to describe such programme material. Melville Dinwiddie, Scottish Regional Director, said in 1947, two years after the Scottish Home Service was introduced, that 'Our job, as I see it, is to select the most suitable items for Scottish listeners, and we are not exercising an option, but operating an agreed policy'.[17] Programme material in the Scottish Home Service was also made available to the other radio networks.

Scottish programmes were sometimes broadcast on the Light and Third Programmes or even taken by the Home Service in London and re-broadcast as repeats in Scotland. During 1950–1, Scotland contributed 400 hours of radio programmes for other BBC services, and this included 88 hours for the Light Programme and 47 hours for the Third Programme.[18] This did, however, only represent a small percentage of the total hours of programmes produced in Scotland (i.e. 1,893 hours, of which 1,493 hours were produced primarily for listeners in Scotland). The bulk of programmes broadcast on the SHS were taken from the Home Service and other BBC services: during 1950–1, this represented 4,473 hours. The total of network contributions from Scotland and the number of programme hours produced primarily for listeners in Scotland fluctuated over the years. Reductions in network contributions and Scottish opt-out programmes tended to be compensated for by increases in the volume of programmes taken from the other networks. Up until the mid-1950s, Scotland was contributing an increasing number of programme hours to the Light Programme, but a more variable number to the Third Programme. Scotland did produce more of her own material than any of the other BBC Regions outside London: Scotland was also a significant contributor to the Third Programme in comparison with other Regions, but less so with regard to contributions to the Light Programme. Contributions to other radio networks gave prestige to producers in Scotland and released more resources for producing other programmes, given that London covered the cost of pro-grammes taken by the radio networks. Producers such as Robert Kemp, George Bruce and A.P. Lee originated many programmes which were taken by the other radio networks. Also, with fewer lines of authority in Scotland compared to London, radio producers in Scotland experienced a greater sense of freedom and authority. Their authority derived to a significant extent from their specialist knowledge in specific subjects. For example, George Bruce stated that he was appointed as programme assistant in December 1946 because of his knowledge of Scottish literature. He argued that the high quality of Scottish programme output up until the mid-1950s derived in part from the BBC's appointment of individuals who had already distinguished themselves in particular fields outwith the BBC.[19] Similarly, Robert Kemp was a distinguished journalist with the *Manchester Guardian* before joining the BBC.

It was a period during which London had great respect for the work of radio producers in Scotland. Scottish staff had freedom to decide how to allocate resources within the given budget, and so they could allocate more funds to some programmes then to others without consulting London. However, by the mid-1950s, television began to attract an increasing number of listeners and claim more resources. There was a diminished role for radio broadcasting after 1955, and, with the greater influence of television, control passed to London because it had the human and technical resources to develop television broadcasting. It was therefore television rather than radio producers who left Scotland to go to London to improve their career prospects and learn new skills. The attitude of radio producers in Scotland who worked for the BBC in the postwar period up until the mid-1950s, and regarded it as a 'golden age', also has some parallels in the interwar period when those who worked in the local stations in the 1920s regretted their replacement under the Regional Scheme. Similarly, staff who worked in the BBC in London during the first few years of broadcasting sometimes found it difficult to adjust to the growth in the size of the BBC and the more formalised hierarchical structure which accompanied such growth. So there was perhaps an element of nostalgia in the use of the term 'golden age'. Radio producers took comfort from audience research statistics which indicated that the Scottish Home Service was more popular in Scotland than the Light Programme, whereas in England the reverse situation applied.[20] Also, a larger proportion of listeners in Scotland tuned into the Third Programme in comparison with other parts of the country, although reception was limited to areas served by local transmitters, in effect the cities of Edinburgh, Glasgow, Aberdeen and Dundee. Radio retained its popularity during daytime hours, and in some parts of Scotland it remained the main source of information and entertainment. It could not, however, ignore the presence of television.

In order to counteract the popularity of television, an increasing number of popular items were broadcast on the Scottish Home Service in the early evening. The SHS did though retain a larger proportion of listeners than other Regional services, despite competition from television. The BBC, however, never regarded the provision of the three radio services and one television service as sacrosanct should audience preferences alter as television coverage spread throughout the country. In a paper prepared in September 1953 on the BBC's ten-year plan for broadcasting, the following point was made:

> Sooner or later, however, the time will come, with the growth of television audiences and a corresponding shrinkage of audiences dependent on sound alone, when the BBC may feel free to calculate that its obligations towards its various audiences can be met by a differently proportioned set of programmes in sound only and in sound and vision.[21]

The question was posed as to when and whether the BBC could reduce its output to two radio services after it took on the additional responsibility of an extra television channel. In Regional terms, the questions the BBC had to consider were: whether the future of Regional broadcasting should be in radio or television; when and under what conditions television should be regionalised; and the financial implications of such changes.

By the early 1950s, each of the three radio networks had reinforced their individual character, thereby discouraging listeners from switching between channels. Nevertheless, the BBC, in a submission to the Beveridge Committee on Broadcasting, which was based on a policy statement prepared in July 1946 on the BBC's Home Services, stated:

> It is important to note that, while each of the three programmes has its individual character, there is no firm line of demarcation dividing them. The programmes shade into each other, the differences between them being much more marked in approach and treatment than in range of content.[22]

Although each radio network was expected to concentrate on what it did best, the BBC stressed the interchangeability of items between the three networks. In practice, after the inauguration of the Third Programme, fewer people began to listen to serious programmes and switched their attention mainly to the Light Programme or to television. This situation was deemed by the BBC to be attributable to the specialist audience which Third Programme material was aimed at.[23] Sir William Haley, BBC Director-General, in a statement on home programme policy, had envisaged the community as a broadly-based cultural pyramid slowly aspiring upwards. This pyramid was served by the three radio programmes, differentiated but broadly overlapping in levels and interest with each programme leading on to the other.[24] The intention was to lead the listener over the years from the good to the better programmes by curiosity and a growth of understanding. In theory, this appeared to be a more graduated approach than under Reith's policy whereby listeners would be exposed to a wide range of subject matter and have to experience rapid gear-changes in programme content. According to Haley, listeners were encouraged to be selective in choosing programmes and so move from the lighter to the more serious material (i.e. from the Light to the Third Programme via the Regionalised Home Service). Haley believed that as the educational and cultural standards of the community rose, then so also would the levels of the BBC's programme pyramid. Unfortunately, in his cultural mission, Haley was wrong to suppose that listeners would tune into all three radio networks. The audience for the Third Programme remained a minority audience and did not reach the ten per cent level which he regarded as an ideal share of the audience to which to aspire. The Board of Governors maintained that the Third Programme was making an important contribution to culture and that conse-quently it had fully justified itself. However, the Board regretted that the numbers listening were not larger, and hoped that improvements in reception would increase the listening figure, with the proviso that standards should not be lowered to achieve this aim.[25]

Five years after the inauguration of the three radio services, the Director-General issued a paper assessing the situation. Despite adjustments in the content of the Home Service, the coverage of local issues by the Regions was praised. The range of content in the Light Programme had been broadened beyond variety to include discussion programmes. But despite the ambitious aims for the Third Programme, there were, as noted, problems with regard to its geographical availability in Scotland and in some other parts of the country, and in its share of the total audience despite higher than average listening figures for this Programme in Scotland. There was, however, support for the Third Programme's cultural innovations and contribution towards the prestige of the BBC. Internal competition among the programme services was credited with widening the range of programme output, although it was acknowledged that it could also lead producers to place undue stress on listening figures rather than on programme quality. There was also support for the postwar programme head-supply system in which programme heads had the absolute right to reject programme material offered by the supply divisions, the latter being responsible for artistic and professional standards. Producers in Scotland were responsible to London for professional and artistic standards. The BBC argued that internal competition was preferable to central planning because the use of the latter to coordinate output would have robbed programmes of their richness and variety by placing weaker items against stronger ones to avoid embarrassing alternatives. So, overall, the advent of limited competition between the sound services, and the introduction of the programme head-supply system, were deemed to have been jointly beneficial with respect to the range and quality of programme output in comparison with the prewar position. The paper by the Director-General went on to state that 'It can be claimed that the B.B.C. today, at the end of five years' postwar broadcasting, is far livelier, more all-embracing, more liberal, less exclusive, less bound by idiosyncrasies or formulae than it was previously'.[26] The expansion in the volume and range of programme output after the war had led to a greater abundance of weaker programmes, but it had also brought about an increase in the number of high-quality programmes as well as a greater professionalism among the staff. It must also not be forgotten that the nature of the programme services provided by the BBC in Scotland depended to a significant extent on technical factors and not merely on organisation or programme policy. The radio and television transmitter development programme in Scotland and the technical, financial and social aspects which have governed the extension of the BBC's broadcasting services in Scotland need to be considered.

A variety of factors influenced the rate of BBC transmitter development not only in Scotland but throughout the UK: the service range of each transmitter; the number of people served by any given station; the costs involved; the practical difficulties in siting and building transmitters; the need to abide by international frequency regulations; and the existing level of social amenities (including broadcasting services) available in particular areas. Not all these factors were given equal priority. Technical factors invariably, but not always, influenced the rate of transmitter development. The broad principle adopted by the BBC in extending broadcasting coverage was to concentrate on the provision of services to the four nations which constituted the United Kingdom, and thereafter to give priority to the size of population to be served. These were the main priorities according to Mr David Gammans, the Assistant Postmaster-General, in a written reply to a parliamentary question concerning broadcasting coverage in Scotland.[27] Inevitably, areas which were expensive and difficult to cover, such as remote areas in Scotland where there were scattered communities, were at a disadvantage in comparison with more populous centres where there was also a more even geographical contour. Transmitter development was also dependent at a more general level upon the capacity of industry to supply the necessary equipment, and on the ability of the Post Office to provide cable or radio links between stations. It should be noted that the shortage of frequencies, which were allocated at international level, also governed the number and locations of transmitters. Indeed, given that there was an insufficient number of frequencies to provide a different one for each transmitting station, stations using the same frequency (such as relay stations) had to be separated geographically and operated on low power to prevent interference from occurring. This governed the maximum power of each station, and, with signals diminishing in strength according to the distance from the transmitter, this influenced the size of each service area. Also, relay stations had to be sited carefully in order to receive signals from existing stations for re-broadcasting at a satisfactory standard of quality. In Scotland, the problems which faced engineering staff included high mountains, deep glens, long distances, a rugged coastline and a scattered population in the Highlands. Also, it was only when electric power was extended to the Highlands that listeners were able to use mains-powered radio receivers rather than battery radio sets. BBC engineering staff visited Scotland to survey possible transmitter sites and consult with Scottish-based engineering staff. Final technical decisions were, however, taken by staff in London because they had the expertise and the responsibility for the overall planning of the transmitter network. Scottish listeners and viewers continually voiced their concern at the BBC in Scotland for perceived deficiencies in broadcasting coverage.

After the war, the BBC sought to improve radio and television coverage. In television, a plan was prepared for nationwide coverage which involved the construction of high-power and medium-power stations. The location of television transmitters was designed to take television to as many people as possible within the resources available. The BBC was also aware that it could not ignore the needs of the listening audience. During the period when work was proceeding for the construction of a television station at Kirk O'Shotts in central Scotland, a General Advisory Council paper on the development of the television service stated:

> The maintenance of a proper balance between the necessity to develop television vigorously and the equal necessity to ensure that the BBC's 12,000,000 Sound licence-holders are given the best possible service insofar as it is effected by capital development is not easy to determine.[28]

Initially, the government only authorised the construction of high-power stations. On 14 March 1951, the government announced that the plan for five medium-power stations, one of which was to be located at Aberdeen, had been postponed indefinitely because it would have interfered with the resources required for the government's defence programme. In December 1952, shortly after all the initial five high-power stations were in operation, the Assistant Postmaster-General stated in the House of Commons that the government believed that it was not in the national interest, at a time when industrial investment was limited due to Britain's defence and export efforts, to devote more resources to the construction of new stations or to the manufacturing of television receivers.[29] The opening of new stations would have boosted the demand for television receivers. So, during 1952, Scotland was served by only one television transmitter located at Kirk O'Shotts covering the central belt. Two years after the arrival of television in Scotland, the Assistant PMG was asked in March 1954 what percentage of the total area of Scotland received television, the cost of providing 100 per cent coverage, and whether areas without any service would have priority over any intention to introduce alternative programmes for areas already covered by a BBC service. Mr Gammans gave the following reply:

> The television station at Kirk O'Shotts gives coverage to 26 per cent of the total area of Scotland; this contains 79 per cent of the total population. When the two additional stations planned for North-East Scotland are working, these percentages will increase to 39 and 89, respectively. An estimate of the cost of providing complete coverage would be quite hypothetical since it is not possible under the BBC's plan to cover 100 per cent of the area of the United Kingdom. Nor are those plans affected in any way by the proposal to introduce an alternative service.[30]

So, although remote areas benefited from a postal service for the same cost as people living in cities, the same principle was not applied to broadcasting.

The BBC in Scotland provided a wider range of programme services in Scotland on radio. In 1950, the transmitters at Westerglen (central Scotland), Burghead (Moray Firth) and Redmoss (near Aberdeen) provided the Scottish Home Service programmes. These transmitters also broadcast the Light Programme; the Third Programme was broadcast from local transmitters based at Edinburgh, Glasgow, Redmoss and Dundee, and so coverage was less than the SHS or the Light Programme. Under the Copenhagen Plan which took effect on 15 March 1950, one medium wavelength was allocated to the SHS. This plan restricted the number of wavelengths available to the UK and so limited the number of transmitters which the BBC could use to overcome poor reception. After the plan took effect, the number of stations operating on medium wavelengths almost doubled in Europe, thereby giving rise to interference in Scotland during the hours of darkness when the atmosphere reflected signals over longer distances. The SHS in fact shared the 371m wavelength with stations in Spain and Yugoslavia. A temporary low-power transmitter was opened at Dumfries on 24 December 1952, but realistically only the higher frequencies of VHF offered the prospect of improving reception, especially with the increase in the number and power of transmitters in Europe. However, government restrictions on BBC capital development continued into 1953. In April of that year, the Assistant PMG outlined the government's position in reply to a parliamentary question expressing concern about poor broadcasting reception in some areas of the country. Mr Gammans stated:

> I am fully aware that in some parts of the country the reception of BBC sound programmes is poor, and I can assure my Hon. friend that both the BBC and the government will keep this fact well in mind in their plans for future development in sound and television. The only satisfactory solution to the problem is VHF, but the rate of progress which can be made with it and other developments must be determined by the amount of capital investment which could be justified in the light of our general economic position.[31]

Restrictions on capital development, together with the disproportionate cost of serving small isolated communities with VHF in mountainous country where signals were screened by hills, placed constraints on the extension of broadcasting services in Scotland. VHF radio broadcasting was certainly significant because of its implications for improving both broadcasting coverage and sound quality, and for permitting the introduction of localised broadcasting services.

The BBC engaged in experimental work on VHF sound broadcasting during the 1950s. This work opened up the possibility of improving broadcasting coverage and sound quality by reinforcing existing radio services on long and medium wavelengths, and of permitting the introduction of more localised radio services in England as well as diversifying the Scottish Home Service output in some parts of Scotland. The BBC initially envisaged a VHF service using a chain of frequency modulation (FM) stations of varying powers, giving near-complete coverage of the Home, Light and Third Programmes. Improving coverage of existing services using VHF was given a higher priority than fragmenting services within Scotland or any of the other Regions. Given the insufficient number of medium and long-wave channels and the consequent problem of interference on medium-wave from too many continental stations, the use of VHF opened up the possibility of increasing the number of channels and in improving reception. Moreover, medium-wave receivers had to be designed to reject as much interference as was possible from foreign stations which used wavelengths similar or close to those of the BBC, but, in making these receivers more selective in picking up signals from the BBC, the quality of sound output deteriorated. In 1950, it was accepted within the BBC that the use of VHF as a solution to the deterioration in reception conditions would be a long-term remedy.[32] The only advantage with the low and medium frequencies was that they covered a much larger service area than the higher frequencies used with VHF. In Scotland, there was a strong case for providing VHF coverage to Angus, the Borders, Orkney and Shetland.

The propagation characteristics of VHF with its shorter wavelengths differed somewhat from those of medium or long wave.[33] VHF coverage was the same at night as during the daytime, but signal strength did decrease rapidly according to distance from the transmitter, hence the need for correspondingly more transmitters. VHF signals were also more likely to be affected by the contours of the terrain over which they travelled, hence the heights of the transmitting and receiving aerials were more important than they were with medium wavelengths, and this obviously influenced the siting of stations. Unlike medium waves, VHF waves were not reflected by the atmosphere but instead escaped into outer space, thereby not producing interference between stations over long distances, especially during the hours of darkness. The problem with VHF was that hills cast partial shadows and so reduced the reception of signals from the transmitter, thus appearing not ideal for serving mountainous areas in the north of Scotland. Indeed, VHF signals could also be distorted before reaching the receiver by being reflected off large buildings (i.e. multi-path reception), and the inability of VHF signals to bend as easily round corners as low and medium frequencies thus gave rise to gaps in broadcasting coverage. It can also be noted that VHF was affected by any form of electrical interference (such as car ignition systems in built-up areas) or bad weather if the signal was weak, and that the signals could not be received on existing radio sets. However, the technical characteristics of VHF made it ideally suitable for providing local radio services with a much better quality of reception than either medium or long waves and with less possibility of mutual interference between stations. The greater number of stations required with VHF was likely to increase capital costs, but it opened up the possibility of again providing local broadcasting in Scotland as the BBC had done during the 1920s.

Given that, on balance, the advantages of VHF outweighed the disadvantages, a decision had to be made regarding which system of modulation to adopt: frequency modulation (FM) or amplitude modulation (AM). FM had advantages over AM with regard to the level of hiss which was noticeable during programme pauses, and to electrical interference from car ignition systems and domestic electrical appliances. This was important because the greater degree of noise suppression with FM permitted a larger area to be served by transmitters before interference became noticeable, particularly in areas where field strength was low due to physical obstructions. In October 1952, the PMG asked the Television Advisory Committee to consider the issue of VHF sound broadcasting and what form of modulation should be adopted. The BBC also conducted experimental VHF broadcasts from Wrotham in Kent. FM required a wider bandwidth than AM, which would result in the use of fewer channels in any given band of frequencies, but it could provide good reception to larger areas than AM and so incur lower capital costs. Tests in fact confirmed that it was more economical to provide a nationwide VHF radio service using FM. On 16 December 1953, the Television Advisory Committee therefore recommended the adoption of FM as the method of modulation to be used for VHF broadcasting.[34] On 10 February 1954, the government accepted this recommendation. The BBC's first VHF station was brought into service at Wrotham in England on 2 May 1955; the first VHF station in Scotland was not to open until 29 March 1956. The construction of VHF stations in Scotland to bolster coverage of existing services and to introduce some localised programmes therefore took place in a later period. A significant development which took place in the early 1950s was, however, not of a technical but of a constitutional nature. It involved the formation of a Broadcasting Council for Scotland.

The Beveridge Report on Broadcasting, published in January 1951, recommended the establishment of Broadcasting Commissions (or Councils as they were later called) in the BBC's national Regions. Before the government responded to the Broadcasting Committee's recommendations, the BBC Governors put forward their own views about the possible introduction of Broadcasting Councils. The Governors feared that this proposal would undermine the unity of the BBC, reduce the volume of Regional contributions to the UK sound networks and impose unreasonable financial burdens if the changes resulted, as they were expected to do, in demands for greater Regional broadcasting. In the absence of more wavelengths, it was argued that a greater volume of Regional broadcasting could only be achieved at the expense of other parts of the UK. It was even stated that an increase in local material would lead to a deterioration in BBC standards. The paper went on to observe that:

> The Commissions would, by their nature, be continually forced to pull against the Corporation. Their policy could not help being expansionist and inflationary. There would be continual pressure upon them to give greater prominence to nationalist activities than was their proper due. Such pressures are already upon the BBC but can be resisted better by the Corporation than would be possible by the Commissions.[35]

Staff in the national Regions would, it was believed, have divided allegiances. For example, if a difference of view arose between the Corporation and the Commissions, this would place the Regional Controller in a difficult position. Also, if the Commissions were only granted control over radio and not television broadcasting, then this would result in unhealthy competition between both broadcasting media. The Board of Governors was similarly not impressed by the proposal that a Scottish, a Welsh and a Northern Ireland Governor should each be a member of the Board. They disliked the concept of a functional or representative Board where individual Governors would naturally protect or promote any particular interest. To prevent sectional rivalries, it was argued that individuals should be chosen for their suitability to be Governors and that therefore the fact of their nationality should be of merely secondary importance. The Governors also wished to retain control over the appointment of the most senior staff in Scotland as well as over capital expenditure.

The Conservative Government's White Paper of May 1952 confirmed that the new Charter would make provision for the establishment of Broadcasting Councils for Scotland, Wales and Northern Ireland. Their primary function would be to control the policy and content of their Home Service programmes.

In fact, only Broadcasting Councils for Scotland and Wales were established; Northern Ireland was nevertheless represented by a national Governor. The White Paper stated that the government would leave it to the BBC to decide upon the detailed definition of powers to be delegated to the Councils. In a debate in the House of Lords just after the publication of the White Paper (Cmd 8550), Lord Reith expressed his dislike of the intention to introduce these Councils. He said that he could foresee confusions, conflicts and divisions of authority and responsibility. He added that these Councils would be subject to constant pressure to extend their powers and spheres of influence, thus ultimately weakening the BBC. He drew attention to the divided loyalty of Regional Controllers – would they owe loyalty primarily to the Councils, or to the Director-General?[36] A paper was prepared for the meeting of the Scottish Advisory Council on 3 June 1952 regarding the renewal of the Charter as it affected Scotland. Devolution was taken in practice to represent control of the Scottish Home Service within the limits of a block grant to cover expenditure on staff, equipment and accommodation. The crucial issue with the formation of the Broadcasting Council was taken to be the problem of combining the maximum of devolution with the minimum of central financial control neces- sary to maintain the unity of the BBC. The problem posed was whether the Council should be given executive power, and, if so, within what limits consistent with the preservation of overall BBC policy and standards.[37] Would the loyalties of BBC staff in Scotland reside with the Council or with London, particularly in the situation where many Scottish programme staff already had a dual responsibility (i.e. to supply material to the sound networks and not simply for Scottish domestic consumption)? Also, if the Council only had control over staff wholly employed on the Scottish Home Service, would the Council be able to resolve conflicts over policy between Scotland and London or would such a task be left to the Board of Governors? It was in any case difficult to determine which staff were wholly employed on the Scottish Home Service because some SHS programmes were taken by the other sound networks for UK transmission. When the Council was established, only some members of staff in Scotland received a letter indicating that they had been transferred to the staff of the Broadcasting Council; posts such as that of Television Programme Organiser were not under the control of the Broadcasting Council because the Council was only given control over sound broadcasting. Members of the Scottish Advisory Council preferred a reconstituted SAC with statutory powers to appoint other advisory bodies, rather than the formation of a Broadcasting Council. The SAC did not believe that it was unduly restricted by being a purely advisory body, although it did accept the need for greater administrative and financial devolution and more technical resources.

The BBC's new Charter came into operation on 1 July 1952 and was to continue in force for ten years. It made provision for the BBC to establish two national Broadcasting Councils in Scotland and Wales respectively.[38] The Broadcasting Council for Scotland (BCS) was to be chaired by a National

Governor for Scotland who automatically became a member of the BBC's Board of Governors in London. The Charter stated that the national Governor should be selected taking into account his knowledge of the culture, characteristics and affairs of Scotland, and his closeness to Scottish opinion.[39] There were eight members of the BCS in addition to the national Governor. These members were selected in late 1952 for appointment by a panel nominated by the BBC's General Advisory Council. It was noted by the Board of Governors that, at the meeting of the GAC on 8 October 1952, the Council would be asked to nominate separate panels for the appointment of members of the national Broadcasting Councils.[40] A GAC panel, chaired by Sir John Falconer (a former Lord Provost of Edinburgh who was Chairman of the SAC), invited organisations to submit the names of individuals for consideration for membership of the BCS. Other members of the GAC panel were Hector McNeil MP, Niall MacPherson MP, Dr Sidney Raybould and Mrs Mary Stocks. The GAC panel, which met in Edinburgh on 31 October, sifted through the names of over one hundred individuals which had been received from organisations. This list had to be reduced to eight names which could then be placed before the Board of Governors for approval. The Board of Governors made the appointments to the Council in December. The national Governor was appointed in the same manner as the other members of the Board of Governors and thus was a political appointment, in contrast to the other members of the Council, who were appointed by the BBC. Lord Clydesmuir, the first BBC National Governor for Scotland, was a former Secretary of State for Scotland. Members of the BCS were expected to represent the public interest, not sectional interests. Five of the eight members were to be selected after consulting representative cultural, religious and other bodies in Scotland whom the GAC panel selected as being concerned with Scottish broadcasting policy; the other three members were to be selected as being representative of local authorities in Scotland. The latter appointments were subject to some criticism, not least because local authority representatives were not seen to be qualified to judge about broadcasting matters. The government, though, regarded the system as more democratic, since members would be more representative of listeners in the national Regions.

The BCS, thus representative of the 'Great and Good' in Scottish society, was designed to keep the BBC conscious of its Scottish dimension. The functions of the Broadcasting Councils as defined by the Charter are worth quoting in full as follows:

> (a) the function of controlling the policy and the content of the programmes of that service among the Home Sound Services which the Corporation provides primarily for reception in the country for which the Council are established, and exercising such control with full regard to the distinctive culture, interests and tastes of Our People in that country; (b) such other functions in relation to the said service as the Corporation may from time to time devolve upon them;

and (c) the function of tendering advice to the Corporation in regard to all matters relating to other broadcasting services of the Corporation which affect the interests of Our People in the country for which the Council are established.[41]

The relationship between the BCS and BBC staff in Scotland was analogous to a certain extent with that between the Board of Governors and the BBC staff as a whole. However, the method of appointment, the power and the responsibilities of the BCS differed from those of the Board of Governors, not least because the Council only had control over radio programmes produced within and for Scotland and neither possessed fiscal autonomy nor was able to appoint senior staff. The BCS was given power to appoint advisory committees, and members of the Council were to be allowed to see the minutes of these committees and to attend their meetings. The list of functions of the BCS was more grandiose in theory than it was to prove to be in practice. This was in some measure a reflection of lack of sufficient knowledge on broadcasting, in that it made the BCS principally reliant on information supplied by senior management and thereby undermined the ability of the Council effectively to determine policy. The Council was useful as an intermediary with London when Scotland lobbied for more resources or wished to convey complaints direct to the Board of Governors. However, the attitude of the Council to the opportunities and influence at its disposal in shaping broadcasting policy did vary over time according to the prevailing broadcasting climate, the amount of information supplied by Scottish management, the personality of the national Governor, the willingness of the Council to use its power, the composition of membership of the Council, the views of the Board of Governors and Board of Management towards Scottish broadcasting, and not least the unity of the BCS on various issues.

The first meeting of the BCS was held on 14 January 1953 at Broadcasting House, Edinburgh. The meeting was also attended by Sir Alexander Cadogan (BBC Chairman), Sir Ian Jacob (Director-General), Mr R.E.L. Wellington (Director of Home Sound Broadcasting) and Melville Dinwiddie (Controller, Scotland). At that meeting, which discussed the terms of reference of the Council and the policy and content of the Scottish Home Service, it was also agreed that future meetings should be held at monthly intervals alternating between Edinburgh and Glasgow with an occasional meeting in Aberdeen. The Scottish Controller normally attended all meetings of the BCS, as did other senior staff in Scotland. The first report of the BCS was submitted by Sir Cecil Graves (acting Chairman), who had been joint Director-General of the BBC from 1942 to 1943, to Sir Alexander Cadogan (BBC Chairman) on 31 March 1953. The Annual Reports of the BCS were incorporated in the BBC's Annual Report which was presented to Parliament. These reports were subject to ultimate sanction by the Board of Governors. The BCS could also prepare special reports on its own initiative or if requested to do so. The minutes of the BCS were more detailed than those of senior management, partly for future reference purposes, and did not contain a day-to-day record of events; and also because members of the Council who held prominent positions in public life did not have extensive experience of broadcasting and so had to have access to reasonably detailed information for their monthly meetings. The minutes of the Council were seen by the Board of Governors and Board of Management, although it should be noted that these minutes too did not necessarily convey the tone of each meeting, act as an absolute guide to how individual members of the Council were thinking, or outline matters discussed over working lunches. Moreover, the reasons behind all policy decisions were not always minuted. Some programme decisions were arrived at in general discussions between programme staff in Scotland and those in London, rather than emerging from formal meetings. BBC Scottish management could propose policy changes which would be placed before the BCS for approval, but it was also open to the Council to propose changes itself.

From the beginning, BBC Scottish management was willing to take advantage of the limited knowledge of Council members regarding BBC operational activities in order to thwart any radical changes in policy. The Scottish Controller wrote on this theme to the Director-General:

> My general feeling of the Council and its members is that they are thoroughly interested and most anxious to learn and give all the help they can. We will do everything we can to guide their enthusiasm into the proper channels so that they keep to their Terms of Reference in dealing with the policy and content of the Scottish Home Service.[42]

Scottish management soon became aware that any differences of opinion on technical or programme policy matters between staff in Scotland and those at Head Office could be brought to the attention of the Board of Governors via the national Governor. For example, the BCS was prepared to pursue at Board of Governors level the need for the Scottish Home Service to be transmitted during the early evening in the non-television hours from the television sound transmitter at Kirk O'Shotts to those people living in the fringe areas of the Westerglen medium-wave transmitter until the SHS could be received from VHF sound transmitters. The Broadcasting Council argued that many fringe areas received television sound with greater clarity than that of the medium-wave radio transmissions. On 5 October 1953, the Board of Management rejected this suggestion on technical and cost grounds. The BBC argued that technically this would generate high voltages in receivers unless sound signals were accompanied by synchronous pulses from the VHF vision transmitter, and also that it would not be cost-effective in relation to the small number of households with television sets who would benefit from such a course of action. Nevertheless, the Scottish Controller asked for the decision to be reconsidered, but the original decision was confirmed. It was then that BCS members decided to ask their Chairman to pursue the matter with the Board of Governors, thus prompting the Scottish Controller to remark that 'This is the first instance of an obvious defect in the organisation of the Council, whereby a difference of opinion between Regional and Head Office staff can be reflected at the Board of Governors level'.[43]

In policy terms, the first general point to note about the BCS was that it was initially authorised to control only the policy and content of programmes in the Scottish Home Service because the Light and Third Programmes were provided for reception in the UK as a whole. According to William Haley, who was Director-General until just before the Broadcasting Councils came into existence, Scotland might be consulted about the content of items of Scottish interest included in the Light and Third Programmes, but only for purposes of accuracy and not as a means of censoring material. On this theme, the first BCS paper defined the general scope of Council policy as follows:

> The broad policy of the Scottish Home Service is to take the best items available from wherever they may be found, so as to provide balanced and satisfying entertainment for Scottish listeners. For the past five years, the Corporation has given almost complete autonomy to the staff in Scotland, to initiate as many items as money and talent will permit. The basis of the programme is, of course, the Home Service from London, and Scottish items or suitable material from other Regions and Overseas are built into this basic schedule.[44]

Control over television programme output produced within Scotland in addition to or to replace UK network output (i.e. the Scottish opt-out programmes) only followed after the publication of the Pilkington Report on Broadcasting in 1962. Indeed, devolution to the BBC Regions with regard to television was not envisaged in the White Paper of 1952 at a time when television was gradually being extended to the Regions. During this period, television was regarded by the BBC as a network operation, and the Regions were expected to operate as reservoirs of programme material for that network. The BCS had responsibility for the content of Scottish-originated items in the Scottish Home Service, but only acted in an advisory capacity with regard to television or other BBC radio services transmitted in Scotland which affected the interests of the people of Scotland.

A fundamental point which must also be stressed about the BCS was that, despite the functions of the Council as outlined in the Royal Charter, this arrangement left the BBC centrally with the power to prescribe the detailed definition of powers to be delegated to the Council. Indeed, the powers of the BCS were subject to such reservations and directions as appeared to the BBC to be necessary from time to time for reasons of finance or in the interests of due coordination and coherent administration in the BBC.[45] These were substantial qualifying clauses. The BCS acted in an advisory capacity in matters such as operating expenditure, capital development and the planning of the transmitter network. The Council had responsibility for the Scottish budget, the largest element of which comprised the programme allowance. When the Broadcasting Council took over from the Scottish Advisory Council, the programme allowance had not been increased for three years and was hindering programme development. During 1952–3, the programme allowance was £104,415 out of a total budget of £210,232 under the Council's control. Many years later, Sir Charles Curran, BBC Director-General, commented upon the constraining factors in the Charter which influenced the operation of the Broadcasting Councils for Scotland and Wales. He stated:

> These were clearly potential major limitations on the freedom of action of the Broadcasting Councils, and they constituted the possible grounds of conflict over the respective jurisdictions of the Board of Governors and the National Broadcasting Councils, and between the national executive in London and the local executives in Scotland and Wales.[46]

In an essentially unitary broadcasting organisation in which Scotland represented only one Region, albeit a national Region, ultimate control remained at the centre (i.e. in London) in matters affecting the whole broadcasting service. The argument pivoted on just how much control London needed to retain. The BCS had control over the balance between Scottish and network material broadcast in Scotland and in the appointment of staff whose duties were solely connected with the broadcasting services in Scotland, but there was no fiscal autonomy. Nevertheless, the presence of the National Governor for Scotland on the BBC Board of Governors appeared to give Scotland an input into the formulation of policy which was denied to any English Region. Also, although the Chairmen of the English Regional Advisory Councils were members of the GAC, the GAC and these Councils did not meet as frequently as the Board of Governors or the Broadcasting Council for Scotland.

The effectiveness of the BCS depended to some extent upon the use which it made of the powers at its disposal, as will be noted. There was a tendency during the early years for members to be unwilling to take risks that would have involved unpopular decisions. They may also have been unable fully to grasp the non-technical implications of technical matters. Given that members were part-time and had few contacts with programme or engineering staff, this prevented them from becoming aware of all aspects of broadcasting in Scotland. Scottish management were in any case never enthusiastic about regular contacts developing between members of the BCS and BBC staff in Scotland. John Gray, a former BBC Chief Assistant in Edinburgh, remarked that members of the BCS needed to find out where the boiler room was and to see for themselves how the system operated.[47] The problem was that members of the BCS too often stayed, in metaphorical terms, on the bridge rather than venture into the engine room.

The years from 1952 to 1954 were significant not merely because of the arrival of television in Scotland, the challenges to radio broadcasting, technical developments such as the prospect of VHF radio, and constitutional changes such as the establishment of the Broadcasting Council for Scotland. These years also covered the period from the government's decision in principle to permit competition in broadcasting, through to the passage of the Television

Act which ended the BBC's monopoly of broadcasting which had remained intact since 1922. The background to the arrival of Independent Television was important since it necessitated a reappraisal of how the BBC Regions should compete with ITV.

The BBC's monopoly of broadcasting, and the coming of Independent Television, 1952–4

An examination of television broadcasting both within the UK in general terms, and within Scotland in particular from the early 1950s, must take into account the background to the events which led to the end of the BBC's monopoly of broadcasting. The monopoly which was initially based on technical and administrative factors was later justified by the BBC according to programme criteria (i.e. the maintenance of a wide range of high-quality programmes). With the limitation on the number of wavelengths and the fact that the Post Office regarded the monopoly as administratively more convenient to supervise, successive governments opted to license one corporation rather than several corporations. Reith did much to establish the BBC as a relatively independent institution with its tradition of public service, high standards and moral responsibility towards the public which it served. The prewar BBC was like a national Church: it was often regarded as elitist, and it sought to provide what it regarded as a balanced programme output to as large an audience as possible. The monopoly was justified by the BBC because it appeared to sustain those high standards. During the war years, the performance of the BBC similarly dampened any critical comment about the monopoly. However, criticism of the monopoly, rather than criticism of programme output as such, became a more prominent issue in the immediate postwar period, thereby ensuring that the Beveridge Committee on Broadcasting, unlike previous committees of inquiry, would be unable to take the monopoly for granted. It is therefore important to consider the background to the criticism which was directed at the BBC's monopoly of broadcasting, and the various arguments which were used both in defence and in opposition to the monopoly. Moreover, the coming of Independent Television and its structure, funding and programme philosophy can be compared with those of the BBC in order to examine how both systems were expected to cater for Regional broadcasting. The period leading up to the arrival of Independent Television can usefully be covered by tracing developments from the publication of the White Paper of 1952 which made provision for competition in broadcasting, through to the period immediately following the passage of the Television Act in 1954.

Several factors emerged which prompted much greater criticism of the BBC's broadcasting monopoly by the early 1950s. British broadcasting, which was often viewed as the best in the world, did not constitute proof that a better non-monopolistic system could not be developed. Equally, there was no reason to suppose that competitive broadcasting services could not be operated in the public interest. The criticism of the American system of broadcasting could not be taken to imply that the only alternative to the British system was one based upon American methods of practice. The BBC had developed a strong link between the concept of monopoly and that of public service, hence it was easy to accept that the only alternatives to the British system consisted either of a state-operated monopoly, or an American commercial system. The continuation of the monopoly did, however, deny alternative outlets for the work of authors and composers as well as alternative sources of employment for broadcasting staff in Scotland, particularly transmitter engineers whose specialised work existed only within broadcasting. It may have been the centralised nature of the BBC which fuelled criticism of the monopoly; a federal system of broadcasting might have avoided the dangers of a concentration of power and been more able adequately to reflect life outside the metropolis, such as in the BBC's national Regions.

During the Second World War, some material was published by former members of staff of the BBC who were critical of the monopoly. An example was the book published by P.P. Eckersley, the BBC's first Chief Engineer.[1] Criticism ranged from concern about the centralised nature of the BBC on Regional programme development, through to concern about freedom of speech in view of the greater influence of broadcasting than the press upon public opinion. Later on, television was regarded as having a greater influence than radio since it was possible to listen to radio with half an ear, but not possible to watch television with half an eye.[2] On this basis, it was in television rather than in sound broadcasting that the BBC's monopoly was most in need of being dismantled. Also, in television the BBC had nothing to compare with the varied radio services and the choice of programme material which they offered to listeners; their Regional element, such as the Scottish Home Service; and their wide geographical coverage throughout the country. In both broadcasting media, the BBC did not broadcast its own editorial opinions, but it did control access to the microphone. What appeared to be needed was a greater diversity of programme outlets within the large monolithic structure of the BBC, and the transfer of more authority from London to the Regions. Four articles published in successive weeks during October and November 1944 in the *Economist* considered the future organisation of broadcasting. They commented that the public-spirited nature of the BBC was no guarantee against the negative effects of monopoly, since the power of broadcasting to influence people was mightier than that of the pen.[3] These articles, which were intended to widen the range of public discussion on the subject, stated that a competitive broadcasting system would widen programme choice in a manner similar to the choice which existed with regard to books, journals, newspapers, theatres and cinemas. The articles published in the *Economist* questioned whether the BBC's monopoly was the best system imaginable: 'Why should we believe that, without experience and without experiment, and almost without thought, we should have hit, at first go, on the perfect system?'[4]

Prior to the expiry of the BBC's Charter in 1946, a series of articles was published which focused on the possibility of introducing competitive broadcasting. In February 1946, Prime Minister Clement Attlee stated that the government had decided that it was not necessary to institute an independent inquiry into the monopoly before the renewal date of the BBC's Charter. This decision was criticised in several press and journal articles.[5] The article by R.H. Coase indicated that there was a need for an examination of issues such as Regional autonomy, the relative merits of VHF broadcasting and the BBC's allocation of funds to the Regions. Sir Frederick Ogilvie, Reith's successor as Director-General from 1938 to 1942, wrote a letter criticising the monopoly, which was published in *The Times* on 26 June 1946. Ogilvie supported greater autonomy for broadcasting in Scotland and Wales. Nevertheless, the White Paper of July 1946 rejected the demand for an inquiry into broadcasting which would have covered the issue of the BBC's monopoly. The government argued that it was too early to foresee the effects of technical progress and that therefore broadcasting ought to remain a monopoly. Although the previous major inquiry into broadcasting had taken place in 1935, the BBC had been operating under new and unfamiliar circumstances for the duration of the war years, and so it could be argued that the Corporation had to be allowed a few years to develop the pattern of its programme services before being subjected to scrutiny by a further major committee of inquiry. The BBC's Charter and Licence were therefore renewed from 1 January 1947, but significantly only for five years.[6] The White Paper indicated that the prewar committees of inquiry on broadcasting had supported the BBC monopoly, but R.H. Coase, who published an influential book in 1950 on the issue of the monopoly, took exception to this line of reasoning. He argued that the Sykes Committee did not recommend that there should be a monopoly, the Crawford Committee only received evidence which supported the monopoly, and the Ullswater Committee accepted the monopoly but without discussing it.[7] On this basis, the assumptions on which the arguments in favour of the monopoly were based had never been questioned, and neither had the organisation or funding of alternative systems been fully examined. By 1950, the problem of the organisation and control of broadcasting was essentially the problem as to whether the BBC's monopoly should continue.[8]

There were several major arguments put forward by the supporters and critics of the monopoly, and these can be classified according to the social, cultural, economic, political, administrative and technical aspects of the issue. Each of these is worth considering in turn. The social and cultural purposes of BBC broadcasting (i.e. to enlarge public taste through the provision of a wide range of high-quality programmes) had to be viewed in the context of the social possibilities offered by the presence of a competitive system (i.e. a wide range of programme output to cater for the interests of all social classes). However, there was the possibility that a system operating on commercial lines might be more concerned with the criterion of popularity than that of merit, although even a mass audience is composed of a number of minority groupings who merely coalesce to form a majority depending upon the subject matter of programmes. The BBC for its part had consistently argued that the popularity of programmes as measured by listener research did not dictate programme policy.[9] The public could, though, not be expected to provide a considered opinion on a non-existent competitive service. There was certainly no widespread public clamour for commercial broadcasting, but equally no evidence of public clamour against it. Supporters of the monopoly within Parliament and throughout the country believed that with the introduction of a commercial system as a competitor for the BBC, the social purpose of broadcasting would be diminished because advertisers would indirectly influence programme content and thus narrow the range of output to those programmes likely to attract the largest audiences. If commercial television stations were to provide a number of majority and minority programmes, then it could be argued that viewing figures would fluctuate and so also would advertising revenue. The argument thus centred on the belief that commercial operators would be more willing to transmit programmes whose popular appeal had been demonstrated, rather than take a financial risk with an unknown programme formula. There was also the possibility that commercial operators might be more concerned with audience ratings than with audience appreciation, although it was not necessarily always the case that only light entertainment programmes attracted the largest audience.

There was in general some concern that a commercially-funded system would result in a narrowing of the range of programme items. This line of argument was neatly summed up by Herbert Morrison (Lord President of the Council and Leader of the House of Commons from 1945 to 1951) when he stated that the man who paid the piper would call the tune.[10] He was right to suppose that it was the larger businesses which would be able to pay television advertising rates, but wrong to suppose that Britain was likely to adopt sponsored television in which advertisers would influence the content and scheduling of programmes to sell their products, thereby resulting in a loss of editorial control. Nevertheless, the fact that the government was proposing to introduce systems of control to obviate dangers inherent in commercial broadcasting was taken by the pro-monopolists as an admission that such dangers did not arise with BBC public service broadcasting. The use of spot advertising was a solution to this problem because it divorced advertisers from any direct influence on programme content. In any case, since advertisements appeared in quality newspapers, then it could be argued that they should not have been excluded from broadcasting. Critics of the monopoly could focus on the newspaper analogy because the existence of the BBC's broadcasting monopoly stood ill at ease with the wide range of local and national newspapers in Scotland. However, the difference between newspapers and commercial broadcasting was that the government was proposing that the latter should be entirely financed through advertising, whereas no newspaper derived its income solely from advertising. This is what seems to have increased concern that commercial broadcasting would be subject to undue financial pressure from advertisers, which in turn would influence programme content. Also, advertising on radio or television would be more intrusive than advertising in the press, because an individual who bought a newspaper was not compelled to look at the advertising columns, whereas he would be unable to avoid advertisements placed within or between programmes unless the television set were switched off. Competition in broadcasting could in theory nevertheless provide an outlet for greater coverage of Scottish topics. Monopolists, such as Herbert Morrison, were not however convinced that competition would lead to anything other than a lowering of programme standards. He stated that 'The promoters and controllers of commercially sponsored TV would have an interest in disregarding decent standards and promoting programmes of a debased character for the purpose of attracting the maximum audience of all ages'.[11] It was this belief, combined with the view that a commercial system would be unable for financial reasons to cater for minority interests or Scottish culture, which posed doubts on the ability of a competitive commercial system to uphold the social purpose of broadcasting and widen cultural horizons. For example, there were likely to be limitations on the number of Scottish-produced programmes transmitted, since network programmes would attract more advertising income. Commercial viability was likely to place some constraints on the extent of Regionalism within commercial broadcasting.

In addition to the social and cultural aspects of the monopoly, several economic arguments were marshalled both for and against the retention of the monopoly. A prosperous commercial system might raise broadcasting standards, but it could not be provided cost-free to the public because advertisers would merely shift their advertising costs to the goods and services which they provided to the public. In comparison with the direct method of funding the BBC via the licence fee, this would represent an indirect method. However, anti-monopolists could argue that in theory advertisements could stimulate the production of goods, lower production costs and thus absorb the cost of such advertisements. But the need for commercial television to attract production and technical staff from the BBC, given that the BBC represented the only major reservoir of skilled personnel, was likely to lead to salary and fee warfare, thereby increasing costs for the BBC and placing more pressure on government to increase the licence fee. However, the government could argue that a commercial system would enable a larger volume of programme material in Scotland and in other parts of the country to be offered to the public without having to increase the licence fee to a significant extent; it was therefore a safer political option in financial terms. Advertising agencies and television manufacturers no doubt foresaw the commercial benefits of competitive television broadcasting, but newspapers were likely to be more cautious for fear of losing advertising revenue. In Regional broadcasting terms, there was the question as to whether a commercial system would be willing to use resources to develop Regional programmes. The Scottish Advisory Council agreed with the BBC view that commercial television would be of no benefit to Scotland, partly because it would only cover populous areas, and partly because programme content would be English-dominated. At its meeting on 3 June 1952, there was unanimous agreement within the Council that the introduction of sponsored items in either radio or television would be inadvisable.[12]

Political factors played a crucial role in the decisions which were made about the monopoly. Lord Woolton, Chairman of the Conservative Party, who took over the chairmanship of the Cabinet's Broadcasting Policy Committee in March 1952, was, like Winston Churchill, not in favour of retaining the monopoly. Also, the influx of Conservative backbenchers (some of whom had interests in advertising and in the electronics industry) after the General Election on 25 October 1951 put pressure on the government to consider ending the BBC's monopoly. Professor H.H. Wilson argued that the Conservative Party leadership was influenced by a group of Conservative backbenchers into supporting the introduction of commercial broadcasting. In his book, he stated:

> This study would seem to establish the fact that a small number of MPs, well organised, with good connections among both Party officials and outside interests, and pushing a definite, limited programme, may exert considerable influence and even overwhelm an unorganised majority in their own party.[13]

Undoubtedly there were pressures, but it may be difficult to isolate the influence of them from so many other factors. Pressure-group activity was present due to the formation of two associations after the publication of the government's White Paper of 1952 indicated an intention to introduce competition in broadcasting. The formation of a National Television Council to oppose the creation of commercial broadcasting was announced in *The Times* on 4 June 1953. Several distinguished individuals, such as Lord Beveridge and Bertrand Russell, supported the NTC. On 2 July, a Popular Television Association was formed to oppose the BBC monopoly in television and to press the case for the introduction of commercial broadcasting. Members of the PTA included Malcolm Muggeridge and the historian A.J.P. Taylor. These pressure groups did not, however, involve the public to any significant extent.

The government had also to take note of the administrative and technical arguments. The Post Office preferred to license one broadcasting organisation because it was administratively less complex than overseeing a multitude of separate corporations. The Post Office would have encountered greater difficulty in allocating wavelengths and Regions between competing broadcasting companies. The number, power, location and wavelengths of stations had been planned centrally. However, the shortage of frequencies, which was the original technical reason for supporting the continuation of the monopoly, was becoming less credible because VHF offered the possibility of overcoming the shortage of wavelengths and thus permitting the establishment of several local stations, each with a restricted radius. The BBC believed that it could use VHF to diversify broadcasting and improve coverage of existing services in remote areas. However, despite restrictions on capital development, the BBC could be accused of technical conservatism at least to the extent that Scotland might have received a television service much sooner than 1952. One of the arguments of critics of the monopoly was that Regional television development would have proceeded at a faster rate if a commercial system had existed. Furthermore, there was the ancillary argument that a commercial system was needed because the BBC did not make full use of its network in that television programmes were not transmitted throughout the whole day. Overall, the demands for greater autonomy in broadcasting in Scotland were related to critical comment on what was regarded as the centralising aspects of the BBC's monopoly, especially the control of broadcasting and the range of television programme output. The technical arguments relating to the monopoly were examined by R.H. Coase. His view was that, although the number of wavelengths limited the number of programmes that could be transmitted at any given time, the number of broadcasting organisations could be greater than the number of wavelengths because time on any station could be shared. He stated that it was not sufficient to demonstrate that the allocation of wavelengths should be carried out by a central authority; it must also be shown that it was desirable that this authority should also operate the broadcasting stations and produce the programmes. Coase stated that the technical argument had never been developed in this manner.[14] The implication was that the allocation of wavelengths, the operation of broadcasting stations and the production of programmes were separate functions and need not be performed by the same organisation. The BBC's monopoly was however in the physical means of broadcasting and did not constitute a monopoly of opinion, since the Corporation was forbidden to broadcast any editorial opinion. The availability of space in band III for another television network, together with the prospect of VHF, made it increasingly difficult to believe that technical factors would in the long term necessitate the continuation of the monopoly. Not surprisingly, the BBC believed that the technical arguments were not the strongest ones to deploy in seeking to defend the monopoly. In an interview with Malcolm Muggeridge over two decades later, Reith recalled: 'Technically, I thought that a monopoly was justifiable, but I was far, far more interested in the monopoly in terms of the intellectual and ethical standards of the content of its programmes.'[15] Reith continued to believe that if he had been in charge of the BBC at the time when the Corporation's monopoly was being threatened, then he would have been better able than Haley to sustain the monopoly by resisting the introduction of commercial television. By 1952, the days of the monopoly were numbered.

As a prelude to the abandonment of the BBC's broadcasting monopoly, the government considered the recommendations of the Broadcasting Committee, the previous government's White Paper (Cmd 8291) and views expressed in debates in both Houses of Parliament. The BBC had enjoyed an exclusive licence to broadcast because successive governments decided that the Postmaster-General should not license anyone other than the BBC. The Conservative Government recognised that the monopoly had helped to establish the excellence and reputation of the Corporation, and that the BBC should be the only broadcasting organisation with any claim on the revenue from the broadcasting receiving licences. However, the government wished to widen programme choice and maintain the high standards of public service broadcasting and was not prepared to accept the previous government's view, in accordance with the majority recommendation of the Broadcasting Committee, that the BBC should continue as the sole authority responsible for broadcasting.

The government's White Paper, which was published on 15 May 1952, indicated that the days of the monopoly were numbered:

> The present Government have come to the conclusion that in the expanding field of television, provision should be made to permit some element of competition when the calls on capital resources at present needed for purposes of greater national importance make this feasible.[16]

The government stated that Parliament would be given an opportunity to consider the conditions under which a competitive system would operate. The BBC felt compelled to prepare a comprehensive plan for the future development of its own services, including the provision of a second television channel with national coverage. The BBC Governors believed that the latter would strengthen the hand of those opposed to the introduction of commercial television.[17] The White Paper indicated that there would be safeguards against abuses in a competitive system and that a controlling body would be required to oversee such a system. The latter was the price that was paid for securing the introduction of commercial television. Significantly, the BBC's sound monopoly was to remain intact, and this could be regarded as a concession. The BBC in any case had a less distinguished record in television broadcasting. It was with this medium that greater programme choice was needed and more advertising revenue could be generated.[18] Asa Briggs noted:

> Indeed, the very idea of introducing competitive television and leaving sound broadcasting as a monopoly was already an initial compromise, at least as far as principle, if not profit, was concerned, and the Government showed itself willing throughout to compromise on basic questions of control.[19]

During the parliamentary debate in February 1953, the government was criticised for proceeding too quickly to introduce commercial television, particularly at a time when coverage of BBC television, such as in large parts of Scotland, was inadequate. The government did not wish to wait until the BBC completed its plan to build more transmitting stations for fear that the BBC might hold back its plans in order to delay the introduction of commercial television. By July 1953, the PMG had received eleven applications for licences to operate a commercial television station in central Scotland. A month later, on 20 August, the BBC's Director-General prepared a paper for the Board of Governors on the Corporation's attitude to competition. One of the greatest fears expressed was that of the loss of a significant proportion of the audience to commercial television, especially given the inability to expand BBC television operations significantly. The BBC had by then also considered the possibility of both better remuneration to retain key staff, and the use of exclusive contracts for some artists. At this stage, the BBC did not wish it to be publicly known that it accepted the need to prepare plans to meet competition, since this would imply that the Corporation had accepted the inevitability of competitive television.[20] Similarly, the BBC was in a dilemma as to whether it should initiate broadcasts on the pros and cons of commercial television, an issue on which it had a direct interest. The BBC in fact received a request from the Popular Television Association to be allowed airtime to state its case in favour of commercial broadcasting. On balance, the Board of Management favoured broadcasts about commercial television since it regarded such broadcasts as being in the public interest. The BBC was, however, concerned to hold on to the mass audience and not just minority audiences in the face of competition, hence it was prepared to compete to retain the attention of the mass audience.[21] It was noted by the BBC that the sound and television services should jointly seek to avoid undesirable programme clashes in order to benefit the Corporation as a whole in a competitive situation with a rival broadcaster. There was also the question as to whether a commercial system not hindered by government restrictions on capital development would be able to bring about a more rapid expansion of television services throughout the country, since the BBC had been accused of treating television as merely an extension of sound broadcasting. The BBC was aware of criticism that it was not making full use of its network.[22]

On 13 November 1953, the government published its memorandum on television policy (Cmd 9005) which developed ideas on the structure of commercial television. The BBC would remain the main instrument of broadcasting, but control over television was not to remain in the hands of a single authority. In order to counter the twin arguments regarding the shortage of frequencies and the effects of a competitive system on programme standards, the government stated that band III would be used for commercial television, that a network system would operate to save costs, and that there would be no sponsoring of programmes.[23] Only spot advertising was to be permitted, to prevent advertisers from influencing programme content. A controlling body would own and operate the transmitting stations and hire its facilities to programme companies who would provide the programmes. The government did not wish to have another monopoly in the form of a single programme company. It was envisaged that the controlling body would be funded from rentals obtained from the programme companies, which would derive their income from spot advertising. The amount of time allocated to spot advertising was not to be so great as to detract from the value of the programmes broadcast. The BBC's Board of Management discussed the financial prospects of commercial television at a meeting in January 1954, and it was decided that a careful estimate should be made of the advertising rates that were likely to be necessary.[24] The government's plan was a recipe for commercial enterprise but under effective public control, in effect a compromise solution to appease critics who focused on the possible abuses of commercial television. The government believed that the controlling body would be able effectively to control the companies, to ensure high programme standards and to satisfy Regional aspirations, by modifying or terminating contracts given that the companies would not have invested large sums of money in fixed assets such as transmitters.

Taking all of the above factors into account, the government summed up its attitude to competition as follows:

> The policy which the Government recommends to Parliament is designed to achieve three objectives – the first is to introduce an element of competition into television and enable private enterprise to play a fuller part in the development of this important and growing factor in our lives; the second is to reduce to a minimum the financial commitments of the State; and the third is to proceed with caution into this new field and to safeguard this medium of information and entertainment from the risk of abuse or lowering of standards.[25]

In the House of Commons on 14 December 1953, the Assistant PMG, Mr David Gammans, sought to defend the government's decision to introduce competition in broadcasting. The Labour Party threatened to revoke the ITV licences when it was returned to power, although the BBC did not view this as a realistic possibility.[26] In a meeting with Regional Controllers, the BBC's Director-General advised them not to speak publicly about the White Paper, but it was noted that there would be no objection to pointing out the following:

(1) that the purpose of commercial television was to sell goods whereas that of public service broadcasting was to provide a public service;

(2) that a second service only provided a choice if it was planned as an alternative service;

(3) that commercial television was unlikely to bring a second service to thinly populated areas, such as in many parts of Scotland.[27]

By the time that the Television Bill was published incorporating the powers which the Independent Television Authority (ITA) was expected to exercise over the programme companies, the Authority was satirically labelled as a 'television aunt'.[28]

The Television Bill was published on 4 March 1954, was subject to numerous amendments, and received Royal assent on 30 July. It was a significant moment in the organisation of broadcasting in Britain, in which regulated monopoly was superseded by regulated competition. The Television Act made provision for television services in addition to those provided by the BBC. It appeared to replace one form of monopoly with another. With regulated competition between the BBC and Independent Television (ITV), there was no true breaking of the monopoly if the BBC and ITA were each to operate as monopoly suppliers of programmes. So there was duopoly rather than true competition in broadcasting. The Television Act established the ITA as the controlling authority and outlined its constitution, powers, duties and financial resources; it also stated the obligations of those companies contracted to provide programmes.[29] The use of the words 'independent' and 'authority' was interesting in the sense that to describe the ITA as independent implied that the BBC was not independent of detailed governmental control; to call it an authority implied that it had authority over the whole field of television, whereas the BBC wished to be viewed as the main instrument of broadcasting in the UK.

The Act, which stipulated that the ITA was to provide television services for ten years, also gave the authority the power to establish, install and operate the transmitting stations. The ITA was to be funded by rentals from the programme companies. The programmes were to be provided by these programme contractors, who would derive their income from advertisements. All members of the ITA were appointed by the PMG, and three of them were selected to look after the interests of Scotland, Wales and Northern Ireland. No member was expected to have any financial interest in either a programme company or in an advertising agency. The ITA, which provided the distribution network between main and relay stations, controlled and appointed, but did not employ the programme makers; it was also granted power to appoint advisory committees. The ITA was not expected to select programme contractors by competitive tender because then it would have been obliged to accept the highest bid; it was expected to ensure adequate competition between the programme companies. There were extensive provisions in the Act to ensure that the ITA would exercise proper control over programme content, such as in the balance of subject matter, the quality of output, a proper proportion of British material televised, adherence to impartiality, and so on. Mindful of BBC Regional television output, section 3 of the Act stated that Regional ITV stations were expected to transmit a suitable proportion of Regional programmes. But with only one programme company in each Region, there was, as will be noted, no genuine competition within ITV. The creation of local commercial monopolies in Scotland and in the other ITV Regions appeared to indicate that a higher priority had been given to providing an alternative service to that of the BBC as opposed to a genuinely competitive service.

On 3 August 1954, the PMG announced the appointments to the ITA. Sir Kenneth Clark, Chairman of the Arts Council, was appointed as Chairman of the ITA. Dr T.J. Honeyman, Director of Glasgow Art Galleries, was expected to make the interests of Scotland his special responsibility. On 25 August, the ITA issued a press advertisement inviting applications from potential programme contractors; the first interviews to select contractors began on 28 September.

Sir Robert Fraser, Director-General of the Central Office of Information, took up his duties as Director-General of the ITA on 1 October. A licence was granted to the ITA on 6 April 1955 to establish the first station in London. This licence continued in force until 29 July 1964.[30] The ITV system split the country up into geographical units, in contrast to the BBC, which essentially provided a UK service with Regional opt-outs. Comparisons can also be drawn between the type of institutional structure chosen for the ITA, and the BBC's Board of Governors. Both were public bodies, but the BBC was incorporated by Royal Charter whereas the ITA came into existence under the terms of the Television Act. The BBC Governors were appointed by the Queen in Council, whereas ITA members were appointed by the PMG. Furthermore, the emphasis in the Television Act on matters such as the balance of programme material or the need to provide sufficient Regional material had no counterpart in the BBC's Charter. Unlike the ITA, the BBC's Governors had no specific power over BBC management to arrange for the supply of material from any agency to ensure a proper balance of programme output. Overall, it thus appeared that the Royal Charter defined the duties of the BBC in a less restrictive manner than did the Television Act with regard to the ITA. This may have reflected the need to appease critics of commercial broadcasting. Bernard Sendall, the former Deputy Director-General of the ITA, stated that 'In the structures and organisation outlined for the competitive service, efforts had clearly been made to build in potential safeguards and responsibilities to allay the fears of critics and doubters'.[31] ITV represented private enterprise under public control. The federal structure of ITV resulted in the establishment of autonomous programme companies, three of which were eventually to be located in Scotland. Each company had its own staff and resources. So, unlike the BBC, the ITA's officers were responsible only for programme matters whereas, in the BBC, Governors had the dual responsibility of acting as trustees in the public interest in programme matters but also exercising control over management. The providers of the television service in ITV were not the employers or servants of the public authority (i.e. the ITA) as was the case in the BBC. Indeed, unlike the BBC Board of Governors, the ITA was separated both physically and organisationally from the various production centres which it supervised.

Apart from the organisational structure, differences in both funding and in programme philosophy between the BBC and ITV influenced the nature of the services provided. Predictably, the BBC stated that high-quality programming and the commercial profit motive were irreconcilable. In a paper on the future of broadcasting, the Governors noted:

> The idea of giving a service to the public may still be there, but it can only be a secondary motive because those who conduct and pay for the service have their own interests which in any clash of arguments are bound to take precedence.[32]

It can be argued, however, that ITV companies would either generate insufficient income to sustain a quality service, or would generate excessive profits and thus antagonise critics of the system. There was also the question as to whether ITV could provide a better Regional television service in Scotland than the BBC. This was likely to depend upon the income generated by the Scottish station(s) and whether this was used to develop a rich reservoir of Scottish material, or mainly used to pay for the cost of transmitting non-Scottish material (i.e. programme material originated from outwith Scotland). In this context, it can be noted that the value of an ITV franchise in terms of potential revenue rose in direct proportion to population served because viewer hours were sold to advertisers. However, costs did not rise in proportion to the number of viewers, hence the reason why large contractors tended to be more profitable. Moreover, the networking system which developed within ITV inhibited competition between companies and so worked against the ability of the smaller companies, such as those which were located in Scotland, to obtain more resources to develop their own production base through getting material networked. The system was, however, more genuinely Regional than the BBC because Scotland was subsequently served by three programme companies in comparison with the BBC's unitary presence in Scotland, and programmes on ITV could often be transmitted at different times on different days in each Region. The financial implication of this structure was that the costs of the commercial network could be expected to be higher than those of the BBC because of the duplication of studios, staff and equipment in each Regional centre. No single ITV company had resources to match those of the BBC; equally, no small ITV company had resources to match those of the network companies which were later formed. Prior to the start of ITV transmissions, the BBC was, however, concerned about the potential impact of ITV on costs within the BBC. In December 1954, Sir Ian Jacob (BBC Director-General) prepared a paper highlighting his discussions with the ITA regarding mutual restrictions on the hours of broadcasting. The BBC was concerned that competition would force it to extend its hours of broadcasting and thus place greater strain on its financial, human and technical resources. The Director-General stated:

> If television is provided by our rivals at hours of the day when we are off the air there is bound to be a considerable demand, particularly from those areas which cannot get the ITA's transmissions, for us to give similar value for money. In my view this demand could only be resisted if there are definite prohibitions in the form of closed periods.[33]

The programme companies in ITV were, however, likely to want to be free to seek out the largest audiences at times of their own choosing and not of the BBC's choosing.

The programme philosophy of ITV differed from that of the BBC. There seemed to be a contrast between the BBC philosophy of providing the public with programmes which the BBC thought was best for them, and the ITV philosophy of giving the public the type of programmes which the public itself wanted. This is of course a very simplistic and misleading statement, for, as Sir

Hugh Greene (a former Director-General of the BBC) once remarked, the 'public' is an abstraction and does not have a common will but rather consists of individuals who have a variety of tastes and interests.[34] But it does indicate differences in perceptions about the type of programme service which each broadcasting organisation was expected to deliver. Almost a year before ITV transmissions commenced, Sir Ian Jacob had still not grasped the potential impact of commercial television on the BBC's own television schedules and programme philosophy. Jacob was aware that as opportunities for television widened, those for radio would diminish. But he did not yet regard sound and television as two separate broadcasting activities, each catering for a different audience. Instead, he regarded both services as complementary. Jacob noted that 'The Corporation in its several services must, therefore, strive to include all types of material than can be conveyed by broadcasting, and should not content itself with an output which satisfies merely the less-discriminating mass'.[35] The BBC's view was that its programme policy and philosophy would not be altered by the arrival of a competitor. In its Annual Report for 1954–5, the BBC commented upon the impending arrival of ITV and stated:

> This fact cannot affect the BBC's aims and obligations under the Charter. There will be no departure from the BBC's purposes nor from the standards which it has set itself. But the existence of an alternative broadcasting system is bound to affect the Corporation's work in many ways.[36]

There was to be competition in programmes and for key staff and artists, and the BBC did eventually seek to compete actively at both national and Regional levels with ITV for audiences. Broadcasters did not wish to endure a situation where few people watched their programmes, even if in broadcasting terms the few might be counted in thousands if the many were counted in millions. The BBC in Scotland had to prepare to meet competition just as the BBC nationally had to do, but commercial television was two years later in arriving in Scotland. With the advent of ITV programmes in September 1955, an era in broadcasting came to an end.

Part Three

Competition, consolidation and expansion, 1955–67

9

The BBC and ITV duopoly: the effects of competition in broadcasting, 1955–61

With the arrival of commercial television in September 1955, broadcasting entered a new phase of development. BBC programme policy was now formulated in the absence of the monopoly, but the Corporation did have the advantage of control over both radio and television which was denied to its competitor. Two years had elapsed since the BBC had announced its ten-year plan of expansion in June 1953, a plan designed to complete the television network, develop television production facilities in London and in the Regions, extend broadcasting coverage and plan for the possibility of colour television and a second channel. It was a plan conceived at a time when the BBC was anxious to demonstrate to the government that it had a blueprint for the future development of its programme services which needed governmental support before priority was given to allocating licences for competitive broadcasting. But Independent Television had now become a reality. Between the years 1955 and 1961, the ITV network was developed and completed. Scotland received commercial television in August 1957, and this, together with the two further ITV stations which were opened in Scotland in 1961, influenced BBC programme policy in Scotland. The development of the ITV network and the response of the BBC to competition in television will be examined both in general terms within the UK and more specifically within Scotland. By 1962, ITA transmitters covered ninety-five per cent of the population of the UK and thus provided competition for the BBC in most parts of the country. During the second half of the 1950s, changes also took place in radio broadcasting, partly because of the possibilities which VHF opened up to introduce area broadcasting in Scotland, and partly because of the need to compete effectively against the increasing hold of television on audiences, especially during the evening hours. This period can be regarded not merely as one of competition between two television services generated by the presence of the duopoly, but also one of competition between radio and television, both BBC and ITV. The latter was a primary reason which led the BBC to abandon the policy of competition between the radio networks which had been endorsed in the postwar reorganisation of the sound services in 1945, and to replace it with a policy of integration of the sound services, both national and Regional.

In early 1955, the BBC discussed arrangements for monitoring ITA programmes when they initially arrived in London. This was intended to cover aspects such as the standard of productions and the names of artists used. It was expected that this task would be extended to the Regions when ITV companies began to be established outside London. Two days before the start of ITV, Sir Ian Jacob (BBC Director-General) sent a memo to the Director of Television Broadcasting in which he stated that 'I am confident that the hard work and enterprise of the kind that has characterised the service up till now will keep it in the lead. The Corporation must and will retain the initiative, and will set the standard of public service by which others will be judged.'[1] The BBC did not have to wait very long, because, after test transmissions at the ITA's Croydon station on 13 September 1955, the first ITV programmes were broadcast on 22 September in the London area. These programmes were interspersed with advertisements (or commercials as they came to be known) for household products such as Gibbs SR toothpaste, Kraft cheese and Surf soap powder. On the following day, an article in the *Glasgow Herald* commented: 'To an accompaniment of high-sounding phrases and suitably patriotic music, commercial television was tonight launched on its restricted sea'.[2] It was a restricted sea because ITV programmes did not reach Scotland. A week after the start of commercial television, the BBC's Director-General reviewed the first week's programmes: it was noted that the general feeling of the BBC's television staff was that although the competitor should not be underrated, nevertheless so far no new ideas had been presented.[3] However, the BBC recognised that it would be unable to identify as closely with Regional audiences in comparison with the ITV companies, hence it accepted the need to extend and improve Regional facilities and programme output. This, it was believed, would strengthen the Corporation's claim to additional wavelengths for the second channel. In preparation for this, it was noted that Regions needed more freedom to substitute local items, and an increased programme allowance to encourage experiment in Regional television material similar to what had been achieved in sound broadcasting.[4] Asa Briggs commented upon these plans in the following terms:

> The arguments both for a second Television channel and for a regional component in the BBC's future pattern of television were derived as much from the experience of Sound – with echoes of the 1920's – as from a sense of the need to compete with the new programme-operating companies.[5]

The BBC was initially unprepared for operating a television service which placed stress on the need to entertain the audience. This was not unexpected, given the absence hitherto of any competitor. As Peter Black stated, 'everything the BBC had done until September 1955 had been done in a vacuum. Nobody knew whether the audience stayed with it because it liked it or because there was no other television to look at.'[6] ITV programmes had the advantage of novelty. The BBC's initial response was to emphasise its experience in television broadcasting, the range of its output, and its public service duty to serve both minority and majority interests. There did not appear to be any desire at this stage to introduce more popular material into the programme schedules. Indeed, the importance of the BBC maintaining its standards and the quality of its programmes in the presence of competition from ITV was re-emphasised at Board of Governors level.[7] ITV did, however, entice many key BBC producers and technical staff to work for commercial television because the BBC represented the only principal source of trained broadcasting staff. This potential problem had been discussed within the BBC two years earlier in 1953 when the Director of Television Broadcasting had asked the Controller (Programmes) to consider the future effect of competitive television and to report back to him by 8 July 1953. A year later, the BBC's Director-General reported that even following the announcement by the ITA of their chosen programme companies, there had been serious attempts to entice away some senior members of the BBC's television staff.[8] Special offers were made to thirteen key staff, and the BBC anticipated that it might have to make similar offers to another twenty-five to thirty members of staff. The BBC's loss was a gain to broadcasting staff, who now had the opportunity of alternative employment and higher salaries. The BBC was forced to offer special contracts to key staff to retain their services. For example, some producers were offered promotion and salaries at the top end of the producer grades if they agreed to remain with the Corporation for five years.

The BBC was also faced with a balancing act between maintaining programme standards and sustaining the interest of the audience:

> The almost impossible task, therefore, which faced the BBC's television service during the next few years was to maintain the audience figures and yet produce programmes of a standard which would be sufficiently different from that of commercial television to ensure that the public could be asked to support the payment of licence fees to the BBC.[9]

The ITV companies sought to capture some of the audience from BBC programmes and create a new audience among those sections of the public for whom BBC programmes had little appeal.[10] This involved the need to pioneer new programme concepts, facilitated by a new and younger generation of producers anxious to prove the merits of an alternative broadcasting system. ITV programmes were more populist in tone than BBC programmes, their presenters were less formal, and regularity was built into the programme schedules to encourage regular viewing habits. Critics were soon to argue that ITV programmes must be poor in quality because they seemed to be popular, yet some programmes were undoubtedly popular because of the quality of their content. The BBC had to learn from ITV's attempt to inculcate channel loyalty. ITV made use of the inheritance factor, whereby the most popular programmes such as *Coronation Street* and *Emergency Ward 10* would be transmitted at peak viewing times, thus encouraging viewers to remain with the channel for the remainder of the evening. The BBC was forced to do likewise in order to retain a respectable share of the audience, but inevitably this did eventually tend to narrow the range of programme output during peak viewing hours. As regards the position of Regional programme output in this competitive situation, Sir Ian Jacob noted in January 1956 that with only one BBC television channel, the Regional effort must find its outlet mainly in contributions to the network, but that, as resources were increased, opting out to provide Regional news would be feasible.[11]

The audience for ITV increased when coverage was extended outwith London to the English Regions and to Scotland. It was also increased with the introduction of more popular programmes and by developing networking. Quiz contests, westerns and American comedy were particularly popular. The difficulty of filling several hours of transmission time each week was eased by the development of networking in the autumn of 1956. Also, networking permitted the best programmes to be broadcast throughout the country. Network and Regional companies had the same contractual relationship with the ITA, but the network companies did not have to produce Regional programmes. The smaller companies, such as the three Scottish companies which were awarded a franchise, affiliated to one of the network companies for the supply of network programmes from all the major companies. But as the system developed it was found that there was less competition than originally intended among the network companies to supply programme material to the smaller Regional companies. Despite the existence of the network, most national programmes were provided by four companies (i.e. ATV, ABC, Associated-Rediffusion and Granada) and not one organisation as occurred with the BBC. ATV, ABC and Granada were based outside London but also had studios in London. From 30 July 1968, the ITA in fact increased the four network companies to five: London Weekend Television (LWT) and Yorkshire Television were the new contractors, and two of the existing companies (ABC and Associated-Rediffusion) merged to form Thames Television. Given that not all ITV network companies operated from London, the system was not as centralised in programme production as that of the BBC. However, as will be noted, there were some similarities with the BBC to the extent that Regions such as Scotland experienced difficulty in securing network transmission for the programmes which they made. Apart from networking, there was one other aspect with ITV which inhibited competition between companies for audiences in any given Region. There was only one programme company in each area because it was technically impossible to arrange for competing services in any Region unless large parts of the country were to be left without any ITV service. The use of the split-week system was therefore used by the ITA to induce some competition into the system and thus prevent undue power from being given to one programme company based in London. This system was not extended to the later smaller companies, such as the Scottish programme companies, because they never supplied a large percentage of their own programme material and were not network companies.

The Scottish companies were therefore all to be awarded seven-day contracts.

With the prospect of the opening of the first commercial television station in Scotland, the BBC had to consider how it would respond. The background to the arrival of commercial television in Scotland can be briefly noted. In 1954, when Roy Thomson, a Canadian, came to Britain, preparations were well advanced for the start of commercial television. On 28 November 1955, the ITA invited applicants as potential programme contractors for the central Scotland station. The financial problems encountered by the first few commercial stations in England (where costs exceeded advertising revenue) acted as a disincentive for businessmen in Scotland to consider becoming involved in tendering for the Scottish franchise. It was not in fact until 1957 that the financial prospects of ITV companies improved. Roy Thomson, however, carefully examined the potential revenue from advertising as well as the likely operating costs of a Scottish station. The advertising rates which could be charged were likely to be much less than those in London because of the smaller potential audience. In his autobiography, however, Thomson stated that he was convinced that commercial television would be a success after the advertising potential had been fully tapped.[12] He also received financial support from Howard and Wyndham, the theatre contractor. Thomson therefore submitted an application for the Scottish franchise. He subscribed eighty per cent of the capital and so held eighty per cent of the voting shares; this was subsequently reduced during the 1960s to fifty-five then to twenty-five per cent. On 28 February 1956, members of the ITA spent time in Edinburgh to interview potential Scottish programme contractors, and on 30 May Scottish Television Ltd (STV) was appointed as programme contractor for central Scotland, the first ITV company to be awarded an all-week contract because its potential audience was insufficient to support more than one programme company. At this stage, the Broadcasting Council for Scotland was concerned that the BBC's Scottish television output of $1\frac{1}{2}$ hours a week would be totally inadequate to deal with competition from commercial television when it arrived in Scotland.[13] Concern about the potential impact of a commercial station on BBC output in Scotland was raised within the Board of Governors by Tom Johnston (BBC National Governor for Scotland, who was a former Secretary of State for Scotland) in March 1956. He reiterated that BBC Scotland's $1\frac{1}{2}$ hours a week of television output would not show up favourably against the larger amount of Scottish material proposed for ITV's first Scottish station. At that time, the Director-General stated that plans were being made to introduce Regional television news periods towards the end of 1956, and that in any case it was doubted whether a commercial operator could afford to originate a large proportion of programmes within Scotland.[14] There was no certainty that viewers in Scotland would prefer more Scottish material in preference to London-based programmes, but equally the BBC in Scotland could not afford to be seen to be failing in its duty towards the Scottish audience. Moreover, BBC Scotland was having to make use of outside broadcast cameras for studio programmes until such time as indoor television equipment could be provided. This diminution of outside broadcasts was regarded with some concern by OB staff since it seemed to be placing BBC Scotland in a disadvantageous position with respect to commercial television. In other words, it was expected that by the time studio cameras were provided and outside broadcast equipment was released in 1958 to cover more sporting events, STV would already have signed lucrative and exclusive contracts to televise, for example, boxing events, and so place the BBC in a difficult position. This prompted James Buchan (Outside Broadcasts Producer, Television) to note in a memo to the Head of Scottish programmes: 'The very real danger that in two years' time we shall start searching for outside broadcast material and find it sewn up by the competitor could, it seems to me, be avoided by the provision of one extra camera to Scotland.'[15]

In October 1956, the Theatre Royal was purchased in Glasgow and Thomson began to convert it into offices and studios. STV also affiliated with Lew Grade's Associated Television (ATV) in order to get access to the programme material of the network companies, and did so on very favourable terms. STV attracted some staff from the BBC, just as the initial programme companies based in England had done in the preceding two years. Thomson's statement in February 1956 that he hoped to schedule twenty to twenty-five per cent of Scottish material prompted the press to enquire about the BBC's response. The BBC's Scottish Controller, according to the minutes, merely noted that the Corporation would continue to fulfil its responsibilities under the Charter to serve the whole community.[16] BBC Scotland was also anxious to bring the temporary studio at Springfield Road in Glasgow into operation before STV began transmissions at the end of August 1957, but in January of that year there were already doubts as to whether the studio would be fully equipped by October, let alone fully operational. In April 1956, the BCS considered whether it might be appropriate for the national Governor to raise with the BBC Governors the question as to whether 'wasteful expenditure' incurred in competition with ITV might be postponed given the plans for television development in Scotland by STV and governmental limitations on BBC finances.[17] In December 1956, with the plans for STV becoming clearer, the BCS minutes read as follows:

> The Scottish Programme Contractor's intention of putting on 25% of Scottish items on commercial television was noted and fear was expressed that unless the BBC could forestall commercial television in this respect a large proportion of the audience might be lost irretrievably.[18]

There was, however, a quantitative difference between transmitting twenty-five per cent of Scottish items and filling twenty-five per cent of airtime with Scottish items. The BBC in Scotland was particularly concerned about the potential impact of competition on its ability to cover entertainment, news and sporting events, particularly football league matches. These concerns were outlined in a BCS paper on the potential impact of commercial television in Scotland on BBC services.[19] BBC Scotland believed that there was insufficient work to offer long-established artists and scriptwriters exclusive contracts, and that therefore these individuals would be presented with more lucrative offers by STV. It was expected that artists who did not wish to be bound to either the BBC or STV would accept the highest offer made and thereby increase fees. With scriptwriters, it was a question of trying to offer exclusive contracts that would guarantee employment for a series or serial; variety artists such as Jimmy Logan and Stanley Baxter were thought likely to accept the highest offer which was made. The BBC was also concerned about the close association between STV and the theatre contractor Howard and Wyndham with regard to the availability of artists, scenery and so on. Charles McQueen (Director of Howard and Wyndham) became a Director of STV. There was also the question of the availability of news material. Roy Thomson had strong newspaper connections (he bought control of *The Scotsman* newspaper in 1953), and so the BBC was understandably concerned about competition in the area of news output, particularly in the absence of a daily BBC Scottish television news bulletin. Nevertheless, the BBC was ready to compete with STV. The BCS paper concluded by stating:

> The obvious conclusion is that Commercial Television in Scotland will aim at attracting a mass lower-middle-class audience because of its potential purchasing power and readiness to view material of little cultural value. It cannot be regarded as true competition, but this challenge has to be met and will be, with vigour.[20]

The main competition for the BBC in Scotland was, however, to emanate from the network programmes shown on STV rather than STV's Scottish-originated output.

On 8 July 1957, Andrew Stewart succeeded Melville Dinwiddie, who had been the BBC's most senior official in Scotland for a period of almost twenty-four years. Andrew Stewart, who had joined the BBC in 1926, had been Scottish Programme Director from 1935 to 1948, and latterly Controller, Northern Ireland (1948–52) and Controller, Home Service (1953–7). Aware of the imminent arrival of commercial television in Scotland, he asked Sir Ian Jacob (BBC Director-General) for adequate resources both to cover Scottish items and to compete effectively against STV. Just over a month later, on 12 August, a Scottish Committee of the ITA was formed in order to advise the ITA on the conduct of commercial televison in Scotland. Unlike the BBC's Broadcasting Council for Scotland, the ITA's Scottish Committee had no executive responsibility over matters such as the allocation of franchises for the Scottish area, transmitter development, or the networking of programmes. STV began transmissions on 31 August 1957 from the Blackhill transmitter, which was situated midway between Glasgow and Edinburgh at a site 900 feet above sea level. It was the fifth transmitter to be opened by the ITA since September 1955 when commercial television first arrived in Britain. At the time when STV began transmissions, the company had a staff of about 150. The opening ceremony began with short speeches from the Lord Provost of Glasgow, the Secretary of State for Scotland, the Chairman of the ITA (Sir Kenneth Clark) and the Chairman of STV (Roy Thomson). The *Glasgow Herald* regarded the arrival of commercial television in Scotland as a promising development:

> To the average Scot in the new reception area the benefit will be unquestionable. For the first time he will taste the joys of that selectivity which has long been the privilege of the listener to sound only. He will also find new vistas opened up by the impact of commercial as opposed to BBC television.[21]

The ITA stipulated in 1956 that STV should originate at least fifteen per cent of programmes itself with the balance taken from the network. In its Annual Report for 1956–7, the ITA reaffirmed this general principle:

> Although it is a necessary feature of the independent television system that the bulk of the programmes should be presented over the whole network, the Authority requires each programme company to ensure that on average the output from its own resources is not less than 15 per cent of its total programme output. It is also desirable, in accordance with the provisions of the Act, that a suitable proportion of material of a company's own origination should appeal specially to regional tastes and outlook.[22]

STV never did transmit twenty to twenty-five per cent of Scottish-originated material as originally planned, but it was a prosperous company because of its monopoly in central Scotland and the popularity of the network programmes which it transmitted. This prosperity was reflected in Roy Thomson's famous phrase, 'a licence to print money'. STV was also, according to Roy Thomson, more attuned than the BBC to popular taste in Scotland. But there were occasional complaints in the press that insufficient money was being reinvested in programmes as opposed to the payment of good dividends to shareholders. The presence of STV prompted the BBC to make changes in its programme output.

The initial evidence that the BBC was actively seeking to compete with STV occurred on 30 August 1957, the day before the start of STV transmissions, when the BBC introduced a five-minute Scottish news summary which was broadcast at 6.05pm. During that same month, the BBC opened television studios in Glasgow. The Corporation hoped to increase the volume of programme items which originated in Scotland. STV for its part pioneered *Here and Now*, the first five-days-a-week news magazine programme in Britain, which followed the evening news. STV also broadcast its own religious and sports programmes such as *Late Call* and *Scotsport*, as well as producing some schools' programmes for the network. There were also the renowned film documentaries with John Grierson in *This Wonderful World*; these weekly thirty-minute programmes were taken by the network. A high proportion of STV programmes in the early years consisted of outside broadcasts, such as at the

Edinburgh International Festival, the Mod, Hogmanay, the General Assembly of the Church of Scotland, and so on. The lack of sufficient studio accommodation was improved somewhat with the subsequent opening of studios at Cowcaddens in Glasgow and at the Gateway Theatre in Edinburgh. By the late 1950s, as a result of competition from commercial television throughout the UK, BBC Regional Controllers wished to increase Regional television opt-outs to provide more local programme material.[23] Within Scotland, both BBC and STV programmes did however attract criticism in the press for being poor in quality, parochial and of little interest to the network. In November 1960, the BCS was still voicing concern about the need to increase the volume of Scottish output to meet competition from STV, and to schedule these programmes during peak viewing hours. The Council believed that programmes such as *The White Heather Club* (Scottish country dance music with Andy Stewart) and *Compass* (a fortnightly programme on current affairs) were being broadcast too early or too late to achieve their full audience potential. Views such as these about the volume and the timing of BBC Scottish programmes were conveyed to Gerald Beadle, BBC Director of Television Broadcasting, who attended a meeting of the Council.[24] In particular, the BCS wanted greater freedom from London with regard to programme timings, given the greater freedom of STV to schedule its programmes at suitable times. This was not so acceptable to London because it was said to hinder the BBC's ability to rearrange programmes at short notice to meet competition from ITV. Moreover, the BCS itself recognised that programme planners in Scotland often found it difficult to decide which network programme to drop in order to substitute a Scottish programme. The latter programmes included plays, sport, news, outside broadcasts, current affairs, drama and religious items. The radio serial *The McFlannels* was adapted for television, there was the discussion programme *Viewpoint*, the arts were covered in *Counterpoint*, *Para Handy* was one of a number of drama serials, outside broadcasts covered a number of events such as the Royal Highland Show and the national Mod of An Comunn, and the traditional New Year Party from the Glasgow studio was taken by the network. BBC network programmes such as *Dixon of Dock Green* (police series), *Laramie* (a western), *Grandstand* (sport) and *Hancock's Half-Hour* (comedy) were popular, but the BBC had no programme to compete with ITV's *Sunday Night at the London Palladium*. This again highlighted the fact that the main competition for the BBC in Scotland tended to emanate from network programmes shown on STV rather than from STV's own programme output. There were some exceptions: STV appeared to be more willing than BBC Scotland to respond to popular culture within Scotland in programmes such as the weekday lunchtime variety programme *One O'Clock Gang*.

During the late 1950s, BBC Scotland began slowly to build up its human and technical resources in television. Some staff began to specialise in television production and gained advice from television producers who came up from London. Engineers who had been trained in sound broadcasting now had to adapt these skills to the different requirements of television. For example, in television it was more important to position microphones carefully out of sight of the camera yet still obtain good sound quality, whereas in radio broadcasting the microphones would not be seen by the audience. Television required a larger staff complement than radio, and this, together with the existence of only one television channel, placed some constraints on the number of television productions which could originate in Scotland for viewers in Scotland or as contributions to the network. STV was the first commercial television station in Scotland, but the BBC also had to take account of the arrival of two additional Scottish-based stations which were opened during 1961 and which assisted in the completion of the ITA network. On 1 September, Border Television went on the air from the Caldbeck transmitting station; the transmitting station at Selkirk opened on 1 December. Sir Robert Fraser, Director-General of the ITA, opened the new station, which was based in Carlisle. Border Television covered a population of 500,000 on both sides of the Scottish-English border and was the second-smallest station in the ITA network. This station affiliated to Granada Television to obtain its network output. It broadcast local news, the discussion programme *Borderline*, farming prices, a country magazine *Time out of Doors* and the light music programme *Beat in the Border*.

Due to its location, Border television was never regarded as a distinctively Scottish station. This could not be said for Grampian Television, the twelfth ITV Regional station, which went on the air on 30 September, just over a year after being selected as programme contractor for North-East Scotland. The smallness of the station, with its news, farming, folk music, sports, religious, discussion and women's programmes, enabled it to remain in close touch with the communities which it served, albeit widely scattered geographically. In the overlap transmission area of Tayside, viewers did however prefer to watch STV programmes rather than those broadcast by Grampian. Grampian, which affiliated with ABC Television to obtain network programmes, prompted BBC Scotland to be concerned about the provision of local programmes, including the need for an interview studio, in the Aberdeen area. The BBC took note, for example, of the interest shown in Grampian Television's *News and Views* magazine news programme, particularly in the absence of a BBC Scotland local news and magazine programme. For the Aberdeen area, the BBC hoped to be able to provide opt-outs in the early evening to provide such local programmes as an alternative to the Scottish news bulletins produced in Glasgow, but pending the availability of finance. By the end of 1961, Scotland therefore had three commercial television companies in addition to the national television service provided by the BBC. The franchise areas of these three companies were determined according to the geographical coverage of the transmitters, thus the ITV structure in Scotland did not necessarily coincide with three separate communities of interest, socially, economically or culturally. Unlike the ITV companies, BBC Scotland for its part has, with some justification, never been sure whether it is Scottish or merely part of a UK broadcasting system.[25] The

BBC's programme output in Scotland was therefore liable to be criticised for being either too Scottish or too British in content.

By the end of 1961, the ITV network was nearing completion. The population coverage of ITV programmes had increased almost fourfold since 1955 to reach over ninety-four per cent of the UK population by the end of 1961.[26] ITV captured part of the BBC audience but also created its own audience among people who rarely watched BBC programmes. ITV programmes reached over eleven million homes in 1961, as against the 200,000 homes able to receive commercial television in 1955 when the first programmes were transmitted. The advent of ITV also boosted the purchase and renting of television receivers in Scotland and in other parts of the country. The BBC's loss of audience to ITV was concealed to some extent during the early years of competition because ITV was not available throughout the whole country. The BBC competed with ITV in order to hold on to fifty per cent of the audience and not return to the BBC:ITV 27:73 share of the audience which it held in 1957, notwithstanding the fact that both BBC and ITV adopted different methods of measuring the audience. BBC audience research used sampling methods to determine the number of individuals who viewed programmes at any particular time, whereas Television Audience Measurement (TAM), the research company used by ITV, made use of meters attached to television receivers in a panel of households to determine the number of sets switched on to a particular channel and then estimated the number of individuals watching these sets. Both systems did not cover identical geographical areas. TAM only sampled areas where ITA transmissions could be received, whereas the BBC covered larger areas and thus its sample included viewers whose sets could not receive ITV programmes. Both systems had their limitations. BBC audience research depended upon the accuracy of the memory of people who were interviewed regarding which programmes they had watched on the previous day. Nevertheless, the BBC did lose a significant proportion of the audience to ITV, even when some allowance was made for the fact that the tammeters attached to television sets could not identify whether each viewer was in fact watching the programmes on the channel which the meter indicated, or indeed how many viewers in households with multi-channel receivers were actually viewing specific programmes. The BBC believed that it could not afford to lose so much of its audience that it became the junior partner in the duopoly, especially with the prospect of a new committee of inquiry into broadcasting and the Corporation's evident desire to operate a second television channel. It also had to strike a satisfactory balance between popular and serious programme material. The change to a more populist and competitive BBC television aimed at capturing the majority audience became more evident after Kenneth Adam was appointed as Director of Television in June 1961. Even prior to that, Hugh Greene, who had succeeded Sir Ian Jacob as Director-General in January 1960, supported the BBC's attainment of a 50:50 share of the audience. The effects of ITV on the BBC were not wholly negative in the sense that the BBC sought to compete programme for programme during peak viewing hours; ITV

in 'fact induced the BBC to introduce some welcome developments in programme content such as in Regional television news, schools' broadcasts and
religious output. The BBC remained a genuine national service in terms of
coverage only until 1961, by which time the chain of ITV stations was completed.

The advent of a more competitive BBC policy in national broadcasting had
repercussions on television policy in Scotland. The fact that much of the earlier
Scottish output, especially on television, was confined to Scottish affairs and
broadcast as opt-outs in off-peak times tended to reinforce the belief that
broadcasting in Scotland was too parochial. The arrival of ITV companies in
Scotland failed to some extent to offer the BBC in Scotland adequate
competition in terms of the generation of new programme ideas and programme formats. The BBC, unlike ITV, was however expected to provide national
rather than local or Regional coverage of events within Scotland; it was also
expected to contribute material to the network. It thus had a dual programme
responsibility. All BBC Regions produced material for both local and network
transmission, but quite rightly had deeper obligations towards the communities
which they served than towards the BBC centrally.[27] With the advent of greater
competition at the national level, the question was to what extent opting out in
television could be permitted at the Regional level. With the development of
Regional television facilities in the late 1950s, the BCS supported the policy of
increasing the number of Scottish programmes which replaced network
programmes for viewers in Scotland. In its Annual Report for 1958–9, the BCS
stated:

> The prime need here is to correct the inescapable predominance of
> English and metropolitan interests in the single service so far allowed
> to the BBC. This is confirmed by the large, growing audience which
> the BBC's Scottish programmes attract in Scotland. The Council
> considers essential a continuing development in this direction.[28]

In the absence of separate transmission networks, Scottish and other Regional
programmes could not operate on a totally independent basis; Scottish opt-out
programmes had to be carried on the same networks which provided UK-wide
programmes. Television network Controllers were, however, cautious about
the volume of opt-outs permitted in the Regions. Gerald Beadle, Director of
Television Broadcasting, stated that 'Regional fragmentation comes to be
regarded as a right of way, which is hotly defended on grounds of local policy. It
could become an inflexible straitjacket for the UK network.'[29] In a paper dated
15 March 1960, the Board of Governors also took the view that, in television,
the main function of Scotland, in common with other BBC Regions, should be as
a contributor to the UK network rather than as an opt-out centre. The fear was
that increased opting-out would lead to greater fragmentation of the network
and a diminution of contributions to that network. This view was expressed in
the following terms:

> The Board feels it is necessary to continue to stress the value to the
> country of the network. Anything that would tend towards weakening

the network would tend to weaken the BBC's contribution to British television. The special position of Scotland and that of Wales within the United Kingdom are fully recognised. On the other hand, Scotland and Wales are both valuable sources of network material. There is the danger, if Scottish and Welsh contributions to the network, and those from other parts of the Kingdom, should be weakened, that the BBC's Television Service might become unduly Metropolitan in character.[30]

During this period, the BCS was seeking parity of responsibility for control over television output within and for Scotland to that which it already exercised with regard to radio output. This was achieved in 1962, but the BBC centrally continued to stress that with the greater variety of radio services in comparison with the single television network, the emphasis in Scotland's dual programme responsibility could not be identical for both radio and television (i.e. radio should provide programmes for Scottish listeners, whereas in television Scotland was expected to place greater emphasis on contributions to the network and much less on opt-out programmes). In radio, BBC Scotland had much greater flexibility in providing items calculated to be of special interest to people in Scotland, and this remained so even after the arrival of BBC2 in Scotland in July 1966 because the BBC's second television channel was not designed to cater for Regional opt-outs. Indeed, BBC2 was designed in part to facilitate Regional contributions to the network since this had been difficult to achieve in practice with only one television network. In general, the BBC television networks were never fragmented to the same extent as the sound services.

There were interesting developments taking place in the sound services during these years. Indeed, the arrival of competition in television must not be allowed to obscure the fact that the effects of competition were extended to the radio networks and to the Scottish Home Service. Although during the 1950s radio suffered to some extent because of the popularity of television, radio was soon to benefit from technical developments such as VHF which improved the quality of reception and made localised services a possibility. The Beveridge Committee on Broadcasting, whose Report was published in 1951, had recognised the benefits of VHF with regard to the improvement of existing coverage of services and of increasing the diversity of programmes through localised services. The committee stated that 'Use of VHF could make it possible not merely to give the existing BBC programmes to people who now fail to get them, such as in the North and West of Scotland, but to establish local stations with independent programmes of their own'.[31] Just over two years later, the BCS voiced concern at the bad reception of the Scottish Home Service, particularly in Angus, Wester Ross, Orkney and Shetland and the Borders. The Council wanted the installation of VHF stations to be pressed on with urgency.[32] The extension of radio services was regarded as a means of coping with rural depopulation in some areas as well as the more general aim of providing a public service of broadcasting for small communities in sparsely-populated areas. The first VHF radio station in Scotland which provided the Home, Light and Third Programmes was opened at Meldrum, serving North-East Scotland, on 29 March 1956. In August 1956, the PMG approved the construction of six VHF radio stations, one of which was to be located at Kirk O'Shotts, serving central Scotland. Coverage of the SHS was indeed improved when on 30 November 1957 the BBC introduced VHF from the Kirk O'Shotts transmitter. A BBC pamphlet on the new service accepted that those people in remote areas would not receive VHF transmissions, but added that BBC policy was to provide services only where it was reasonably practicable to do so, the problems of remote areas only being noted for future consideration.[33] In areas which received VHF signals, listeners had either to purchase a new receiver or to have an adaptor fitted to their existing receiver. The higher cost of VHF receivers and the need to use an outdoor aerial in some areas was a disincentive to purchasing these receivers. The BBC wanted all new receivers to be equipped to receive VHF, preferably with push-button tuning to facilitate switching between channels. Transistors, which later became increasingly popular, were not initially equipped to receive VHF. It should also be noted that daytime reception on medium frequency and low frequency was adequate for many people and that fewer people listened to radio during the dark winter evenings, when medium-wave reception was poor and VHF would have been beneficial, because many tended to watch television instead. It was difficult to persuade listeners to equip themselves to receive VHF, so that even by the 1970s the BBC could not regard the VHF networks as the main carrier of its programmes. The BBC sought to use VHF not only to reinforce existing services, but also to vary national programmes.

In December 1957, the Broadcasting Council for Scotland approved proposals for some area broadcasting from the VHF transmitters at Meldrum, Rosemarkie and Sandale (and later from Orkney). These programmes were expected to consist of local news, sport and topical magazines.[34] These local variations, which were introduced during 1958, involved the broadcasting of a ten-minute weekly newsletter, with Meldrum and Rosemarkie also transmitting a weekly fifteen-minute magazine. Area broadcasting from Rosemarkie began on 12 October, but it was not possible to fragment the SHS from the Kirk O'Shotts transmitter serving central Scotland because it operated on high power. It was in the north of Scotland that the BBC was able to take advantage of the smaller coverage areas of the VHF stations to vary SHS transmissions in some areas as a means of introducing this limited amount of local programming. Apart from the provision of area programmes, listeners and viewers in Scotland benefited from the provision of new radio and television transmitters during this period. In addition to the VHF radio station at Kirk O'Shotts, which served over four million people, television stations were opened at Meldrum, Rosemarkie (on the Black Isle opposite Inverness) and at Sandale (near Carlisle), the last serving both England and Scotland. Nevertheless, in its Annual Report for 1956–7, the Broadcasting Council recognised that some people would have to accept something short of a first-class service. The Council stated that 'To provide first-class reception for every area is more than the present wavelength and financial situation will allow, but in some fringe areas, the radio relay system has helped local reception'.[35] The opening of the Rosemarkie transmitter on 16 August 1957 in fact brought television to ninety-three per cent of the population of Scotland and left only the Western Highlands, the Islands and parts of the Borders without any television service. The BCS urged BBC Scottish management to give a high priority to extending coverage to remote areas. In the following year's Annual Report, the Council stated:

> There is a general agreement among the Council, the Highland panel, members of Parliament and local bodies of the urgent need to extend the television and sound broadcasting services and the Council brings this to the notice of the Board and the Postmaster-General.[36]

For many years, the government had recognised the social problems encountered in areas which suffered from a lack of adequate broadcasting services. In a parliamentary reply to Mr Jo Grimond (MP for Orkney and Shetland) in May 1957, Kenneth Thompson (Assistant PMG) referred to the social and cultural aspects of broadcasting coverage:

> We have every sympathy with what the hon. Gentleman has said about the desirability of extending the BBC services to those remote parts, and the advantages which would accrue to the people receiving those services. We know and share the views which he has expressed about sound and television programmes for rural communities, which are often denied the more normal forms of pleasure and entertainment upon which other communities in more populous areas have come to rely.[37]

However, social and cultural considerations have never been accorded a high priority in determining the extension of broadcasting services. Remote communities in Scotland experienced higher food and transport costs and often had few leisure facilities. Newspapers and postal services were delayed, and there were often no cinemas or touring theatre companies. These areas sometimes wished to attract labour and encourage tourism, but the absence or poor provision of broadcasting services made this task that much more difficult. In extending broadcasting coverage, priority was given to providing the Scottish Home Service because of its high content of Scottish programme material. When television arrived in remote areas, there was however the possibility that mixed feelings would emerge because it could be regarded either as a threat to indigenous culture or as a means of stimulating local culture. Rural areas with their own cultural traditions did want access to the wide range of programme material which reflected life in other parts of the country. Broadcasting was of value during the long, dark winter evenings in the north of Scotland and in the Islands. School broadcasts which schoolchildren in other parts of the country took for granted were welcome, and so also was material which helped to sustain Gaelic language and culture. During the late 1950s, new VHF radio stations in Scotland were opened at Rosemarkie and in Orkney. A station at Sandale near Carlisle provided VHF programmes for South-West Scotland from England until several years later, when the television transmitter at Kirk O'Shotts was linked with Sandale to relay BBC Scotland programmes. Television stations were also opened in Orkney and at Thrumster near Wick. On 20 May 1960, the PMG approved stage II of the BBC's television/VHF radio plan, stage I having been authorised in June 1959. However, stage II was still expected to leave gaps in coverage, such as in the central Highlands, the Islands and South-West Scotland. In general, it can certainly be said that as the broadcasting services were extended to fill pockets of non-reception, many low-power stations were needed and this therefore increased capital costs.[38] The BBC sought as a public-service broadcaster to bring services to as many people as possible, but there were no guarantees of 100 per cent coverage. Despite the ongoing transmitter programme, the BBC was not under any obligation either to provide 100 per cent broadcasting coverage or to supply transmitters for many of the small Scottish communities. These were the type of communities which relied upon radio for many years after the arrival of television in the more populated areas.

For a number of years, Scottish radio programmes retained their popularity, and Scottish programme output remained greater than any other Region except London. During 1950–1, there were 1,893 hours of radio broadcasting produced in Scotland, of which 400 hours were produced for other BBC services.[39] During 1959–60, 1,877 hours of radio programmes were produced in Scotland, of which 431 hours were taken by other BBC services.[40] Over this period, Scotland contributed an increasing number of programme hours to the Light Programme, but a stable number to the Third Programme. However, in comparison with the other Regions, the BBC in Scotland tended to be a more significant contributor to the Third Programme than to the Light Programme. The bulk of programmes broadcast on the SHS continued to be taken from London and the other Home Services. For example, during 1950–1, the 1,493 hours of programme output for listeners in Scotland were supplemented by 4,473 hours taken from other Home Services, giving a total Scottish Regional output of 5,966 hours. Similarly, during 1959–60, the 1,446 hours of output for listeners in Scotland were supplemented by 4,869 hours taken from other Home Services, giving a total Scottish Regional output of 6,315 hours. The composition of Scottish-originated programmes for listeners in Scotland did undergo changes throughout the 1950s. During 1950–1, 317 hours of serious music were produced in Scotland for Scottish listeners, but this figure fell to 238 hours during 1959–60; there was also a significant reduction in hours of output for features and drama from 177 hours during 1950–1 to 56 hours in 1959–60. In contrast to this, the 89 hours of light music produced in Scotland during 1950–1 increased to 224 hours during 1959–60; news output more than doubled from 125 hours (1950–1) to 260 hours (1959–60).

The pattern built into the programme schedules – for example, serious music and discussions broadcast on Wednesdays, sport and Scottish dance music on Saturdays, religious programmes on Sundays – could not prepare radio in Scotland for competition from television. Although the Scottish Home Service offered a balanced rather than a specialised programme output, the closed hour for television from 6–7pm each evening was used for the broadcasting of popular items on the SHS. However, when the closed period was ended during 1956–7 and thereafter used for the broadcasting of television programmes, this presented a strong counterattraction in Scotland to the SHS. The BBC continued to provide a wide range of radio programmes which were particularly valued by those listeners who relied upon radio after the arrival of television in Scotland either out of choice or out of necessity. Those programmes included *Arts Review* (a monthly review of the arts in Scotland), *Farm Forum* (a weekly series on Scottish agriculture), *Industrial Inquiry* (a monthly series on key issues affecting industry), *Scotland in Parliament, Scope, Scottish Life and Letters, Annals of Scotland* (a series on Scottish writing), *Ere I Sleep* (the nightly epilogue), outside broadcasts of sporting events, schools' programmes, music from the BBC Scottish Orchestra, and drama such as *Master John Knox* (a play by Robert Kemp specially for the fourth centenary of the Reformation in Scotland). There were also area broadcasts on VHF only for the North-East and for Orkney, such as the magazine programmes and special items for farmers. In addition to these Scottish-originated programmes, listeners in most parts of Scotland also had access to the Light and Third Programmes and other items taken from other Home Services and incorporated in the Scottish Home Service. But all of this programme output was subject in varying degrees to competition from television. The adverse effect of television, both BBC and commercial, on audience figures for radio programmes during the evening, combined with rising costs and the downward trend in listening to radio because of changing social habits, prompted the BBC to propose changes in its network services and re-evaluate the role of the Regions in national broadcasting terms.

During 1956, a Sound Coordinating Committee within the BBC sought to reduce the total volume of radio broadcasting, partly to save money and partly to develop radio in a stronger direction in the competitive presence of television. It was recognised that programmes, such as radio features, could not compete effectively with filmed documentaries shown on television. This situation prevailed to an even greater extent in other subject areas such as sport. Competition between the radio services was now to be replaced by a policy of integration. London and the Regions were expected to pool their resources, as they already did in television, to provide the best possible material for national broadcasting. In practice, this was taken to mean more simultaneous broadcasts and less duplication of programme material by London and the Regions. The role of the Regions was not fundamentally altered, but Regions were expected like London to be subject to a reduction in their programme allowance.

Integration, according to the Director of Sound Broadcasting, was not meant to imply any reduction of Regional autonomy, but merely greater cooperation between London and the Regions.[41] In practice, cooperation was taken to mean the establishment of a close working relationship between the supply departments in London and programme heads and producers in the Regions to end narrow departmentalism. The aim was to find good programme material wherever it could be found, for presentation to programme Controllers who had the power to accept or reject material. It also meant that programme budgets were to be arrived at by joint discussion between the programme Controllers and the supply heads rather than being the sole responsibility of the former. Supply heads would continue to remain responsible for artistic and professional standards and so also remain the ultimate source of authority in these matters for Regional staff. Integration resulted in the production of fewer Regional programmes, but a higher percentage of those produced were taken by the radio networks. With the exception of programmes which were genuinely Regional in character, Regions were expected to take more programmes from each other and from London. Integration already existed in television because there was only one network and Regions were therefore expected to contribute material to this network rather than embark on extensive opting-out. The BBC rejected any suggestion that, under the new policy for radio, London would merely cream off the best Regional artists, writers, producers and ideas.

The days of competition among the three sound services were over. With the decline of the radio audience, the BBC wished to reduce the frequency of opting out in the Regions. The report of a working party set up by Lindsay Wellington, Director of Sound Broadcasting, on 9 November 1956 was ready by January 1957, and this was followed by a policy document issued on 9 April in which Wellington stated:

> it is felt strongly that the element of internal competition which is reflected in the present programme organisation should now entirely disappear. The reasons for it were good at the time but they no longer apply. The last vestiges of rivalry and competition between the Programmes should cease. The output of Sound radio should be planned as a whole so as to ensure contrasting choices wherever possible.[42]

The BBC wished to streamline output in order to reduce expenditure over the period 1957 to 1960 by £1 million and so be in a stronger position to face any future committee of inquiry and to counter the possibility of commercial radio. What appeared to be required was a reduction of £200,000 in 1957–8, £300,000 for 1958–9, and £100,000 for 1959–60. This cumulative reduction of £600,000 in the annual rate was expected to result in a saving of expenditure of £1 million by March 1960. It was ironic that these savings and the consequent proposed cuts in programme allowance for London and the Regions, as well as the administrative savings, were to take place at a time when area broadcasting was likely to result in the need for additional Regional expenditure. Scotland needed more resources to develop area services without adversely affecting the main SHS programme output. Regional expenditure could now only be sanctioned if regarded as essential and if proportionate savings were made in other areas.[43] It was on 31 January 1957 that the BBC indicated that there would be adjustments in the pattern of the radio services. At a meeting in March, the Board of Governors stated that no mention should be made about financial economies (i.e. cuts in programme budgets and staff) in the press statement on the changes due to be issued in April.[44]

On 8 April, the BBC issued a press statement which indicated that the Third Programme would be cut to three hours each evening; a new network entitled Network Three would be introduced in October 1957 on the same wavelength as the Third Programme but would operate earlier in the evening outside the hours of the Third Programme; the Light Programme would be extended by two hours each day and its output made 'lighter' in content by reducing the number of talks and by increasing the volume of popular music and variety; and the Home Service would join the Light programme to form a single programme at some periods during the day, thereby removing the element of competition between these two programme services, although the Home Service would continue to be the vehicle for Regional broadcasting. The introduction of Network Three was expected to cost less than the savings made by cutting hours in the Third Programme. This new network was expected to provide specialised programmes such as natural history, hobbies and languages for sizeable majorities who had practical rather than intellectual interests which were not of a sufficiently wide appeal to be catered for on the Light and Home Programmes or indeed on television; it was also designed to accommodate further education broadcasts. As regards the existing networks, there was a shift of material between them in order to give each service a consistent character and so provide listeners with a clearer choice of programmes and hence a more informed expectation of what they would find on each network. For example, light music and variety on the Home Service were transferred to the Light Programme, and minority interest subjects on the Home Service and Light Programme went to the new Network Three. The Light Programme, according to the BBC, was to be relieved of the duty consciously to educate and improve the taste of listeners; and the Third Programme was regarded as too highbrow and elitist. There was a promise of increased contributions from the Regions being taken by the three sound services, as well as continuing development to some extent of VHF area broadcasting.

These changes in radio broadcasting generated external criticism. The changes appeared to represent a cultural retreat in the face of competition from television, particularly commercial television. Interestingly, the audience for cultural items on the Third Programme had remained fairly constant despite the presence of competition from television, whereas the Home Service and its Regional elements had suffered much more from the attraction of television. On 24 March 1957, a Third Programme Defence Society (known from 7 June as the Sound Broadcasting Society to indicate that concern was not confined to the Third Programme) was formed to press for changes to the BBC's plans. A pamphlet was printed by the Society to outline the case for the retention of a separate Third Programme not merged in any form with the basic Home Service. It also criticised what it regarded as the BBC's attempt to sacrifice quality programmes in the competitive struggle with ITV for audiences.[45] On 18 July, the Society sent a deputation to the BBC to oppose the cuts in the Third Programme and the emphasis on more 'lighter' programme material, but the BBC was not anxious to give in to the wishes of a pressure group. The BBC's proposed changes did represent a departure from the Reithian ethos, as the following comment would confirm: 'The Corporation wants each listener to make his own choice according to his own taste and mood. The Corporation does not want to force a choice upon him ...'.[46] The BBC was thus seeking to cater for the tastes of its audiences without attempting to alter and improve them. Entertainment was no longer to be undervalued or merely regarded as a stepping stone to more serious programme material. Nevertheless, the BBC stated that the Third Programme, even in its shortened form, comprised almost one tenth of total transmission time for an audience which was no more than one hundredth of the total audience.[47] The Corporation argued that it would continue to educate, entertain and inform majority and minority audiences to the fullest extent possible but within the resources available.

There were also negative aspects to the changes. The BBC accepted that the audience for further education broadcasts on Network Three was smaller than it was when these programmes had been transmitted in the other services. The reduction in the amount of money available to radio broadcasting as a whole was felt to a lesser extent in Scotland, where there was a five per cent cut in the Scottish programme allowance and a reduction in the volume of Scottish-originated items. The weekly Gaelic news on radio was, for example, replaced by a monthly programme in August 1957. In its Annual Report for 1957–8, the BCS commented upon the changes in relation to Scotland:

> The revised plans for sound broadcasting in the United Kingdom, introduced last Autumn, aroused comparatively little reaction in Scotland. The Council think that this is because the strong national interest of the Scots in broadcasting is well understood by the BBC and the Council, who took care to maintain unimpaired the main Scottish programme activities.[48]

The changes in the radio services and the effects of competition in broadcasting were two of the topics which were brought to the attention of the Pilkington Committee on Broadcasting which was appointed in July 1960 to consider the current and future pattern of broadcasting services.

The Pilkington Report on Broadcasting:
submissions, recommendations and responses, 1960–2

On 13 July 1960, the Postmaster-General, Mr Reginald Bevans, announced in the House of Commons that the government was setting up a committee to examine the future pattern of broadcasting services in the United Kingdom. The committee was expected to consider the future of the domestic broadcasting services, and to advise which services should in future be provided by the BBC and the ITA; to recommend whether any additional services should be provided by any other organisation; and to propose what financial and other conditions should apply to the conduct of all these services. The committee was chaired by the industrialist Sir Harry Pilkington of Pilkington Brothers, the glass manufacturer. Given that the BBC and the ITA were to remain in existence, the Pilkington Committee was thus precluded from recommending that broadcasting should again be organised on a monopolistic basis. Unlike previous Committees of Inquiry, the Pilkington Committee was the first to examine broadcasting in a period in which television had eclipsed radio broadcasting to become the dominant medium. It highlighted questions about the BBC's radio services which had never been needed to be raised on previous occasions: whether the BBC's sound broadcasting monopoly should remain; how radio services should be planned during a period in which the use of radio services by listeners was changing; and whether localised services should be provided, and if so, by whom. Despite the fall in the number of radio licences purchased and the decline in listening audiences during evening hours, the transistor, the car radio, VHF local radio and stereophonic broadcasts offered prospects for sustaining the interest of the public in radio. An article in *The Times* published in April 1960 stated that 'It may be that as the novelty of television wears off, the more discriminating will once again be prepared to consider the choices offered by the Sound services for their evening's entertainment, but there is little evidence that that has begun to happen yet'.[1] Radio though remained in a stronger position than television to cater for minority interests. Overall, the possibility of local radio (BBC and/or commercial) and changes in the format of the existing BBC radio networks were issues which needed to be considered in any future plans for sound broadcasting. The Pilkington Committee received 636 memoranda from a wide variety of individuals and organisations involved in, or having close links with, broadcasting. Many of these submissions were published on 13 September 1962 in separate volumes to the main report which appeared on 27 June 1962, but all the meetings were held in private. The Pilkington Committee was significant to the extent that it was the first time that a major Committee of Inquiry had been asked to examine a broadcasting authority other than the BBC. In order to allow time for the results of the inquiry to be absorbed, the BBC's Charter and Licence were extended from 30 June 1962 to 29 July 1964 (i.e. to coincide with the expiry date of the Television Act).

One of the main topics on which the committee received submissions of evidence was that of the competition between the BBC and ITV. The committee asked the BBC to give its views about the effects of the introduction of competition in television broadcasting. In February 1961, the BBC submitted a memorandum in which it stated that competition had not increased the range of programmes available. The BBC wished to plan two channels in order to gain flexibility in scheduling programmes not necessarily during peak viewing hours and so avoid the programme clashes which developed because of competition with ITV. Indeed, the complementary planning of the BBC's radio networks could be contrasted with the negative effects of direct competition between BBC and ITV. The BBC had lost much of its audience to ITV in the first years of competition because it refused to reduce the number of serious programmes during peak viewing hours. In fact, the BBC's share of the audience, according to its own statistical evidence, did not exceed that of ITV until the period October–December 1962. In a separate memorandum dated January 1961, the BBC recognised that ITV continued to attract larger audiences but went on to state that 'In the BBC's opinion, this result has been achieved by the programme companies by a process of concentrating on the less demanding types of entertainment during the main viewing hours'.[2] The BBC argued that the negative effects of competition included increased costs, the loss of some producers and technical staff to ITV and the narrowing of the range of programme output. However, the BBC did benefit from competition in that it improved its production techniques in light entertainment, encouraged greater professionalism in general, and enabled benefits to be derived from studying the ITV schedules. For example, the BBC discovered that audiences for minority interest programmes could be increased by placing them after popular BBC programmes, or opposite ITV's minority interest programmes. However, the Association of Broadcasting Staff stated in a memorandum that it was not convinced that competition had led to any major improvements in programme standards which would not have been inevitable as and when improved technical facilities were brought into service. Other submissions, such as that from the TUC, were critical of the BBC for allowing itself to be drawn into the competitive process by matching programme with programme, thereby reducing choice for viewers.[3] Criticism of competition between the BBC and ITV formed part of a wider criticism of the networking arrangements within ITV. The absence of directly competing companies in each service area resulted in the creation of local broadcasting monopolies within ITV. STV, for example, had a local monopoly in central Scotland. Also, the networking arrangements restricted competition among ITV network companies to supply programmes to the Regional companies and made the network companies reluctant to accept Regional material. The difficulty which Regional companies, such as STV, experienced in breaking into the network began to mirror the opportunities available for BBC Scotland to do likewise. Within ITV, the network companies offered the same financial terms to the smaller companies which affiliated to them in order to pay for the supply of programmes from all network companies. Although the ITA wished to overcome any disincentives in the production of programmes by the small Regional companies and to encourage a greater exchange of programmes between companies, the Authority could claim that, unlike the BBC, most network material was not produced in London.

One of the issues which the Pilkington Committee was to consider was to advise on what future services should be provided. With this in mind, a BBC memorandum on future programme policy argued that the third television channel should go to the BBC. The BBC sought to justify this as follows:

> A second service would enable the BBC to increase the number of serious, cultural, and informational programmes, to cater more fully for Regional needs and aspirations, to extend educational broadcasts, to experiment on the screen (because closed-circuit experiment is much less effective as well as being expensive), and to serve more interests.[4]

The BBC also envisaged that an additional channel would enable it to provide a home for Regional opt-out programmes, and this appeared to offer the prospect of developing BBC Scotland's television output, since there had been constraints on Regional opt-outs on BBC1. The BBC added that a commercially-based system could not fulfil all the tasks which the Corporation hoped to implement using a second television channel because advertisers would be reluctant to advertise on a less popular channel.

With regard to television programme output in Scotland, the Pilkington Committee received several submissions which commented upon the nature of the BBC's Scottish programme service. In its memorandum of November 1960, the Saltire Society stated that it wanted to see the encouragement of the production of programmes of the highest quality suited to Scottish needs and tastes. In broadcasting terms, it wanted Scotland to be treated as a nation, and also commented upon the image of Scotland projected in programmes:

> We do not ask for a larger quota of material built round a Scottish parish pump. While there are, under present arrangements, some good Scottish programmes, too many project an image of the Scot as a being with none but the most parochial and shallow of interests.[5]

The Saltire Society wanted programmes which showed a Scottish perspective on world events rather than a perspective filtered through English lenses. The Scottish National Party believed that the BBC was treating Scotland as a province of England rather than as a nation. In particular, the SNP drew attention to the fact that the BCS had no control over television output within and for Scotland, and that therefore the constitutional arrangements for broadcasting in Scotland did not meet the wishes or the cultural and social needs of the Scottish nation. The SNP was also critical of BBC news, which it regarded as being too parochial because it emanated from London and therefore was too metropolitan. It also wanted the BBC in Scotland to have suitably qualified announcers and producers who could take control of Scottish items of interest to the network, thus avoiding the need to import staff from outwith Scotland. The Scottish Trades Union Congress (STUC) General Council considered the issue as to whether priority should be given to introducing a third television network rather than expanding broadcasting coverage of existing services in remote parts of Scotland. The STUC favoured the latter option, as did Ness Edwards, the former PMG, who wanted the country to receive two good television services before any part of the country was offered three services. The BCS and the Church of Scotland Committee on Church and Nation also wanted television services to be provided for the whole country before the allocation of a third television channel was considered.

In 1959, a few months prior to the appointment of the Broadcasting Committee, the BCS submitted a memorandum to the Board of Governors on the Council's attitude to television in Scotland, and in particular the need to operate one policy in sound and television.[6] At that time, the Scottish Controller was directly answerable to the Director-General and not to the Broadcasting Council on matters such as television opt-outs. In a memo to the Director-General in January 1960, Gerald Beadle (Director of Television Broadcasting) noted that 'It does seem logical to me that the two Councils should have authority over the content of programmes mounted exclusively for their own people'.[7] He was not prepared to go so far as to recommend that television personnel should be classed as Council staff, because he believed that television staff would continue to play a large part in the network operation rather than in programme output purely for Regional audiences. In the early 1950s, television was principally a network operation with Regions expected to contribute material to this network, whereas by the early 1960s the Regions wanted greater latitude to produce and transmit material for their own Regional audience. Beadle recognised that pressure for fragmentation of the network had programme planning and financial implications: it caused Regional audiences to miss the network programmes; it made Regions press the Controller of Programmes (Television) to plan weak output in order to prevent Regional audiences from believing that they were missing good network programmes, and this in turn would lower network standards and reduce the BBC's competitive strength in relation to ITV; and fragmentation utilised more staff and technical resources which could be used for network contributions, thus preventing the network from becoming more metropolitan. In short, although Gerald Beadle was prepared to concede that the powers of the Broadcasting Councils should be extended to cover television output, he did not think that the Councils should take this to imply any acceptance of greater fragmentation.

On 15 March 1960, the Board of Governors stated that to give the Broadcasting Councils authority equivalent to that which they already possessed in sound broadcasting implied the provision of broadcasting services in television on an equivalent scale to those available to listeners on radio. But with only one television channel, the BBC could not provide a Scottish television equivalent to the Scottish Home Service on radio. This implied that the constitutional change in the powers of the BCS would only take place when more television channels became available. The Board noted that constitutional change would not by itself increase the amount of opt-out time, since the latter was governed by limitations on the resources available such as money, wavelengths and staff. However, in a memorandum to the Pilkington Committee in December 1960, the BCS stated that because the audience for BBC television in Scotland was greater than that of the combined audience for all three radio services, the Council should be given the same responsibility in television as it exercised in sound broadcasting. This was also a sensible course of action because it was evident from the minutes of the Council that television was taking up an increasing amount of time at meetings of the BCS. In May 1961, the BCS was informed of the BBC's verbal recommendation to the Pilkington Committee that the Council's powers should be extended to cover television, although Sir Arthur fforde (BBC Chairman) stated that full implementation would only be possible when the BBC was permitted to operate a second channel.[8] In August 1961, the BBC formally stated that it favoured extending the power of the Broadcasting Councils to cover television output, but the BBC still believed that the rearrangement of programmes at short notice to cope with competition from ITV would be impaired if there were a significant increase in opting out.

The Pilkington Committee also received many comments on radio broadcasting. In a memorandum to the committee, the BBC recommended that the national Broadcasting Councils for Scotland and Wales should be given the additional function of controlling the policy and content of programmes from local radio stations, should any of these stations be opened in Scotland and Wales. The Broadcasting Council for Scotland stated that it was interested in, and had considered establishing, local stations. The Council recommended that the BBC should be authorised to carry out a local broadcasting experiment over a two-year period because this would demonstrate whether there was any public interest in local radio. However, the BCS added that local radio should not develop to the point of financially damaging either the BBC's national service of broadcasting within and for Scotland, or Scotland's contribution to network output.[9] Local radio in Scotland was therefore regarded as a third objective, the main and secondary objectives being to improve the output of the Scottish Home Service and to contribute some programme items to the other radio networks. Indeed, the BCS regarded local radio as a modest service of local items to supplement the output of the Scottish Home Service. The Sound Broadcasting Society argued that if the government authorised local radio, then only the BBC and not a commercial system should be allowed to operate it. This view was echoed by the STUC General Council, which believed that local radio would provide better opportunities for covering community affairs in Scotland. The Church of Scotland Committee on Church and Nation stated that any local stations should not be operated under a commercial system. As regards network services, the Sound Broadcasting Society regretted what it regarded as the deterioration in the cultural, educational and informative content of BBC radio output which began in 1957 when the Corporation introduced changes to the programme schedules involving an alteration of the balance between 'serious' and 'light' programme material. The Society wanted the BBC to extend the broadcasting hours of the Third Programme. The 1957 changes had been introduced in order to reduce radio expenditure and take account of alterations in listening habits because of competition from television. In May 1951, the Director of Home Broadcasting had stated that, under a system of central planning, 'some of the richness and variety of our present programme offerings would have been eliminated in the attempt to avoid embarrassing alternatives by placing weaker programmes against the stronger'.[10] Yet in 1957 it was central planning and the policy of integration which superseded competition between the radio services.

There were a few other matters relating to broadcasting in Scotland on which the committee received evidence. In December 1960, the memorandum by the SNP expressed concern about the status of broadcasting in Scotland. The SNP stated that 'If Scotland is not to be submerged in a stream of Anglo-American ideas and culture, it is imperative that a Scottish Broadcasting Corporation be formed to control the services at present provided by the BBC'.[11] The SNP was critical of the level of administrative and financial control exercised over the BBC in Scotland. The Saltire Society stated that the powers of the BCS over the policy and content of the Scottish Home Service were too limited. The Society wanted Scottish broadcasting to have real financial and executive autonomy. It also believed that Scottish programme output under the control of the BCS was too Scottish and provincial in content and therefore less likely to be of interest to a non-Scottish audience.[12] Sir David Milne, Chairman of the BCS, submitted a paper to the Pilkington Committee on BBC financial practice in relation to Scotland. He noted that, by the end of the 1950s, the number of combined licences had overtaken the number of sound-only licences, thus narrowing the gap between BBC income and expenditure in Scotland, given that the income from combined licences was much greater than that from radio licences. He stated that there were differentials in expenditure within Scotland because the BBC spent a larger amount of income per head of population in the Highlands and other remote areas in comparison with the populous central belt. However, there remained gaps in transmitter coverage in Scotland. In its memorandum of January 1960, the Advisory Panel on the Highlands and Islands expressed concern about the extent of social amenities in the Highlands and Islands and drew the committee's attention to the poor reception of BBC radio output in

North-West Scotland, the Western Isles and Shetland.[13] The Advisory Panel made the comparison between the indifferent reception of BBC radio in Scotland and the fact that many other parts of the country had access to good radio and television services. By 1962, coverage of the three radio networks on VHF in Scotland was ninety-three per cent, but the remaining seven per cent comprised many communities in the North-West Highlands and Islands and in the central Highland area. The social dimension of broadcasting coverage was also brought to the committee's attention because An Comunn (the Highland Association) stated that 'Our desire is that adequate provision be made, in time and resources, to ensure that the needs of the Gaelic-speaking communities in the Highlands are met'.[14] The committee considered these and other topics on which it had received both oral and written evidence.

The Pilkington Report was published on 27 June 1962. The BBC welcomed the report, and it was agreed that detailed comment should be reserved until after the government's White Paper had been published.[15] The committee's report was particularly critical of ITV programme output for what it regarded as its failure to raise the level of public taste, to cater for minority audiences or to provide a sufficient volume of Regional material. This obviously ran counter to the ITA's view that ITV programmes were operating in broad conformity with the requirements of proper balance and that the system of programme control which it was expected to oversee was working satisfactorily. The committee was particularly critical of ITV's entertainment programmes. Improvements in technique and in presentation skills were deemed not to have been matched by improvements in programme content. The ITA was regarded as acting more as a mouthpiece for the programme companies than as a guardian of the public interest. The committee not only rejected the ITV programme philosophy of giving the public what it wanted, but also rejected the BBC philosophy of giving the public the programmes which the broadcasters thought were in the public interest, since this was regarded as too patronising. The committee indicated that it believed that the pressure of competition had caused the BBC to depart somewhat from its public service ideals, but it stated that, in view of the submissions which it had received, the causes of disquiet about television were not to any great extent attributable to the BBC's service.[16] It can be argued that if the BBC had not engaged in competitive scheduling with ITV, then those viewers who had access only to BBC television would have been presented with a narrower range of programme choice. The BBC did not want to leave ITV to put out the more popular programmes, especially during peak viewing hours in the early evening. The committee criticised the lack of Regional programmes within ITV, and stated that programmes produced outside London were local more in origin than in appeal:

> Thus, though the smaller independent television companies produced more hours of programming than did the BBC Regions, items of local appeal still formed only a small part of each company's programme: and most of these items were shown at off-peak hours.[17]

This was understandable to the extent that small companies, such as STV, earned most advertising revenue from transmitting the popular programmes made by the network companies; they could not match the standard of network output; and there was no incentive to substitute too many local programmes for network programmes if the latter had already been paid for as a percentage of net advertising revenue. As regards the third television channel, the Pilkington Report recommended that this channel should be allocated to the BBC.[18] The committee recognised that an additional channel could provide more opportunities for programmes catering for interests in the BBC's national and English Regions without depriving viewers of network programmes. Furthermore, the committee noted that few programmes were produced in Scotland, and that, of those which were, the consensus which emerged from the various written submissions and oral evidence was that these programmes often failed to reflect distinctive Scottish culture. The committee took note of the various submissions advocating an extension in the responsibilities of the Broadcasting Councils and stated that 'We recommend that the National Broadcasting Council for Scotland be vested, in respect of the BBC's television service in Scotland, with rights and duties comparable with those it exercises in respect of Sound radio'.[19] The committee rejected the idea of establishing a Scottish Broadcasting Corporation; the dangers of 'Londonisation' were deemed to be less than those of isolation.[20]

The committee also offered recommendations on network and local radio broadcasting services. As regards the network radio services, the committee stated that it had received evidence criticising the segregation of programme material in the networks which, it was believed, had gone too far in separating popular from more demanding programmes. The committee wanted a greater interchange of material between the Home, Light and Third/Network Three Programmes to enable listeners to be exposed to a wider range of programme material. The Pilkington Report did, however, recognise that because listeners were more selective in their choice of programmes, the BBC could best serve them by providing three services, each of a recognisably different character. Listeners were now less likely to give undivided attention to a variety of programmes on one channel and more likely to prefer homogeneous networks with familiar but different types of programme material on each of them. The committee however suspected that the BBC's policy had inherent dangers, in that segregating programmes into classes might lead to a segregation of listeners into classes, and therefore what it sought was some overlapping of majority and minority interests in the planning of programmes on all three radio services.[21] For example, the committee argued that the BBC had underestimated its audience by transferring some programmes from the Home Service, where they would give pleasure to a large audience, to Network Three where the audience was much smaller. In general, however, the committee endorsed the BBC's radio services, both network and Regional. It accepted BBC recommendations about the need to extend the broadcasting hours for the Light

Programme, to use the Third Network transmitters to provide a daytime service of music, and to introduce localised services on VHF.

The Pilkington Report envisaged no need for additional national radio services, but local services on VHF were an entirely different matter. The committee stated that commercial companies which had proposed to engage in local radio broadcasting had not developed their views about the character and composition of the service as much as the BBC had done.[22] Moreover, it was suggested that commercial local radio would serve the interests of advertisers rather than the public interest. Relying upon BBC evidence that there was sufficient local material to sustain a service of BBC local radio, the committee stated that 'We are, however, satisfied that the evidence of available local material justifies a sustained and broadly-based trial, in the expectation that an extensive pattern of local stations might follow'.[23] The Pilkington Report stated that only a public corporation should be responsible for developing a service of local radio covering as many communities as possible, but that this development should not delay the completion of VHF coverage of the BBC's existing three radio services. The committee stated that commercial television companies which had been unable to realise the purposes of broadcasting were unlikely to fare much better with local radio. The question of participation of local newspapers in local radio companies and that of competition for advertising revenue at the local level were, it was recognised, not problems that would arise if the BBC were permitted to operate local stations financed from licence income. Furthermore, BBC local stations could rely upon the three radio networks for sustaining material and thus in theory provide a larger reservoir of programme material and at a cheaper cost than a commercial system could achieve. Overall, the committee believed that only the BBC could provide a satisfactory local radio service to small communities unable to sustain a commercial service. The committee summed up its views on local broadcasting by stating:

> Accordingly, we recommend that one service, and one only, of local sound broadcasting be planned; that it be provided by the BBC and financed from licence revenue; and that the frequencies available be so deployed as to enable it to be provided for the largest possible number of distinctive communities.[24]

The issue of local radio broadcasting, the closed-circuit BBC experiments in the early 1960s and the establishment of local stations on an experimental basis in the late 1960s are discussed in a later chapter. It can be noted, however, that whoever was eventually permitted to operate local radio would in essence be the provider of a monopoly service unless two or more competing services were provided in each locality.

The submissions of evidence to the committee about the conduct of the Scottish Home Service did not indicate any significant dissatisfaction about the quality of the service provided. Where there was criticism, it related more to constitutional issues and broadcasting coverage in Scotland. The committee noted that there was criticism of the way in which the BBC's General Advisory Council selected members of the Broadcasting Councils for Scotland and Wales, both of which had control over the policy and content of their Home Service radio programmes. The committee stated that in Scotland it was considered unsatisfactory that the members of the GAC panel who chose the members of the BCS were not Scots living in Scotland. It was noted that because the BCS contained individuals who were representative of the Scottish people and active in the life of Scotland, the same principle should apply to members of the GAC panel.[25] The Pilkington Report also recommended that the requirement that three members of the Broadcasting Councils for Scotland and for Wales should be selected as being representative of local authorities in each of these two countries should no longer be imposed. On the issue of Scottish party political broadcasts, the committee stated that the BBC's Licence and Agreement should be revised in order to permit the inclusion of additional party political broadcasts addressed specifically to Scotland and to Wales. On the geographical coverage of programme services, there was support for the need to improve reception, but also an implicit acceptance that there were no guarantees of 100 per cent coverage:

> The concept of the comprehensive service applies not only to programme content, but also to the geographical range or coverage of the transmissions. It has never been accepted that services of broadcasting should be available only to those for whom they can be provided easily, or economically. Both the BBC and the ITA have regarded it as their duty, as public corporations, to see that their existing services are as nearly as possible available to everybody in the whole of the country.[26]

The Pilkington Committee, unlike the previous Committee of Inquiry, delivered a unanimous report, so, as Tom Driberg pointed out, there was no minority report for the government to fall back on if it wished to adopt a different approach to the main lines of argument developed in the Pilkington Report.[27] On 4 July 1962, the government issued its White Paper on Broadcasting. It agreed with the Pilkington Report that no independent Scottish or Welsh broadcasting corporation should be established, but accepted that the Broadcasting Councils for Scotland and Wales should exercise the same powers in relation to the content of television services as they already did for sound broadcasting.[28] This change was to be incorporated in the new Charter, due to be renewed for twelve years from 30 July 1964. The BBC was, however, prepared to treat the period 1962 to 1964 as a transitional one during which the new powers of the Councils would be considered as already in existence and thus could be introduced within the limits of available finance and technical resources. This had the merit of providing practical experience in the operation of these powers before the new Charter came into force and thereby not requiring the introduction of a supplemental Charter as suggested in the White Paper. The Chairman of the BCS supported this view, although the

Council agreed that if in nine months they found a lack of cooperation between Scotland and London over the issue of opt-out television programmes for Scotland, then they would review the situation and ask for a supplemental charter.[29] The government's White Paper also indicated that it wished to see the development of two more television networks on UHF 625 lines (bands IV and V), and agreed that the BBC should be permitted to start one of these new services by mid-1964. The government also stated that any colour service should only commence on 625 lines UHF, and that in due course the BBC would be allowed to start transmitting some programmes in colour on their second channel. As regards the selection of members of the Broadcasting Councils, the government accepted that the GAC should contain individuals who were active in the life of Scotland and Wales, given that this Council had duties with regard to the selection of members of the Broadcasting Councils for Scotland and Wales; it also accepted that there should no longer be any requirement that some members of these Councils should be selected as being representative of local authorities. With regard to radio broadcasting in general, the government agreed that no additional national radio broadcasting services were needed, but that the BBC should be authorised to extend broadcasting hours in the Light Programme and the Third Programme/Network Three.[30] As regards local radio, the government exercised caution, and so although the committee had recommended that an experimental service of local broadcasting should begin, the government nevertheless stated that because of the extra demand on resources and the lack of evidence of public demand for local radio, no such local radio experiment should be authorised.[31] These and other contentious issues were covered by a further White Paper issued later that year.

In December 1962, the government issued its second White Paper in response to the recommendations of the Pilkington Report. This covered the more contentious aspects of broadcasting raised by the committee, such as reforms of the structure of ITV and the question of local radio. The government stated that it did not believe that criticism of ITV justified major restructuring of the type suggested by the committee whereby the ITA would plan the programmes and sell advertising time, so leaving the ITV companies to produce and sell to the ITA programmes for inclusion in the programme schedule planned by the Authority. The government argued that it did not want to introduce a centralised system with the ITA acting as the monopoly buyer of programmes. The government did however recognise that the financial arrangements between network and Regional companies had discouraged the production of Regional programmes, hence the proposal that the ITA should control the networking of programme material and that it should supervise the arrangements for the buying and selling of programmes.[32] The aim was to facilitate the networking of material produced by the Regional companies, such as the three ITV Scottish contractors. As regards the creation of a second ITV channel, the government did not propose at the time to authorise such a channel. On the issue of local radio, the White Paper stated that this should not command a high priority in the allocation of resources, but that the possibility of localised services was to be reviewed at a later date.[33] The White Paper was reviewed by the BBC Board of Governors at their meeting on 20 December. The Board took note of the fact that a second ITV channel was not to be expected for several years, and that the issue of local broadcasting was kept open. The Pilkington Report, as Asa Briggs noted, helped to shape the mood in which problems and opportunities in broadcasting were viewed during the 1960s, a decade of expansion within the BBC.[34]

BBC television development in Scotland and the origins, programme policy and influence of BBC2, 1962–7

The 1960s can be regarded as a period of rapid expansion within the BBC, much of it as a result of the proposals of the Pilkington Report of 1962. It was also a period in which the BBC appeared to be less stuffy, more enterprising, more populist and more controversial, especially in satire, drama and current affairs output under the guidance of Hugh Greene, who had assumed the Director-Generalship of the Corporation in January 1960. This new attitude which permeated network programme output was not necessarily replicated in Regional output. In many ways, Scotland remained more conservative and adhered more strictly to Reithian ideals. But Scotland was influenced to some extent by the expansion in programme activities during this period. The Pilkington Report's recommendation that the Broadcasting Council for Scotland should be given powers in relation to television broadcasting in Scotland analogous to those which it exercised with regard to sound broadcasting was subsequently accepted by the government, put into practice by the BBC and incorporated in the new Royal Charter of 1964. The practical impact of this widening of responsibilities was to culminate in the preparation of a five-year television development plan for programmes in Scotland. Moreover, the government's decision to sanction a second television channel for the BBC had mixed blessings for Scotland. It offered the prospect of increasing television output in Scotland for the network, but also threatened to place constraints on improving coverage of existing programme services in Scotland. These were also years of exciting technical developments which were initially applied to the BBC's second television channel, BBC2, and were subsequently extended to both BBC1 and to ITV. The two principal developments were the introduction of UHF 625-line transmissions which improved picture quality, and the introduction of colour television which added a new sense of realism to images on television screens. Scotland also benefited from these programme and technical developments, although not at the same rate as other parts of the country. By late 1967, some viewers in Scotland had access to the experimental colour television service available on BBC2; it took many more years after that before almost all people in Scotland had access to three television networks transmitting colour programmes.

The new Royal Charter of 1964 stated that each national Broadcasting

Council would have the following additional function which would be exercised with full regard to the distinctive culture, language, interests and tastes of the people in the BBC's national Regions:

> the function of controlling the policy and content of those pro-
> grammes in the Television Services which the Council decides shall
> be provided primarily for reception in that country in replacement of
> or in addition to programmes provided by the Corporation for general
> reception in Our United Kingdom of Great Britain and Northern
> Ireland.[1]

These powers were in fact put into practice by the Corporation prior to the publication of the new Charter, and so, towards the end of 1962, the BCS was able to consider future television development in Scotland. It was noted that the BBC's second television network would present the Corporation with a strong challenge in terms of planning and development, but that contributions to BBC2 would be expected from Scotland, at least in order to put Scottish interests before a network audience. On programme output, Council members thought that the current output was on the right lines and that the main objective in the first stage of television development was to expand existing work between 1963 and 1967 and seek finance for programmes rather than for capital expenditure on studios.[2] Until such time as Regional resources throughout the UK could be converted to 625 lines (the line standard to be used for BBC2), Regional contributions to the network had to be confined to BBC1, thus prompting the formation in late 1962 of a working party to study the potential for increases in Regional contributions to the BBC's single television network.[3] In Scotland, the five-year development plan for television was designed to give effect to the new powers of the BCS over television programme output within and for Scotland by seeking to double this output by 1970. It was expected that the main period from 1965 to 1970 covered by the plan would be divided into at least two phases comprising 1963 to 1967 and 1967 to 1970. For the year ending 31 March 1962, gross expenditure on television in Scotland was £856,000, with net expenditure (i.e. gross expenditure minus amounts charged to the network) of £702,000.[4] This expenditure comprised the Scottish programme allowance, staff costs, studios and premises, engineering and transmitting costs. The largest element within the total was represented by the staff costs (£227,000 gross expenditure; £189,000 net after allowance was made for £38,000 charged to the network). The programme allowance for television was £163,000 gross, moderately greater than the radio programme allowance of £148,000. In 1961, the BBC's Director-General had envisaged that the television programme allowance would increase from £165,000 during 1962–3 to approximately £477,000 by 1969–70, and would do so by five yearly increases of £40,000, beginning on 1 October 1965. These phased increases were reproduced in a memorandum from the Controller, Scotland to the Controller of Programme Services, Television.[5] The engineering and transmitting costs were consider-ably greater for television than for radio, but the gap between gross expenditure on television and that on radio was narrowed only because of the additional costs involved in radio in transmitting the Light Programme, the Third Programme and Network Three.

In its Annual Report for 1961–2, the BCS stated that it was seeking to achieve an output of ten hours a week on television from Scotland by 1970. The Council argued that the main Scottish needs in television in terms of subject areas were news, religion, current affairs, drama, entertainment, folk music and dancing, sport and arts programmes. For example, at that time, BBC Scotland's Glasgow newsroom had no staff reporters and so had to make use of freelances to cover Scottish news items. Furthermore, the problem of providing Scottish news and documentary programmes for the rest of the UK was aggravated by the use of English reporters to cover newsworthy events in Scotland, such as the subsequent opening of the Forth Road Bridge in September 1964. The limited range of programme material produced by the BBC in Scotland made it more vulnerable to criticism in the press. In the House of Commons, Mr Norman Buchan (Renfrew, West) said that the Broadcasting Council had failed to ensure that the BBC paid full regard to the distinctive culture, language, interests and tastes of the people of Scotland. He remarked that 'Scottish BBC has singularly failed to serve the Scottish people and this is equally true of commercial Scottish television, both in quality and in quantity'.[6] On television, the programmes which the BBC in Scotland was producing included *Compass* (a fortnightly current affairs magazine programme), *Counterpoint* (covering the arts in Scotland), *Jimmy Logan Entertains, Six-Ten* (a daily news and magazine programme), *Dr Finlay's Casebook* (the popular programme based on a rural medical practice, and which was taken by the network), *The Kilt is my Delight* (Scottish country dancing), *Scotland in Parliament* (a monthly programme which was also covered in the Scottish Home Service), *Music of the Gael* (the first Gaelic television programme, initially transmitted on 7 March 1962), *Sportsreel* (sports coverage on Saturday evenings), *The Vital Spark* (light entertainment), *Between the Lines* (light entertainment programme shown on both BBC networks), a limited volume of drama output, such as *The Master of Ballantrae* (a serial version of the novel by Robert Louis Stevenson), and a number of other programme items, including the nightly epilogues and special programmes for New Year's Eve which were normally taken by the network.

In general, the programme output by the BBC in Scotland on television was certainly limited, partly because of financial constraints, and partly because programme Controllers in London were wary of permitting too much opting out by Scotland or indeed any Region while there was only a single BBC television network. Moreover, any increase in opting out could only be achieved by denying viewers in Scotland access to popular network programmes. Indeed, it was the BBC's popular network programmes which had to compete against the popular programme items produced by the ITV network companies and which were transmitted by the three Regional Scottish ITV companies. STV, for example, attracted large audiences for programmes produced by the network companies. These programmes included *Coronation Street* (produced by Granada), *Double Your Money* and *Take Your Pick* (quiz programmes produced by Associated-Rediffusion), *Bootsie and Snudge* (comedy programme produced by Granada), *World in Action* (current affairs from Granada Television), *The Avengers* (drama series produced by ABC Television), *Emergency Ward 10* (hospital drama from ATV) and *All Our Yesterdays* (historical documentary programme series produced by Granada). In order to counter the popularity of these programmes in Scotland, the BBC in Scotland had to rely on the popularity of programmes mainly produced in London for the network. These BBC programmes included *Steptoe and Son* (light entertainment), *Z-Cars* (police drama), *Juke Box Jury* (pop music), *That Was the Week That Was* (satire programme, and its successor *Not So Much a Programme, More a Way of Life*), *Dixon of Dock Green* (police series), *Tonight* (magazine programme, and its successor in 1965, *24 Hours*), *Harry Worth* (comedy) and the popular light entertainment programmes *The Billy Cotton Band Show* and *The Black and White Minstrel Show*. The progress of the BBC's Scottish television development plan was dependent upon the allocation of funds by London. These funds were in turn dependent upon the ability of the Corporation to secure adequate increases in the licence fee.

In October 1964, the BBC had requested an increase from £4 to £6 for combined licences, and from £1 to £1 5s for sound-only licences. However, the government increased the combined licence to £5 and the sound-only licence to £1 5s, and only from 1 August 1965. This placed some constraints on the expansion of programme output. Total television programme output produced in Scotland for both viewers in Scotland and for the network, which had increased significantly from 339 hours (1963–4)[7] to 481 hours (1964–5),[8] increased at a more moderate rate for the following two years and stabilised from 1967 to 1969 at over 500 hours each year. Within these totals, the decline in contributions to the network in and after 1965–6 was compensated for by the increase in television programme hours produced by the BBC in Scotland for viewers in Scotland. For example, although contributions from Scotland to the network declined each year from 122 hours (1964–5) to 80 hours (1967–8), television programme output for viewers only in Scotland increased from 359 hours (1964–5) to 444 hours (1967–8). The bulk of the television programme output in Scotland consisted of programmes taken by Scotland from the network and the other Regions. During 1963–4, for example, within the total programme output of 3,675 hours, 3,336 hours of programmes were taken by Scotland from the network and only 339 hours were produced in Scotland, of which 62 hours were for the network and 277 hours were for viewers in Scotland. In the mid-1960s, the BBC as a whole had to curtail expansion, as indicated in the White Paper of December 1966.[9] This shortfall in income to meet rapid expansion led to a two-year standstill in television development in Scotland, which represented Scotland's contribution to the BBC's overall financial cutbacks. The television development plan for Scotland did not resume until the autumn of 1969 when financial resources again became available to continue with the programme of development.

The issue of the availability of financial resources raises some important points about BBC financial policy and resources in Scotland. Scotland was allocated an annual budget which could be spent at the discretion of the Scottish Controller and his senior staff. Overspending on any individual programme or series of programmes normally had to be compensated for by altering the allocation of resources to other projects. Some BBC Regions generated a surplus of income whereas others, such as Scotland, tended consistently to operate at a deficit. The surplus of income in some Regions was used to meet deficits in other Regions. If the BBC in Scotland had received funding in direct proportion to the number of licence-payers in Scotland, then on this basis Scotland would have received much less income than it did receive. So the BBC argued that, on a per capita basis, Scotland received proportionally more money than the English Regions, although programme resources were more thinly spread compared to London. No BBC Region could consistently support the complete service of television and Home, Light and Third Programmes it received out of the income arising from within each Region. The BBC therefore expected each Region to meet the expenditure on its own programme service and to contribute towards shared services in accordance with its capacity to pay which was determined by licence income. This contribution towards shared services in television (i.e. access to network programmes) was consistently greater than actual television operating expenditure in Scotland. Moreover, the contribution towards shared services was also invariably much greater than any financial credit obtained by Scotland from programmes contributed by Scotland to the network where costs in such cases would be borne by London. So, with the large amount designated as Scotland's share of television network programmes and central costs, and with few Scottish-originated programmes produced by Scotland and hence taken by the network, Scotland remained on paper with a financial deficit each year. For example, as at 31 March 1962, the BBC in Scotland had a deficit of £672,000 because the total income generated of £3,439,000 was less than the total expenditure of £4,111,000 which represented the total of radio (£1,571,000) and television (£2,161,000) operating expenditure (£3,732,000) as well as capital expenditure (£379,000) in Scotland. However, given that the surplus in some Regions was used to offset the deficit in others, the overall surplus of £1,776,000 in England helped to offset the deficit in other Regions, and so the BBC deficit as at 31 March 1962 was £83,000. From 1962-3 onwards, the BBC Scotland deficit began to increase at an accelerated level. This deficit, which had previously remained at over £600,000 for about four years, rose to over £1 million as at 31 March 1963.[10] This was mainly attributable initially to the increase in television expenditure in Scotland and latterly by increases in capital expenditure due to the opening of new studios and the extension of the transmitter network. The BBC centrally, however, subsidised the cost of extending BBC services to remote and scattered communities in Scotland. The greater deficit as at the end of March 1963 was not unique to Scotland because the overall BBC deficit increased significantly, mainly because of the conversion of the surplus in England into a deficit primarily caused by preparations for BBC2. The increase in operating expenditure due to the arrival of BBC2 was followed by a significant increase in capital expenditure when BBC2 was extended outwith London and the Corporation sought to extend the UHF transmitter network which carried the BBC2 programmes. In Scotland, the much greater deficit evident during 1962–3 continued to increase until 1965–6, when it was again reduced to over £600,000 for two years. During 1967–8, the Scottish deficit again increased appreciably because of significant increases in both television operating and capital expenditure, whereas radio expenditure remained at a more constant level. Expenditure on television in Scotland first exceeded that of radio expenditure during 1962–3 if no allowance is made for Scotland's share of network and central costs. The gap between television and radio expenditure in Scotland widened thereafter, reflecting the much higher cost of television programmes rather than the volume of television output as measured by hours of television broadcasting.

The BBC is a large and complex organisation whose staff and programme activities have increased significantly in the postwar period. With the expansion of television, the BBC's overall costs increased considerably because television was a more costly medium than radio. Competition from ITV also served to increase costs, yet the BBC, unlike ITV, could not increase its charges to compensate for increased expenditure. This was less of a problem when income from increased sales of licences was able to cover costs, but it became a problem when, during periods of expansion, licence fees were not increased sufficiently frequently and at realistic levels to cover such costs. During the 1960s, the BBC as a whole experienced a period of rapid expansion because of a variety of factors: the introduction of BBC2; the extension of UHF television coverage which required the provision of many relay stations; colour television; the extension of VHF radio coverage; increases in broadcasting hours; the changeover to a new line standard in television; the reorganisation of the radio networks; and the introduction of local radio. The effects of increased costs during this period would have been more severe if there had not been a steadily increasing yield of income from broadcasting licences combined with improved methods to detect licence evasion. The expansion in programme services was reflected in organsational changes within Scotland. By 1960, the total number of programme services staff based at Glasgow was 260, almost exactly four times the number of programme staff based at Edinburgh;[11] there were also 117 engineering staff.

In the early 1960s, programme staff in Glasgow began to be grouped into distinct departments covering subject areas such as Music, News, Current Affairs, Religion, Drama, Light Entertainment, and Sport and Outside Broadcasts. A film unit was also formed, staffed by a Producer (later designated

Manager, Films), Film Editors and Film Cameramen. With the advent of Gaelic television programmes in March 1962, a Television Production Assistant for Gaelic joined Production Assistants in other areas. With the division of programme services into more clearly-defined subject areas, the number of specialist staff in some areas such a News and Current Affairs became evident. News staff now comprised as News Editor (James Kemp), News Assistants and an Industrial Correspondent. By the mid-1960s, News and Current Affairs was staffed by a Scottish Editor, an Assistant Scottish Editor, a Chief News Assistant, Senior News Assistants, News Assistants, an Industrial Correspondent and a Current Affairs Producer. Gaelic radio programmes were provided by Fred MacAulay (Senior Gaelic Producer) and two Gaelic Producers; from the mid-1970s, one Producer specialised in radio, the other in television. In Music, BBC Scotland had the services of James Loughran as Conductor of the BBC Scottish Symphony Orchestra (previously known as the BBC Scottish Orchestra) and Ian Sutherland as Conductor of the Scottish Radio Orchestra (previously known as the BBC Scottish Variety Orchestra). In Drama, there were Producers covering both radio (Stewart Conn) and television (Pharic MacLaren), and in Light Entertainment there was a Senior Television Producer. In 1966, the total number of programme staff at Glasgow had reached 481, with an additional 168 attached to Engineering Division. [12] At that time, there were approximately seventy programme staff at Edinburgh, with a further fourteen attached to the Engineering Division. The organisational structure at Edinburgh was less complex in comparison with the BBC's headquarters in Glasgow. Also, Edinburgh specialised more in radio than in television broadcasting. It was also the base of the Clerk to the Broadcasting Council for Scotland and the Secretary of the School Broadcasting Council for Scotland. During the 1950s, an Administrative Assistant and the Publicity Officer (Scotland) were based in Edinburgh, but in the early 1960s the post of Chief Assistant (Edinburgh) was created, although this post lapsed on 1 September 1970 when it was replaced by a Manager in charge of the BBC's Edinburgh operation. The BBC in Scotland also had the services of a Head of Administration from October 1963 (which replaced the post of Administrative Officer (Scotland) and was based in Glasgow). The two posts of Assistant Head of Programmes for radio and for television were replaced in the 1960s by those of Chief Assistant (Edinburgh), held by Aidan Thomson, and Chief Assistant (Planning and Programme Services), held by G.D. Runcie. These changes left just one Assistant Head of Programmes who was based in Glasgow, rather than two posts split between Edinburgh and Glasgow. The production staff at Aberdeen remained under the control of the Aberdeen Representative until 1 September 1970 when this post lapsed and was replaced by that of Senior Producer, the position being filled by Pat Chalmers.

The most significant expansion of staff numbers in the BBC coincided with the introduction of a second television service in April 1964. Even before the arrival of commercial television in 1955, the BBC, in the face of potential competition, had argued that its obligations to the viewing public could only be fulfilled if it operated a second television channel. In a paper written as early as August 1953, the Director-General stated that 'Our intention of starting an alternative Programme must be realised as quickly as possible so as to ease the burden thrown on the Service by having to satisfy the Corporation's obligations within so small an output'.[13] This view was endorsed by the Board of Governors. When commercial television did arrive, the BBC indicated that a second television channel was necessary to enable the Corporation to fulfil the requirements of the Charter to inform, to educate and to entertain the public. In January 1955, the questions of programme hours, facilities and transmitter development for a second television channel were discussed by the Board of Management.[14] In July 1955, the BBC made an application to the Postmaster-General for the use of frequencies in band III for a second service. The BBC hoped that if approval for a second channel was given, then transmissions could begin in October 1957. The ITA was however allocated frequencies in band III for the ITV service. The BBC then.argued that competition from ITV would narrow rather than widen programme choice, hence the need for a second BBC television channel to provide complementary planned schedules.[15] In order to cater for a wide variety of tastes and so develop a full public service operation, the BBC had extended its sound broadcasting services; this principle was now equally applied to television broadcasting and formed the basis for the BBC's contention that it should operate two television channels.

In a pamphlet published in 1958, Sir Arthur fforde, BBC Chairman, argued that a third UK television channel should be allocated to the BBC rather than to ITV because only the BBC could raise the proportion of 'serious' programmes within peak viewing hours.[16] In a published article later that year, Sir Ian Jacob, BBC Director-General, stated that the BBC needed a second channel to enable it to perform its public service obligations, and this included the provision of a balanced yet diverse range of programmes.[17] In March of the following year, the PMG stated that no third television channel would be authorised until the Television Advisory Committee had decided on the line standard to be used (i.e. 405 or 625 lines). In August 1960, the BBC submitted a paper to the Pilkington Committee in which it emphasised that a second BBC television channel would provide a greater outlet for Regional programme material. The ITA was, however, in consultation with the PMG about the allocation of the third television network. The ITA's view was that the existing single channel made it impossible for the Authority to stimulate competition within ITV given the absence of more than one programme company in each area. This, together with the development of networking in ITV, had reduced competition within the system and lowered the volume of Regional programme output. The ITA was therefore arguing that if the third television channel was allocated to ITV, then it would be able to appoint more programme companies and so overcome these obstacles, which had not been fully envisaged in the Television Act of 1954. At the very least, the ITA believed that any new television service should be independent of the existing two networks, rather than two services being under the control of any single broadcasting organisation. The ITA stated that it would even prefer the third service to be run by a single, separate, state-financed corporation than operated by the BBC or by a programme company already providing programmes.[18] But the Pilkington Report, which was published in June 1962, recommended that an additional television channel should be authorised and be allocated to the BBC. The White Paper of July 1962 stated that the government proposed to authorise the BBC to start an additional television channel on 625 lines in UHF.[19]

The decision by the government to opt for a change in the line definition standard from 405 to 625 lines using ultra-high frequencies in fact followed the recommendation which had been made by the Television Advisory Committee in May 1960. The use of UHF on 625 lines (bands IV and V), approved by the PMG in July 1963 to carry BBC2 programmes, offered the prospect of better picture quality, particularly at a time when consideration was being given to introducing a colour television service on the third television network and an increase in the size of the screen in television receivers. However, these changes did require a wider frequency channel (i.e. eight megacycles on UHF as opposed to five Mc/s with VHF), and so fewer television services were possible. It also required the building of many relay transmitters because UHF covered a more limited transmission area than VHF, hence there was likely to be a greater delay in extending coverage in Scotland given the topography of the country. It was not possible to avoid having to place UHF stations closer together than VHF stations by using larger transmitting and receiving aerials or by using more powerful transmitters. UHF transmissions were also more easily impeded by obstacles because, unlike VHF signals, they tended to travel in straight lines rather than follow ground contours, hence the need for more transmitters and careful siting of those which were built. Also, many UHF transmitters were designed for unattended operation, and so the additional equipment required for this, together with the greater number of transmitters used, therefore increased capital costs. Nevertheless, there were advantages in using UHF because, apart from better picture quality due to a reduction in the visibility of the scanning lines, there were also fewer ghost images on the screen because of the use of more highly directional aerials, and there was no need to use standard converters which degraded picture quality when moving from 405 lines to a higher line standard. The BBC used the first line converter in 1963, which was subsequently used to convert programmes made on 625 lines to the BBC1 405-line standard. The latter process did not degrade picture quality because the conversion took place from a higher to a lower line standard. It can also be noted that the BBC's 405-line VHF transmissions in band I had in any case been subject to interference in some parts of Scotland and in various other areas throughout the country because of the 'Sporadic E' effect. This name was used to denote the drifting clouds of ionised gases formed in the upper atmosphere by solar radiation, which tended during the summer months to reflect television signals from continental stations which shared the same channels as the UK. This interference would have been more unacceptable if colour rather than monochrome signals had been transmitted on 405 lines VHF as opposed to 625 lines UHF.

A change in linage offered the prospect of relieving the radio industry from having to produce 405-line receivers capable of being adapted to 625 lines, as they had been doing since 1961, as well as assisting manufacturers to compete in overseas markets. Few 405-line sets were manufactured after 1964, when BBC2 was transmitted on 625 lines; dual standard 405/625-line sets continued to be produced until 1975, when they were also phased out. Given that there were advantages in using the higher line standard, the main question which had to be answered was how the changeover should take place. The two main possibilities were the duplication method and the switchover method. The duplication method involved duplicating existing programmes on 625 lines and then transmitting them in UHF simultaneously with VHF 405 lines. The VHF 405-line services would thus not cease in any area until UHF coverage was complete. In contrast to this, the switchover method would require equipment capable of 625-line operation to be installed nationwide, with 405-line transmissions ceasing on an appointed day. This method was likely to pose problems, not least because all viewers might not have purchased new receivers or had old sets converted in time, there would have been a sudden loss of sales of old receivers prior to the switchover date, and viewers would be forced to replace 405-line sets before their useful life had expired. The duplication method had several advantages: it permitted viewers to receive 625-line services much sooner; it permitted ongoing experiments in the range and coverage of UHF transmissions; and it ensured a steady level of sales and replacement of old receivers during the changeover period. Taking all these factors into account, the Television Advisory Committee and the Pilkington Committee of Inquiry recommended the use of the duplication method for existing BBC1 and ITV services. Apart from these technical issues, the main factor which appeared to be of concern to Scotland during the early 1960s was the timing of the introduction of the BBC's second television service.

There was some concern in Scotland as to whether the decision to start a new channel should take priority over extending coverage of the existing BBC channel. The PMG had however consistently refused to agree to hold back the sanctioning of a third channel until all viewers in the Highlands, the Islands and in parts of the Borders received at least one television channel. In September 1962, the Broadcasting Council for Scotland noted that BBC2 might start in London in spring 1964, although Scottish transmitter development already sanctioned would not be completed until much later. The Council argued that this conflicted with its stated view that those people with no television service should receive one before other people were provided with a choice of three television channels.[20] By 1962, television was available to ninety-five per cent and VHF radio to ninety-three per cent of the population of Scotland. This   ·

masked special problems, such as viewers in South-West Scotland who received their programmes from the BBC's North Region via the Sandale transmitter or from Northern Ireland via the Divis transmitter and so were unable to receive BBC Scotland. The Islands wished to receive a service before viewers on the mainland received alternative television services. It should also be noted that the use of UK statistics on broadcasting coverage often tended to mask problems experienced in the Highlands and Islands, where most of the few per cent of the population who could not receive television services lived. In a discussion with Sir Harold Bishop (BBC Director of Engineering), the BCS questioned whether the Corporation as a public service body was failing in its duty to isolated and homogeneous communities.[21] The BCS hoped that the new television studio in Glasgow, which was to be equipped for 625 lines to supply programmes on video tape for London, would not unduly interfere with the provision of programmes on the existing channel for viewers in Scotland. At a meeting in June 1962, the Council also hoped that a senior member of the Scottish staff would be included on the planning committee for BBC2. Moreover, there was also the question as to whether it would be possible or indeed fair to repeat on BBC1 in Scotland programmes which had been recorded in Scotland for BBC2. In other words, was it proper to agree that the location of a studio determined which parts of the country should be given the opportunity to see programmes originated in it, given that this principle might apply to all Regions, at least until coverage of BBC2 was extended throughout the country? It could be argued that a second channel was likely to provide more opportunities for opt-out programmes and for contributions towards network programmes, but for technical reasons BBC2 was initially unlikely to draw much on Regional material because studios and equipment had to be converted for 625-line operation. Scottish opt-outs were dependent upon finance and technical resources, and this was likely to be a longer-term prospect than direct contributions from Scotland to BBC2.

The presence of a second channel was deemed to be likely to offer an opportunity to overcome existing obstacles which prevented a fragmentation of the BBC1 network between 7.00 and 10.00pm. Programme planners in London were believed by BBC Scotland to be resistant to allowing Scotland to schedule its own programmes at more suitable times (i.e. during the early evening, and at regular time-slots). The BCS commented upon central planning staff by stating that London 'looked inward rather than outward and appeared to think it knew best and resisted the Council's attempts at effective representation of Scottish interests at effective times'.[22] The Director-General, Hugh Greene, reaffirmed that in cases of disagreement between Scotland and London programme planners, matters could be referred to him, although any disagreement had to be settled before *Radio Times* programme listings were sent to the printers. Greene was more inclined to believe that the BCS should give as much thought to Scotland's representation on the network as to opt-out programmes. In the last Annual Report to be published before the start of BBC2, the BCS regretted that the decision to introduce the new channel had taken priority over the aim of improving broadcasting coverage in Scotland to ensure that almost everyone had the opportunity of access to one television service:

> The Council has repeatedly stated its conviction that the people in the remoter places should have one dependable service before the people in the populous parts of the country are offered a third television service. Much as it welcomed the Government's decision that the BBC should start a second television service in 1964, it cannot but regret the order of priority.[23]

The BBC did not wish to delay the start of a second channel until it achieved almost complete coverage of BBC1, because the costs of providing a service to remote areas increased significantly as gaps in coverage were filled.

By the autumn of 1963, Hugh Greene had stated that the target date for the opening of the new channel would be 20 April 1964. Until national coverage of the new channel could be achieved, BBC1 was expected to continue for a few years to present a balanced programme output for viewers who could only receive the one channel. It was intended that BBC1 and BBC2 would be planned together to provide a genuine choice of programmes, in contrast to the programme similarities which had developed because of competition between the BBC and ITV. The new channel was not expected to capture a large audience, given that its remit would include the provision of programmes for minority interests and more Regional material. Neither was it to be an educational channel to the exclusion of information and entertainment, since this would not have a broad appeal. It was expected to be distinguishable from BBC1 in terms of faces, styles and formats. Transmissions were expected to start in London and the South-East in the peak viewing hours and so be immediately available to upwards of ten million viewers. The BBC's plan for the extension of BBC2 throughout the country was that the new service should be introduced quickly and to a restricted audience rather than slowly and to a larger audience. The BBC's Director of Engineering told the Broadcasting Council for Scotland in 1962 that a master plan covering the whole of the UK would be prepared and the high-power stations covering the most populated areas would be built first.[24] The Corporation planned a promotion campaign on a Regional basis and timed to coincide with the extension of BBC2 to new areas. The BBC had no desire, for example, for Aberdeen to be subjected to such promotional material well in advance of the arrival of a transmitter. Also, the BCS appeared to be concerned that difficulties might arise if viewers in Scotland had to pay a higher licence fee before the new service reached them. In a BBC Lunchtime Lecture delivered four months prior to the start of BBC2, Stuart Hood, Controller of Programmes (Television), stated that 'our basic endeavour must be to give viewers, during the hours of maximum audience availability, the widest possible choice we can devise within the limits of our money and resources'.[25] Competition between the BBC and ITV for a share of the audience, especially during peak viewing hours, had for some time been held to be responsible for diminishing effective programme choice. Now BBC2 was expected to provide such a choice because the new channel was not envisaged as likely to be in direct competition with ITV.

The BBC outlined in its Annual Report for 1962–3 the general programme policy for the new channel, how it would integrate with the existing BBC television channel, and how this in turn would govern the relationship between both BBC channels and the single commercial channel. The BBC stated:

> The aim when the second BBC television service opens will be to try to provide the public with alternative programmes of quality and interest and the widest possible range of choice, as recommended by the Committee on Broadcasting. This will not mean that the BBC will compete with independent television in the sense of trying to pit two BBC programmes against a single commercial programme simply in an effort to attract viewers; but it will mean competition with independent television in the broad sense of trying to take advantage of the new freedom of two channels in order to put better television on both.[26]

The BBC's attempt to draw the distinction between healthy competition (i.e. the provision of better-quality programmes on two BBC networks) and unhealthy competition (i.e. competition with ITV for greater audiences) had yet to be put to the test. Also, the Corporation did not state precisely how BBC1 and BBC2 programmes would differ from each other, and whether it was intended for quality productions and Scottish Regional material to find a natural home on BBC2, thereby leaving BBC1 as the main competitor to ITV. Indeed, a memo from Michael Peacock (Chief of Programmes, BBC2) to Stuart Hood (Controller Programmes, Television), written two weeks before the start of BBC2, indicated uncertainty as to the relationship between the Regions and the new channel in terms of both network contributions and opt-out programmes.[27] Discussions had by then proceeded with Regional programme heads and Regional engineers about the interchange of production and engineering staff. Also, it had already been decided by the planning committee that on BBC2 each evening, one item would be treated in depth and that other programmes, such as Regional material, would be built around these items. It was an attempt to give the new channel a distinctive character. To prepare for the advent of the new service, the BBC re-equipped studios to operate on 625 lines, planned the sites for new UHF transmitters, recruited and trained additional production and technical staff (68 extra production staff, 154 engineers, 176 technical assistants and 189 technical operators) and created four output groups to supply programme material to both networks. These output groups consisted of current affairs, drama, light entertainment and outside broadcasts. Overall, the introduction of the new channel resulted in growth and increased complexity for the BBC. Test transmissions for BBC2 began on 4 January 1964 from Crystal Palace in London in order to assist the radio trade in the installation of new receivers prior to the official opening of the service. From March 1964, the BBC produced all its programmes on the 625-line standard, with BBC1 programmes being converted down to 405 lines using a standards converter.

On 20 April 1964, BBC2 began transmissions from Crystal Palace to the London area on 625 lines UHF, two years after the planning of the network had begun. One million people were equipped with television sets capable of receiving BBC2, but unfortunately on the opening night a power failure at Battersea power station, which supplied electricity to the transmitters, blacked out Television Centre. A smaller proportion of viewers were equipped to receive BBC2 on its opening night in comparison with the first day of ITV transmissions over eight years earlier. Indeed, the BBC's second channel became technically within reach of a larger percentage of the population than those people who were willing to equip themselves with receivers to obtain the new channel. The government's agreement that the additional service should be provided by the BBC was not, though, accompanied by any increase in the licence fee to help cover the costs of the new service. However, it might have been unfair for an additional charge to be imposed on all licence-holders when initially only a minority of viewers could receive BBC2. Manufacturers of receivers were understandably anxious for the new service to be extended throughout the country as quickly as resources would permit. BBC2 was expected to develop into a national network within five years, although there would remain persistent pockets of poor reception in remote areas shielded by hills, particularly in Scotland, until many relay stations could be built. As regards programme policy, given that BBC2 would not need to be tied to the same schedules as BBC1, differentially timed programmes could be catered for. However, within a short period of time, viewing figures were found to be disappointing, and so corrective action was required prior to the launch of the 1964 autumn programme schedules.[28]

By September 1964, the BBC had accepted the need to introduce changes in programme planning to take effect in the winter programme schedules for 1964–5. The original BBC2 programme policy, which was devised in 1962 and was known as 'seven faces of the week', had offered viewers a different category of programme material each evening: light entertainment on Mondays, education on Tuesdays, repeats on Wednesdays, minority interest programmes on Thursdays, drama on Fridays, serials and documentaries on Saturdays, and plays, films and opera on Sundays. This policy gave BBC2 a distinctiveness, but it complicated any attempt to make the channel complementary to the programme material available on BBC1, given that the aim was to avoid contrasting programmes, for example by deliberately scheduling a serious programme on BBC2 against lighter programme material on BBC1. It also segregated viewers to such an extent each evening that it lost audiences to the other channels. During some evenings, viewers understandably often found very few items which were of interest to them. The BBC wanted them to watch on all nights of the week, not just on some nights, and so the 'seven faces' policy was transformed into a 'seven days' policy. It also appeared that the channel had acquired a highbrow image to such an extent that viewers tended to remain with the existing networks which broadcast familiar programmes in familiar time-slots. The abandonment of the 'seven faces' planning principle avoided clashes of programme material on both BBC channels, and this facilitated the introduction of common programme junctions (i.e. common starting times for programmes). Continuity announcers could thus state which programmes were about to be broadcast on the opposite channel. The use of complementary planning enabled a mix of minority and majority interest programmes to be broadcast on BBC2 on any evening during the week. This achieved both horizontal scheduling (i.e. programmes complementary to those on BBC1) and vertical scheduling (i.e. a balance of programme material on BBC2 each evening). It also incidentally resulted in BBC2 gaining a higher proportion of its viewers from BBC1 than from ITV, and so the BBC:ITV share of the audience remained 50:50 rather than reaching an expected 66:34. The change in policy also sought to remove the impression that BBC2 was the television equivalent to the Third Programme on radio and thus designed only to cater for more cultural, specialised and by definition minority audiences. David Attenborough (Controller, BBC2) stated in 1966 that it would have been wrong for BBC1 to concentrate primarily on light entertainment programmes and leave all the highbrow material to the second channel, because many viewers, such as those in Scotland, could not yet receive BBC2.[29] The public, however, continued to view BBC2 selectively, although it should be noted that the so-called minority interest programmes were sometimes viewed by millions of people and could reach a wider audience if they were re-broadcast on BBC1. A point worth noting about the small audiences for BBC2 was that this channel was for many years only available to a small percentage of the population, it was broadcast for fewer hours each day, and it started transmissions later in the day than BBC1.

BBC2 programmes were initially expected to reach Scotland on 12 December 1965 from the Blackhill transmitter. However, with delays in the construction of masts and aerials caused by bad weather, it was not until June 1966 that the BBC began test transmissions from the transmitter. Regular transmissions began on 9 July 1966, and programmes began at 7.00pm when David Attenborough introduced BBC2 to Scotland.[30] Production facilities in Scotland for contributing material to BBC2 had been in service since 17 February 1964, when Studio A in Glasgow was opened. This was the first Regional studio to be equipped for dual standard operation (i.e. 405 and 625 lines). In the absence of a programme link to carry the 625-line signals from Glasgow to London, programmes had to be recorded on tape and sent to London. Now, just over two years later in July 1966, BBC2 programmes became available in central Scotland; the service was extended to the Aberdeenshire area with the opening of the Durris transmitter on 29 July 1967. Blackhill and Durris began transmitting BBC2 colour programmes on 30 October 1967. The Glasgow studio continued to specialise in the production of drama serials for BBC2 until the late 1960s, by which time the network had moved into colour production and the Glasgow studio could no longer supply programme material until it was converted for colour operation, which took place by 1972.

The background to the introduction of colour television on BBC2 in July 1967 has a long history which involved the interplay of technical, economic and political factors. In May 1953, the Television Advisory Committee recommended that any colour television system should be compatible, in that colour transmissions should be capable of being received on monochrome sets. In the following year, the Postmaster-General asked the TAC specifically to consider the issue of colour television.[31] From October 1955, the BBC began to work on an adaptation (using 405 lines) of the American National Television Systems Committee (NTSC) system. These initial series of tests took place in cooperation with the Post Office and the radio industry outwith normal television transmission hours. The aim of the tests was to promote receiver development, to test colour television equipment, to check the compatibility of the system and to review any problems arising in the transmission and reception of colour signals. The BBC was anxious to start a limited colour service on 405 lines, even though a higher line standard was more likely to be suitable for producing colour images on receivers. However, in May 1960, the TAC recommended that colour television should only be introduced on the line standard which would eventually be adopted for monochrome transmissions.[32] A decision therefore had to be reached on line standards before any decision could be made about the introduction of colour. Given that, as already indicated, the TAC believed that television should be transmitted on 625 lines in bands IV and V, the implication was that any colour system should only be introduced on this line standard. On 9 December 1960, the BBC sought the approval of the PMG to introduce a limited experimental colour service of studio programmes and films from November 1961, but this request was turned down. The PMG indicated in the House of Commons that the arguments of the TAC against the introduction of such a service were convincing.[33] The PMG was unwilling to make any decision until the Pilkington Committee had completed its examination of broadcasting. In February 1961, the BBC submitted a memorandum on colour television to this committee arguing that any delay in authorising the start of colour television pending an ultimate decision on line standards would be detrimental to the development of colour television in Britain and to Britain's export opportunities.[34] On 13 April 1961, the BBC made further representations to the PMG on this issue, but on 10 May the PMG again rejected the BBC's request to start a limited colour service on the existing 405-line standard. The PMG believed that it would be both unwise and unfair to the public to encourage the sale of colour sets on the lower line standard, and that there was no export market for colour sets on 405 lines that might benefit British manufacturers. Also, a dual-standard set that could receive programmes in colour would have been unnecessarily complicated. The Pilkington Report, published in June 1962, in fact recommended that only a compatible 625-line colour system should be considered.

With a decision reached on the type of transmission to be used for colour television, attention was switched to a consideration of the type of colour systems which could be adopted. During 1963, the BBC began field tests to assess critically the French SECAM colour system and compare it with the American NTSC system. A variant of the American system developed by the German Telefunken Company and known as phase alternation line (PAL) was also being developed. All three systems had ninety-five per cent of their parts in common; the differences were located in the coding, decoding and transmission of signals. The PAL and SECAM systems contained simpler electronics than NTSC at the transmitting end, but more complicated circuitry in the television receivers. For example, unlike the American system, SECAM transmitted colour signals during alternative lines rather than simultaneously, and so receivers using the French system had to include a means of storing the colour signals for the duration of one line. The PAL system had the advantage that it was European and compatible with the American system and so could act as a compromise choice. The PAL signal was less subject to distortion than the NTSC signal, the PAL receivers were only four per cent more expensive than NTSC receivers. So, by late 1965, the choice of a common colour system for Europe in effect involved a choice between PAL and SECAM. Subsequent improvements in the PAL system, involving the elimination – by averaging out the colour errors between lines – of errors in hue caused by reflected signals in mountainous country, tended to bring it more in favour with British engineers in the British Radio Equipment Manufacturers' Association (BREMA). Nothing was regarded as likely to irritate viewers more than unnatural shades of colour. So, taking all these factors into account, on 3 March 1966 the government granted permission for the introduction of colour on BBC2 at 625 lines UHF using the PAL system. In 1967, the government authorised the BBC and ITA to proceed with establishing a UHF transmitter network to duplicate 405-line services, and to introduce colour in these services in accordance with what the Television Advisory Committee had recommended in its 1967 report.[35]

On 1 July 1967, the BBC introduced an experimental colour television service on BBC2, the first colour service in Europe. This launching period gave an opportunity to engineering and production staff to assess colour television, and it also offered retailers an opportunity to demonstrate colour sets to potential customers. The original starting date was intended to be late 1967, but the Television Service pressed for an earlier start in order to make use of the outside broadcast unit at summer sporting events such as Wimbledon. This colour service, which was not available in Scotland, was limited to about five hours a week. As noted earlier, colour programmes on BBC2 became available in parts of Scotland on 30 October 1967. The full colour service began on 2 December, accompanied by an increase in colour transmissions to over thirty hours a week. This increase persuaded a small but growing number of people to purchase or to rent colour sets, and gave producers more regular experience of working with colour. Colour television was regarded as natural television, but it was also costlier. For the BBC, there were additional costs such as colour cameras, more powerful lighting, better air conditioning to cope with the heat generated by more powerful studio lights, larger technical areas within studios, and more staff to operate colour equipment. For the public, there were additional costs involved in renting or purchasing colour receivers. The use of transistors in television sets did in time assist in reducing costs and the size and power consumption of sets as well as in improving reliability. When the colour service did arrive, objects on the screen often appeared unusually brighter than they would appear in the real world, partly because of problems with colour tuning, and partly because, unlike the real world, images were concentrated in a small area on the television screen. The addition of colour enhanced and enriched the visual image for those viewers with colour sets. Plans proceeded for the introduction of colour on all three networks, but this provoked criticism because some viewers in Scotland could only receive one channel, and only in black-and-white. Edward Short (PMG) dismissed any idea of suspending plans to extend colour services until all viewers in Scotland had access to equivalent services. He stated that 'It would be wrong to deny the vast majority of viewers the opportunity to see colour television because a relatively small number of people are not within reach ˚of either service'.[36] For those people in Scotland who were able to receive BBC2, the programmes available were wide-ranging. Programmes included *The Forsyte Saga* (a twenty-six part drama serial later shown on BBC1), *The Virginian* (a very popular 'western' imported from America), *Wheelbase* (a motoring programme), *Chronicle* (a monthly programme on archaeology and history), *Horizon* (science), *Jazz 625* (jazz music), *The Money Programme* (business and finance), *Theatre 625* (drama), *Late Night Line-Up* (arts and discussion programme), and a number of notable co-productions which from the late 1960s to the early 1970s included Sir Kenneth Clark's *Civilisation*, Alistair Cooke's *America* and Dr Jacob Bronowski's *The Ascent of Man*. Many of these programmes did much to establish the reputation of BBC2 in Scotland. Scotland also produced drama series for BBC2, such as *This Man Craig* (featuring John Cairney, and based on a comprehensive school), which was later shown on BBC1. Other programmes produced in Scotland were not designed to be taken by the network, and these programmes included *'Se Ur Beatha* (Gaelic songs), *Lobby Talk* (on parliamentary matters affecting Scotland), and a number of comedy programmes and outside broadcasts. Scottish light entertainment programmes featured artists such as Stanley Baxter, Andy Stewart, Moira Anderson, Rikki Fulton and Jimmy Logan. Outside broadcasts were taken from events ranging from the Edinburgh International Festival through to coverage of sporting events. By the late 1960s, many viewers in Scotland were therefore able to benefit from a wide range of programmes on three networks and from the associated technical developments which had come to fruition by that time.

Localised broadcasting and the influence of offshore pirate radio on BBC programme policy, 1962–7

BBC radio began in the 1920s on a local basis because the transmitters which were used (i.e. low-power medium-wave) had limited geograpical coverage. With the advent of high-power transmitters capable of extending broadcasting coverage on a simultaneous basis quickly throughout the country, the BBC began to close down its local stations and introduce a Regional Scheme in 1929. Scotland was to be designated as one of these BBC Regions. The new high-power stations soon began to provide both a national broadcasting service and a Regional broadcasting service in Scotland. It was only in the 1950s that the development of VHF made it possible realistically to consider opening genuine local stations catering for identifiable community interests and distinguishable from Regional or area broadcasting services. Local radio therefore existed before there was a network, and this can be contrasted with television, whose development was planned as a network operation in the absence of existing local stations. This chapter begins by focusing on the background to the BBC's plans for operating local radio services. It covers the period from the closed-circuit local radio experiments in the early 1960s through to the establishment of BBC local radio stations in 1967, and how these developments can be viewed in relation to the provision of existing radio broadcasting services in Scotland. This revival of local broadcasting was also matched by changes taking place in network broadcasting, which also influenced the conduct of broadcasting services in Scotland. The arrival in 1964 of offshore pirate radio stations, one of which was later located off the Scottish coast, prompted the BBC to examine critically the nature of its network services. Pirate radio was outlawed in August 1967, to be followed a month later by the restructuring of the BBC radio networks. The significance of all these developments for broadcasting in Scotland will be considered in the period up until 1967, when important changes in both local and network radio took place.

During the 1950s, radio suffered to a certain extent from the increasing popularity of television, but radio was soon to benefit from technical developments such as VHF, which improved broadcasting coverage and made localised broadcasting a possibility. The widespread use of transistors, which were more reliable than valve sets, were portable and had a low power consumption as well as being relatively cheap to purchase, all helped to sustain an interest in radio.

Those who worked in radio did not wish this medium to become the poor relation of television. Radio was in any case still popular with a large number of listeners. That popularity was likely to be enhanced if the possibility of local radio became a reality. In February 1955, Frank Gillard (Controller, West Region) prepared an interesting paper on how Regional broadcasting might be extended and developed to cater for more local cultures. He stated that Regions were most effective and popular as sources of information (i.e. news, talks, outside broadcasts and features) rather than as sources of music and entertainment. He argued that listeners would seek out the best entertainment they could find, regardless of place of origin. Gillard's main aim was to press for more localised broadcasting than was possible with the large BBC Regions and so provide what he termed community broadcasting. Taking a cue from Regional broadcasting, he argued that the basis for localised broadcasting would not be entertainment as it had been with the BBC's local stations during the 1920s, but instead would be solidly based on information programmes. VHF would provide the technical means of permitting local broadcasting. Gillard was anxious for the BBC to attempt this in order to pre-empt commercial interests from doing so.

It was not until 1958, after having concentrated resources on improving coverage of national services by using VHF, that the BBC began to think realistically about using VHF for local broadcasting. At that time, VHF was being used to introduce a limited amount of area broadcasting in Scotland, but this was not identical to local radio because the area services opted out from the Scottish Home Service. In January 1960, the Board of Governors decided that the BBC should move experimentally into the field of local broadcasting.[1] The BBC's Director-General agreed to produce a plan for such a limited experiment in local radio. So, by the early 1960s, when the Pilkington Committee was considering the future of broadcasting, the BBC was gathering information about the viability of introducing local stations. There was no evidence of public demand for local radio, but arguably public demand could not be gauged accurately until local radio services were actually provided. The BBC was aware that if it reduced its sound broadcasting services based on evidence of the declining audience for radio, then it would find it progressively more difficult to defend its sound-broadcasting monopoly. The BBC's twin aims for local stations were that they should serve local communities and also enrich the national networks. They were also viewed as a means of decelerating the decline in radio audiences because of television, and of stemming the possible introduction of commercial radio. Local radio, unlike Regional radio or area broadcasting, would be able to serve discrete communities with programmes of local interest, given that the coverage of Regional radio depended upon transmitters which were initially sited to give the best coverage for national broadcasting, and that, unlike area services, local radio would not operate on an opt-out basis from the radio networks. Given that there was a limit to the amount of opting out from the Scottish Home Service that the public thought was desirable, local stations, unlike area services, offered the prospect of an increase in the number of local interest programmes without depriving listeners of access to nationally networked programmes. The justification for opt-outs in radio in any case became less tenable during the evenings, when television offered strong competition to the sound networks.

At the start of the decade in which local radio was introduced, *The Times* noted in the second of a two-part study on the future of broadcasting:

> The ideal of local broadcasting has an obvious appeal. One sees it in a visionary sort of way as a cherished local institution, propagating an intelligent interest in local affairs, watering the roots of local culture, a nursery of local talent, an audible counterpart to the local newspaper. Unfortunately, there is no evidence that it would be accepted by the listening public in this spirit.[2]

These were, however, early days. In any case, the BBC's Assistant Director of Sound Broadcasting, R.D'A. Marriott, recognised that the attractiveness of local radio for listeners might not depend principally on the provision of local information as Frank Gillard was suggesting in a paper written in August 1961, but rather might depend upon the broadcasting of popular music, especially if network radio was used as a benchmark. In a memo to the Director of Sound Broadcasting, he stated:

> I believe that we shall provide a useful service for a minority of listeners who will be attracted by and come to value the local information we provide, but I think our hold on listeners will depend to a large extent on the attractiveness of the music which cements each local broadcasting station's programme.[3]

In its Annual Report for 1959–60, the BBC was anxious to stress the merits of VHF for providing a foundation to develop local broadcasting: 'The Corporation believes that there is great value in the idea of a local service of news and other programmes for self-contained communities, set in the framework of the BBC's national and regional programmes.'[4] At this stage, there was no mention of replacing Regional with local stations. What was envisaged was a tripartite division of radio services. This arrangement was only modified in 1970 with the dismantling of the Regional structure in England.

In May 1960, the BBC approached the government for permission to operate local radio services, but the Postmaster-General told the BBC Chairman that such stations would not be authorised pending the outcome of the Pilkington Inquiry into the future of broadcasting.[5] As noted below, the BBC subsequently resorted to closed-circuit experiments, some of which took place in Scotland. The BBC outlined its plans for local radio services in a memorandum to the Pilkington Committee in February 1961 in which it envisaged the provision of local radio for self-contained identifiable communities to complement network radio. In doing so it took a number of key considerations into account. The BBC's plan involved the building of eighty to ninety stations in a mixture of urban areas, small towns and larger geographical areas where identifiable communities could be found. These local stations were expected to use VHF channels in band II rather than the congested medium waveband, but by doing so the number of potential listeners was initially likely to be limited because of the slow sales of VHF receivers. The BBC began its own series of closed-circuit local radio experiments in thirteen areas, beginning in 1961, in order to ascertain whether a sufficient number of hours of quality programmes could be sustained over a period of time, and also to explore the techniques involved in local radio. The results were recorded on tape and not broadcast to the public, hence it was not possible to ascertain the views of listeners with regard to programme content. It was, though, intended as a means of providing the Pilkington Committee with some information on the practicalities of operating local radio. The first local experiment took place at Bristol on 22 March 1961. Further experiments were conducted in chronological order in the following areas: Portsmouth, Norwich, Hull, Dundee, Poole, the Potteries, Swansea, Wrexham, Durham, London, Dumfries and Reading. Two of these local radio experiments were thus held in Scotland, at Dundee in 1961 with Harry Hogan in charge, and at Dumfries in March 1962 with John Gray; the Scottish experiments lasted one week.

In his address to the Programme Board towards the end of 1961, the Controller of BBC Scotland stated that the Radio Dundee experiment had shown that BBC Scotland had the skills required to operate local broadcasting.[6] The BBC wished to operate local services itself rather than leave this task to commercial competitors. The Dumfries experiment, which lasted from 20 to 23 March 1962, and at which Frank Gillard had attended, provided an opportunity to study the technical and staffing implications of local radio and to see whether the area could provide sufficient material for four hours of local broadcasting each day. What was not considered was the potential grievance likely to develop in rural districts denied access to local stations, given that these stations were likely to be sited initially in urban areas. Frank Gillard, the pioneer of BBC local radio, believed that any scheme of local broadcasting should be prepared to include small towns and rural areas which might serve several communities (i.e. a form of area as well as local broadcasting).[7] Area services operating on an opt-out basis from the networks would provide more local services for rural areas, but unlike local radio stations they would consequently have a smaller output of purely local programme material, probably up to about two hours each day. There were, however, likely to be insufficient funds to cover both area and local broadcasting; local stations were expected to cost from £15,000 to £20,000 to establish, with an additional £30,000 needed for operating costs. Moreover, Regions would have had to assume responsibility for supervising a more complex structure of broadcasting services (i.e. local, area and Regional). The BBC was not in favour of an extensive development of area broadcasting on the lines which Gillard was suggesting. After studying the results of the local radio experiments, the BBC concluded:

> These exercises confirmed the Corporation's belief that a community
> of reasonable size and cohesion would be able to provide sufficient

programme material to sustain as much as four or five hours a day of
local programme output of good quality.[8]
The experiments enabled the BBC to assess to some extent the demands of local
stations on staff, premises, technical equipment and programme costs.

The BBC sought to justify why it should be permitted to operate local radio.
The Corporation stated that, unlike commercial stations, its own stations would
be more financially viable because they could draw upon sustaining material
from the BBC networks. Each station would also be free from control by
commercial interests, such as advertisers and the local press. BBC stations were
expected to conform to the public service standards characteristic of the
network services. Unlike commercial stations, they would not exist as rivals to
local newspapers with regard to advertising revenue, and might even stimulate
greater interest in local events which could then be covered in more detail by
local newspapers. The BBC's public service ethic, its programme and technical
resources, and its commitment to providing a wide range of high-quality
programmes, were contrasted with commercial companies whose profit motive
would lead to an undue emphasis on entertainment and consequently a
narrower range of programme output. The BBC argued that a commercial
service would not be financially viable and, if it were, then it could only be so at
the expense of the quality and variety of programmes produced, or by serving
larger catchment areas than the proposed BBC local stations. The possibility of a
networking arrangement which would circumvent the genuine local character
of stations operating on a commercial basis was one of the negative aspects of
commercial local radio which Hugh Greene, BBC Director-General, emphasised when he stated that 'commercial television, which was supposed to be
decentralised, has become a highly integrated network and the economic
pressures which have brought this about would also tend to operate, at any
rate in the long run, in the field of sound'.[9] However, even BBC local stations
could not be expected to originate all their own programme material, and
so they would have to rely upon network programmes. Indeed, Gillard noted
that 'It is one of the great strengths of the BBC's position that it would not
have to fill every hour of the day with locally originated material on its local
stations'.[10]

The publication of the Pilkington Report in June 1962 appeared to bring the
prospect of BBC local radio that much closer, because the committee recommended that the BBC should be permitted to establish local stations on a trial
basis. The prospect of local radio offered sound broadcasting an opportunity to
expand its role, a role which had been greatly diminished because of television.
But the government decided to defer judgement on the introduction of local
radio stations, much to the disappointment of the BBC.[11] On 18 December
1962, a further White Paper was issued which covered the more contentious
issues which had not been dealt with fully in the previous White Paper. But
the prospects for localised broadcasting were no better. The White Paper
stated:

Further consideration has confirmed the Government in its view that this development should not command a high priority in the allocation of national resources, though it does not discount a possible latent demand for local sound services. It will later review the situation in the light of the other developments in broadcasting dealt with in this and the previous White Paper.[12]

Just over three years later, on 4 March 1966, the BBC published a pamphlet entitled *Local Radio in the Public Interest: the BBC's Plan*.[13] According to this plan, the BBC offered to launch up to nine local radio stations in a pilot scheme without involving any increase in the licence fee, nor relying upon any income from advertising. It was stated that the service provided would not be parochial because it would merely represent one service within a comprehensive and balanced system of broadcasting covering local, Regional, national and international affairs. The purpose of each local station, it was argued, was not to reach the maximum number of listeners, but rather to give the fullest possible service to a community of people holding the maximum number of interests in common. The BBC stated that freedom from detailed central control would be granted to each local station and that a Local Advisory Council would provide the link between each station and the community which it served. The aim was to make listeners regard each station as their own station rather than merely the BBC station in their town. In an article in the BBC *Handbook* for 1967, Frank Gillard, Director of Sound Broadcasting, looked forward to the possibility of government authorisation of local radio and again justified the need for local services:

If in the whole span of newspaper journalism an undisputed place exists for the local unit, so also in the full spectrum of broadcasting there is a real and valuable place for the local radio station. A BBC local system would work alongside the local papers, complementing but not competing, providing at the local level the sort of service which in national life has long since proved its worth and become fully accepted.[14]

On 20 December 1966, the White Paper on Broadcasting gave approval for the BBC to begin a local radio experiment in nine areas on VHF and in cooperation with local interests.[15] There was no authorisation for any extensive local radio development. This experiment was to be reviewed by the PMG after its completion in two years, and then a decision was to be made about the future of local radio. The White Paper ruled out the possibility of any commercial local stations funded by advertising. Each BBC local station would be funded locally, not through the licence fee which the Pilkington Committee had advocated in 1962, and would be provided with a Local Broadcasting Council appointed by the PMG in consultation with the BBC. The purpose of the local radio experiment was to determine whether sufficient financial support would be forthcoming which would justify the extension of local radio to other areas, and whether there was sufficient programme material to sustain a genuine local service. The government stated that the decision to allow the BBC to conduct the local radio experiment did not imply any commitment on behalf of the government that the BBC should eventually provide a permanent local radio service, should one be authorised after the experiment was completed.[16] On 27 January 1967, the BBC held a conference of local authorities which were interested in having local stations in their communities. The BBC subsequently received over twenty applications from local authorities wishing to participate in the local radio experiment. No local authority in Scotland was prepared to provide financial contributions for such a service, although Edinburgh Town Council did express an interest in securing such a station. Stations were selected over a four-month period and were expected to provide a nursery slope for new broadcasters. After the rapid expansion of television in the 1950s and 1960s, it appeared that, as the 1970s approached, local radio would be the only significant area left in which the BBC could expand its operations. It was also to highlight the need to reconsider the justification for the retention of Regional radio. With the prospect of local radio in England, Scotland was left to be served by the Scottish Home Service, which provided a national service of sound broadcasting supplemented by a very limited amount of area broadcasting. There was to be no BBC local radio in Scotland in 1967. The first local radio station in Scotland did not appear until December 1973, and it was to be a commercial, not a BBC local station.

During a period in which the BBC was engaged in examining the possibilities and prospects of local radio services, the nature of the network services also came under scrutiny because of the presence of offshore pirate radio broadcasting. In March 1964, the first of several offshore pirate radio stations began broadcasting, and these broadcasts highlighted programme deficiencies in existing BBC radio programmes. The first pirate radio station, Radio Caroline, began transmitting on 28 March 1964 off Felixstowe. It was followed on 23 December 1964 by Radio London and on 23 September 1965 by Radio 390. Scotland had its own pirate station, aptly named Radio Scotland, which went on the air on 31 December 1965. These stations created a demand for continuous pop music among young people and forced the BBC to take a more radical look at its own programme output. BBC programme policy changed to accommodate competition from television and the need for more popular music. The pirate stations, however, remained in existence until August 1967, when legislation was passed to outlaw pirate radio; most pirate stations, including pirate Radio Scotland, ceased broadcasting in mid-August. Six weeks later, the BBC's radio networks were restructured to take account of the arrival of a new channel devoted to pop music and regarded as a replacement for the pirate radio stations.

Since 1963, the BBC had taken some tentative steps to respond to shifts in the popularity of radio in relation to both television and the increasing popularity of pop music among a significant section of the public. In July 1963, the BBC established a Popular Music Department responsible for all pop music, including programmes such as *Saturday Club*, *Top Gear* and *Easy Beat*. This new department took over this responsibility from the Light Entertainment and Light Music departments. The BBC also sought to extend the Light Programme by starting this programme earlier at 5.30am and closing down at 2.00am, although the Musicians' Union was initially concerned about allowing the BBC to increase the number of hours devoted to playing gramophone records because this denied employment opportunities for musicians. These extensions to the Light Programme in order to increase the output of light music had been sanctioned by the government in July 1962 immediately following the publication of the Pilkington Report on Broadcasting.[17] It was not until June 1964 that the BBC was able to conclude a satisfactory 'needletime' agreement with Phonographic Performance Limited which allowed for an increase in the number of hours for which gramophone records could be broadcast, from 28 in the 280-hour week, to 75 in the increased weekly output of 374 hours.[18] This increase in programme output was shared between the Light Programme and the Third Network. The Light Programme, as noted, began an hour earlier on weekdays and closed down two hours later; and a new service called the Music Programme was introduced on the Third Network from 7.00am to 6.30pm on most days of the week. The latter programme was regarded by the Broadcasting Council for Scotland as providing a greater opportunity for broadcasting music from Scotland. The Music Programme was followed by Study Session from 6.30 to 7.30pm, with the remainder of the evening devoted to the Third Programme. The BBC increased the output of light and popular music on the Light Programme, partly by increasing broadcasting hours, and partly by moving some speech programmes to the Home Service. However, the increase in the amount of time devoted to pop music within the overall total allocated for entertainment music did not satisfy the desire for more pop music from a significant section of listeners, mainly younger people who had access to transistors. The BBC indicated the constraints on catering adequately for those listeners who wished to listen mainly to pop music. The Corporation stated that:

> large as it is, the 'pop' audience is only a minority of the Light
> Programme's total audience, and if too great a quota of 'pop' music
> were provided, the total amount of listening to the Programme would
> certainly decline.[19]

The pirate radio stations responded to this desire for more continuous pop music which the BBC did not satisfy. The popularity of the pirate stations may also have been, as the BBC had argued, a reflection of the illegality of their operations because they infringed copyright regulations and deprived many musicians of royalties. The popularity of the stations highlighted the need to find a method of satisfactorily catering for changes in public taste. Although the pirate stations did not achieve national coverage, they did capture part of the audience for the Light Programme, especially at times when this programme did not broadcast pop music. The Light Programme provided a mixture of pop and popular music, whereas the pirate stations provided a more continuous output of pop music. The BBC could not increase needletime (i.e. time spent playing pop records) because the Musicians' Union was still concerned that this would deprive 'live' musicians of additional employment opportunities. In its Annual Report for 1964–5, the BBC stated:

> Within the agreed limits for the BBC's use of gramophone records the BBC has done much in its extended programmes to meet the demand for continuous music, especially of the pop music so much favoured by the young, which the pirate radios concentrate almost exclusively on meeting.[20]

This did not, apparently, satisfy some sections of the listening audience, who now began to tune in to the increasing number of pirate stations which began broadcasting off the British coastline.

In 1964, plans were prepared for a pirate radio station to operate off the Scottish coast. The idea for such a pirate station, later known as pirate Radio Scotland, came from Mr Tommy Shields, a public relations officer with STV who left that ITV programme company in 1963. On 14 October 1964, he formed City and County Commercial Radio (Scotland) Ltd, which was an advertising agency. Shields hoped that if the Conservative Party won the 1964 General Election, then they would introduce legislation permitting the establishment of commercial radio stations. However, the Labour Party won the election, and so it was likely that, if local radio were permitted, this task would be entrusted to the BBC. The commercial success and popularity of the other pirate radio stations did, however, give encouragement to those individuals who hoped for commercial radio in Scotland. An offshore station was unlikely to be as convenient to operate or as economical as a land-based station, but Shields hoped that his efforts would place him in a strong position to operate such a station, should commercial local radio be authorised by a future Conservative Government. Plans were therefore prepared for opening a pirate radio station in Scotland towards the end of 1965. A 1904 Clyde-built 485-ton converted lightship, the *Comet*, which had previously served off the east coast of Ireland, was acquired and converted in Dublin in order to transmit the station's broadcasts. The engineless ship was provided with a 170-foot aerial and two transmitters and generators, and had the words 'Radio Scotland' painted along her 100-foot length. The station was to be staffed on a shift basis by five or six disc jockeys as well as engineers; operating expenditure was to be derived from advertising. The initial capital costs, which were high, would have been offset to a greater extent if a larger number of potential advertisers had been contacted at an early stage. About seventy-five per cent of the programme output was expected to consist of pop music, with some provision for programmes utilising Scottish theatre, radio and television artists. It was just before midnight on 31 December 1965 that pirate Radio Scotland began transmissions on 242 metres on the medium waveband, serving Scotland and northern England. The station initially broadcast for up to twenty hours each day from the Firth of Forth, and subsequently from the Firth of Clyde where it could reach a larger number of listeners in the west of Scotland, fill vacant advertising slots and thereby increase advertising revenue. Lack of advertising income was to be a recurring problem for the station. Also, in the absence of an engine, the ship had to incur the cost of towing fees, and loss of advertising during the towing procedure, each time a move to a different location was contemplated.

With the growing popularity of offshore pirate radio broadcasts, the government felt compelled to respond in order to end these broadcasts. During the 1964 General Election, neither major political party had made pirate radio an election issue for fear of losing votes, but in 1966 the Labour Party was returned to power with an increased majority and so was in a stronger position to counter pirate radio. The writing was on the wall for pirate radio because, even in December of the previous year, Anthony Wedgwood Benn (the PMG) had stated that sanctions to silence the pirate radio stations would be introduced soon. He had no intention of granting pirate operators licences, or of being pressurised to make such changes by a commercial radio lobby. Scottish Conservative backbenchers were critical of any attempt to ban pirate radio stations, particularly if no alternative commercial stations were to be provided. In Scotland, it was left to the Light Programme rather than the Scottish Home Service to provide programmes for those listeners who were inclined to tune in to the pirate broadcasts. The natural home for light entertainment was the Light Programme. BBC radio in Scotland did not cater for Scottish popular culture, but this task was taken on by pirate radio. During 1964–5, 328 hours were devoted to serious music, in contrast to only 23 hours of light entertainment on the SHS.[21] An article in the *Economist* commented upon the broad implications of the ability of pirate stations to capture a significant proportion of the local audience, and stated:

> The biggest argument for abolishing the pirates and allowing legitimate commercial radio stations is that they might provide the right sort of lively innovation in local news and features that has eluded the Corporation's own men in the provinces up to now.[22]

The issue became party political because Scottish Conservative MPs criticised the Labour Government for devoting more attention to seeking to outlaw pirate radio than in meeting the demand for continuous pop music by permitting legitimate, land-based commercial stations even on an experimental basis. A motion was even tabled in the House of Commons drawing attention to the better quality of reception of pirate Radio Scotland programmes in comparison with BBC programmes in some parts of Scotland. The BBC had in fact opened several new transmitting stations in the post-Pilkington period. On 22 June 1963, a television and VHF radio station was opened at Oban, thereby completing the Great Glen chain of low-power relay stations which improved reception in the South-West Highlands. Shortly afterwards, a television and VHF radio station came into operation at Ashkirk in the Borders on 1 July 1963. On 22 December 1964, the PMG approved stage IV of the relay station programme. The Sandale (Scottish) television transmitter came into service on

27 September 1965, and on 14 March 1966 a television and VHF radio relay station was opened at Skriaig, thus bringing BBC1 VHF coverage to 97.6 per cent and VHF radio to 95 per cent of the population of Scotland. Later that year, on 19 December, a television and VHF radio station at Kingussie and a television relay station at Girvan came into service. Plans continued during 1966 for the outlawing of pirate radio.

In its Annual Report for 1965–6, the BBC argued that there were constraints on its ability to offer a service comparable to that provided by the pirate stations:

> Although willing to do so, the BBC has not been free to provide such a service on its legally allocated frequencies since it has to use its three networks to serve the community as a whole. It must also conform to the requirement of the law of copyright and respect the legitimate desire of musicians to protect their own future by insisting that there must be no unrestricted use of records on the air.[23]

The government pressed ahead with its plans to outlaw pirate stations, and on 29 July 1966 the Marine etc. Broadcasting (Offences) Bill was published, which sought to make pirate radio broadcasting illegal both inside and outside British territorial waters. No attempt had been made either to bring the pirate stations within the law under special circumstances, or to offer an alternative to these stations, the demand for which had already been proven. In July 1967, the PMG announced in the House of Commons that the Bill to outlaw pirate stations was awaiting Royal assent and would become law on 15 August 1967. The Act was passed and came into effect on that day.[24] Only five pirate ships were left operating just before the Act came into effect (i.e. Radio Scotland, two Radio Caroline vessels, Radio London and Radio 270). Only Radio Caroline continued broadcasting after 15 August. The Act made it unlawful for any broadcast to be made from a ship while in UK or external waters or for anyone to assist in the making of such a broadcast by supplying a ship with any equipment or goods.

With the passage of the Act, the final broadcast from the pirate station Radio Scotland took place on 14 August 1967. The station was losing money and could in any case not afford to continue broadcasting illegally beyond 14 August. The last hour of broadcasting from the station was introduced by Tommy Shields, the founder and Managing Director. Pirate Radio Scotland's nineteen-month period on the air provided a strong indication of the type of programmes which many listeners in Scotland wanted and which the BBC Scottish Home Service could not provide. It also generated interest in the possible introduction of legal commercial radio. The Scottish Home Service could not fill the gap left by pirate radio because radio in Scotland did not in general cater for Scottish pop music. Programmes which were broadcast on the SHS included *Scottish Life and Letters* (on Scottish literature), *In Scotland Now* (covering current affairs on a weekly basis), *University Notebook* (a monthly programme on events in the Scottish universities which was first broadcast in October 1963), *Farming Journal* (the programme which replaced the long-running *Farm Forum*), *From Today's Papers* (extended in scope to cover the Scottish press), *Today in Scotland* (news magazine presented on weekdays), daily news bulletins (including a Gaelic bulletin) and concerts given by the BBC Scottish Orchestra. There was light entertainment on the Scottish Home Service, but this tended to be represented by programmes such as *Laugh with Lex* (featuring the comedian Lex McLean) and *Heather Mixture* (music from Jimmy Shand and his Band, which was also broadcast weekly on the Light Programme). BBC Scotland believed that those listeners who were interested in continuous pop music would be adequately catered for by the new popular music programme being planned by the BBC to operate as a network service. This new programme had been authorised by the government in its White Paper of December 1966 at the time when legislation was being introduced to end pirate radio.[25] Given that the new popular music programme would not be Regionalised, there was consequently little Scottish input to the programme. The new service operated as a network, and so failed adequately to represent Scottish popular culture. The introduction of the new programme and the restructuring of the radio networks took effect from 30 September 1967.[26] The first programme broadcast on the new network was *The Tony Blackburn Show*, which played pop music from 7.00am. In the absence of an additional wavelength, the changes involved the splitting of the Light Programme at certain times of the day to create two networks: Radio 1 on 247 metres on the medium waveband (i.e. the wavelength formerly used by the Light Programme to supplement coverage on 1500 metres long-wave and on VHF) to provide pop music to many areas of the country from sixteen medium-wave transmitters; and Radio 2 on 1500 metres long-wave and on VHF to provide the more traditional programmes which had previously been broadcast on the Light Programme. The medium-wave channel was allocated to Radio 1 because Radio 2 on long-wave was reinforced by VHF transmissions, both of which had achieved almost complete population coverage. Additional stations broadcasting on 242 metres medium-wave were now required for Radio 1 in order to form a national network, given that this wavelength had, as noted, previously been used only to supplement and not duplicate long-wave and VHF transmissions on the Light Programme. The BBC stated that coverage of Radio 1 would be greater and more uniformly spread than that provided by the pirate radio stations, even with its single wavelength in the medium waveband.

With the introduction of the new networks on 30 September 1967, there was a change from names to numbers in identifying the networks. Four networks (Radios 1, 2, 3 and 4) replaced the three former networks (Light Programme, Network Three and the Home Service with its Scottish Regional element). Radio 1 was to be the new service, but without the rather mid-Atlantic style used by pirate radio. Radio 2 achieved better geographical coverage, and sound fidelity was superior because of the use of VHF. The BBC sought to separate Radios 1 and 2 as much as possible during peak listening daytime hours within financial and needletime restrictions. During the evenings, programmes on

Radio 1 were broadcast as on Radio 2. Radios 1 and 2 increased the output of the previous Light Programme by up to forty per cent. The Third Network was designated Radio 3, although the Music Programme broadcast during the daytime and the Third Programme broadcast in the late evening on Radio 3, retained their separate identities. The Study Session in the early evening and the Sports Service on Saturdays continued to be broadcast on this network. The Home Service, which included the Scottish opt-out programmes, now came within the umbrella of Radio 4. The coverage of Radio 1 was expected to reach eighty per cent by day, but much less during the hours of darkness, when interference from continental stations on medium-wave would be audible. Coverage of Radio 2 was about ninety-five per cent on medium-wave and ninety-nine per cent on VHF; the coverage of the other two services remained unchanged. In Scotland, Radio 1 was transmitted on medium-wave from Burghead, Redmoss and Westerglen. Radio 2 was served by the high-power long-wave transmitter at Droitwich. Unfortunately, the absence of Radio 2 on medium-wave prevented many people in Scotland from receiving this network (on long-wave), and so two low-power stations operating on 202 metres medium-wave were subsequently opened in Edinburgh and Glasgow in December 1967 to improve reception of Radio 2. Radio 3 was transmitted from Dundee, Edinburgh, Glasgow and Redmoss, and Radio 4 from Burghead, Dumfries, Redmoss and Westerglen. Radios 2, 3 and 4 were also available in many parts of Scotland on VHF.

A central question to consider is the extent to which these changes in network radio compensated for the demise of pirate radio. Frank Gillard, Director of BBC Radio, argued that the BBC was not claiming that Radio 1 would be a replacement for pirate radio because the BBC would have to observe needletime restrictions, and so less than one third of the music output from Radio 1 could come from records, the remainder being provided by session musicians.[27] The restrictions on needletime and technical constraints hindered the separation of Radios 1 and 2. The BBC sought greater credibility with the new network by employing some of the better-known disc jockeys who had previously worked on the pirate stations. Jingles were extensively used in order to make the new station attractive to the younger audience and to lessen the BBC's 'auntie' image. However, the changes appeared to some observers as marking something less than a genuine revolution in BBC attitudes to more popular tastes in music. It could be argued that Radio 1 represented only a postponed rationalisation of the Light Programme in the sense that, if changes in programme policy on the Light Programme had taken place much sooner, then the change brought about by the introduction of Radio 1 would not have appeared so momentous.[28] The novelty of Radio 1 could be taken as an indication of the extent to which the Light Programme had lost touch with many younger listeners, although the BBC had often emphasised the technical and needletime constraints which prevented it from catering more fully for pop music. As a public service, the BBC justified the need to cater for all tastes, including those who preferred more pop music, and could point out that Radio 1 served a larger audience and at a lower operating cost than any of the other networks. The launch of the Music Programme in 1964 had catered for listeners who preferred serious music, and so it was only fair that a service should now be provided for those who preferred pop music. The universality of the licence fee provided the theoretical justification for the provision of comprehensive services catering for all tastes. It simply took that much longer than expected to bring this to fruition.

Part Four

*Local broadcasting, structural change and competition
in radio, 1967–74*

*BBC local radio, and changes to network radio and
non-metropolitan broadcasting, 1967–70*

Between the years 1967 and 1970, significant changes took place in the structure of BBC Regional broadcasting. The first of the BBC's local radio stations which had been sanctioned by the government in December 1966 began broadcasting in November 1967. This station, and the subsequent stations which came on air between then and the middle of 1968, were all located in England because no local authority in Scotland was willing to provide financial guarantees as a contribution towards the cost of operating such stations. These experimental stations were expected to be funded partly from local sources, such as local authorities, and partly by the BBC. They were not to be funded entirely from the licence fee, because the stations were initially confined to eight areas, and it was only proper that those areas which wanted a local station should be prepared to contribute towards the operating costs of local radio. The advent of local radio in England did, however, serve to highlight the need to examine the provision of radio services in Scotland and in doing so thereby indicate the views of BBC Scotland and of the Broadcasting Council for Scotland towards the provision of local services. The outcome of the eight experimental stations was reviewed in 1969 and, later that year, the Labour Government indicated that the BBC would be permitted to establish up to forty local stations. However, these plans were abandoned in the following year by the new Conservative Government because plans were being prepared for the introduction of commercial local radio, plans which were published in March 1971. During the years 1968 and 1969, the BBC utilised the services of a firm of management consultants, McKinsey. The proposals which emerged from this study of BBC managerial practice and cost control influenced BBC organisation, the management of resources and the provision of programme services, both in London and in the Regions. There were to be radical changes in network radio and in the structure of non-metropolitan broadcasting. A further rationalisation of network radio, indicated by plans published by the BBC in July 1969, was to result in the emergence of a new structure for network radio in April 1970; it was also to result in the replacement of the existing three large English Regions by eight smaller Regional centres, three of which were to be designated network production centres. All these changes were of immediate relevance to broadcasting in England, but they also had implications for the type of radio and television broadcasting services which the BBC was providing in Scotland. In this context, useful comparisions can be made between the operation and development of BBC television in Scotland and BBC English Regional television, as well as Independent Television in Scotland. The desire to seek a wider transmission of Scottish programme material through networking and yet not compromise either the identity or the volume of items produced for the audience in Scotland (i.e. Scotland's dual programme responsibility) was to be subject to review in the late 1960s by the new Controller of BBC Scotland, Alasdair Milne.

On 8 November 1967, the first of the BBC's experimental VHF local radio stations, Radio Leicester, went on the air. Seven further local stations were opened, all of them located in England: Radio Sheffield opened on 15 November 1967; Radio Merseyside on 22 November; Radio Nottingham on 31 January 1968; Radio Brighton on 14 February; Radio Stoke-on-Trent on 14 March; Radio Leeds on 24 June; and Radio Durham on 3 July. Manchester withdrew, and so stations were sited in only eight of the planned nine areas. The VHF channels for low-power local radio stations had been obtained at the Stockholm conference in 1961 when VHF frequencies were also obtained for four high-power radio networks, three of which were later used for Radios 2, 3 and 4. BBC Scotland supported the development of national rather than local radio within Scotland. This did ensure a more equitable distribution of broadcasting services throughout Scotland, covering both low- and high-density population centres. In general, the BBC's national Regions, in contrast to the English regions, resisted subdivision within their Regions to cater for more clearly-defined audiences. Andrew Stewart, Controller of BBC Scotland, stated that he was not in favour of local radio experiments in Scotland. He believed that local radio would have been more appropriate had it been introduced in the immediate postwar period, when there could have been a single Scottish radio service with local stations opting out at different times of the day. He argued that local radio was of less relevance in the 1960s because of the growing influence of television.[1] However, genuine local stations needed to be much more than merely opt-outs from an existing Scottish radio service. Furthermore, as John Gray (Chief Assistant, BBC Scotland) pointed out, the reluctance of Scottish management to generate enthusiasm about local radio may have been because of fear of surrendering some degree of power to autonomous local stations if it was decided that these stations should only be responsible to Frank Gillard (Director of Sound Broadcasting) in London.[2] Local stations would also have had to reflect accurately the social and cultural mix of the areas which they served, and this was contrary to the Reithian mixed programming philosophy favoured by BBC Scotland whereby a wide range of items would be offered in order to constitute a balanced programme output. The BBC believed that it already served homogeneous communities in the national Regions with the Regional Home Services, and so local radio appeared to be more relevant in England. A BBC pamphlet stated that 'Basic to the concept of BBC local radio was that each station should reflect the characteristics of its own neighbourhood. It should not seek to conform to some general programme pattern.'[3] BBC Scotland was not in favour of local stations whose programme output would have to reflect the social and cultural mix of the areas which they served.

In the experimental local stations which were established, the Station Managers were given editorial charge of their stations and were subject to central control only in general policy matters. They were allocated a programme allowance, although London set the level of this allowance. The local stations were not answerable to any Regional Controller; the Station Manager decided when to broadcast local programmes, what material to use, how many hours to broadcast and when to take material from any of the radio networks. Each station was advised by a Local Radio Council broadly representative of the local community. The members of these Councils were initially appointed by the Postmaster-General and later by the BBC when the Minister of Posts and Telecommunications (a post which replaced that of the PMG) relinquished his right to make such appointments. The BBC retained editorial responsibility for programme output, but Local Councils could offer advice on programmes. In particular, the Chairman of each Council discussed progress with senior staff in London on a regular basis. This mode of operation was chosen partly in order to convince critics that a centralised BBC could allow local stations to have a sufficient degree of independence from London control. Local authorities used money from investments rather than from the rates to help fund local stations, and these contributions from all stations totalled £350,000 in the period to 31 March 1969; the balance of operating expenditure (£450,000), which represented about fifty-six per cent of total operating expenditure, was underwritten by the BBC in order to give some degree of security to programme staff as regards forward planning; the BBC also covered the capital costs (£300,000) and did not charge local stations for any programmes which they supplied to them.[4]

In July 1968, when all eight BBC experimental stations were broadcasting, the PMG was asked in the House of Commons what consideration the government was giving to the development of local radio stations in Scotland. Mr John Stonehouse (PMG) stated that plans for further BBC local stations beyond the eight which were initially authorised would need to await the review of the local radio experiment due in 1969. He added that he had not received any further proposals from local authorities in Scotland regarding the establishment of any such station in Scotland.[5] There was no conclusive evidence that listeners in Scotland wanted local radio, but arguably the BBC's most successful programmes have never been asked for and thus have tended to precede demand. There was no reason to suppose that the same situation did not apply to local broadcasting as it had applied to network radio and television.

On 10 March 1969, the Estimates Committee reviewed BBC local radio, and the PMG was preparing to announce the government's intentions for the future of local stations. On 14 August 1969, the government stated that the BBC would be allowed to operate up to forty stations and hoped that some of these would be located outside England. Towards the end of November, the BBC was authorised to establish twelve stations in addition to the existing eight stations. They were, in common with the existing stations, also expected to operate only on VHF, hence their appeal was limited because of the slow growth in the number of listeners who were equipped with VHF receivers. The twelve stations were located in the following areas: Blackburn, Birmingham, Bristol, Derby, Humberside, London, Manchester, Medway, Newcastle, Oxford, Solent and Teesside. These stations were to be financed totally from licence income, rather than being partly dependent upon local contributions towards operating expenditure as the experimental stations had been. This raised the question as to whether licence-payers in Scotland should subsidise the extension of local radio in England in the absence of a commitment to extend localised broadcasting to Scotland. However, within a year, the planned forty stations were frozen because on 5 August 1970 the new Conservative Government set a ceiling on the existing twenty BBC stations which had covered about seventy per cent of the population of England. The new government was committed in principle to introducing commercial stations; the outgoing Labour Government had wanted some of the original forty stations to be located in Scotland and the other national Regions. In these changed circumstances, no BBC local stations were therefore located in Scotland. The BBC suggested that, in Scotland, what was needed was a limited form of local broadcasting based on the major Scottish cities, a local service for the Highlands and Islands, and a stronger Scottish opt-out service on Radio 4 (the successor to the Home Service). During 1972, Charles Curran, BBC Director-General, stated that he was in favour of the introduction of local radio in Scotland, but no doubt as a means of enabling the BBC to compete with the impending start of commercial local radio. Up until then, the desire to establish a national identity in Scotland had lessened the need for local radio. On 2 September 1972, the BBC local stations in England were allowed to operate on medium-wave rather than merely on VHF. It enabled them to reach larger audiences and compete with the incoming commercial stations, but it resulted in the English Regions losing their opt-out programmes on medium-wave; Scotland did not lose its medium-frequency channels and so had access to these and to VHF. By the early 1970s, BBC local radio was entering a new phase of development because of the advent of the Independent Local Radio (ILR) stations.

During the period that the BBC was establishing its experimental local radio stations, BBC managerial practice and cost-control methods came under the scrutiny of an external firm of management consultants who were brought in on the BBC's own initiative. In 1967, Prime Minister Harold Wilson asked Lord Hill, BBC Chairman, to instigate a review of BBC finances. By using an external firm of consultants, Hill hoped to convince critics that the BBC was continually seeking to operate on a cost-effective basis. Charles Curran accepted that the public relations aspect was not insignificant.[6] The expansion of BBC services had exerted pressure on financial resources, but Ministers had been reluctant to increase the licence fee to a level which would comfortably cover operating costs. The BBC had grown within a relatively short timespan into an industrial complex with a proliferation of professional specialisms. By the late 1960s, BBC management needed to tighten financial control procedures without stifling the creative talents of producers. The McKinsey diagnostic report, intended only for internal circulation on the advice of the management consultants, was placed before the BBC. The McKinsey recommendations were examined by a BBC internal committee headed by Gerald Mansell (Controller, Radio 4 and subsequently Director of Programmes, Radio). The report was presented to the Board of Governors in May 1969.

McKinsey reported that BBC management had done a satisfactory job of planning and controlling resources, but they nevertheless believed that the BBC should redefine its managerial responsibilities. They were thinking in terms of the need to delegate accountability for the operation of individual budgets as well as ensuring that management had better access to more detailed information about costs. At the beginning of their investigation, McKinsey encountered two distinct factors which appeared to place constraints on the efficient management of resources as judged in comparison with any typical business organisation. These two factors were the public service ethos in broadcasting and the in-built constraints on existing management methods. According to the first factor, it can be argued that the whole philosophy of public-service broadcasting implied that there were particular standards which could be applied to judge the worth of any individual programme other than the benchmark of cost-effectiveness. A more cost-effective programme was not necessarily a better-quality programme. To attempt to streamline programme output by drawing comparisons with, for example, a car assembly line was likely to be unproductive since each individual programme represented a unique, one-off product. A varied and complex mix of staff and technical resources was used on each programme, whether it originated in London or in Scotland. Also, there was the possibility that excessive cost control might stifle producer creativity, the baseline in public-service broadcasting. The second factor which McKinsey had to take note of was the existing constraints on management methods. McKinsey soon realised that the BBC was an atypical organisation, in the products which it produced, but more fundamentally because there were so many decision-makers. Unlike any other organisation of similar size, the BBC had a far greater number of decision-makers because many day-to-day decisions were delegated to the level of producers. This rather diffuse and apparently decentralised decision-making structure was a product of the nature of broadcasting as an activity. McKinsey had to devise a managerial structure relevant to the needs of broadcasting. The aim was to streamline the decision-making structure by reducing the number of key decision-makers and by simplifying the chains of command. This was combined with an emphasis on competitive scheduling, more co-productions, and the adoption of stranded programming (i.e. a series of programmes perhaps with a common theme, broadcast in a regular time-slot, and invariably aimed at a majority audience). This, as will be noted, was to have an adverse effect on the ability of BBC Scotland to secure network transmission for some of its programme output.

Since October 1933, Reith's distinction between the role of administration and that of creative staff had been maintained. The practical outcome of the McKinsey study was that creative staff were no longer shielded from the burdens of administration, since they were expected to be responsible for programme costings. Full responsibility for current and capital expenditure was entrusted to the three Heads of Television, Radio and External Services. They were now designated as Managing Directors directly answerable to the Director-General, thus becoming the Corporation's senior line management. These changes therefore placed the stress on managerial accountability combined with greater delegated authority. The requirement for individual programmes to be costed and kept within a given budget was designed to make production staff more accountable for the requisition and deployment of resources at their disposal. The BBC, though, maintained that managerial efficiency and artistic excellence were not necessarily incompatible.[7] Devolution permitted a greater degree of central control over the allocation of resources because management was provided with more adequate and up-to-date information on the disposition of programme resources. Producers now tended to feel financially accountable rather than responsible generally for the deployment of resources. This was more so in television than in radio because the lower costs of radio production did not require control over the total cost of each programme. In radio, it was possible to submit plans to network Controllers consisting of an aggregate of individual programme budgets. However, in television, producers were allocated production budgets which linked in with the overall fiscal budget, and were now expected to be accountable for the whole cost of each of their productions, not merely part of them. The system of budgeting for individual programmes was to be supplemented by departmental budgets so that departments could set their own productivity targets. Savings targets which had previously been represented by overall sums were now expected to be linked to specific proposals for economies. In July 1969, the Estimates Committee concluded that, on the evidence available to them, their impression was that the BBC was fully cost-conscious and that its methods of financial control were adequate to ensure the efficient use of its resources.[8]

The problem with the introduction of production budgets was that there was a temptation for the previous year's costs to be taken as the baseline for current costs, and that there was a possibility that producers might spend up to the budget allowed for each programme for fear that the subsequent year's budget might be cut. These factors would therefore reduce the incentive to make savings. As regards capital rather than operating expenditure, it can be noted that, unlike most business enterprises, increases in BBC capital expenditure did not increase the Corporation's income, with perhaps one exception: the extension of transmitters did bring an increasing number of people within range of BBC radio and television services and so indirectly increased licence income by increasing the potential number of licence-holders. Nevertheless, as the extension of the transmitter network neared 100 per cent, the BBC's costs increased significantly because of the high cost of providing many relay stations in sparsely populated areas, such as in the north of Scotland and on the western seaboard. It thus appears to be difficult to establish precise criteria for efficiency in the use of capital in the BBC compared to commercial companies. In recommending that the BBC should seek to apply cost-conscious methods to capital projects and not simply to operating expenditure, McKinsey suggested changes that went beyond the BBC's existing costing procedures.

The McKinsey reforms had implications for organisational structure, resource control and programme output within BBC Scotland. McKinsey were asked to include a review of the Regions. The McKinsey team visited Glasgow, and the reforms which followed tended, in common with the BBC as a whole, to affect television more than radio because of the greater costs and complexity of television productions. It was much easier for radio producers to set and then keep within a workable budget. Productivity targets were set and there was a strengthening of central control of information on the deployment of resources. Producers in Scotland were expected to estimate costs before embarking on any production, and then seek to try and keep within these costings. Producers were therefore given control over their own budgets rather than having to negotiate for funds from several central budgets; it invariably involved making producers more accountable for these budgets. Management could now compare the actual costs of a programme with the expected production costs. In Scotland, there was a greater need for television producers to work out their costs in some detail, particularly as they were only beginning to gain experience of large-scale productions and new technical developments in comparison with the larger television production facilities in London. For many years, some staff in Scotland had worked in both radio and television production and so did not specialise in television. In common with the stress on managerialism elsewhere in the BBC, similar changes took place in Scotland in which some senior posts were retitled and given managerial status. The head of Engineering (W.A. Jackson) was redesignated Head of Programme Services and Engineering. Similarly, the Engineer-in-Charge, Operations Scotland (B.J. Slamin), who was also based in Glasgow, became known as Manager, Operations (Scotland). Some other engineering posts were also given Manager/Deputy Manager status, and the Engineering Division itself became known as Programme Services and Engineering. Also, the BBC's Edinburgh operation was placed under the control of a Manager which superseded the previous post of Chief Assistant (Edinburgh). The title of 'Edinburgh Manager' lapsed in the mid-1970s and was replaced by that of Chief Assistant, Radio, because the BBC's radio operations were mainly centred in Edinburgh. Changes also affected the BBC's production centre in Aberdeen. Originally Aberdeen had come under the control of a Director, later known as the Aberdeen Representative, and in charge of Programme Assistants (known from the mid-1950s as Programme Producers) and an Engineering Division. But from September 1970 the station came under the control of a Senior Producer when the post of Aberdeen Representative lapsed. There was no change in the post of Controller, Scotland, but with the replacement of Directors by Managing Directors, the Scottish Controller was now responsible to Frank Gillard (Managing Director, Radio), Huw Wheldon (Managing Director, Television) and James Redmond (Director of Engineering).[9] Apart from these issues of the control over resources and the retitling of posts and regrouping of responsibilities, there is one other aspect of the McKinsey study which had important implications for Scotland, and this was in the area of programme output.

The greater emphasis on strands of programme output to fit in with predetermined budgets did have an adverse effect on the networking of Scottish material. The emphasis on programme series, such as the documentary series *Horizon*, rather than on a sequence of individual programmes, each involving separate producers, was disadvantageous to Scotland. Stranded programming was less costly and facilitated greater financial and organisational control in comparison with individual, and often expensive, productions. However, this made it increasingly difficult for BBC Scotland to contribute the occasional individual production, except perhaps in an area such as drama, particularly since editorial control over programme strands increasingly took place outwith Scotland. In a series of pyramids, each representing different programme areas, the top of the pyramid of stranded programming was invariably London, thereby making it increasingly difficult for BBC Scotland to get material taken by the networks. Production staff in Scotland naturally wished to see their credit on work that would be networked, and in any case the financial investment in material taken by the networks could be recovered from the BBC centrally, thereby releasing more resources within BBC Scotland for local or network programmes. Scotland continued to be successful in getting, for example, drama serials taken by the network, such as *Sunset Song*, the six-part dramatisation of Lewis Grassic Gibbon's famous novel, which was shown on BBC2.

The outcome of the McKinsey study can be viewed against the background of the development of professionalism within the BBC which pre-dated the stress on managerialism from the late 1960s onwards. By the time the BBC decided to call in McKinsey, there was already a transition within the Corporation from the Reithian public service ethos to a professional ethos. This was noted in 1965 by Richard Hoggart, who had been a member of the Pilkington Committee on Broadcasting.[10] In Reith's time, the goal of professionalism had been subordinate to the task of using broadcasting to raise public taste. During the 1950s and 1960s, the growth in the size and complexity of the BBC tended to undermine the rather gentlemanly club which had been characteristic of the sound broadcasting service during the formative years of the BBC. In his autobiography, Reith recalled that he was interested in people who wanted to work in the BBC and nowhere else.[11] He did not want them to treat the BBC as just another employer. However, changes occurred thereafter because of the growth of the BBC and the influx of many new younger staff eager to develop the possibilities of the medium of television. The interchange of staff, artists and ideas between the BBC and ITV reduced the uniqueness of the BBC and was also accompanied by internal tension within the Corporation for audiences and for resources. The BBC became just another employer with its own professional career structure and staffed by professional broadcasters who did not all adhere to the strict Reithian definition of public-service broadcasting. It seemed as if loyalty towards the BBC and the public-service principles it represented was being replaced by loyalty to a career path. By the late 1960s, the BBC began to resemble an industry in which reference was made to terms such as management techniques, productivity, cost control, programmes as commodities which were bought and sold, and audience research which was widely used as a guide to the popularity of programmes. Tom Burns drew the distinction between working *for* the BBC and working *in* the BBC, in which the latter was deemed to have replaced the former.[12] There appeared to be a conflict of interest between the desire to devote one's energies in a commitment to public service (i.e. working *for* the BBC as a vocation), and careerism (i.e. working *in* the BBC as a career structure). Burns went on to argue that professionalism, with its emphasis on professional judgements as to what constituted excellence in programme standards, did appear to be croding the whole concept of public service broadcasting:

> The increasing salience of such preoccupations is a further, and definitive, mark of the transition of broadcasting from an occupation dominated by the ethos of public service, in which the central concern is with quality in terms of the public good, and of public betterment, to one dominated by the ethos of professionalism, in which the central concern is with quality of performance in terms of standards of appraisal by fellow professionals; in brief, a shift from treating broadcasting as a means to treating broadcasting as an end.[13]

The emergence of managerialism after the McKinsey reforms was not unexpected and could be regarded as one of the consequences of the greater professionalism within the Corporation, in the sense that a means had to be devised to oversee the work of a diverse number of specialisms. This differed somewhat in emphasis from the traditional view of senior broadcasters as editors who also had managerial functions. It now seemed that the latter function was to be emphasised at the expense of the former.

McKinsey provided a blueprint for giving greater control to management via acccss to more detailed and up-to-date programming costs, and by making producers responsible for their own programme budgets. Control was increasingly shifted from production departments to central administration staffed by many ex-producers. In Reith's BBC, the staff had worked towards one goal, namely the provision of programmes geared to raising public information and cultural taste. From the late 1960s, this goal was supplemented by a diversity of goals which included professionalism and financial efficiency. On 11 December 1963, just prior to the introduction of BBC2, Stuart Hood (Controller of BBC Television) commented in a BBC Lunchtime Lecture that with the imminent arrival of BBC2, funds would be available to support creativity and experimentation because the primacy of programmes in the BBC had priority over the actions of the accountants, whereas in commercial television the reverse was deemed to be the case.[14] By the end of the 1960s, this situation had altered appreciably, given the primacy of cost control throughout the BBC.

In November 1968, a policy study group composed of senior BBC executives and advisers from McKinsey was formed in order to examine the future of network radio and Regional broadcasting. The background to the BBC's proposals for changes in radio broadcasting stemmed from the need to make financial economies and to plan the nature of the programme services provided to enable them to meet the changing tastes and needs of the audience which it served. The delay in achieving a £6 licence fee (which was only granted on 1 January 1969), combined with a static income from the radio licence and higher costs in other areas, such as national insurance contributions and Post Office charges for collecting licence fees, left the BBC with a deficit of over £3 million by 31 March 1969. The BBC therefore sought to look for economies in radio and determine what type of radio services should be planned for the 1970s. Local radio was to be exempt from these economies because the intention was to allocate additional funds to develop local radio services. The outcome of the BBC study was considered by the Board of Management and Board of Governors, and in July 1969 the BBC published a pamphlet in which it outlined its plans for changes in the radio networks and the reorganisation of non-metropolitan broadcasting.[15] Sixty thousand copies of this pamphlet were printed, and it was widely distributed and discussed. The nature of the proposals had implications for Scotland, although not to the same extent as English Regional broadcasting. Those proposals most likely to affect broadcasting in Scotland included: the BBC's desire to disband the Scottish Symphony Orchestra as an integral element in the McKinsey recommendation that the Corporation should reduce its commitment to its 'house' orchestras; the development of local radio and the phasing-out of Regional radio in England which highlighted the need to review the provision of more localised services in Scotland; and the restructuring of the radio networks and the implications of changes in the structure of Regional television in England for the networking of programmes produced in Scotland. The nature of the BBC's proposals, the controversy which they generated and the introduction of the new network structure in radio in April 1970 can all be noted.

In a foreword to the BBC's pamphlet on the proposed changes to network radio and non-metropolitan broadcasting, Lord Hill, BBC Chairman, stated that BBC radio had to adapt to meet changing tastes and needs. The pamphlet outlined what it took those changing tastes and needs to be, and what the implications were for public-service broadcasting. The evening audience for radio had been falling for many years because of the attraction of television. BBC radio therefore had to place much greater emphasis on daytime programmes because few listeners appeared to use radio as a means of entertainment during the evenings. Indeed, even during daytime hours, radio was regarded less as a medium for family entertainment and more as a provider of background music. The proposals which the BBC began to outline challenged the traditional Reithian idea of mixed programming, whereby listeners would be exposed to a wide range of programmes and so enlarge their cultural horizons. Instead, the Corporation was convinced that the public wanted more predictable and specialised networks involving segmented programming because these networks could be tailored to cater for different audiences. According to the BBC, listeners were now tending to select stations rather than programmes.

By 1969, Radios 1 and 2, which attracted the largest percentage of the listening audience, had been operating in tandem for some periods during the day for just over a year because of the lack of resources to separate both networks (i.e. to separate pop from light music). The BBC wanted to continue Radio 1 as an all-pop network and convert Radio 2 to a separate, mainly light music, network. To achieve this clearer separation of these two networks, it was necessary to extend needletime on Radio 1 and transfer speech programmes from Radio 2 to Radio 4. During the period in which the BBC was seeking to reduce overall costs, it was predictable that attention would focus on Radios 3 and 4, the two most expensive networks. Radio 3 generated higher costs per programme hour than any of the other networks, yet it continued to attract the smallest audience because of the specialised nature of much of its output. Audience research figures indicated that the Third Programme attracted larger audiences when individual programmes were repeated on Radio 4. This suggested that the Music/Third Programme labels deterred many people from tuning into this network. The proposed solution was to abandon the separate labels of Music Programme and Third Programme in order to include all music and arts programmes under the single heading of Radio 3. Documentaries previously broadcast on the Third Programme were to be transferred to Radio 4 in line with the policy of transforming the latter into a mainly speech network with a few entertainment programmes. So, although Radios 1 and 2 would provide news summaries, only Radio 4 would provide a longer and more detailed news analysis. More controversially, the BBC wanted all educational programmes (schools and Open University) to be broadcast only on Radio 4 VHF, thereby separating them from Radio 4 on medium-wave to avoid costly duplication of services. This proposal was likely to present problems for those people, particularly in the north and north-west of Scotland, who did not have access to VHF receivers or to VHF radio. The BBC expected that, during those hours when educational programmes were not broadcast on VHF, Radio 4 general programmes could be broadcast on these higher frequencies. The transfer of schools programmes to Radio 4 VHF did not take place until September 1973. All these proposed changes represented an attempt to introduce greater specialisation into the networks. It was expected that this generic pattern would therefore make it possible to distinguish more easily between the networks: Radio 1 concentrating on pop music with hourly news summaries; Radio 2 focusing mainly on light music with hourly news summaries, but merged with Radio 1 during the evening; Radio 3 as a provider of classical music, drama, the arts, serious discussions and literature; and Radio 4 as primarily a speech network covering news, current affairs, plays, discussions, documentaries and some light entertainment.[16] The BBC argued that choice of programmes was being preserved, and that choice between programmes was being made more convenient for listeners by the streamlining of the radio networks. However, upon closer inspection, the technical and financial aspects of these changes and their implications for programme output generated controversy.

Radio 1 as a national service could not be provided on VHF using high-power stations because of the lack of frequencies; VHF on low-power was available, but this was suitable only for local stations, not for Radio 1, which required national coverage. Radio 2 operated on long-wave and VHF. There was some disappointment that Radio 1 could not be allocated its own VHF wavelength. The BBC also wished to develop local radio on VHF with some support on medium-wave, although the Corporation argued that local radio was not an addition to existing radio services but rather an element in a reorganised radio structure. But this proposal caused concern that the replacement of local stations for existing Regional services would be detrimental to those areas in England which lost their Regional services but were not allocated a local radio station. However, it was the proposals for changes in Radios 3 and 4 which aroused most controversy within, and to some extent, outwith the BBC. The proposal to move educational programmes on Radio 4 to VHF would mean that medium-wave coverage on Radio 4 would need to be improved to compensate for the partial loss of VHF, and it was expected that this would be achieved by ending Regional and area opt-outs on Radio 4 in England. The BBC argued that this would be compensated for by the establishment of more local radio stations.[17] Even more controversial was the proposal to reallocate the medium waves on Radio 3 to benefit the other networks and the local stations; this would leave Radio 3 only on VHF, although the BBC had argued that the musical content of Radio 3 programmes would benefit from the superior quality of VHF transmissions. This proposal was, however, later withdrawn in the face of public opposition. The proposal was controversial because those listeners without VHF receivers would be deprived of receiving Radio 3, which they had been able to receive on medium-wave. Indeed, the loss of the medium-wave from Radio 3 and part of VHF from Radio 4 appeared to outweigh any gains. The BBC regarded those gains as comprising the greater separation of Radios 1 and 2, more specialised output on Radios 3 and 4, improved medium-wave coverage on Radios 1 and 4, a separate VHF channel on Radio 4 for educational broadcasts, and proposals to extend the number of local radio stations to forty to cover ninety per cent of the population in England. The BBC envisaged the future of non-network services in the provision of local rather than Regional services. This implied that Regional opt-outs from Radio 4 in England would cease as local radio stations were developed and were able to supply more local programme material than the Regional opt-out services. The proposed changes in radio were an attempt to move from a three-tier structure comprising the network, Regions and areas (within Regions) to a two-tier structure comprising the network and local stations. The emphasis on local radio could be regarded as a means of enabling the BBC to compete with commercial local radio if and when such stations should be authorised, hence the changes could be regarded as in the BBC's institutional interest rather than simply in the public interest. The Conservative Government's decision in 1970 to limit the number of local radio stations to twenty obliged the BBC to maintain some Regional radio presence on VHF in areas not yet served by local stations.

The first aspect of the changes which was of immediate relevance to Scotland was the proposal to disband the Scottish Symphony Orchestra (SSO) as part of an overall reduction of musicians employed in the BBC's 'house' orchestras. McKinsey believed that the BBC Regions represented a significant proportion of total expenditure, yet the productivity of Regional centres was regarded as poor in comparison with London. Cutbacks in the orchestras could therefore reduce Regional expenditure. The BBC wished to make greater use of recorded music and reduce its reliance upon 'live' orchestral music. This was one of the more controversial of the BBC's proposals. The BBC confirmed to the Estimates Committee in 1969 that McKinsey were asked as part of their overall study to look at the position of the orchestras.[18] When the proposals for network radio were published in July 1969, the BBC stated that in order to economise on the employment of orchestral musicians, it could no longer continue to fund the SSO. As a result of external criticism and governmental pressure during 1969, this proposal was later withdrawn. The Broadcasting Council for Scotland had, however, not sought to resist BBC attempts to disband the SSO. In its Annual Report for 1969–70, the Council stated:

> faced with a general BBC need to economise on the employment of orchestral musicians, the Council felt it could not dispute the BBC's proposal that it could no longer continue to finance the Scottish Symphony Orchestra; fully recognising that this decision would be disastrous for the musical life of Scotland but nevertheless seeing that step as the least injurious to broadcasting in Scotland open to it.[19]

The maintenance of an orchestra has always appeared to have been an important ingredient culturally, artistically and symbolically of Regional programme activity, hence the concern expressed then and subsequently in 1980 when threats to the continuation of an orchestra were posed. As regards the implications for Scotland of the replacement of Regional radio programmes in

England by local radio stations, the BCS stated that these changes would not be immediately applicable to Scotland because the Council believed that Scotland should continue to be provided by a national Scottish output. The reorganisation of the Regional structure in England did not alter the BBC's attitude that Scotland should primarily continue to be regarded as a single unit in broadcasting terms. The possibility of developing local radio stations in Scotland did not alter this basic premise, but the changes taking place in England highlighted the issue of introducing some form of localised broadcasting in Scotland, not necessarily analogous to the English local stations, alongside the BBC's national radio service for Scottish listeners. The changes in the radio networks also had an impact on BBC radio in Scotland. The changes made it more difficult for Radio 4 Scotland to attract a large audience because, unlike the 1950s when many people listened to the Scottish Home Service, the bulk of the audience now tended to listen to Radios 1 and 2. As a primarily speech network, Radio 4 could not command the same audience levels as the other two networks, and so the Scottish opt-outs on Radio 4 likewise had a reduced audience. The only method of increasing the audience for BBC radio in Scotland was therefore to extend the opt-outs on Radio 4 to include Radio 2 also, given that Radio 2 commanded a larger audience than Radio 4. The creation of network production centres in England and the greater reliance upon stranded programming in network radio also made it increasingly difficult for Scottish producers to contribute individual programmes of merit for network transmission.

The restructuring of the radio networks represented one major element in BBC policy. The other major element consisted of the BBC's plans for reorganising Regional broadcasting in England. For technical and financial reasons, television, unlike radio, could not provide extensive localised broadcasting services. Television services did not offer the same precision as geographical boundaries. The siting of transmitters and the cost of television productions placed constraints on BBC Regional policy. The three large English Regions, prior to their reorganisation in 1970, could not claim to be serving as homogeneous an audience as the BBC's Scottish Region. A reorganisation of Regional broadcasting was long overdue, as BBC Chairman Lord Hill admitted.[20] The position of the national Regions, such as Scotland, differed from the situation in England. The BBC believed that the three national Regions served homogeneous communities, whereas the three English Regions (North, Midlands, South and West) could not be regarded as serving any definable communities, given the size of these Regions and the arbitrary nature of their boundaries, which were governed by the range of the high-power medium-wave transmitters. In order to bring the English Regional structure more in line with prevailing needs and aspirations, given the decline in the audience for Regional radio programmes, the BBC wished to replace the three large Regions with eight smaller geographical Regions. The existence of ITV's Regional structure had in any case for many years called into question the size of the BBC's English Regions.

In July 1970, the three large English Regions were replaced by three network production centres and smaller television Regions serving more manageable communities, but in Scotland the BBC maintained a unitary presence with headquarters in Glasgow and smaller studio centres in Edinburgh and Aberdeen. The BBC's three principal Regional centres outside London, which were based in Birmingham (Midlands Region), Bristol (South and West Region) and Manchester (North Region), now formed the nucleus of the network production centres. These centres were expected to reflect the character of the areas which they served and to contribute material to the networks. They assisted in lessening the concentration of production facilities in London to the extent that each centre specialised in a particular type of programme output: Birmingham specialised in drama, Bristol in natural history, and Manchester in light entertainment and industrial affairs. It was a recognition that London had no monopoly in innovative programme ideas, but it had adverse implications for the networking of BBC Scottish television output because Scotland's status as a national Region prevented it from specialising in any single programme area. As regards the eight television Regions, the BBC had sought over the years prior to reorganisation in 1970 to serve smaller communities by creating five additional areas within the three large English Regions (i.e. Leeds and Newcastle within North Region, Plymouth and Southampton within the South and West Region, and Norwich within the Midlands Region). These were replaced in the reorganisation by eight television Regions located as follows: South (Southampton), West (Bristol), South-West (Plymouth), Midlands (Birmingham), East Anglia (Norwich), North-West (Manchester), North (Leeds) and North-East (Newcastle). Each of the eight television Regions was designed to provide more localised services than had been possible previously with the three large Regions. These stations, which opted out of BBC1 to provide a news and magazine programme, covered a larger area than any local radio stations, but they broadcast for a shorter period of time each day and so did not provide such a wide range of programmes. They did, however, reach a large audience when material was broadcast on the BBC1 network. The BBC regarded these stations as complementary, not competing, services on the same lines as network radio and television.[21] Within the Regions, staff feared that the replacement of the large Regions by smaller ones would reduce the influence of the English Regions in London in comparison with the national Regions, such as Scotland, and also threaten job prospects. The BBC, however, created the new post of Controller of English Regions, which was of equal status to that of the Scottish Controller and based at Pebble Mill in Birmingham.[22] The task of the new Controller was to supervise the output from the eight Regional centres and act as a link with central management in London. The change in the Regional structure was an attempt to reflect cultural diversity and lessen metropolitan predominance in television, but the eight television Regions, although each represented a smaller operational base than BBC Scotland, exhibited similarities with Scotland in that there were deficiencies in finance and facilities, and sometimes film crews were sent from London to cover items of interest in these Regions for network transmission. This was particularly so with regard to those five English stations which were not based in the same cities as the three large network production centres, hence, like Scotland, there was concern about metropolitan bias and lack of autonomy.

The development of BBC television in Scotland can also be considered in relation to the presence of the three Scottish ITV programme companies. The smaller size of the ITV Regions did call into question the size of the BBC Regions. The federal structure of ITV was expected to keep the programme-makers in close touch with the communities they served. The extent to which ITV was genuinely Regional does, however, have to be viewed in relation to the disproportionate influence of the major English network production companies. The Scottish ITV companies had to rely upon material from the large programme companies in England for sustaining output, just as BBC Scotland relied upon network material for most of its programme output. There was never perfect competition within ITV.[23] The network provided the smaller companies with a regular supply of programmes, but it also acted as a disincentive for these companies to produce programmes above their minimal contractual commitment to the ITA. The Scottish ITV companies, like BBC Scotland, found it difficult to break into the network. The major programme companies, however, had a guarantee of network transmission of their pro-grammes before production commenced. In its Annual Report for 1964–5, the ITA offered the following comment on the networking of Regional programmes:

> Whilst the Authority regards the first task of Regional companies to
> be the provision of programmes serving the tastes and interests of
> their areas, it believes that material for wider showing will emerge
> from time to time, and that the arrangements for the mutual use of
> programmes should be flexible enough to make this practicable.[24]

However, given that programmes made for networking by Regional companies were not guaranteed to be taken by network companies before production commenced, it was thus much more risky for small companies such as STV to make these programmes, because less money would be recouped if only some companies took these programmes. The absence of competition between programme companies in any area (given that only one programme company was appointed in each area), and the disincentives to Regional programme production, were the two principal criticisms of ITV. In ITV, the franchise which had been allocated by the ITA to programme companies on a geographical and Regional basis (i.e. three Scottish ITV companies covering different Regions) was reassembled by the network companies and divided by time (i.e. time-slots for different programmes produced by different network companies and supplemented by a smaller number of Scottish-originated programmes). What Regional broadcasting centres in the BBC and in ITV wanted was a wider transmission of their programme material without compromising their sense of Regional identity. This was the policy of Alasdair Milne, who became Controller of BBC Scotland in 1968.

In general, the BBC's changes of 1970, particularly in network radio, were designed to readjust the services available to cater for the preferences of listeners, to attract a larger audience to radio and to introduce a more rational use of resources. The move away from the Reithian idea of mixed programming in the direction of more rationally planned specialised networks was reminiscent of a Haleyite reform, discussed in Chapter 5, but without Haley's intentions. Haley's cultural pyramid was abandoned. The BBC accepted that listeners would mainly listen to one or two networks, thus in theory they were now exposed to a narrower range of programme material. The BBC appeared to be prepared to abandon balanced programming on any single channel. In an article in the *New Statesman*, the changes were unfavourably reviewed, and it was argued that the type of radio which would emerge from the BBC's plan would be commercial radio without the advertising.[25] This was symptomatic of the deep concern both within and outwith the BBC about various aspects of the BBC's proposals. For example, radio appeared to be moving away from its role as a cultural medium to one as a provider of news and music. Furthermore, criticism was also generated because of the lack of adequate consultation on the issues before the BBC's plans were published.[26] It was announced on 16 October 1969 that the proposals, modified to some extent, were eventually to be implemented. On 14 February 1970, a letter was published in *The Times*, signed by 134 members of London radio programme staff who were critical of the plans.[27] Ian Trethowan (Managing Director, Radio) nevertheless stated that the changes would proceed as planned. On 4 April 1970, the new network structure in radio was introduced. Each network was now more clearly identifiable with regard to purpose and content. The BBC had consistently argued that the proposals were based on a recognition that listeners were already more selective in their choice of programmes and that the changes would not lead to a reduction in cultural standards. The Corporation stated that it would continue to adhere to its public-service function to provide balanced programming, but now this would take place across the networks rather than within any individual network. The BBC summed up its plans as follows:

> The purpose of the BBC's plans, as outlined in 'Broadcasting in the Seventies', has been twofold: to adapt services to a changing world to meet changing tastes and needs, and to make it possible for BBC Radio to live within its prospective income in the five years 1969–74. The first objective is well on the way to being achieved; the second is more problematical.[28]

Never before in recent history had any BBC proposal given rise to such controversy, particularly at the start of a decade in which the BBC would, for the first time in fifty years, lose its radio broadcasting monopoly.

The advent of Independent Local Radio, and BBC radio and television development in Scotland, 1971–4

The 1970s began with a threat to the BBC's radio broadcasting monopoly, which had remained intact for almost fifty years. It culminated in the publication in March 1971 of a White Paper which outlined the government's plans for introducing Independent Local Radio (ILR) stations. Within just over a year, a Sound Broadcasting Act was passed, and this permitted the establishment of ILR stations and outlined the conditions under which these stations were expected to operate. The BBC now had to consider how it would respond to the imminent arrival of competition in radio. This issue was particularly important for BBC Scotland because, unlike England, no BBC local stations had been established in Scotland in the late 1960s, stations which might have provided fair competition with ILR. BBC Scotland's views on competition from commercial stations, and on the changes in programme schedules on the Radio 4 Scottish opt-out service which were mainly attributable to the presence of the first ILR station in Scotland in December 1973, need to be considered. In television, different considerations need to be noted. BBC Scotland's policy under Alasdair Milne and his successor Robert Coulter, who became Controller designate in December 1972, was to concentrate more resources on programmes which might be taken by the networks. This provided an opportunity for the cost of such programmes to be covered centrally and in theory also for lessening the metropolitan content of network output, but it also highlighted the need to consider the relative emphasis to be accorded to both aspects of BBC Scotland's dual programme responsibility (i.e. programmes for viewers in Scotland and for the larger network audience). On a broader level, there was the question of the images of Scotland which were projected in programme output, and the transmitting mechanisms available, such as Regional opt-outs and networking, for projecting those images. In particular, with the resurgence of national consciousness in Scotland in the early 1970s, there was a need fully to reflect social, economic and political change in programme output. The quantity and quality of Scottish television programmes was one matter, but the geographical availability of radio and television services was also an important issue during this period. In 1973, the government appointed a committee to examine broadcasting coverage and the nature of the programme services provided in the national and English Regions. The proposals of the

Crawford Committee's Report, published in November 1974, highlighted as far as Scotland was concerned issues such as the Regionalisation of television within Scotland and the provision of local radio services, and above all the need for the social dimension of broadcasting to be kept in view in considering the implications of rapid economic development in remote areas.

In 1962, the Pilkington Committee had supported the BBC's plans for local broadcasting, but the government at the time deferred the idea of introducing local radio. It was not until December 1966 that the White Paper on Broadcasting had authorised the BBC to conduct a local radio experiment in cooperation with local interests. There was no provision made for commercial local radio. It was only with the advent of a Conservative Government in June 1970 that the possibility of a commercial system drew that much nearer. This was confirmed on 29 March 1971 with the publication of a White Paper outlining plans for the introduction of several commercial local radio stations. There was no organised pressure group which campaigned in favour of commercial stations, and so this differed from the early 1950s when the pressure-group element was present prior to the introduction of commercial television. The era of pirate radio did, however, to some extent provide increased support for the provision of legal commercial radio. Moreover, the reluctance of many local authorities in England, and of all local authorities in Scotland, to fund the operating costs of the first few experimental BBC local stations did present a strong argument for allowing commercial local radio. The commercial viability of local stations depended upon technical factors and not simply the nature of programme content and the catchment area served. It seemed that commercial stations would have to operate on medium-wave and not just on VHF in order to reach a larger audience. The question was whether they would provide a community radio service or merely entertainment at the local level. There was also the question as to whether sufficient advertising revenue could be generated at the local level because these stations would incur heavier costs than the pirate radio stations, and whether the relationship between commercial stations and local newspapers could create a local monopoly of news. On the first point, large advertisers would certainly have preferred a national commercial radio service, and on the second point a monopoly of news would be potentially more dangerous at the local than at the national level because of the scarcity of news outlets at the local level. There was justification for a commercial service to the extent that the BBC could not provide local services for all parts of the country which wished to have a service without unreasonable demands being placed on the licence fee.

Many of the arguments both for and against both systems (i.e. BBC and commercial) mirrored some of the arguments which were used in the early 1950s during the debates on the merits of introducing commercial television. However, the BBC monopoly in radio was of a different nature to the television monopoly, given that in radio the BBC already offered a choice of networks with some degree of in-built competition. The BBC could also claim that local radio should be funded from the licence fee because, unlike a commercial service, people living in remote areas would be able to receive a local service subsidised by those living in more densely-populated areas. Potential commercial operators were aware that they would not be allowed to ignore needletime restrictions or disregard copyright laws in order to reduce operating costs as the pirate radio stations had done. The government was aware that although there was a need to ensure minimum programme standards and a satisfactory output of locally-originated material, commercial operators had to be given an opportunity to generate reasonable profits. It appeared that local commercial stations would have to opt for mixed programming, which was at variance with the results of audience research which indicated that listeners preferred more specialised networks.[1] The nature of programme content was significant, particularly at a time when the BBC was introducing more specialised radio networks which could be expected, together with BBC local radio stations, to compete to some extent with any commercial local radio stations.

In its 1970 election manifesto, the Conservative Party promised to introduce commercial local radio under the supervision of a controlling authority. With the prospect of commercial stations, the BBC began to express its own reaction to the demise of the sound broadcasting monopoly. In January 1971, Ian Trethowan, Managing Director of BBC Radio, stated that the Corporation was not fighting to defend its monopoly in radio. What was deemed to be of concern was the precise nature of the government's plans for local radio: were these stations to supplement or to replace BBC radio, and would competition provide listeners with a wider choice of programmes?[2] The BBC's view was that its existing services which were planned in conjunction with each other did provide reasonable choice for listeners, and that if BBC local stations were closed down, then the Corporation would need to maintain some Regional radio presence outwith London in order to provide additional material to sustain the expanded news and current affairs output of the networks. The BBC believed not only that local stations were a counter to metropolitanism, but also that there was room for additional VHF stations to enable the BBC and commercial stations to coexist. If only commercial stations were permitted to operate, then this would represent a monopoly at the local level. Those who worked for BBC radio may have felt under threat not only from the prospect of commercial stations but also by the abolition of the radio-only licence in February 1971, the existence of which had provided a visible case for adequate funding for radio.[3] This remained so, even although income derived from receiving licences was never distributed to television and to radio in proportion to the number of separate television and radio licences purchased.

On 29 March 1971, the government issued its White Paper outlining plans for an alternative service of radio broadcasting at the local level. The government stated that competition in television had been beneficial and was accompanied with little support for any return to the monopoly, hence there was no reason to object to a competitive source of programmes in radio broadcasting: 'the case which is now largely accepted for competition in television is no less strong in radio'.[4] The government argued that it was offering an extended choice of public-service broadcasting: it would be a public service because the system would be under the supervision of an Independent Broadcasting Authority (IBA), which would be responsible for appointing programme companies, providing facilities for the transmission of programmes, supervising programme standards, and controlling the amount and nature of advertising. The ITA's organisation was deemed to be suitable for the supervision of local radio, hence it was renamed the IBA and given control over Independent Television and Radio. The BBC was allowed to retain its twenty local stations in England, and in Scotland the Scottish opt-outs from Radio 4 were to continue. The government's plan for commercial local radio envisaged a network of up to sixty stations throughout the UK. Furthermore, having taken account of the limited audience for BBC local radio on VHF, the government agreed that the medium waveband would also be used to support BBC and commercial stations in order to make programmes available to a larger number of people.[5] It was possible to do this only by closing English Regional programmes on Radio 4, thereby releasing additional frequencies. Moreover, because of the need to share frequencies and consequently limit the power of the transmitters, the service areas of the local stations on medium-wave, especially during the hours of darkness, were likely to be much smaller than VHF areas.

The government's White Paper did not specify where the local stations would be sited, but they were expected to serve recognisable communities initially in large conurbations and would seek to combine popular programming with an attempt to stimulate greater public awareness of local affairs. Their main source of competition was envisaged as coming from BBC Radios 1 and 2. The ILR stations were to derive their income from spot advertising, each company was to be appointed using a system of three-year rolling contract periods, and they were to pay a rental to the IBA to cover transmission costs. Labour opponents of ILR believed that some companies would regard local radio as a purely commercial venture rather than as a means of providing genuine alternative services. As regards competition between these local stations and the local press, the government made three provisos:

(1) local newspapers with a circulation which was significant in relation to the population served by a local station were to have the right to acquire an interest in it;

(2) where a newspaper had a monopoly in an area, it was not to be allowed to acquire a controlling interest in a local station;

(3) a television company was not to be allowed a controlling interest in local radio in the area of its television franchise.

In an article in *The Listener* in March 1972, Frank Gillard, the pioneer of BBC local radio, did not believe that the commercial radio stations would be able to generate the same profits as the commercial television stations, except perhaps in the larger urban areas. He argued that only by relying upon extensive use of gramophone records would commercial stations be able to exist financially in competition with the BBC's radio services. In an amusing play on words, he stated: 'Get yourself a microphone, an amiable ape and a pile of pop discs, and you are in business.'[6] He argued that the intrusion of advertising on radio would be even more evident than on television because of the absence of any visual image. On 12 June 1972, the Sound Broadcasting Act, which made provision for commercial local radio, was passed.[7] The Act stipulated that no contractor was to be permitted to provide both radio and television services for any area. The IBA was to appoint local advisory committees for all areas in which there would be local stations. Members of these committees were expected to reflect the range of tastes and interests of people residing in the areas for which the committees were appointed. The IBA was authorised to provide television and local radio broadcasting services until 31 July 1976. It seemed likely at the time that Scotland might be able to support four or five commercial stations. To take account of all these changes, an Act was passed on 23 May 1973 to consolidate the Television Act of 1964 and the Sound Broadcasting Act of 1972.[8]

BBC local stations, which had a self-sustaining output supported by material from Radios 1 and 2, did not plan any major changes in advance of the arrival of ILR stations, because it was expected that these stations would compete mainly with Radios 1 and 2 rather than with BBC local radio. The BBC's balance of speech and music in its local programmes tended in any case to appeal to middle-aged and elderly listeners, whereas commercial radio was expected to appeal to younger listeners. In November 1972, Hugh Pierce, General Manager of BBC Local Radio, stated that BBC local stations would however have to engage in competition with commercial stations at least to some extent:

> When commercial radio comes, we must ensure that our popular
> programmes are as popular as the other fellow's. But our job must be
> to remain loyal to our original concept of public service local radio,
> and we shall continue to carry those programmes for minorities
> which, though highly appreciated by a few, would break an adman's
> heart.[9]

With the de-restriction of broadcasting hours on 19 January 1972, BBC radio had already had to cope with greater competition from television during the daytime hours; now it had to face competition from another source, commercial radio. The IBA began the process of awarding the first five franchises to large urban areas, one of which was located in Glasgow. The ILR stations by now seemed likely to compete directly with BBC Radio 1, which could not be Regionalised. In Scotland, there was no BBC local radio station to offer competition to ILR stations, and neither was the Scottish opt-out service on Radio 4 likely to be a principal competitor to commercial stations. In September 1972, Alasdair Milne, Controller of BBC Scotland, stated that when ILR did arrive in Scotland, the BBC would be in a disadvantageous position in competitive terms because of the absence of BBC local radio in Scotland and the intention of the government to sanction the creation of sixty commercial stations to compete with only twenty BBC local stations, all of them located in England.[10] Milne's view was echoed by that of the Broadcasting Council for Scotland, which stated in its Annual Report for 1971–2: 'The Council did not feel that the present structure of Radio 4 Scotland, committed as it is to serving the whole nation, could reasonably be regarded as fair competition for commercial radio established on a localised basis.'[11] Ian Trethowan, Managing Director of BBC Radio, recognised that although radio had been used to reinforce national identity, localised radio in Scotland and in the other national Regions might develop at a later date.

In March 1973, the IBA announced that the contract for the Glasgow area had been awarded to Radio Clyde. Radio Clyde was the first Scottish station and Britain's third ILR station; the first ILR station, London Broadcasting Company, opened on 8 October 1973, closely followed on 16 October by Capital Radio, also serving London. Radio Clyde was expected to employ up to seventy staff and serve a potential audience of 1.9 million people in the West of Scotland. It broadcast on 261 metres medium-wave and on VHF in stereo. The station began transmissions on 31 December 1973, and within a short period of time it made inroads into the listening figures for BBC radio. It attracted a much larger share of the audience in the West of Scotland than Radio Scotland or any other radio network could achieve. Radio Clyde's popularity was partly attributable to its attempt to study the character and needs of the listeners which it served, and partly because of the novelty of commercial radio, particularly in the absence of BBC local radio. The large geographical area covered by Radio Clyde meant that the station was only 'local' if this term was liberally interpreted. Nevertheless, the BBC's national radio service in Scotland, with its mixed programming output, suffered to some extent in popularity because it opted out of Radio 4 which was basically a speech network. Listeners who did not normally tune in to Radio 4 therefore often missed the Scottish programmes. Radio Clyde sought to reflect Glasgow and West of Scotland culture, which the BBC in Scotland found difficult to achieve with only an opt-out service from Radio 4 which was expected to serve the whole of Scotland. The arrival of commercial radio led to changes in BBC Scotland's radio schedules, even although BBC Scotland's Controller, Robert Coulter, did not envisage the BBC as being in direct competition with ILR. From 1 January 1974, BBC Radio 4 programmes in Scotland on 371 metres medium-wave and on VHF became known as 'Radio Scotland' in the *Radio Times*.[12] The new BBC Radio Scotland remained an opt-out service from Radio 4, but there were programme changes designed to reflect a more distinctive Scottish flavour, and the number of hours of opt-outs from Radio 4 was increased. From New Year's Day 1974, the BBC introduced an hourly Scottish news bulletin entitled *News from Scotland*; there was also a new two-hour current affairs programme, *Good Morning Scotland*, which was broadcast every morning from the Glasgow studios, although the programme did not find favour with those listeners who were now denied access to the *Today* programme from London. It was expected that the output of Scottish music, drama and light entertainment would also be increased over a period of time. These and other changes were aimed at increasing the volume of Scottish material which was broadcast (i.e. more opt-outs for Scotland were permitted), and as a means of rescheduling minority interest programmes away from peak listening times. They were an attempt to cater for the competitive presence of Radio Clyde and the increasing salience of Scottish economic, industrial and political issues in the country. Competition from Radio Clyde acted as a stimulus to Scottish radio broadcasting in terms of techniques, such as the use of production teams rather than single producers by BBC Scotland, in programme content as noted above, and in terms of the provision of localised BBC radio services in Scotland. There were also important considerations affecting television during this period.

In 1968, Alasdair Milne, aged 37, became the youngest Regional Controller in the BBC's history when he succeeded Andrew Stewart as Controller of BBC Scotland. He inherited programme-making which had frequently been criticised in the Scottish press as being too conservative, too establishment-minded, and not sufficiently controversial by relying too much on official statements rather than based on more widespread investigative journalism. Milne was viewed as someone who would undermine the Reithian ideals firmly held by the retiring Controller, Andrew Stewart. In this sense, he shared the more open and enquiring approach to the function of broadcasting which Sir Hugh Greene as Director-General espoused. Alasdair Milne's policy was one of concentrating resources on high-quality productions which could be offered to the network. Milne wanted Scotland to increase its programme contributions to both BBC television networks, and he re-emphasised this approach in an article in a book published in 1970[13] and in his autobiography published in 1988.[14] He maintained that if too much attention were focused on catering for local programmes, then new ideas for network programmes would come increasingly from London, thereby reinforcing their metropolitan content. On the other hand, the cost of programmes which were networked would be covered by London, thus releasing more resources for network or Scottish programmes. This contrasted with the views of a former Editor of News in Scotland, James Kemp, who argued that BBC Scotland should focus primarily on local programmes which, if of a sufficiently high standard, would be taken by the networks. His view was that Scottish-originated programmes tailored for the network would lose their Scottish identity. Alasdair Milne wanted Scotland to play a fuller part in UK broadcasting without losing its Scottish identity. This appeared to represent an attempt to break away from the resistance to innovation and the establishment-mindedness of which Stuart Hood had been critical about BBC Scottish management in an article in 1967 before Milne succeeded Andrew Stewart as Controller.[15] Alasdair Milne sought to concentrate on programmes in the high-cost areas of drama, documentary and light entertainment which were more likely to be accepted by the network and would challenge ITV more effectively in Scotland.

Scotland did contribute drama serials such as *The Vital Spark, Scobie in September* and *Dr Finlay's Casebook* to the networks from Studio A in Glasgow. Drama serials were, however, later withdrawn from Glasgow because of the lack of colour facilities. Colour television was in fact available on all three channels from 15 November 1969; colour was available on 13 December from the Blackhill transmitter serving central Scotland. At the time, there were only 9,160 colour licences in Scotland, but this had increased to almost 24,000 within twelve months. In Edinburgh, a three-camera studio was brought into service on 29 December 1969. In January of the following year, BBC Scotland gained a colour outside broadcast unit. Viewers still complained about the lack of colour in coverage of association football in *Sportsreel*, but the BBC placed the blame on the inadequate lighting at football grounds which was not sufficiently strong for colour cameras to provide a clear image. In news and current affairs, programmes such as *Reporting Scotland* and *Current Account*, both introduced in 1968, offered some opportunities for Scotland to contribute items to the network. Also, some documentary films were shown on BBC2 after the formation of a Television Documentary Unit within BBC Scotland. In the autumn of 1969, coverage of parliamentary and local government affairs was extended with the televising of the monthly programme *Right, Left and Centre*. Light entertainment could be regarded as a more difficult area in which to get material networked, but programmes such as *The Stanley Baxter Show* were transmitted on BBC1. The BCS believed that it was vital for Scottish entertainment programmes to be seen throughout Britain.[16] Some light entertainment programmes produced in Scotland, such as the late-night Saturday show *One Over the Eight* and a successor entitled *Saturday Round about Sunday*, received adverse comment in the press. Programmes such as *First Person Singular* (interviews with well-known personalities conducted by Mary Marquis, for many years a main presenter of *Reporting Scotland*), *Moira Anderson Sings*, *The View from Daniel Pike* (a drama serial shown on BBC2) and *Who are the Scots?* (a documentary with Dr Ian Grimble), attracted rather more praise. Emphasis was placed on these three subject areas of drama, documentaries and light entertainment when the five-year television development plan resumed in the autumn of 1969 after a two-year standstill because of financial constraints. Although programmes primarily for viewers in Scotland were not neglected and new programmes such as *Scope* (covering the arts in Scotland) were introduced, the main priority was to divert resources into programmes capable of being taken by the networks. With the development of stranded programming from the late 1960s, as noted in the previous chapter, there were, however, fewer opportunities for Scotland to contribute single, quality programmes. Scotland did not have the advantages of the network production centres in England, which could develop a strand of programming without abandoning local interests. These network centres produced programmes such as *The World*

About Us (natural history shown on BBC2 and produced in Bristol), *A Question of Sport* (a sports quiz for BBC1 produced in Manchester), *The Good Old Days* (variety programme also produced in Manchester) and *The Doctors* (a twice-weekly serial produced in Birmingham). The lack of technical facilities in Scotland was just as much a problem as that of the inability to specialise. For example, Studio A in Glasgow was fully colourised by August 1971, but the Edinburgh and Aberdeen studios remained in monochrome. This difference was noticeable to viewers in a programme such as *Reporting Scotland*, where the picture switched between the Glasgow, Edinburgh and Aberdeen studios to obtain news reports throughout the country. Likewise, the desire for better production facilities was a reflection of the contrasts believed to exist between the technically high standard of network output and that of some Scottish programmes. The lack of facilities, such as to produce programmes in colour, did adversely affect opportunities for the networking of Scottish material. The Edinburgh studio was colourised in March 1975, followed shortly afterwards by the Aberdeen studio. Despite these technical constraints and the greater use of stranded programming, Scotland continued to produce drama output for the network because drama was a programme area where the network continued to accept one-off productions; light entertainment material was more difficult to export to the network.

Alasdair Milne succeeded in obtaining more resources for programme-making, partly because of his ability to demonstrate that Scotland could contribute material worthy of network transmission. His critics argued that he adopted a more romantic than realistic view of Scotland, to the extent that contemporary social issues such as unemployment and industrial change were not covered as fully as they might have been in programme output. This was as much a reflection of the content of drama and documentary output. Early documentary films, such as *The Northern Lights* about lighthouse men, were followed in the early 1970s by documentaries on current themes, such as the North Sea oil boom, which was covered in the television programme *Undersea Strike!*, a programme which received an award from the Radio Industries Club as the best television programme produced in Scotland for the year 1972–3. Drama output consisted of a mixture of contemporary and traditional themes; the popular *Weir of Hermiston* which was shown on BBC2 was based on the unfinished novel by Robert Louis Stevenson. But equally, the best drama output produced outside Scotland for the network, such as *The Onedin Line* (about a shipping line in the mid-nineteenth century), was not based on contemporary themes.

In 1972, Huw Wheldon informed Alasdair Milne that David Attenborough wished to leave his post as Director of Programmes (Television). Milne agreed to take on this new post and so left for London, to be succeeded by Robert Coulter (Head of Programmes, Scotland), who became Controller designate on 5 December. Robert Coulter succeeded Alasdair Milne as Controller of BBC Scotland on 1 January 1973. Coulter was, for health reasons and because he was two years short of retirement, not in a strong position to carry through Milne's policies and to steer BBC Scotland through a challenging period both in terms of pressure for devolution within the BBC and the need to reflect social, economic and political change in Scotland in programme output, as well as face the challenge from commercial local radio.[17] Scotland needed someone who had greater influence in London. The challenges facing the BBC in Scotland were recognised by the BCS at the beginning of its Annual Report for 1973–4. The celebration and exhibition at Broadcasting House in Glasgow in March 1973, which was attended by BBC Chairman Sir Michael Swann and Director-General Charles Curran to mark fifty years of broadcasting in Scotland, offered a brief opportunity to take a retrospective view of Scottish broadcasting. Throughout the week, special radio programmes were broadcast, including older programmes such as *Children's Hour* and *The McFlannels*. But it was to the future that broadcasters urgently had to turn their attention. There was the technical challenge of improving UHF television coverage, and the programming challenge of ensuring that a greater proportion of Scottish material could enrich UK output. Some programmes were networked on BBC1, in particular *Sutherland's Law* (which dealt with the life of a procurator fiscal in a small Scottish town and featured Iain Cuthbertson) and *Moira in Person* (featuring the singer Moira Anderson). Scottish output did come under greater scrutiny, and this generated external criticism. In January 1974, a Better Scottish Television Association was formed in order to suggest methods for improving broadcasting output in Scotland. This Association, which was based in Edinburgh and whose members included the MP Nicholas Fairbairn and the author Bill Williams, arranged for a survey of public opinion on broadcasting to be conducted by System Three (Scotland) Ltd. This survey was published on 29 October 1974.[18] Despite the inherent limitations of such a survey and the fact that the questions asked were often general in nature, the results indicated that BBC and ITV programmes in Scotland were regarded as less professional, less experimental and less controversial than network programmes, and that life in Scotland was not adequately represented by broadcasting output in Scotland.

Unlike radio, Scottish television programmes could only be provided instead of, rather than in addition to, any network programme. This often irritated those viewers in Scotland who preferred network output. There appeared to be less objection to opting out in television when all BBC Regions opted out together, such as in the *Nationwide* news and magazine programme which was first introduced in 1969. The BBC sought to avoid clashes of popular network programmes with Regional programmes, but where this was unavoidable the network output was on some occasions repeated at another time. The BBC's dual programme responsibility in Scotland did lead to criticism either that the output was too Scottish or that it contained an insufficient proportion of Scottish material. In both radio and television, Scotland had the option of opting out from the main networks to provide programmes likely to be of interest to a Scottish audience; but equally it was a duty of the BBC to bring

Scottish items to a UK audience in order to prevent insularity and parochialism from permeating Scottish output, and also to give opportunities to Scottish-based producers consistently to aim to produce material to network standards. Most producers welcomed the opportunity to display the product of their skills to a wider listening and viewing public. It was also a means of maintaining a strong production base in Scotland by preventing an imbalance occurring between the numbers of staff leaving Scotland to seek wider experience in London and the English Regions and those with greater professional experience who returned to Scotland. There were, in any case, financial incentives involved in getting material networked, in that the costs of programmes which were taken by the networks were covered by the BBC centrally.

Problems regarding the volume of Scottish material which was broadcast both within Scotland and to a wider network audience were connected in part with the image of Scotland projected by the BBC in its programme output. Some critics argued that for many years the broadcasters in Scotland presented restricted images of Scotland for both Scottish and UK consumption.[19] There was deemed to be an absence of images of contemporary Scotland in, for example, television plays. This heavy reliance upon traditional themes reinforced the parochial quality of Scottish output. The use of the term 'parochialism' seemed to imply that programme material was too local in nature and second-rate in quality. Scottish country dancing, the traditional heavy industries in the west of Scotland, and the more traditional sectors in the north of Scotland such as fishing and agriculture, all formed the basis of some of the Scottish images in broadcasting. Regional variations in culture and lifestyle were less accurately portrayed. STV also at times focused on an image of Scotland which concentrated on a static past, thus ignoring contemporary issues or future possibilities. Popular Scottish soap operas tended to be set in rural rather than urban settings, although this did not necessarily diminish their appeal to either a Scottish or a network audience. In BBC Scotland's drama output, dramatisations of classic literature tended to take precedence over contemporary literature. It was in news and current affairs that Scottish programmes slowly began to have an influence on Scottish matters and Scottish culture, perhaps by emphasising differences in public policy, such as in education or the arts, between Scotland and the rest of Britain. However, the tendency of broadcasting in Scotland for many years to avoid adequate treatment of contemporary issues has on several occasions prompted critical comment. John Gray, a former BBC Chief Assistant (Radio) in Scotland, in commenting upon the relationship between, and influence of, broadcasting on culture in Scotland, stated that 'In more than fifty years, broadcasting in Scotland has done little or nothing to evolve a distinctly Scottish broadcasting identity, rather it has consistently looked backwards'.[20] This tendency to look backwards, combined with the use of marked Scottish accents, sometimes made programmes less acceptable for UK transmission than they would otherwise have been and reinforced their parochial quality. Dr Robert McIntyre,

President of the Scottish National Party from 1958 to 1980, was critical of the BBC's choice of Scottish accents which tended, he believed, to present a very unfavourable image of Scottish people to the rest of the UK, but equally he recalled criticising Melville Dinwiddie (Controller, BBC Scotland until 1957) about the use of English accents in Scottish programmes.[21]

The critical comments on the image of Scotland which the BBC projected to the rest of the UK were accompanied by criticism of the quality and quantity of Scottish programme output, particularly on television. Programmes were regarded as too dull, too parochial, or too trivial in comparison with network output. This may be partly explained by the difference in resources available for television productions in Scotland in comparison with London-based productions. Indeed, the audience tended to apply the same standards when judging Scottish and network output without taking account of the funds or facilities available for both. During the 1960s, Scottish news and current affairs was criticised for not engaging sufficiently in investigative reporting or in conducting adequate background research on contemporary issues. Programmes such as *Current Account* did bring about some improvement, but there still remained criticism that too few Scottish programmes were seen outside Scotland.[22] Acceptance of material for network transmission had to be based on quality, since there was no quota system in which London guaranteed to take a proportion of Scottish programme output. Network output tended more to reflect Sir Hugh Greene's belief that broadcasting should encourage the examination of views in an atmosphere of healthy scepticism, should take account of social change, and should be ahead of public opinion because, in his words, today's heresies might prove to be tomorrow's dogmas. For much of the 1960s, BBC Scotland appeared to be out of step with the greater freedom in manners and morals of network output during Hugh Greene's Director-Generalship. By the early 1970s, there was certainly a need to develop programme policy because of the imminent arrival of commercial local radio, pressure for devolution and the need to reflect in programme output the resurgence of Scottish national identity as well as political and economic change in Scotland. But it also involved the need to produce material which was not necessarily Scottish in content. Also, Scotland had always been a country with international links, but this had never been evident from broadcasting output. It could, however, also be argued that the term 'parochialism' could be ascribed to London, where artists and production staff came into frequent contact with each other yet often knew little of Regional or non-metropolitan culture.

The social dimension of broadcasting coverage was an issue which was evident during the 1970s because of the resurgence of Scottish national identity and the social implications of rapid economic development in remote areas.[23] The extension of the 625-line UHF transmitter network posed greater problems in filling gaps in coverage in Scotland compared to the 405-line VHF system because of its different propagation characteristics (i.e. shorter range, and signals deflected by obstacles). There was, though, criticism that the BBC was unfair to Scotland on a population and on an area basis.[24] This has to be viewed against the background of the technical factors which influenced the rate of transmitter development. In planning relay stations in remote areas of Scotland, as elsewhere, the BBC initially tested different sites to determine which ones could provide the best coverage with the minimum transmitter power. Many relay stations were built during the 1970s to fill most gaps in broadcasting coverage. Sites for these stations were carefully chosen in order to be capable of receiving signals from an existing station and re-broadcasting them with translators which used a channel and power level that would not interfere with other transmitters yet would also provide the maximum coverage possible. It was preferable for sites to be reasonably level in order to avoid large building costs. Access to sites could be difficult over uneven terrain or where long access roads were needed, as in the north and west of Scotland. It was necessary to have good access during the building phase, but less so when stations became operational, since most were designed for unattended operation. After surveying and testing sites capable of receiving an electricity supply, sites would have to be bought or leased because the BBC had no powers of compulsory purchase. Planning permission would delay the building of transmitter stations if the BBC encountered legal or administrative problems. In remote, scenic landscape in Scotland, the BBC could be forced to provide a building or mast which blended in with the landscape. On purely technical rather than aesthetic grounds, when the UHF 625-line stations began to replace the VHF 405-line stations, the new stations had to be sited on high ground because of the propagation characteristics of UHF signals. However, suitable high ground was not necessarily near to convenient access roads. The need to supply many UHF relay stations for remote areas meant that they had to be designed for unattended operation, thus requiring reliable computerised equipment. Whenever equipment broke down, this was most likely to pose problems for BBC engineers during the winter months, when many parts of the Highlands of Scotland become inaccessible because of heavy snowfalls. Indeed, breakdowns in the electricity supply, particularly if that supply was carried on a poled route, were more likely to occur during the winter. To compensate for such an eventuality, stations could be provided with a diesel alternator, but this presupposed the existence of good access roads to deliver the diesel oil. In practice, the BBC normally provided reserve transmitting equipment which would become operational automatically if a fault occurred in the main transmitter. But since this could only provide a sustaining service at twenty-five per cent of normal power, it was regarded as a temporary expedient. In any case, if a fault persisted and there were delays in getting access to a site due to bad weather, the public experienced a greater degree of inconvenience. The provision of a full-power reserve transmitter to obviate this problem inevitably involved higher capital costs both for the extra equipment and the space required to house such equipment. In summary, a variety of technical factors determined to a significant extent the ability of the BBC to extend transmitter coverage in Scotland. Some, but not all, of the technical constraints could be overcome by a commitment to utilise financial, human and material resources. Progress depended upon the BBC's estimation of the various priorities requiring capital development.

By the early 1970s, about one third of BBC transmitters had been sited in Scotland, thus emphasising the much greater problems which the BBC experienced in Scotland in extending coverage of its programme services. As a consequence of the serial nature of extending broadcasting coverage (i.e. remote areas tend to be the last to be served), in 1970 a lower percentage of the population in Scotland in comparison with England had received television. The BBC was working on plans to extend UHF television coverage to communities of 1,000 or more people – this became known as phase 1 of the UHF project. It was not practical at the time to extend coverage to 100 per cent of the population, as the Television Advisory Committee had acknowledged.[25] The use of VHF to fill in gaps in coverage would have prevented its use for other television services, so what was required were more UHF relay stations. The problem was that the UHF transmitter programme required four or five times as many transmitters as had been used to extend VHF television during the 1950s and 1960s, primarily because of the shorter range of UHF signals. Also, the UHF transmitter programme was serial in nature, in that the location of stations later in the programme depended upon the coverage obtained by earlier stations. The aim was to bring the UHF service to as many people as quickly and as economically as possible, as well as trying to maintain a geographical balance to enable the four countries of the UK and the BBC Regions in England to be treated on roughly equal terms. Main transmitters covering populous areas were built first, followed by the relay stations. In order to economise on capital expenditure, the programme feed from a relay station had to be obtained direct from another transmitter without the use of additional links, and this therefore dictated the sequence in which relay transmitters were built.

By March 1970, BBC2, which had initially been transmitted in Scotland from Blackhill in central Scotland and from 29 July 1967 extended to the Aberdeenshire area via the Durris transmitter, had reached a population coverage of seventy-five per cent in Scotland because of the opening of two further stations at Angus (on 28 July 1969) and Craigkelly (on 27 October 1969).[26] Reception of the BBC1 405-line VHF service and Radios 2, 3 and 4 on VHF had reached ninety-eight per cent of the population of Scotland. All these figures were lower than the UK broadcasting coverage figures because, as at March 1970, the BBC1 405-line service was available to 99.5 per cent of the population, BBC2 to 87 per cent, and Radios 2, 3 and 4 on VHF to just over 99 per cent. However, VHF radio coverage in Scotland was much higher than coverage of Radios 1, 3 and 4 on medium-wave and Radio 2 on long-wave and medium-wave during daytime hours, and even more so during the hours of darkness. With the UHF network for BBC1 replacing the 405-line VHF service, the coverage of BBC1 on UHF was much less than the 98 per cent figure achieved on VHF. Indeed, by March 1971 when coverage of BBC2 (UHF) had reached 76 per cent in Scotland, the figure for BBC1 (UHF) was only 53 per cent. BBC2 was transmitted from Rosemarkie in July 1970. In addition to the extension of both BBC1 and BBC2 on UHF and of VHF radio in Scotland, the BBC was also seeking to extend colour television. From 13 December 1969, BBC1 in Scotland was duplicated in colour when the UHF transmitter at Blackhill was brought into service, thereby reaching 50 per cent of the population in Scotland; viewers had already received BBC2 colour programmes since 1967. During 1971, the transmitters at Angus and Craigkelly began to transmit BBC2 in colour. By March 1973, when BBC1 in colour had been radiated from the transmitter at Rosemarkie, BBC1 and BBC2 coverage of colour transmissions increased to 83 per cent. The extension of colour reception throughout Scotland persuaded an increasing number of people to purchase colour receivers. Fewer people relied upon monochrome transmissions on the BBC1 405-line VHF network, which ceased to be expanded in Scotland. Indeed, stage V of the VHF television transmitter programme was completed on 7 April 1969, when the television relay station at Millburn Muir was brought into service.

The important issues involved in broadcasting coverage were examined during 1973 and 1974 by a committee appointed by the government. In March 1973, the government stated that it did not propose to establish a new major inquiry into broadcasting because the Television Advisory Committee had indicated that no major technical developments would be likely before the early 1980s. However, the government did wish to sanction a study of the coverage of broadcasting services in Scotland, Wales, Northern Ireland and rural parts of England. On 3 May 1973, Sir John Eden (Minister of Posts and Telecommunications) announced that the government had appointed a committee chaired by Sir Stewart Crawford to examine the coverage of the broadcasting services in the national and the English Regions. The committee's report was published on 21 November 1974. Several organisations and individuals submitted written or oral evidence to the committee, and committee members visited several parts of the country, including Inverness in February 1974 as well as Glasgow and Edinburgh, in order to gain information on Regional broadcasting coverage. In Scotland, the Highlands and Islands Development Board (HIDB) emphasised the need to improve television coverage as a social amenity in order to halt depopulation, attract labour and not discourage tourists who were accustomed to a wider range of broadcasting services. With its concern to encourage social and economic development in the Highlands and Islands, the Board stated:

> It is our belief that the development of broadcasting services in the UK
> takes too little account of regional development policy. The allocation
> of resources and the setting of priorities are determined by reference
> to the needs of the majority, not to meeting requirements arising from
> the social and economic aims of government's regional development
> programmes.[27]

Attention was drawn to the fact that, despite the existence of a uniform licence fee, licence-payers in remote areas did not receive the same quality or range of services as those available to people living in more populated areas. A differentiated licence-fee system based on Regional variations was not a practical possibility. The Post Office had for many years consistently argued that the licence fee only covered the use of a receiving set and that this fee could not be adjusted in accordance with the amount of its use or the quality of the reception received. The HIDB argued that if the national interest was benefiting from industrial development in rural areas (because of North Sea oil) then the nation should help to pay for the cost of improving social amenities, including broadcasting coverage, in these areas. The Committee on Broadcasting Coverage accepted that the lack of television in some areas was a discouragement to tourists and would not stem depopulation. The latter posed a social and economic threat to some areas by causing an imbalance in the age structure of the population. The committee stated that broadcasting could help to bolster Gaelic language and culture, to reinforce Scottish national identity and to cover the social and economic changes brought about by North Sea oil development and the corresponding rapid industrial development in hitherto isolated rural areas in Scotland.

The Crawford Committee examined phase 1 of the UHF plan to extend television to communities of 1,000 or more people and offered the following comment:

> It should also be said that a cut-off point of population groups of 1,000 and more is liable to bear harshly on the smaller communities in the more mountainous areas of the United Kingdom, where employment opportunties are limited, where there are usually few other educational and entertainment amenities, and where there is often a danger of depopulation in consequence.[28]

So the committee advocated for social reasons that coverage should be extended to communities of between 500 and 1,000 people. The committee's report stated that social rather than merely technical factors (i.e. the availability of programme feeds) should influence the sequence in which gaps in coverage were filled during phase 2 of the UHF plan. It was hoped that within phase 2, priority would be given to northern Scotland; phase 2 of the UHF construction programme was later approved by the government in December 1976, and it was hoped that this would bring UHF coverage up to that of VHF coverage by the early 1980s. The BBC in any case wished to end duplication of VHF services to avoid wasting resources, but could not realistically achieve this until UHF coverage matched VHF coverage. By March 1974, only about ten per cent of households still relied upon 405-line VHF television, but in North-West Scotland only the 405-line service was available. Two years earlier, the Television Advisory Committee had recommended that 1980 should be adopted as the target date for the closure of VHF 405-line services, assuming that UHF coverage had reached ninety-six per cent by this date.[29] The Crawford

Committee also wanted measures to be taken to develop Regional variations in television to counter centralism and to reflect Regional identities.

The Crawford Report indicated that because BBC Scotland served a large community, a case could be made for subdividing Scotland in a way similar to that achieved by ITV. This did not entail the creation of independent BBC production centres in Scotland but rather the introduction of an element of Regional diversification in the transmission of programmes on a sub-opt-out basis.[30] In addition to the possibility of sub-opt-outs in the north of Scotland, the Crawford Committee also wanted the BBC to consider the allocation of funds and technical apparatus to permit opt-outs on BBC2, and not just on BBC1, for the provision of local interest programmes. This proposal was influenced by comparisons with ITV because the commercial programme companies were regarded by the committee as catering more fully for Regional needs than the BBC. The committee therefore supported the retention of the three separate ITV companies in Scotland rather than their amalgamation into one large company. As regards radio broadcasting coverage, the committee recommended that the BBC should seek to identify unserved areas of VHF transmitters and extend VHF radio coverage to as many areas as possible, particularly in northern Scotland where separate services could be provided, and also in other areas which experienced poor medium-frequency reception. The Crawford Report also drew attention to the need for the BBC to extend local radio to Scotland after an adequate national service had been developed, and then only to extend it to smaller populated areas than the ILR stations covered in Scotland.

With the appointment of the Annan Committee on Broadcasting in April 1974, the recommendations of the Crawford Committee on Broadcasting Coverage were left to be considered by the Annan Committee, particularly because, as a major committee of inquiry, it had a wider remit. Material was prepared by the BBC for submission to the Annan Committee, and the broadcasters now had to await publication of its report and of the government's response to it in order to judge the future direction of broadcasting both within Scotland and throughout the UK.

Part Five

Centralisation, devolution and new challenges, 1974–83

The Annan Report on Broadcasting: submissions, recommendations and responses, 1974–7

In 1969, the Labour Government planned to appoint a committee to examine broadcasting. In May 1970, John Stonehouse, Minister of Posts and Telecommunications, announced that there would be a new inquiry into broadcasting to be chaired by Lord Annan. But these plans were abandoned, much to the relief of the BBC, when Labour lost the General Election a month later to the Conservative Party. It was therefore not until 1974, with the return of the Labour Party to power, that the committee was eventually established. On 10 April 1974, Roy Jenkins, Home Secretary, announced in the House of Commons that a committee would be formed to consider the future of broadcasting services in the UK, including the possible provision of additional services. It would also examine the constitutional, organisational and financial arrangements involved. The committee was also expected to comment on the recommendations of the Crawford Committee on Broadcasting Coverage, whose report was expected to be published towards the end of 1974. Lord Annan, Provost of University College London, was appointed to chair the committee; the appointment of other members was announced on 12 July. The committee received a large volume of both written and oral evidence. Unlike the Beveridge and Pilkington inquiries, this evidence was not published. The Annan Committee, which first met in July 1974, held forty-four meetings. The Home Secretary asked the committee to report in two-and-a-half years, and so he extended the BBC's Charter and Licence and Agreement from July 1976 until July 1979 to allow adequate time for the completion of the committee's work, debate on the report when it was published, and for any legislation that would require to be implemented. This was the first major inquiry to examine the operation of competitive local radio services. The committee set itself three objectives:

(1) to preserve British broadcasting as a public service;

(2) to plan a new structure for broadcasting capable of meeting changes over the following fifteen years;

(3) to retain the editorial independence of the BBC and the IBA free from political pressure or interest groups, yet ensure the public accountability of the broadcasters.

The committee began its study during a period of expansion, and concluded in

1977 during a period of greater pessimism about the resources available for expansion in broadcasting. In one respect, it was thus no different from previous committees which also provided snapshots of broadcasting at specific periods of time. This chapter outlines the submissions of evidence to the committee with regard to broadcasting in Scotland, the recommendations of the Annan Committee on the pattern of broadcasting services which should be provided, and the outcome of the publication of the Annan Report in terms of government policy on the future direction of broadcasting.

In 1975, the Broadcasting Council for Scotland submitted a memorandum to the committee in which it stated that UHF 625-line television should be extended to all communities of more than 500 people before provision was made for a fourth television channel. Furthermore, the Council did not want 405-line VHF television to be withdrawn from any area until UHF services could be provided on a uniform basis. It also wanted more Scottish-originated material to be networked on BBC1 and BBC2 and to be produced for viewers in Scotland. Apart from the volume of programme output, the BCS sought more flexibility in deciding whether to opt out from BBC1 or BBC2. The Council noted that Scotland needed the finance and the facilities to transmit its own programme mix; in particular, there was a need for greater financial freedom when committing funds for major series prior to receiving sanction by London, and for freedom to opt out from the networks in order to substitute Scottish material. The BCS also looked towards the possibility of greater freedom for the regions of Scotland to create their own programmes at some periods during the day and to contribute material for both a Scottish and a UK audience. On the image of Scotland which the BCS wanted the BBC in Scotland to project, the Council stated:

> To those who are not Scots it should be said that the Scotland that we seek to project is not only the known land of romance and matchless scenic beauty but also the newer Scotland of off-shore oil, industrial growth, artistic renaissance and self-government – not parochial, but outward-looking and international in its approach.[1]

BBC Scotland NUJ chapel supported the BCS view that there was a need for more Regional contributions to the network, more Scottish opt-outs and more resources to take on major productions without having to depend upon production teams being brought up to Scotland from London. It supported greater decentralisation of power and authority within the BBC, but not the creation of an autonomous Scottish Broadcasting Corporation. James Kemp, BBC Scottish Editor of News and Current Affairs from 1965 to 1972, stated that the lack of Scottish contributions of material to the television networks denied Scottish-based producers an opportunity to raise their professional standards and that this in turn provided justification for London taking even fewer Scottish programmes.[2]

The Scottish National Party supported greater freedom for Scotland to opt out during peak viewing hours and to have the resources to reflect adequately social and economic change in Scotland. The SNP believed that staff and resources had been spread too thinly because the BBC (and ITV) had too many special responsibilities in programming in Scotland. The SNP summarised its views on Scottish broadcasting in general by stating:

> Scottish broadcasting suffers from being neither fully 'National', nor purely 'regional'. There is too little cash, too few facilities, and too much duplication of effort. So long as BBC London and the ITV Big Five dominate the programme schedules and sign the cheques, Scottish broadcasting will remain provincial.[3]

The need to get more material networked was not unique to BBC Scotland. In a submission to the Annan Committee, STV stated that it wanted more Scottish material to be networked because this would strengthen the Scottish programming base and attract talented producers to work in Scotland. STV did not favour the creation of a separate Scottish broadcasting system, but it did want the Scottish influence in the IBA in London to be increased. The Labour Party's Scottish Council wanted better television facilities in Scotland, more opportunities to contribute Scottish items to the networks, and arrangements for BBC Scotland to opt out from the network without reference to London.[4] The intention was to give greater freedom of control to programme planners in Scotland, but not to press for a separate broadcasting organisation for Scotland for fear that this would lead to an unacceptable degree of parochialism in programme output. It also suggested that BBC2 should be reorganised into a number of Regional centres similar to the federal structure of ITV. The Conservative Party in Scotland supported the greater networking of Scottish programmes – especially documentaries during a period of economic and industrial change in Scotland – in order to provide viewers outside Scotland with a more contemporary perspective on events within Scotland. The Conservative Party also hoped that broadcasting would play its part in helping to assist social integration in areas involved in North Sea oil development which had experienced the influx of many people. The HIDB stressed the need to extend television as a social amenity in areas undergoing rapid economic and industrial development arising from North Sea oil discoveries. It was also important to provide programme material which was not always Scottish in content. On this theme, Alastair Hetherington (Controller, BBC Scotland) commented:

> In thinking of network output, Scotland needs to emerge from being type-cast as always producing 'Scottish' programmes. That tends to perpetuate parochialism, and it cuts off our writers and producers from mainstream British and European work. They shouldn't have to go to London to secure international reputations.[5]

The ability to reflect social, economic and political change in Scotland in programme output depended upon the financial and technical resources available. On 2 July 1975, the Association of Broadcasting Staff (ABS) (Edinburgh branch) sent a submission to the committee in which it stated that there were strong reasons for redirecting the resources of BBC Scotland to Edinburgh because of its position as the headquarters of government in Scotland, as a financial and cultural centre and as the home of traditional institutions such as the law and the Church. The ABS stated that, within BBC Scotland, Edinburgh had the status of an underequipped and understaffed branch office with no facilities for film processing or editing, thereby giving undue influence to Glasgow in television output. Reference was made to Edinburgh being one of the last television studios to be converted for colour operation. The ABS favoured a weekly output from *Reporting Scotland* to allow Edinburgh to provide its own television news magazine covering the east of Scotland. The ABS also argued that the BBC should not merely have been planning to open new studios in Edinburgh but should also, at a time of radical political and economic change, move the Corporation's Scottish headquarters to Edinburgh. The Association argued that unless change of this nature was contemplated, then the resources of the BBC in Edinburgh would be inadequate to cope with the new demands posed by a future Scottish Assembly, should political devolution become a reality.[6] Staff in Aberdeen were also critical of the centralisation of programmes and administration within Scotland based on Glasgow. What was desired was the devolution of responsibilities to Regional centres within Scotland. Within the BBC, the issue of mini-devolution was a theme dealt with in several of the submissions of evidence to the Annan Committee. So whereas the ABS (Edinburgh branch) and staff in Aberdeen drew attention to the negative effects of centralisation of resources within Scotland, what was of concern to many of the other individuals and organisations were the effects of centralisation in the BBC as a whole and its influence on the development of broadcasting in Scotland.

The SNP wanted broadcasting to be devolved to the proposed Scottish Assembly, but had no wish to create an inward-looking Scottish broadcasting system. The SNP sought a wider range of high-quality programmes produced in Scotland; for Scottish broadcasters both to reflect and to assert Scottish national identity; and for a high priority to be given to the expansion of existing broadcasting services in Scotland. If the SNP's aim of self-government came to fruition, then the Party proposed the formation of a Scottish Broadcasting Commission financed through licence fees, an advertising levy and a Treasury grant, and responsible for allocating and funding radio and television channels. Money would be disbursed through a Scottish Broadcasting Authority which would be responsible for directing overall programme policy. The ABS supported the maximum possible decentralisation of programme-making but within existing constitutional and financial limitations. It rejected the idea of establishing autonomous broadcasting organisations in the national Regions because of the potential disruptive effects on the terms of employment and career development of staff.[7] Likewise, it did not support the breaking-up of the BBC into individual units, since this would undermine centralised bargaining arrangements for salaries and conditions of service. The STUC advocated an expansion of BBC Scotland programme activities, better geographical coverage of services and greater devolution in decision-making, but it did not support the creation of a separate BBC Scottish Corporation. On the general theme of the autonomy of broadcasting in Scotland, the Scottish Arts Council concluded its submission of evidence to the committee by stating:

> While we are conscious of the benefits which partaking in a truly British broadcasting service – both as consumers and as producers – could bring, we believe it would accord better with the concensus of opinion in Scotland if more power to take decisions, and more resources to make them effective, were given to people in Scotland. Not out of a narrow sense of nationalism or even separatism, but simply because it is neither necessary nor desirable that so many decisions about broadcasting should be taken, directly or indirectly, in London 400 miles away.[8]

The BCS stated that BBC Scotland must have direct control over a greater proportion of operating and capital expenditure in relation to broadcasting within and for Scotland. The Church of Scotland Committee on Church and Nation also emphasised the need for the Broadcasting Council to have adequate financial, technical and staff resources to discharge its duties to safeguard the interests of Scottish broadcasting. The Church of Scotland Committee went on to state:

> If the Council is being baulked in carrying out its function to the full by decisions taken by BBC London it must demonstrate publicly if all else fails, that it will not be frustrated in carrying out its duties. If, on the other hand, it is satisfied that it is already having full regard to the distinctive culture, language, interests and tastes of the people of Scotland in the radio and television programmes now provided let it say so and allow the licence holders to judge its performance.[9]

The Scottish Controller, Alastair Hetherington, blamed the centralised nature of the BBC for the failure of BBC Scotland to get a higher proportion of material taken by the networks; he hoped that it would be possible to build up staff and resources in Scotland and secure greater access to network time. He supported greater financial and administrative autonomy for Scotland, but not an independent BBC Scotland.

The Annan Committee also received many views about the allocation of the fourth television channel. The SNP supported improvements in existing services before any decision was made regarding the allocation of the fourth channel. The SNP, in common with the BCS, wanted the fourth channel to be used for community, minority interest and experimental programmes when it was eventually authorised; they did not want it to operate as an ITV2. The BBC also argued that this channel should not be operated by commercial interests because, it was stated, this would create a fierce competitive situation between the BBC's two television channels and two commercial channels (i.e. it would reimpose the negative aspects of competition in television which prevailed in the late 1950s and early 1960s). The Corporation went on to state that 'In the view of the BBC, the formula – the asymmetrical allocation of channels between the public and the commercial services and the symmetrical division of the audience between them in the present 50:50 share – serves the public well'.[10] The ABS also did not support the operation of the fourth channel as a commercial service, although it believed that the IBA should provide the transmitter network and distribution links. It wanted the fourth channel to be used to cover specialist interests, including Open University programmes. The Labour Party Scottish Council, the STUC and the Scottish Arts Council supported the improvement of reception of existing television services; the development of the fourth channel was regarded as a longer-term considera-tion. The Scottish Office argued that the fourth channel should not be used for exclusively educational purposes or a combination of that and Welsh language broadcasts because this would restrict the audience for the new channel. With regard to schools' broadcasts, the School Broadcasting Council for Scotland stated that schools' series which consisted mainly of network rather than Scottish material did not take fully into account the different needs of Scottish schools under their separate education system (i.e. different terms, examina-tions, curricula, age of transfer from primary to secondary education). The Council therefore advocated the need for an extension of schools' series produced in Scotland.[11] As regards Gaelic television broadcasting, An Comunn (the Highland Association) criticised the lack of time and resources allocated to coverage of Gaelic language and culture. In particular, the small allocation of television time and its restriction to the North and North-West of Scotland was criticised given that Gaelic speakers were scattered throughout Scotland. An Comunn disliked the fact that the Crawford Committee on Broadcasting Coverage had been more generous in recommending improvements in Welsh television output in comparison with Gaelic television output in Scotland. It stated that the future aim should be to establish a Gaelic television service broadcasting for four hours each day to Gaelic areas (i.e. initially on an area opt-out basis in the Highlands and Islands, but with some output also broadcast on all Scottish transmitters). Television was regarded as a more important medium than radio for sustaining Gaelic language and culture. Furthermore, An Comunn went on to remark that 'We should add here that we would also expect some Gaelic to be broadcast in England and Wales in order to help broaden the general level of awareness concerning non-English-based cultures indigenous to the United Kingdom'.[12] The Highland Regional Council drew the Annan Committee's attention to the need to take account of Gaelic-speaking areas in broadcasting output. The SNP supported the expansion of Gaelic coverage on television and regretted that the Crawford Committee had not given the same priority to television coverage of Gaelic as it did to Welsh, but did not support the use of the fourth channel for Gaelic broadcasting because Gaels represented only 1½ per cent of the population.

The Annan Committee received several submissions of evidence which commented upon the radio services. In a memorandum submitted by the BCS, the Council stated that in radio it wanted Scotland to provide its own coherent programme services without depriving listeners of the opportunity to hear UK services. This implied the provision of a full Radio Scotland service on VHF and medium-wave which would not merely be an opt-out service from Radio 4. In remoter areas, the BCS wanted the development of several community stations. The Council noted:

> The development of community radio, especially in towns outside the central belt, is urgently desirable. This latter would be of particular value in furthering community identity in northern regions suffering the social disruption of rapid industrial development.[13]

Community radio on VHF as an opt-out service from Radio Scotland would develop from the periphery inwards, rather than from the centre to the periphery as was the norm with broadcasting services. The BCS attached great importance to the development of community radio as a means of serving the many small communities scattered throughout Scotland. Drawing the distinction between existing BBC local radio stations and the small community stations proposed for Scotland, the Council went on to state that 'A development of community radio rather than urban local radio has unlimited potential as a medium of communi-cation and as a resource for personal and group development'.[14] The Council welcomed the preparations for a radio station based in Inverness which was designed to provide Gaelic as well as English-language programmes to people in the Highlands and Islands and to contribute material on oil-related develop-ments to the Scottish and UK networks. However, the BCS also hoped that Oban and Stornoway would be centres of Gaelic broadcasting. Furthermore, the Council drew attention to the need to expand the Edinburgh studios and to extend broadcasting services to all communities of more than 500 people, particularly as many such communities were geographically isolated and lacked the amenities taken for granted in urban areas. In particular, in parts of Scotland, listeners had to rely on VHF transmissions for their radio service and were there-fore denied the general programmes available on long-wave and medium-wave. The percentage coverage figures for broadcasting services in the UK gave a mis-leading impression of the situation in Scotland, where many people living in remote areas experienced either poor or no reception of some programme services. The SNP wanted Scottish services to continue to be provided through Radio 4 and later extended to Radio 2, but also supported the establishment of localised radio services in Scotland in the Highlands and in the Borders and at a later stage in Shetland and the Western Isles.[15] The SNP wanted at least four hours of Gaelic radio broadcasting each day in the Highland area and one hour broadcast on national radio. The SNP also wanted future local stations to be provided in the remote areas where the need for such a service was deemed to be much greater than in more populous areas. The SNP supported the strengthening of the BBC's all-Scotland identity on Radio Scotland and also emphasised the need to improve VHF radio coverage in Scotland.

In its submission to the Annan Committee, An Comunn criticised BBC Scotland for its decision in April 1974 to confine most Gaelic radio programmes to VHF, because listeners in areas which could not receive VHF were denied Gaelic broadcasts, and people in VHF reception areas were forced to purchase VHF receivers if they wished to obtain such broadcasts. An Comunn doubted the commitment to Gaelic community radio despite the BBC's plans for a local station in Inverness. What was hoped for was community radio, providing a comprehensive range of programmes to all Gaelic-speaking areas and broadcasting initially for at least four hours each day. An Comunn did not believe that the station planned for Inverness would fulfil this requirement, because Gaelic output would represent only one aspect of the station's programme activities, the programme output would be minimal, and it would not serve all Gaelic-speaking areas.[16] Furthermore, the Association stated that it was confident that demand existed for increased Gaelic radio output for Gaelic speakers resident outside the traditional Gaelic areas. As regards local radio, BBC staff in Aberdeen expressed disappointment that Scotland had been denied any BBC local radio, and in particular supported the establishment of a separate Gaelic radio service for the Highlands and Islands. These developments were viewed as meriting a higher priority than a Scottish presence on Radio 2. At some stage, it was hoped that provision could be made for small, two-man stations for the scattered communities in the Highlands and Islands which could also provide material for the BBC's national services. The paper submitted by BBC staff in Aberdeen also highlighted the need to extend stereo transmissions to the north of Scotland. The STUC regretted that it was commercial rather than BBC local radio which had been developed in Scotland. The ABS supported what it termed a planned expansion of BBC local radio, but did not indicate whether this expansion was confined to England or was to embrace the establishment of local radio stations in Scotland; the ABS did support the development of national radio in Scotland. The Scottish Arts Council regretted that the BBC had not opened any local radio stations in Scotland. The Council also noted that the concentration of network drama in London, Birmingham and Manchester made it difficult to attract actors and actresses to work in 'live' theatre in Scotland. This implied the need to alter the locational imbalance in the production of drama in favour of Scotland. A BBC submission which summarised the development of its programme services from 1962 to 1974 referred to the absence of local radio stations in Scotland but stated:

> It is, however, open to question whether the most desirable form of localised radio broadcasting in Scotland would very closely resemble the stations in operation in England. With few exceptions, the population of Scotland is not concentrated in urban centres and is, in the Highlands and Islands, scattered over very large distances.[17]

In Scotland, radio development took the form of increasing the Scottish output and Scottish identity of the opt-out service on Radio 4, combined with plans to develop community radio on an opt-out basis from Radio Scotland.

The Annan Report on Broadcasting was published in March 1977. The report indicated that the BBC should develop its production base in Scotland to provide more material both for Scottish and particularly network transmission.[18] The committee acknowledged that the BCS wanted opt-outs on BBC2 and not only on BBC1, but stated that the proposed fourth television channel (under the control of a new Open Broadcasting Authority) rather than BBC2 should provide opportunities for a distinctively Scottish television service which would include Gaelic programmes. The committee did not envisage the fourth channel as developing into an ITV2 in competition with the other three channels. It did envisage that the new channel would transmit programmes drawn from a wide range of sources, and that the OBA would ensure that programmes in Scotland, Wales and Northern Ireland met the needs and interests of people living in these countries. The prospect of Regional television, as highlighted by the 1974 Crawford Report, was regarded by the Annan Committee as a more distant prospect. The committee stated that it did not wish to place too many burdens on the BBC, and so it recommended that the Corporation should continue to provide a basically national television service in Scotland rather than extensive Regional variations within Scotland. It did, however, suggest that BBC Scotland should be given more flexibility over the scheduling of programmes specifically for viewers in Scotland to replace network programmes.[19] The committee wanted both BBC Scotland and the ITV Regional companies to contribute more material to the network, but it rejected the view expressed by the SNP and the Labour Party Scottish Council that there should only be one ITV contractor in Scotland to facilitate the networking of material. The committee stated that the three ITV Regional companies in Scotland were needed because the BBC in Scotland essentially provided a service for the whole of Scotland. The report supported the extension of production facilities in Scotland, but, on the image of Scotland which BBC television presented to the network audience, the committee stated:

> Something is wrong with the image of Scotland which television projects to the rest of the United Kingdom. The national culture is reflected too much by hackneyed symbols, and too little importance is given to the new opportunities and hopes, the shifts in pattern of industry and occupations, as well as the dour problems and grim realities of life in some parts of Scotland today.[20]

On this basis, it seemed that little had changed since television had arrived in Scotland a quarter of a century previously.

With the prospect of political devolution for Scotland, there was the question as to what the relationship would be between any Scottish Assembly and the broadcasting organisations. The broadcasters were opposed to the creation of separate broadcasting authorities answerable to Assemblies in Scotland and Wales, for fear that the latter would bring political influence to bear on programme content. In any case, frequency planning had to remain under central control because of the UK's international obligations and also because the same frequencies were used throughout the country but allocated to stations separated geographically in order to prevent mutual interference from occurring. The cost of broadcasting was another matter. On this, the Annan Report stated:

> If therefore broadcasting in Scotland and Wales were to be separated from broadcasting services in England, it would cost the people of Scotland and Wales dear, particularly if the Scottish and Welsh broadcasting authorities had to pay the English authorities for popular programmes.[21]

The committee wanted the BBC to remain the main instrument of broadcasting in the UK and to continue to be financed by licence fees, but to have particular responsibilities in the national Regions. The SNP's proposal that there should be a completely autonomous broadcasting authority in Scotland was rejected. The report did, however, advocate that the BCS should be allocated money for programmes made specifically for transmission in Scotland, and that the Council should be permitted to decide how to divide this allocation of funds between radio and television. It also suggested that the BBC's national Regions should have a limited annual budget for minor capital investment. The committee also questioned whether the national Broadcasting Councils were representative of the communities which they served, hence the suggestion that the range of interests and views on these Councils should be widened. Summing up the case against the creation of separate broadcasting authorities for the national Regions, the committee stated:

> To talk of devolving responsibility for broadcasting to some body in the national regions is meaningless unless the power to plan the use of frequencies goes with it and that would be impracticable. Since the same frequencies are used many times throughout the country, the strategic decisions on the number of services and the frequencies to be used to provide them must continue to be taken centrally, unless there is to be a drastic reduction in the number of services everywhere.[22]

The committee stressed that it was not suggesting that improvements could not be made in the provision of, and control over, broadcasting services in Scotland. Indeed, as already noted, the committee's support for increased Scottish contributions to the network was one step in this direction. As regards UHF television coverage, the committee wanted a high priority to be given to the provision of UHF services to populations of more than 500 people, particularly in northern Scotland, the Scottish Islands and mid-Wales.

With regard to the provision of radio services, the Annan Report stated that the BBC should continue to operate four national radio networks, but that efforts should be made to encourage listeners to switch between radio channels by the use of methods such as cross-trailing the programmes on alternative networks. This was deemed to be of importance, given the presence of generic radio broadcasting with its specialised networks. The committee believed that local radio was useful because it checked the tendency for national radio to become dominated by London and the three large English network production centres. However, given the differences between local radio and network broadcasting, the committee argued that the former should come under the control of a Local Broadcasting Authority (LBA) and not remain under the control of the BBC and the IBA. In these circumstances, the IBA would require to be renamed the Regional Television Authority. The proposed LBA would be funded by rentals from local radio stations and be expected to give high priority to the opening of local stations in areas such as the Highlands and Islands. The LBA would award franchises to those organisations which appeared most likely to provide the kind of service which was best suited to what the people in these areas stated they needed. The committee argued that if local radio continued to remain the responsibility of the BBC or the IBA, then it was likely to develop only in the shadow of the network services and in their image, whereas local stations needed to reflect the image of the communities which they served.[23]

The committee looked at the provision of broadcasting services in the BBC's national Regions and recommended that urgent attention should be given to filling gaps in VHF radio coverage in Scotland. Scotland could set the priorities in terms of extending BBC services within Scotland, but decisions on the overall planning of frequencies would continue to be taken centrally in London. As regards radio programme output, the committee wanted the BBC Controller in Scotland to be given greater flexibility over the scheduling in Scotland of radio programmes produced specifically for listeners in Scotland. It also wanted Radio Scotland to increase its programme output both for the Scottish audience and for other network radio services. With the committee's proposal that local radio, both BBC and ILR, should be the responsibility of a new authority (i.e. the LBA), it therefore followed that the committee's report did recommend that the BBC should not provide community radio services in Scotland.[24] The committee did, however, state that the BBC should continue to operate a community radio station in Inverness until radio services there could be provided by the proposed LBA. It was also recommended that the LBA should establish a committee in Scotland to advise on the arrangements for the provision of Scottish local radio services, particularly in the Highlands and Islands. On the issue of Gaelic broadcasting, the Annan Committee recommended, much to the subsequent dismay of An Comunn, that responsibility for providing programmes in Gaelic to the Gaelic-speaking areas should be shared between Grampian Television and the proposed LBA; the BBC would, however, continue to be responsible for providing some Gaelic programmes on radio throughout Scotland. An Comunn believed that neither Grampian Television nor the proposed LBA would have the Gaelic specialists that the BBC had.

A variety of responses flowed from the publication of the committee's report. The BBC Board of Governors held a special meeting on 24 March 1977 to discuss initial impressions of the Annan Report. The BBC accepted that its national role should not be purely metropolitan in character and that therefore there was a need to strengthen Regional and local broadcasting, hence there was concern about the Report's proposal that local radio should be placed under a Local Broadcasting Authority. In its Annual Report for 1976–7, the BBC stated:

> In our view the Committee's proposal for local broadcasting would not make possible the kind of community service which we in the BBC have provided, and to which the Committee itself has paid tribute. The proposed LBA's primary commercial base would of necessity reflect that base and give a different kind of service. It would eventually result in a reduced choice for the listener.[25]

To emphasise the importance of preserving localised services, the BBC stated that there was no essential difference of principle between spending licence money on Radio 3 for minorities of taste and spending it on local radio's geographical minorities. The BBC wished to extend local radio in England and community radio in Scotland and thus was against the committee's proposal to place control of localised broadcasting under an LBA. The BCS also wanted the BBC to retain control over local radio development. The Council hoped that BBC Scotland would be able to set up further local radio stations based in Dundee, Dumfries, Melrose and the Western Isles. It agreed with the committee about the need to expand output on Radio Scotland and for improvements to take place in VHF radio coverage, especially in the north and west of Scotland. The Broadcasting Council issued a press statement on 9 May in which it welcomed Annan's recognition of the need for BBC Scotland to exercise greater financial and managerial authority. Alastair Hetherington (Controller, BBC Scotland) and Professor Alan Thompson (BBC National Governor for Scotland) both welcomed most of the Scottish recommendations contained in the report, particularly those advocating that BBC Scotland should produce more network television programmes and have greater control over capital and operating expenditure. There was more concern in England about the Annan Report's recommendation that the BBC should cut back on its Regional centres to concentrate programme-making at the large network production centres because the small BBC centres were deemed to have inadequate equipment and insufficient resources for bold programming.

In July 1978, the government published its White Paper on Broadcasting. The government agreed that the BBC should remain the national instrument of broadcasting in the UK with responsibility for providing services catering for the particular needs of people in Scotland, Wales and Northern Ireland. This ruled out any possibility of creating a separate broadcasting authority in Scotland. The government did, however, agree that a greater degree of autonomy should be given to the national Broadcasting Councils. In particular, the White Paper stated that these Councils should be allocated money for programmes made specifically for transmission in Scotland and Wales, and should themselves decide how to divide this allocation between radio and television; it also stated that they should have an annual budget for minor capital investment.[26] The government, much to the dismay of the BCS, which was concerned about governmental interference in broadcasting, also indicated that changes in the method of appointment of members to the Broadcasting Councils should take place. The government wanted lay members, other than the national Governors, to be appointed by the Home Secretary after consultation with the Secretary of State for Scotland or Wales and the BBC Chairman, rather than by a panel of the BBC's General Advisory Council. This was broadly similar to the arrangement proposed for the new Service Management Boards. It reflected the government's view on structural changes in the BBC which it deemed were needed in order clearly to separate the twin functions of the Governors, namely to safeguard the public interest and to oversee BBC management. The government wanted changes in order to distance the Governors from detailed involvement in management. The Governors were expected to delegate to the Service Management Boards for Television, Radio, and External Services, many of the managerial functions which the Governors already held. The theory was that the Governors would then be able to concentrate more fully on their functions as guardians of the public interest. These proposed changes reflected the government's view that the BBC had become too bureaucratic, too concerned with the concept of professionalism and not sufficiently attuned to the public interest. But the government's proposals for the creation of these new Boards seemed themselves unnecessarily complicated and bureaucratic. As regards the fourth television channel, the government stated that it should be supervised by an Open Broadcasting Authority which would acquire but not produce programmes. Also, a phased programme would operate for closing existing 405-line transmitters, so that eventually the whole country would be provided with 625-line UHF services. The White Paper indicated that the plan to extend UHF television to all communities of 500 or more people, many of which were located in Scotland, would not be hindered by the development of a fourth channel.[27] The government encouraged the extension of local radio, but did not agree with the Annan Committee that control over local radio should be taken away from the BBC and IBA and given to a separate authority, the LBA. The government was anxious for as many areas of the country as possible to have access to two local radio services (i.e. BBC and ILR), and agreed with the committee that the opening of local stations in Scotland should therefore be given a high priority within the general expansion of local radio.[28] The BCS welcomed support for community radio under BBC control; proposals for an OBA and Service Management Boards never materialised.

BBC *Scotland and regional devolution, 1975–9*

The centralised nature of the BBC has over the years inhibited the devolution of responsibility for many functions to the Regions. Various aspects of centralisation in the period up until about 1975 are therefore worth noting in order to place in context the greater efforts made during the second half of the 1970s to devolve more responsibility to the BBC in Scotland. John Reith, the BBC's first Director-General, favoured central control of broadcasting for reasons of efficiency and the maintenance of high programme standards. His belief in central control pre-dated the reconstitution of the British Broadcasting Company into a public corporation on 1 January 1927. There is little doubt that the BBC's monopoly had for many years both encouraged and justified centralisation. The monopoly was defended by the BBC because it guaranteed high programme standards, served the interests of minorities and majorities among the listening public, upheld public service ideals, was economically efficient and enabled the transmitter network to be planned to serve rural and sparsely-populated areas and not just the main centres of population. In the absence of governmental intervention in the BBC's day-to-day administration or programme-making, the Corporation had latitude in deciding how much central control would be retained by London and how much control would be delegated to the Regions. As will be noted, this can be traced from the early 1920s up until the 1970s. During the early 1970s, there was a renewal of nationalist sentiment in Scotland and concern about the growth in the size and complexity of the BBC and the ability to manage it under the existing organisational structure. These factors, together with a belief that, despite the existence and extended functions of the BCS, there was too much central control from London, increased pressure for a greater devolution of powers to Scotland. By 1975, there was broad agreement within the BBC that there was a need to devolve more responsibility to the Regions. What was not so easily agreed upon was the extent of Regional devolution and the implications this would have for BBC broadcasting as a whole. This chapter considers the practical steps which were taken in and after 1975 to bring about devolution against the background of wider political devolution; the differing expectations within the BBC regarding how much power would be devolved; plans for development of BBC Scotland services; the conflicts between BBC Scotland and

London over the extent and progress of Regional devolution; and finally the outcome of these conflicts.

Broadcasting which began on a localised basis, and which included the establishment of local stations at Glasgow, Aberdeen, Edinburgh and Dundee, did not remain local. The policy of centralisation and the advent of the Regional Scheme which became fully operational in Scotland in 1932 resulted in the closure of the local stations and their replacement by a Scottish Regional programme. Certainly the Regional Scheme extended radio services to cover parts of Scotland which had previously been denied any broadcasting service, but it was unable to cater adequately for regional cultural diversity within Scotland, and it also led to the predominance of metropolitan interests at the expense of local or regional interests. London had access to the best talent and facilities, and so the policy which emerged was one whereby Regions were not expected to embark on programmes which could be better produced in London. The in-built constraints on the free exchange of programme material between the National and the Regional programmes, and the concern over the policy of centralisation, surfaced in the 1936 report by the BBC's Director of Regional Relations. This report, which drew attention to the lack of facilities in the Regions and the inability of Regional staff to specialise to the same extent as their counterparts in London, also stated that centralisation represented a short-sighted policy because the Regions could exist as a useful reservoir of programme material.[1] The autonomy of the Scottish Region did however remain limited within an essentially centralised broadcasting organisation. Indeed, even the Reithian public-service ethos tended to become associated with metropolitan rather than regional or local culture.

Scottish Regional radio, which closed during the war years, was revitalised after the war with the introduction of the Scottish Home Service on 29 July 1945. However, many of the questions about the implications of central control which became evident during the interwar years had to be addressed in the postwar period. Was the BBC, for example, prepared to treat Scotland as a nation of regions rather than a region of the United Kingdom; and was the BBC prepared to concede more autonomy to its national Regions, given that there was no intention to create a separate broadcasting corporation for Scotland? These were the type of issues which were of concern to the Saltire Society's Broadcasting Committee. At the root of the proposals which emanated from the Society in this period was the concern that effective control over broadcasting in Scotland should reside in Scotland. The proposal for a Scottish Board of Governors did not come to fruition, but the government recommended in the 1946 White Paper that the BBC should appoint Regional Advisory Councils in order to advise the Corporation on matters affecting Regional programme policy.[2] Although this was noted in the White Paper under the heading 'Regional Devolution', these Councils, which included the Scottish Advisory Council, were by definition purely advisory bodies and therefore had no executive control over programme policy. It was not until the publication of the

Beveridge Report on Broadcasting in 1951 that it was proposed that Broadcasting Councils or Commissions should be established with executive powers. However, the proposal that these Councils should be established in the BBC's national Regions was not warmly welcomed by the BBC for fear that they might undermine the unity of the Corporation by generating internal tensions between these Regions and the BBC centrally.[3] Nevertheless, the government accepted the views of the Beveridge Committee about the need for further devolution of powers and for the creation of Broadcasting Councils for Scotland and Wales as a means to this end, but the government also agreed that the BBC centrally must have overall responsibility for finance and capital development.[4] In the latter two crucial areas, the Councils only had advisory powers. It appeared that the formation of the Broadcasting Councils was an attempt to lessen the impact of the centralised nature of the BBC within the national Regions. However, it must be noted that the Royal Charter of July 1952 stated that each national Broadcasting Council was to be subject to 'such reservations and directions as may appear to the Corporation to be necessary from time to time for reasons of finance or in the interest of due coordination and coherent administration of the operations and affairs of the Corporation'.[5] Also, the BCS was confined for a decade to controlling only the policy and content of the Scottish Home Service; these powers were not extended to cover television output until 1962. The Broadcasting Councils have often been regarded as a counterbalancing force to centralism within the BBC. In December 1965, Lord Normanbrook (BBC Chairman) noted in a BBC Lunchtime Lecture: 'The existence of these National Councils is a recognition of the rights of national minorities, and provides a valuable safeguard against the tendency towards centralisation which is natural to any large-scale organisation.'[6] The existence of the BCS also appeared to give more influence for Scotland in comparison with the English Regions at Board of Governors level, but the effectiveness of the Council depended upon a great many factors, not least the personality of the national Governor and on the flow of information from Scottish management to the Council.

The centralised nature of the BBC was also evident in the development of the television and radio services. To facilitate the rapid expansion of television throughout the country, the BBC decided to concentrate on providing studios and equipment in London before developing facilities in the Regions. Regional contributions to television output were confined for several years to outside broadcasts. Inevitably, Scottish services appeared deficient in certain respects when compared to the highly organised and concentrated resources in London serving over fifty million people. But even with important television outside broadcasts which were taken by the network, such as the State visit to Scotland by King Olaf of Norway in October 1962, the BBC chose Richard Dimbleby as principal commentator because there was no experienced Scottish television commentator. The disparity in resources between London and the Regions stemmed from the need to make the most efficient and economical use of resources and to be near the available pool of artistic talent. The BBC regarded it as uneconomical to spend money in an attempt to create an artificial equality among Regions which were naturally unequal in several respects, such as artistic talent. In England, the disparities in resources between London and the Regions were partially narrowed when these Regions began to specialise in specific types of programme output, such as natural history at Bristol. However, the BBC's dual programme responsibility in Scotland resulted in less specialisation in programme output, fewer opportunities to network material and recover the cost of items taken by the network, and less concentration of programme resources. Perhaps it can be argued that many of the criticisms about broadcasting resources in Scotland are unfair to the extent that people tended to make direct comparisons between Scottish and London production facilities rather than make comparisons with European countries of similar size to Scotland. The BBC justified the centralisation of broadcasting resources because it enabled the Corporation to pool engineering and programme skills in order to provide the best programmes to the widest audience in the shortest period of time within the resources available. But the arrival in 1955 of ITV with its federal structure contrasted with the more centralised organisation of the BBC, so that, although it was duopoly rather than diversity which replaced the BBC monopoly when the ITV network was developed by 1962, the arrival of ITV companies did represent a greater decentralisation of production facilities in Scotland in comparison with the BBC in Scotland. The presence of the ITV companies prompted the BBC Regions to press for more fragmentation of the network, a trend resisted by network Controllers in London. In Scotland, these trends, together with the increased popularity of television at the expense of the Scottish Home Service, prompted the BCS to press for parity of responsibility over television output.[7] The BBC was concerned about greater fragmentation of the network and the devolution of responsibility to the BCS for television output, and argued that competition with ITV had increased costs which could be more easily dealt with by centralising television production facilities. The lower costs involved in radio broadcasting, the diversity of services and the absence of commercial competition increased the likelihood that the BBC would consider using radio as a vehicle for decentralising programme production as in the establishment of local stations. Since the advent of the Regional Scheme in 1929, wavelength restrictions had been used as the justification for the BBC's inability to reintroduce localised radio services. However, the use of VHF opened up the possibility of introducing local stations by overcoming the historic wavelength restrictions. In February 1955, Frank Gillard, a fervent supporter of local broadcasting within the BBC, stated that 'Since a healthy national culture is based on healthy regional cultures, broadcasting which is one of the greatest instruments of our day for the nourishment of culture must accept some responsibility for the whole plant from the roots up'.[8] The local stations which were established in England in and after 1967 were given some degree of independence from London; Scotland continued to be served by the opt-out service from Radio 4 serving Scotland as a whole until area and community stations were opened during and after 1976.

All these attempts at diversification of programme services represented diversity through unity, not diversity through fragmentation. In other words, the BBC argued that the strength of its programme services lay in unity – a unity which gave strength to resist incursions on editorial independence. The BBC sought to meet regional needs yet retain its unitary character. The BBC did not wish to be subdivided into independent units or establish separate broadcasting corporations in Scotland and Wales. There were technical constraints on devolving responsibility for broadcasting to the extent that the transmitter networks had to be planned centrally. From the late 1960s, the BBC was however faced with the twin pressures of the need to increase central control over resources after a period of rapid expansion since the early 1960s, yet also to devolve a greater measure of power and responsibility to the Regions. The increasing financial pressures facing the Corporation and the outcome of the McKinsey study during 1968 and 1969 prompted the need for the BBC centrally to exercise tighter financial and managerial control. It was only a recognition of the political dimension regarding the need to decentralise managerial authority which ensured a commitment by the Board of Governors to work for Regional devolution. The Board of Management was less enthusiastic about devolving power. Management believed in the retention of the 'one BBC' concept, whereas the Board of Governors was more inclined to believe that it was politically sensible to take devolution seriously and thereby deflect external pressure for the creation of a separate Scottish broadcasting corporation or a BBC Scotland under the direct control of a future Scottish Assembly. The Governors sought greater autonomy for the national Regions within the existing structure and thus stressed the adverse implications of complete autonomy on matters such as transmitter development, programme planning and production, administration, financial resources, staff movement and conditions of employment.

In Scotland, there are social, economic, cultural and geographical divisions, although much greater differences exist between Scotland and the rest of the United Kingdom than within Scotland, such as between the Highlands and the Lowlands. Despite the absence of an obvious linguistic basis to nationalism in Scotland – since Gaelic is a minority language and culture and mainly confined to the north and west – Scottish institutions have helped to define the distinctiveness of Scotland. These include the law, central and local government, the Church and the educational system, the Scottish press, pressure groups and the existence of bodies such as the Scottish Arts Council, the National Trust for Scotland, and the Scottish Football Association. The BBC is therefore a relatively recent institution in comparison with some older Scottish institutions; it is also part of a UK institution. At the political level, there has always been in Scotland criticism in varying degrees about remote control from London. Scotland is more remote from London than any English region, and so Scottish people have regarded themselves as at a distance from the key decision-making centres. This has conditioned attitudes towards decision-making within the BBC, though not necessarily in other branches of the media such as the Scottish press. For many years, a high proportion of Sunday newspapers purchased in Scotland have been in fact written and printed in Scotland. Even many Scottish daily newspapers, such as the *Scotsman* and the *Glasgow Herald*, have been chosen in preference to English newspapers. This does not include the wide range of local newspapers published in Scotland, such as the *Aberdeen Press and Journal* or the *Dundee Courier*. Interestingly, Scottish people have consistently preferred Scottish newspapers as a source of information, whereas in broadcasting they tended to prefer network rather than Scottish programme output. The public tended to turn to the press for news of local or Scottish events, but preferred broadcasting for information on UK matters of interest. This trend has been somewhat less evident in recent years partly because of the reduction in the number of newspapers produced in Scotland, partly because of the increasing number of Scottish features in non-Scottish-based newspapers, and also partly because of the improvement in both the quality and quantity of broadcasting output on Scottish themes. A crucial point which has to be borne in mind when making comparisons between broadcasting and the press is that whereas the BBC in Scotland segregated Scottish news in separate bulletins, Scottish newspapers placed Scottish items of interest in close proximity to items of both national and international importance. This difference in the method of presenting material helps to explain why BBC Scottish-originated output was regarded as parochial whereas newspaper items escaped much of this criticism, and also why the public tended to prefer broadcasting rather than the Scottish press for the dissemination of information of national and international importance. The close proximity of items of Scottish interest in BBC bulletins tended to imply that the Corporation regarded anything Scottish as of merely regional or peripheral interest, particularly when Scottish items of general interest had to be relegated to the Scottish bulletins. A paper by the BCS commented on this theme as follows:

> As the reason for the relegation of major items of Scottish news to the separate Scottish bulletin is known to be their exclusion from the main bulletins prepared by the BBC in London, the critics regard the BBC's handling of news as an example of a more general complaint that London headquarters of nationalised concerns look on Scotland as a 'region' rather than a country with an intense national consciousness.[9]

The sense of national consciousness was to become more evident during the 1970s and could not easily be ignored by the BBC. What was then envisaged with devolution was a delegation of powers, not merely the transference of functions.

In a pamphlet published in 1972, Charles Curran (BBC Director-General) outlined a defence of the unitary nature of the BBC.[10] Yet the BBC had to be truly seen to represent the sum of its parts rather than merely London with Regional outposts. It was the task of Sir Michael Swann (Principal and Vice-Chancellor of Edinburgh University), who succeeded Lord Hill as Chairman of the BBC in January 1973, to consider how to retain the unity of the BBC, avoid undue centralisation, devolve reasonable powers and redeploy resources to the Regions. There were likely to be technical and financial limits to devolution, and so Scotland had to aim for a workable solution within these constraints. In its Annual Report for 1973–4, the BCS stated that 'the totality of a national Region now evolving in the Scottish context would appear to justify maximum autonomy in the deployment of assured and developing resources'.[11] The BCS wished to offer greater programme opportunities to retain high-calibre staff and thereby counter the centripetal pull of London and ensure adequate coverage of the rapid social, economic and political developments taking place in Scotland during this period, both for Scottish and for network consumption. Indeed, in a BBC Lunchtime Lecture on Regional broadcasting, Owen Edwards (Controller, Wales) noted that 'Within the United Kingdom the effectiveness with which nation shall speak unto nation depends on the extent to which nation can adequately discharge its prime function and its privilege of properly speaking unto itself'.[12] This was more difficult to achieve in television than in radio for technical and financial reasons. Nevertheless, the Crawford Committee on Broadcasting Coverage, in its report published in November 1974, stated that measures should be taken to develop Regional variations in television in order to counter centralism and to reflect both national and Regional identities. The committee stated that because BBC Scotland served a large community, a case could be made for subdividing this community similar to that achieved with commercial television: 'we think that in Scotland, where they are making provision for some decentralisation of programme-making, the BBC should when they have the resources to do so introduce an element of regional diversification in the transmission of programmes on a sub-opt-out basis'.[13] The committee suggested that funds should be forthcoming to enable additional communication links to be provided in Scotland for simultaneous opting-out on both BBC television networks when funds became available. The Crawford Committee welcomed the BBC's movement towards regionalism in England but added that the same development should also occur within Scotland.[14] In its Annual Report for 1975–6, the BBC argued that not only would an increase in the share of resources for the Regions involve additional responsibility for decisions about the use of such resources, but also that there was room for debate about which areas of responsibility should be devolved. The Corporation commented that 'As long as the BBC remains a unified organisation, however, there will remain the problem of the point at which the lines have to be drawn between central and devolved decision-making'.[15] There already existed greater autonomy with regard to the production and scheduling of programmes within the resources available to BBC Scotland, but there needed to be some relaxation of administrative and financial control from London. The BBC was to remain a national institution, but plans for

Regional devolution now had to be translated into practical policy proposals.

In November 1975, the Labour Government published its White Paper on devolution to Scotland and Wales. Political pressures and the renewed sense of Scottish national identity put pressure upon the government to plan for the devolution of power. It was an attempt to meet the legitimate needs of Scotland and Wales but also to preserve the unity of the United Kingdom. The White Paper stated that the unity of the UK did not necessarily entail uniform treatment for all its constituent parts. The government rejected separation for Scotland and Wales, yet wished to preserve the separate identity and cultural traditions and institutions of these two countries. The White Paper indicated that 'The need is to achieve balance – to reconcile unity and diversity in a stronger and better system, offering more achievement and satisfaction to the parts while improving the efficiency and stability of the whole'.[16] In its plan to devolve greater power to the national Regions, the BBC was thinking along similar lines. The parallel with political devolution in the wider context was that the BBC sought to devolve greater power out of necessity rather than out of desire, and to do so in a manner which would not undermine the unity of the Corporation. This ruled out the possibility of creating a separate Scottish Broadcasting Corporation. The White Paper stated that it would not be possible to decide whether broadcasting should be a devolved matter until after the Annan Committee on Broadcasting had published its report. During this period, the committee received several submissions of evidence which urged the need for greater decentralisation. In June 1975, BBC staff in Aberdeen sent a paper to the committee arguing the need for greater devolution based on four factors:

(1) the trend within Britain towards decentralisation and devolution;

(2) the desire of political parties in Scotland to see the establishment of an Assembly in Edinburgh;

(3) the movement of economic power and industrial investment from west central Scotland to the north-east because of North Sea oil developments;

(4) the creation of new social pressures causing threats to indigenous cultural traditions, combined with the reassertion of local identities.[17]

What was envisaged was a redeployment of staff and resources to Aberdeen. There was criticism of the centralisation of administration and the lack of access to decision-makers, and a belief that the BCS had failed to grasp the views of staff or appreciate the problems of broadcasting in Scotland. Favourable comment was made on the federalist structure of ITV in Scotland, and it was hoped that some examination would be made of the problem of network scheduling and its influence on Regional output. For example, whereas oil developments were reflected in network news, there was deemed to be less opportunity to examine the issues raised in local programmes. James Kemp, former BBC Scottish Editor of News and Current Affairs, was also critical of centralisation within the BBC. He believed that the BBC centrally had been able to retain so much power because of the weakness of the BCS. Other submissions to the committee, such as that from the ABS, supported the maximum possible decentralisation of programme-making within given financial and constitutional limitations.

In 1975, Alastair Hetherington, former Editor of the *Guardian*, was appointed Controller of BBC Scotland to succeed Robert Coulter. Sir Michael Swann, BBC Chairman, was aware that Hetherington wished to return to Scotland and was in favour of his becoming the new Controller. Central management believed that there were compelling reasons for appointing someone outside the BBC to take charge of the BBC's operations in Scotland. It was envisaged that Alastair Hetherington would be more likely to be effective in supporting and implementing a policy of devolution – or mini-devolution, as Charles Curran, the Director-General, referred to it – and in strengthening BBC Scotland output both within Scotland and to the rest of the UK. It was expected that his background as Editor of the *Guardian* would provide him with the experience to deal with changes in a rapidly-changing political climate. Given that devolution for BBC Scotland was likely to be a highly political issue, especially with the expectation of a Scottish Assembly, there was some degree of fear within the BBC that, with political devolution, control of BBC Scotland might pass to the Assembly. The Board of Governors and the BCS wanted a strong, independent person of standing who would be able to put Scotland on the UK broadcasting map and develop it without allowing it to come under political control from any future Scottish Assembly. Alastair Hetherington thus sought to implement mini-devolution to demonstrate that Scottish needs could be met within the existing system.[18]

The appointment of a new Controller was significant at a crucial period in the history of the BBC in Scotland, since the appointment was viewed as a recognition of the increasing importance which the BBC placed on affairs in Scotland. Increasing devolution of power and responsibilities to the BBC in Scotland appeared to be a safer option than adhering to the status quo, which would only have increased pressure for an independent BBC Scotland. Much depended upon the type of change and the speed at which it would take place. In a memorandum to the Annan Committee, the BCS commented on these changes:

> We warmly commend the need for greater devolution and we welcome the BBC's statement at the time of the appointment of the new Controller, Scotland, who is to take up his post in January 1976, that it intends to pursue a policy of giving greater autonomy to Scotland.[19]

The Council believed that the national Controllers should be allowed to play a part in the formulation of policy for the BBC as a whole. Furthermore, it wanted BBC Scotland to have direct control over a greater proportion of expenditure in the light of political devolution, to be able to retain key executives and programme-makers, and to produce programmes that would adequately reflect Scottish life and culture both for the audience in Scotland and for the wider network audience. Overall, the Council believed that the Scottish influence should be more strongly represented at the highest levels of BBC management, no doubt to forestall pressure for more radical reforms.

Alastair Hetherington left the *Guardian* in September 1975 and took up his appointment as Controller of BBC Scotland in January 1976. He knew that he had the support of the Board of Governors to increase the degree of autonomy of BBC Scotland as well as to introduce improvements in both the quantity and quality of Scottish programme output. The intention was to expand BBC operations in Scotland, but all factors were to be subject to continuous negotiation, and so there was uncertainty as to precisely what Scotland would be offered. Sir Michael Swann and the Governors wished to give Scotland more independence than any other BBC Region, but Alastair Hetherington may have mistakenly believed that he would have as much freedom as the Editor of the *Guardian*, the post which he previously held. But BBC Scotland represented only one part of the BBC as a whole, and so ultimate control remained with the BBC centrally in London. There were therefore limitations on the degree of freedom exercised by the Scottish Controller. Also, increasing financial pressure on the BBC at the national level increased the difficulty of allocating sufficient resources to develop Scottish broadcasting. The BBC ended the financial year 1974–5 with a £17 million deficit, primarily attributable to higher staff and material costs fuelled by inflation. Alastair Hetherington stated that Charles Curran supported the line of the Governors that more power should be devolved to BBC Scotland, but that when he joined the BBC he found that the Board of Management was not agreed on this policy and that there were strong opponents of any idea to devolve administrative and programme-making control to Scotland or to allocate more funds to Scotland.[20] For example, Ian Trethowan (Managing Director, Television, and Director-General from October 1977) was deemed to be more sympathetic than Alasdair Milne (Director of Programmes, Television, and subsequently Managing Director, Television). Within BBC Scotland, Hetherington stated that there was support for decentralisation from programme-makers but resistance from some administrators who disliked change. This was understandable to the extent that programme-makers would benefit from the expansion of programme services whereas administrators would suffer from attempts to streamline administration and shift more resources into programme production. Hetherington believed that senior staff in Scotland supported his plans, although he underestimated the degree of resistance from within the Board of Management to the shifting of more resources to BBC Scotland.

Alastair Hetherington's plans for the development of BBC Scotland services fell into four broad areas:

(1) the need to gain greater freedom from London, both administratively and financially, without breaking up the BBC into national or regional units;

(2) to secure a larger volume of Scottish-originated material on the networks;

(3) to improve broadcasting coverage in Scotland;

(4) to introduce several community radio stations and develop national radio in Scotland.

In practical terms, the first task involved the need to retain close ties with the BBC centrally, yet to reduce the number of occasions on which Scotland would have to consult London in areas such as staff appointments and capital expenditure. Hetherington wanted all functions of staff administration (i.e. appointments, salaries, grading, personnel matters) to be devolved except for the most senior staff. The Scottish Controller did have the right of veto over appointments, and so London could not impose staff on a reluctant Scottish management, but the right of veto was reciprocal because London could veto the appointment of Scottish staff who wished to work in London. The Scottish Controller did however wish to retain freedom of movement for staff between Scotland and other parts of the UK. With regard to the streamlining of administration in Scotland, the Scottish Controller wished to make arrangements for the early retirement of a number of administrative staff in order to save costs and shift more resources into programme production, but this was resisted by London. He also wanted decision-making on minor items of capital expenditure to be devolved to Scotland, thereby eliminating the cumbersome negotiating machinery with the Television Development Committee and the Radio Planning Group which considered expenditure on capital projects. Scotland had either to have its own capital budget or to have delegated authority for minor items involving capital expenditure. As regards operating expenditure, there was a need to obtain more resources to develop and enrich Scottish programme output and get more material networked in order to recover costs. Funds released in this way could then be used to produce more Scottish programmes and lessen dependence upon network output. London budgeted each year for a percentage of Regional output which might be capable of being networked and where costs would thus be borne by the BBC centrally. In addition to covering the cost of programmes produced for the Scottish audience, BBC Scotland, like other Regions, was also expected to contribute towards the cost of shared services. The problem for Scotland was that, since the cost of shared services was allocated between Regions according to the proportion of net licence revenue and hours of shared service provided, it did not take account of the ability or the willingness of the audience in Scotland to listen to or to view non-Scottish-originated programmes. For example, listeners in Scotland made greater use of their Home Service than other radio networks in comparison with listeners in other Regions, yet the Scottish contribution to shared services was not correspondingly reduced. A similar argument applied to those radio services where reception was poor in Scotland but where this did not result in any diminution of Scotland's contribution towards shared costs. In other words, greater programme expenditure on Scottish programmes could not be offset by any reduction in Scotland's contribution to shared services, but rather was more likely to increase the Scottish deficit.

The breakdown in Regional expenditure was a by-product of the Beveridge Report on Broadcasting which favoured a means of indicating how income was being spent in the Regions. This was difficult to determine because of the operational characteristics of the system. For example, since no Region could consistently exist on the income which the licences produced within each Region, they were thus dependent upon the networks for sustaining material. Also, capital expenditure on facilities in London was of direct benefit to all the Regions and not just to London, and the BBC centrally funded the high cost of extending transmitter coverage in Scotland. This partly explains the BBC formula for apportioning capital expenditure in accordance with licence income within each Region and not according to the actual level of expenditure incurred. This had the effect of blurring variations in actual rates of capital expenditure between the Regions. Rates of operating expenditure were however factual. By far the most significant element in BBC Scotland's annual operating costs related to staff costs. In 1980, these represented 69.1 per cent of operating costs.[21] Radio and television expenditure increased in the late 1970s, but, significantly, Scotland's share of radio and television network programmes and other costs rose steeply from the mid-1970s, although an increasing proportion of money was recovered by BBC Scotland for radio and especially television programmes which were contributed to the networks. The Scottish Controller was critical of BBC Scotland's large contribution towards shared costs and the close supervision by London over Scottish requests for additional revenue. More than this, it was believed that, if Scotland had been allowed to control its own finances, then quicker solutions to problems could have been found, given the complexity of dealing with various administrative departments in London. In an article in the *New Statesman*, Alastair Hetherington argued that BBC Scotland wanted devolution within the BBC for efficiency rather than for political reasons – the aim was to encourage broadcasters to cut down on bureaucratic red tape.[22] He believed that Scotland would be less separatist if it were seen to enjoy better opportunities within the UK, particularly since informal contacts between Scotland and London were not achieving the desired objectives.

The second broad aim which was pursued by the new Controller was the need to secure a greater proportion of Scottish material on the networks. The intention was to double Scottish-originated television output for the network from 1:60 to 1:30 within twelve months because, as the BCS remarked, one television programme in 140 (or one hour in 60) contributed to the network was an inadequate representation for Scotland, which held one tenth of the population of the UK and significant economic potential. The BCS went on to state:

> Scotland wishes to give as well as to take, and the maintenance of Scotland within the British broadcasting service demands an influence upon, and a participation in, the network commensurate with its importance as a contributor to national strength and national unity as exemplified in the abiding virtues of its traditions and its people.[23]

The Scottish Controller wanted Scotland to become a major network production centre as well as to foster local talent, because this would stem the drain of staff southwards and prevent Scottish output from becoming too inward-looking. Professor Alan Thompson (BBC National Governor for Scotland, 1976–9) accepted that Scotland was not as successful in getting material networked as he would have liked.[24] Given the growing importance of devolution and North Sea oil issues within news and current affairs, BBC Scotland also needed to be capable of reflecting these developments and the awakened sense of national identity both to a Scottish and to a network audience. This process began with some organisational changes within BBC Scotland. The News Department in Glasgow was bolstered by the appointment of an Economics Correspondent and later by a Political Correspondent (James Cox, who replaced Chris Baur who had been based in Edinburgh). The Regional News Assistants now became known as News Sub-Editors. By October 1977, the Radio 4 Scotland opt-out service had an Executive Producer (Current Affairs) when the post of Senior Producer Topicality, Radio, lapsed. Other programme areas were not neglected. For example, the new post of Head of Drama Television (Scotland) was created, and in Light Entertainment a Senior Producer for Popular Music joined the existing Senior Light Entertainment Producers for Television and Radio. Two years later, the post of Religious Broadcasting Organiser was finally renamed Head of Religious Programmes (Scotland). By that time, Current Affairs, which had previously been headed by a Senior Producer (Matthew Spicer), was retitled Editor, Current Affairs, in the same way that News Division had for several years been under the overall control of an Editor. Another occasion in which prominence had been given to current affairs was prior to the introduction of television news bulletins in Scotland in 1957, just before the start of STV transmissions in central Scotland. The most significant changes in the staffing structure in Edinburgh took place during 1975 and 1976 with the appointment of a Political Correspondent (Chris Baur) and a UK North Sea Energy Correspondent (Michael Buerk, from March 1976). During this period, when changes in staffing were taking place in Glasgow and Edinburgh to take account of wider political and economic developments, these changes were reflected in the Aberdeen staffing structure with the designation of a Chief News Assistant and a News Sub-Editor. Within BBC Scotland, some new senior posts were also created, including a Chief Assistant, General (later retitled Chief Assistant to the Controller, Scotland), and an Accountant, Scotland. In 1977, the BBC appointed Mr B. Mitchell to the newly-created post of Head of Finance; Mitchell had previously been the Scottish Programme Executive, but this latter post had now lapsed. By 1980, senior staff in Scotland below the level of Controller included: Assistant Controller (Pat Walker), the Secretary (Christopher Irwin), Head of Information (William Carrocher), Head of Television (Pat Chalmers), Head of Radio (John Pickles), Head of Finance (B. Mitchell), Head of Administration and Development Services

(A.M. Brown) and Head of Production Resources and Engineering (J.J. Jarvie).

Changes in organisational structure were also accompanied by developments in programme output. Several documentaries on the issue of devolution, including *Power of Scotland* and *Scotland 1980?*, were produced for television. Radio covered these issues in *Good Morning Scotland* and in a special programme for Radio 4 entitled *At the Crossroads*. North Sea oil developments were covered in *The Energy File* which was taken by the network, and in the weekly series *Current Account*. In other subject areas, the drama production *Huntingtower* and the series featuring singer Lena Martell in *Lena's Music* were both taken by the network, whereas the popular programme *The Beechgrove Garden* and the comedy series *Scotch and Wry* with comedian Rikki Fulton were broadcast to the audience in Scotland. BBC Scotland sought the resources, both human and technical, to cover the increasing number of Scottish items of interest to a UK audience. It also sought to prepare for the possibility of televising a Scottish Assembly and to reflect adequately the implications of the new balance of political forces affecting Scottish politics. In this context, it is therefore worth recalling the background to the SNP's attempt to achieve adequate coverage on radio and television. It was at the General Election of 1935 that the SNP had first applied for permission to participate in pre-election broadcasts, but then, and as at subsequent elections, no broadcasts were allowed because the SNP did not contest a sufficient number of constituencies (i.e. twenty constituencies). In 1939, the SNP again raised the issue of separate broadcasts on Scottish topics. The SNP believed that a fairer system of qualification to take part in these broadcasts was to base them on the number of votes cast in the preceding election rather than on the number of constituencies contested, which was raised to fifty before the 1949 election. In 1949, the Scottish Advisory Council argued that Scottish political affairs should have separate treatment via special party political series on the Scottish Home Service.[25] The problem for many years was that arrangements for broadcasts were made according to the number of candidates put forward by political parties in the United Kingdom as a whole rather than by reference to Scotland alone. Not surprisingly, this worked to the disadvantage of a small party such as the SNP, which might contest a large number of constituencies within Scotland but which would represent only a small percentage when viewed in relation to constituencies throughout the UK. In 1955, the SNP protested to the PMG about the regulations which prevented a separate series of party political broadcasts for Scotland and Wales. At a meeting in the House of Commons on 21 July 1958, Lord Balfour (BBC National Governor for Scotland) was critical that nationalists were denied party political broadcasts.[26] Criticism of the existing arrangements surfaced again in 1962 when two party political broadcasts timed to precede local government elections in England were transmitted in Scotland. The results of the Scottish local elections had been announced a week earlier, yet, under the PMG's direction of 27 July 1955, these broadcasts had to be transmitted throughout the UK. The BCS therefore stated that the transmission of the English election results was an imposition on Scottish listeners and viewers.[27] Just over a year later, the SNP was allocated an allowance of five minutes on radio and on television based on votes cast in Scotland for the party at the 1964 General Election. The PMG's prescription which forbade separate party political broadcasts in Scotland and Wales was withdrawn on 1 June 1965. On 29 September, the SNP made its first party political broadcast. However, apart from party political broadcasts, the SNP subsequently complained about the poor coverage of party speeches. Andrew Stewart (Controller, BBC Scotland) nevertheless argued that better coverage would have been possible if the SNP had appointed a publicity officer, because the BBC needed direct contacts with the political parties to enable speeches to be instantly quoted and inserted into news bulletins. In 1969, the SNP appointed Douglas Crawford to the newly-created post of Director of Communications to facilitate liaison with the media in Scotland. During the 1970s, the allocation of time awarded to the SNP for party political and party election broadcasts rose significantly because of the spectacular increase in the number of votes cast for the party at General Elections. The SNP was awarded two ten-minute election broadcasts on both television and Radio 4 Scotland in October 1974, based on votes cast for the SNP at the February 1974 General Election. At the October 1974 General Election, the SNP won eleven seats and took 30 per cent of the Scottish vote to become the second-largest party in Scotland. In doing so, the SNP was guaranteed an enhanced allocation of time for party political broadcasts totalling thirty minutes on television and twenty-five minutes on radio. After the Devolution Referendum and General Election of 1979, the lower level of interest in nationalist politics was reflected in radio and television output.

The third of the four broad aims of BBC Scotland's development programme concerned the desirability of improving broadcasting coverage. Scottish broadcasting coverage was poor in comparison with other parts of the UK because of a variety of technical, economic and geographical factors. Scotland gave London advice on transmitter development but had no control over the planning of the networks. In return, Scotland benefited by having access to the services of central engineering staff. However, Scotland hoped that the gaps in transmitter coverage, particularly UHF television, which were highlighted in the Report of the Committee on Broadcasting Coverage in 1974, would be given priority by the BBC. The Crawford Committee had recommended that broadcasting services should be extended to all communities over 500 people for social, cultural and economic reasons. BBC Scotland hoped for a speedy extension of services to these often remote and scattered communities under what became known as phase 2 of the UHF plan for transmitter development. Towards the end of the 1970s, an increasing number of UHF relay stations had to be built to fill gaps in broadcasting coverage. By 31 March 1975, there were nine main and eight relay stations in Scotland, bringing UHF television coverage to eighty-seven per cent of the population compared to a UK coverage figure of ninety-five per cent. There was a significant increase in the number of relay stations required to serve a small percentage of the population, hence the cost per viewer rose dramatically. Nineteen UHF transmitters were brought into service during 1975–6 and a further twenty-six stations followed in 1976–7, thereby increasing coverage to ninety-five per cent by March 1977 and doubling the number of transmitters in operation.[28] The law of diminishing returns appeared to operate because, under phase 2 of the UHF plan, about 250 relay stations were required throughout the UK in order to reach an additional 0.3 per cent of the population (i.e. about 175,000 people).

The fourth principal aim of BBC Scotland was to develop community radio and expand national radio, both of which are discussed more fully in the following chapter. Plans for a community radio station in Inverness were already in the pipeline before Alastair Hetherington was appointed as Controller. Radio Highland in Inverness was opened in March 1976, and between then and October 1979 further area and community radio stations were opened at Aberdeen, Orkney, Shetland and Stornoway. Scotland also sought to expand the output of the Radio Scotland opt-out service on Radio 4 by broadcasting material on Radio 2. The ultimate aim was to enable Radio Scotland to stand independently in full competition with other networks. This came to fruition on 23 November 1978 when Radio Scotland became a self-contained service after the changes in wavelengths had made this technically possible. The BBC also wished to compete more effectively with the commercial local stations in Scotland, but there were technical problems in introducing a Scottish element to Radio 1; the task of catering for more popular music was thus left to Radio Scotland.

The progress of Regional devolution in all these key areas came under close scrutiny. In referring to its submission to the Annan Committee, the BCS noted in its Annual Report for 1975–6 that 'The Council's submission has brought about an awakened and sympathetic interest in the affairs of BBC Scotland at the highest levels of BBC management'.[29] But there was concern within BBC Scotland with what was regarded as slow progress towards Regional devolution. BBC Scotland sought progress with devolution within the BBC structure, but it became obvious to some staff in Scotland that, within the first nine months of Alastair Hetherington's appointment as Controller, there were severe constraints on his ability to do all he had set out to achieve. The course of developments may have taken a different direction if political devolution had materialised at an early stage; it did not, and a series of disagreements with London followed which were made public.

During 1977, the Board of Governors reaffirmed the view that within certain limits required for the coordination of matters such as technical development, programme quality and conditions of employment, the intention was to give Scotland a steadily increasing measure of authority to run its own affairs. There was no intention of encouraging Scotland to move in a separatist direction. Likewise, the intention of the review by Huw Wheldon (Managing Director,

Television) of English Regional broadcasting was designed at most to devolve more authority. The Wheldon Report, which was submitted to the Board of Governors in January 1977, led to Regional Controllers being given greater discretion in financial and administrative matters, and a new post of Chief Assistant to the Director-General (Regions) was created. But concern over the rate of progress towards devolution had prompted the BBC to make the following statement in its Annual Report for 1976–7:

> In the Regions it has been our policy during the year to encourage greater devolution without sacrificing the advantages of corporate unity in certain fields ... In Scotland our policy has sometimes been misunderstood and regarded as an English attempt to put a brake on what is seen there as an inexorably advancing vehicle of constitutional change. This is not our policy. Nor do we believe that the interests of viewers and listeners in the United Kingdom or its constituent parts would be best served by separate national broadcasting organisations. Diversity of devolved functions within a sensible constitutional unity is our aim.[30]

The BCS believed that it was important that political events should be anticipated by BBC measures of financial and administrative devolution. But the use to which those resources was put was also important, especially given the discovery in 1977 that overspending on the Scottish programme allowance had taken place within the first half of the financial year 1977–8. At Board of Governors level, the National Governor for Scotland had to balance his responsibility for broadcasting in Scotland with responsibility for UK broadcasting. Professor Alan Thompson, national Governor from 1976 to 1979, stated that he did not encounter any anti-Scottish bias at Board level and that it was the centralised nature of the BBC rather than personal factors which militated against Scotland.[31] Alastair Hetherington was however inclined to place more emphasis on the personality factor within the Board of Management rather than merely on the centralised structure in explaining slow progress towards devolution.[32]

Conflict between Scotland and London reached a more intense level in September 1978 when Alastair Hetherington criticised the continual rejection by television network Controllers of Scottish material.[33] It was believed that London was setting very stringent standards regarding the acceptance of material for networking. This, together with criticism that London was interfering too much in the new Radio Scotland developments, was mentioned at the press conference in Edinburgh on 6 September 1978 held to discuss the reactions of the BCS to the White Paper on Broadcasting, which supported more autonomy for the national Broadcasting Councils.[34] In its Annual Report for 1977–8, the BCS had stated that it believed that subjectivity had influenced the decisions taken by the BBC centrally regarding the networking of Scottish material. The Council therefore wanted the bases of acceptance or rejection of material to be made more specific. There was no desire for the acceptance of material to be based on any Goschen formula of $^{11}/_{80}$, because a quota system would merely have lowered the status of Scottish productions. In November 1978, during this period of uneasy relations with London, the BCS appointed Professor Sir Robert Grieve, a former Chairman of the HIDB, as Vice-Chairman in order to strengthen links both with the BBC centrally and with Scottish management and to emphasise that they were seeking to safeguard the interests of Scottish broadcasting without threatening the unity of the BBC.

The conflict with London reached a climax in December 1978 when the Board of Management took a dim view of a briefing which the Scottish Controller gave to the BCS about the lack of funds for radio development in Scotland. The Board disliked the fact that its decisions were being questioned and then disagreements were being communicated to the BCS. Professor Alan Thompson stated that the Council was broadly in agreement with Alastair Hetherington's views, although there were differences of emphasis in the goals sought.[35] The upshot of the disagreements with London was that Alastair Hetherington had to vacate the post of Controller. Andrew Todd (Deputy Director, News and Current Affairs) was brought in as temporary Controller in January 1979. The BCS was consulted about who should fill the vacancy. Pat Ramsay, who was born in England but of Scots ancestry, was later chosen as the new Controller of BBC Scotland. He took up his duties on 9 May 1979. Ramsay had served for many years within the BBC, knew its procedures, and had many contacts within the Corporation. He had previously been Controller, Programme Services, Television, in London. This was a safe appointment because Ramsay adopted a more moderate approach to the management of BBC Scotland suited to his own background and temperament. His immediate task was to stabilise the relationship between BBC Scotland and central management in London and to deal with the problems of programme policy on Radio Scotland and the increasing financial pressures which affected the BBC as a whole. Also, with the failure of the Referendum of March 1979 to produce a decisive vote in favour of establishing a Scottish Assembly, the progress of mini-devolution within the BBC was adversely affected. Indeed, in the absence of political devolution there was, according to Professor Alan Thompson, a drop in temperature over the issue of devolution within the Board of Governors. He argued that the Scottish dimension of devolving power flowed in more strongly at the Board of Governors level than at the Board of Management level because the Governors were in a stronger position than management to take note of, and to appreciate, the broader public and political issues over devolution. A decisive pro-devolution vote would have brought about intense political pressure behind BBC Scotland for greater autonomy, but no plans ever existed for creating a separate Scottish BBC.

BBC community radio and the development of Radio Scotland, 1976–80

During the second half of the 1970s, there was an expansion in the provision of radio services in Scotland which was accompanied by a corresponding increase in the volume of radio programme output. These changes took place during a period in which, within the BBC, attempts were more to devolve more power to BBC Scotland, and outwith the BBC there was a resurgence of nationalist consciousness. These factors, discussed in the previous chapter, were instrumental in shaping the type of programme expansion envisaged for radio in Scotland. From 1976, community and area radio stations provided a means of catering to some extent for the needs of listeners, including Gaelic listeners, in some remote areas and as a means of demonstrating that, despite the presence of BBC local radio in England and the ILR stations throughout the country, the BBC in Scotland wished to provide some form of localised radio broadcasting. These developments were complemented by the introduction of Radio Scotland as a self-contained national service in November 1978 in place of the opt-out service from Radio 4. It appeared to be a sensible option in line with the new mood of national consciousness within Scotland, but the problems generated by the new service highlighted important questions which needed to be answered about the role of radio in Scotland.

Since the early 1970s, BBC Scotland's emphasis on its national role in radio broadcasting in Scotland had needed to be complemented by the provision of local radio services, particularly with the presence of ILR stations opening throughout the country and the success of BBC local radio in England. Referring to the arrival of ILR in Scotland, the Broadcasting Council for Scotland stated:

> In the competitive context, the Council has consistently emphasised the 'BBC in Scotland' with its four generic networks plus BBC Scotland's role as a national service for the whole country. At the same time we cannot ignore local needs and loyalties and the community radio success elsewhere.[1]

The BBC in Scotland regarded its principal aim in the early 1970s to build up Radio Scotland as a network service throughout Scotland before considering the development of local radio services. In November 1974, the Crawford Committee on Broadcasting Coverage stated that the first objective of radio in Scotland should be to meet national requirements and only then consider the possibility of local stations. Given the presence of ILR, the committee wanted BBC local broadcasting to be extended to Scotland when the financial resources and frequencies made this feasible.[2] The Crawford Committee wanted first consideration in these circumstances to be given by the BBC to small population centres rather than to duplicate the more populous areas served by commercial local radio. The type of local broadcasting which the BBC planned for Scotland consisted of a number of community radio stations. These stations differed from BBC local radio in England because they operated as an opt-out service. In Scotland, the BBC community and area stations operated on an opt-out, *not* opt-in, basis from Radio Scotland. In England, the BBC local stations had their own transmission facilities and airtime, and, with a self-sustaining output of six to eight hours each day, they were opt-in rather than opt-out services. The Scottish community stations therefore had to take most of their programme material from Radio Scotland and to opt out for only limited periods each day. Their output could only be expanded at the expense of Radio Scotland's programme output. Both in 1962 and in 1976, BBC Scotland did not favour the establishment of self-sustaining local radio stations in Scotland. If a local station had been established in 1967 at the time when the first experimental BBC local stations were introduced in England, then the decisions in 1976 about local services in Scotland might have been qualitatively different.

The possibility of community stations in Scotland appeared to offer a means of catering more fully for Gaelic listeners. Indeed, the BBC in Scotland had sought with mixed success to reflect the interests of the Gaelic community, which was mainly located in the western seaboard, North-West Scotland, the Western Isles and with a substantial minority in the Glasgow area. Nationalists declared an interest in Gaelic broadcasting because, as they argued, language is an important criteria in distinguishing a nation. The Gaels believed that there was a role for broadcasting in helping to sustain Gaelic language and culture. There was, however, a stronger linguistic basis to national sentiment in Wales compared to Scotland, and in any case there was, outwith the Gaelic-speaking areas, no 'Scottish' language, only Scottish dialects. Nevertheless, the BBC, which first established a Gaelic department in 1935, came under increasing pressure to improve the volume of Gaelic programme output. In the late 1950s, the BBC's Audience Research Department carried out a survey of Gaelic-speaking areas in order to ascertain the extent to which Gaelic programmes were being listened to. Listening levels were found to be high, and listener preferences were taken into account in programme planning, such as in the broadcast of Gaelic news on a weekly rather than on a monthly basis. Despite these modest programme changes, the BBC's view has always been that with conflicting demands on airtime it was difficult fully to meet the demands of the Gaelic community. The Gaels tended to be treated as a minority group in broadcasting terms akin to the minorities who preferred, for example, classical music, yet Gaeldom contained within its ranks several minorities and could not be equated with a random number of individuals linked by interest in any specialist subject. The principal centres of broadcasting lay outwith Gaelic-speaking areas, but there was also criticism that the BBC in Glasgow produced a stereotyped image of the Gael by relying too much on the advice of expatriate Gaels who lived in Glasgow.[3]

The BBC attracted most of the criticism for its policy towards Gaelic broadcasts simply because the main obligation to provide broadcasts for the Gaelic community has always rested with the BBC. The early Gaelic output was confined to radio, but on 7 March 1962 the BBC transmitted the first fifteen-minute Gaelic television programme, entitled *Music of the Gael*.[4] However, reception in Gaelic-speaking areas was poor, and the programme was introduced in English rather than in Gaelic. These programmes existed as one method by which Gaelic people could be brought in closer touch with their literary and musical traditions, although there was criticism that Gaelic output was too dull in presentation and lacking in artistic imagination.[5] More fundamentally than this, Gaels were concerned that, with a monopoly of English language programmes on all radio and television channels, there would be an anglicisation of Gaels. The Gaels wanted the BBC to pay full regard to its Charter obligations which stated that the Corporation should cover the distinctive culture, language, interests and tastes of the people of Scotland. Not surprisingly, An Comunn (the Highland Association) was therefore disappointed that the 1974 Crawford Report on Broadcasting Coverage stated that, given the size of the Gaelic population, no substantial increase in Gaelic television programmes was possible for financial reasons, yet the committee was prepared to recommend that a fourth television channel should make provision for separate Welsh language programmes.[6] The committee suggested that radio, a less expensive medium, should make the main provision for Gaelic. An Comunn wanted four hours of Gaelic each day on television, a community radio service for Gaelic-speaking areas and a significant increase in Gaelic output on Radio Scotland. The opening of Radio Highland as a bilingual opt-out station from Radio Scotland in 1976 did increase Gaelic output; but it was technically and financially more difficult to provide a sustained Gaelic service on television.

On 25 March 1976, Radio Highland, the first community radio station, began broadcasting on VHF. This station, which was based in Inverness, served a bilingual population to some extent, in that twenty-five per cent were Gaelic speakers. This was a form of area broadcasting because it served a much larger area than some of the smaller stations which were later opened and which could justifiably be regarded as community stations. Radio Highland was staffed by a Station Manager (William Carrocher), a Senior General Programme Producer, a General Programme Producer, a Senior Gaelic Producer, two general Gaelic Producers, a News Sub-Editor and an Engineering Operations Manager. Alastair Hetherington took over as Station Manager after vacating the post of Controller, Scotland, in December 1978; in 1980 Fred MacAulay succeeded him as Manager of the station. Radio Highland, which served an area larger than Belgium, operated on an opt-out basis on VHF from Radio Scotland. The first programme broadcast on the new station was *The Morning Report*, which reviewed events in the north of Scotland.[7] From 17 May 1976, Radio Highland began to broadcast *Studio Two*, a half-hour lunchtime programme. The station also broadcast some Gaelic schools' programmes. By 1978, the output of Gaelic and English programmes from the station was over ten hours a week. Music was found to be useful as a means of bridging the gap between Gaelic and non-Gaelic cultures. Another station, Radio Aberdeen, began broadcasting on 19 April 1976. This station broadcast two opt-out programmes on VHF from Radio Scotland: *Bon Accord*, a half-hour lunchtime programme, and *Northern News Desk*, a half-hour evening programme. The news on the latter programme was followed by a varied format on different days of the week as follows: local culture on Mondays, current affairs on Tuesdays, clubs on Wednesdays, agriculture on Thursdays and sport on Fridays. By 1978, Radio Aberdeen was broadcasting over five hours a week.

Radios Highland and Aberdeen were followed in 1977 by the opening of the two-man community stations, Orkney and Shetland. Radios Orkney and Shetland began broadcasting on 9 May 1977 and both produced about two-and-a-half hours of programmes each week on VHF. Howard Firth was appointed Manager of Radio Orkney, and Jonathan Wills, who worked for the *Shetland Times*, became Manager of Radio Shetland. Each station was staffed by a Senior Producer/Presenter and a Producer/Presenter. Radio Orkney broadcast programmes as on Radio Aberdeen, but opted out in the morning for the twenty-five-minute *Morning Magazine* which covered news of people and events in Orkney; the programme was produced and presented by Howie Firth. Radio Shetland used the Shetland VHF transmitters and broadcast as on Radio Orkney except for a twenty-minute evening programme, *Good Evening Shetland*, covering local news and music. This programme was produced and presented by Jonathan Wills and Suzanne Gibbs. Radios Orkney and Shetland were unique within the BBC because they were each staffed by only two producers, who also presented the programmes. Jo Grimond, the MP for Orkney and Shetland, lobbied BBC Scotland to provide local broadcasting stations for these two communities, which often had different interests from people on the mainland. Alastair Hetherington, then still Controller of BBC Scotland, stated that central management in London, unlike BBC Scotland, was initially more sceptical about the viability of these stations.[8] Ian Trethowan, BBC Director-General, was willing to provide some funds if the remaining financial resources could be found within the BBC Scotland budget. These stations at least did not require resident engineering, administrative and secretarial staff. The types of topics which were covered by these stations included the impact of North Sea oil development, pressures on traditional crofting, fishing and knitwear industries, and political devolution. After the publication in July 1978 of the government's White Paper on Broadcasting, the BCS was anxious to introduce more community stations in Scotland. Area radio stations were favoured for the

Borders, Dumfries and Galloway, Tayside, and the Western Isles. The next development was the opening of Radio nan Eilean (Radio of the Isles), a small bilingual station with a staff of four which was opened in Stornoway on 5 October 1979 and opted out from Radio Highland to broadcast a morning and an evening programme to people living in the Outer Hebrides, part of Skye, and the western coast of Sutherland and Wester Ross. With the introduction of these new services, an expansion took place in the BBC's advisory structure in Scotland. Towards the end of the 1970s, three new committees were formed: the Gaelic Advisory Committee, the Orkney Advisory Committee and the Shetland Advisory Committee. These committees had a smaller membership than other advisory committees, and normally averaged four to six members. Further BBC community radio stations were opened during the 1980s, thereby developing a radio structure where Scotland was provided by a national service in the form of Radio Scotland, supplemented by a pattern of area and community radio stations.

The other significant radio development during the late 1970s, apart from the introduction of area and community broadcasting, was the introduction of Radio Scotland as a self-contained service in 1978. The reallocation of wavelengths after the Geneva Conference of October 1975 made it possible to launch Radio Scotland as a separate radio service on 23 November 1978. On that day, the BBC changed the frequencies of many radio transmitters. Radio 4 on the MF band moved to LF, and Radio 2 moved from LF to the MF band; Radios 1 and 3 continued on the MF band. The VHF services remained unchanged. With the movement of Radio 4 from the medium to the long frequency band, Radio Scotland took over from the previous Scottish opt-out service on Radio 4 and broadcast on 371 metres medium-wave. It now had the task of competing with the four UK radio networks as well as commercial radio. For several years, Radio Scotland had opted out of Radio 4 and so had been unable to develop its own identity, but now there was an opportunity to plan a separate Scottish radio service with an expanded treatment of Scottish issues. It is therefore important to examine the BBC's plans for the start of Radio Scotland, the type of service which it was expected to provide, the problems which emerged over programme policy after the new service had begun, and the efforts which were subsequently made to improve audience figures.

With the change in wavelengths, Scotland did not have to carry the UK service of Radio 4, and so it was possible to plan a Scottish alternative to the mainly London-based programme output. After the changes, Radio 4 became a purely UK network in Scotland on long-wave without any Regional opt-outs. The changes offered the possibility of developing a richer programming base in Scotland which might help to stem the drift of talented staff to London and even encourage some staff to return to Scotland. The BCS commented in its Annual Report for 1976–7 on the projected nature of the new channel:

> It is felt that Radio Scotland must be the authoritative voice for news, current affairs and sport in Scotland, and must reflect all aspects of

Scottish life in politics, religion and the arts. It must spread its wings to cover serious Scottish interests and minority groups who would otherwise not be catered for. At the same time the new channel must broaden its base and offer a programme with mass appeal and a recognised Scottish flavour, which can at certain times of the day hold its own with the popular music channels and to a certain extent with commercial radio.[9]

This was a very ambitious set of criteria for the new station and, as will be seen, was responsible for the problems which later emerged after the new service had begun.

The new Radio Scotland service was expected to be unitary in character in the sense that it would provide a single service for the whole of Scotland yet still be capable of drawing upon material from the developing community and area radio stations. Radio Scotland was therefore not based on the generic principle used by the UK radio networks. The BCS argued that a single channel serving the whole nation was the best means of serving and reflecting the new mood of national consciousness within Scotland as well as facilitating the most economical use of resources.[10] The new channel was expected to be more popular in content than the previous opt-out service on Radio 4, given that the latter was primarily a speech-based network to which not all listeners in Scotland regularly tuned in. Up until then, BBC Scotland had not catered in radio for Scottish popular culture, but the increase in broadcasting hours on the new service made this feasible to some extent. Popular culture was confined to Radios 1 and 2, which were planned in London and which inevitably focused on a UK rather than a distinctively Scottish popular culture. To cover both traditional and popular Scottish culture, what was required were six, not five, radio services (i.e. Radios 1 to 4, Radio Scotland and local stations), but this was too costly to provide. Scotland had to decide whether to develop Radio Scotland as a national service or to develop local radio; it chose the former option. The advent of Radio Scotland as a self-contained Scottish radio service in 1978 was an attempt to resolve this dilemma.[11] However, it failed to a significant extent, and so BBC Scotland had to abandon any attempt to provide a strong output of popular culture of interest to Scottish people and therefore revert to the more traditional Radio 4 format. It highlighted the need to re-examine the role of radio in Scotland: should radio be national or primarily local; should it focus on cultural unity or cultural diversity; and should it concentrate primarily on Scottish matters and perhaps be criticised for being too provincial, or should it provide a Scottish perspective on UK and international events without listeners having to tune in to Radio 4 UK, as Neal Ascherson argued in an article in the *Scotsman?*[12] This highlighted the question as to whether Radio Scotland should be a mixed service, or a core service with the choice of developing local stations. A link can be established between the formation of Radio Scotland and mini-devolution within the BBC. Indeed, as Alastair Hetherington confirmed, Radio Scotland was part of the general expansion of programme services, and was partly also needed because of the expectation that there might be a Scottish Assembly.[13] The need for a comprehensive radio service for Scotland had been agreed in principle before the end of 1976.

Various preparations were initiated before the start of Radio Scotland. A new radio studio was provided in Edinburgh to cope with the increase in hours of output from the new service. The headquarters of Radio Scotland was to be based in Edinburgh. With the expected expansion of programme services in Scotland and the need to replace the existing premises in Edinburgh, a site was purchased at Greenside Place in 1976 as the location for a new Broadcasting Centre, not least because it was close to the former Royal High School, the meeting place of the proposed Scottish Assembly. However, with the increased financial pressures experienced by the BBC as a whole and the failure of the 1979 Devolution Referendum to produce a decisive vote in favour of establishing a Scottish Assembly, plans for the new centre were later revised and then abandoned, so that the new BH, scheduled for completion in 1983, did not materialise. A programme of refurbishment of the Edinburgh premises, the BBC's oldest existing building in the country, took place and was completed in 1990. In addition to the technical preparations for Radio Scotland, there were also staffing preparations. In September 1977, the BBC announced that John Pickles, a Glaswegian and Station Manager at BBC Radio Oxford since 1971, was to be the new Head of Radio Scotland. The BBC planned almost to double the radio output in Scotland when Radio 4 and Radio Scotland separated, thereby bringing the fifty hours of output up to eighty per week, with further increases planned by the early 1980s.[14] This increase in programme output was required if Radio Scotland was to operate as a genuinely separate radio channel in contrast to the previous Radio 4 opt-out service. Listeners would have a greater choice of programmes, because Radio 4 programmes would continue to be available in Scotland together with the expected increased output from Radio Scotland. BBC Scotland expected to spend more than £750,000 annually in operating the new service. London agreed to increase BBC Scotland's budget to meet the additional expenditure, mainly consisting of staff costs. The search for additional staff began in January 1978. Thirty additional production staff were recruited and trained, most of whom were based in Edinburgh, and the news and current affairs teams were also moved to Edinburgh. John Gray, who had previously been a Senior Producer, General Features (Radio), became Chief Assistant, Radio; in June 1978, Leslie Robinson replaced John Gray in this post. Other changes included the appointment of a Managing Editor, News (Edinburgh). Other noticeable changes in staffing in Edinburgh occurred in News with the presence of an Editor, a Chief News Assistant, News Sub-Editors and two special Correspondents – Scottish Correspondent (Michael Buerk), and an Economics Correspondent (Peter Clarke). Current Affairs was headed by an Editor assisted by a Senior Producer and four Producers.

On 23 November 1978, the changeover in the wavelengths took place and the new Radio Scotland service began. These changes prompted complaints from listeners who experienced interference on Radio 4, which had now been moved to long-wave. There was little prospect of introducing Radio 4 on VHF, because Scotland only had three VHF wavelengths (i.e. Radios 1/2, 3 and Radio Scotland). With the changes, programmes such as *The Archers* and *Women's Hour* were now broadcast only on Radio 4 UK and not on Radio Scotland. The output of Scottish material increased with the arrival of new programmes such as *Tom Ferrie* (mid-morning pop and popular music), *The Gerry Davis Show* (music and chat in the afternoons), *Rhythm and News* (news, music and interviews in the late afternoon), *The Tartan Terror Show* (with Gerry McKenzie) and *Night Beat* (late-night music with Ken Bruce).[15] Two weeks after the start of the new service, John Pickles emphasised the basis on which the station was expected to operate:

> It was the very conception of Radio 4, with its UK mantle, which allowed Radio Scotland its own frequency and determined its programme policy. We have never suggested that Radio Scotland has the resources to replace Radio 4 and we have planned our schedules to provide something different – something which we believe fills a gap between the 4 U.K. Networks on the one hand, and the much more localised broadcasting provided by our own stations in Aberdeen, Inverness, Orkney and Shetland and the ILR stations, Clyde and Forth, on the other.[16]

The problem for Radio Scotland, which soon became evident, was that it fell into this gap and lost its way.

Within a short period of time, the new service began to act as a magnet for criticism. The original programme policy had to be modified because of public criticism and a decline in audience figures. Radio Scotland's share of the audience was particularly low in the West of Scotland, where Radio Clyde offered strong competition to all radio networks.[17] Programme planners at Radio Scotland were concerned that their premier service covering the whole of Scotland was of interest only to a minority of listeners. Indeed, Radio Scotland had reached a larger audience when it was merely an opt-out service from Radio 4. By the end of 1979, research figures indicated that Radio Scotland was listened to on weekdays by 4.6 per cent of the audience as opposed to 5.7 per cent for Radio 4, 18.6 per cent (Radio 1), 9.6 per cent (Radio 2) and less than 1 per cent (Radio 3). The problem with Radio Scotland was that it sought to place itself between Radio 1 and ILR output, and Radio 4 output, and so failed to achieve a coherent mix of programmes. It faced the dilemma of trying to be popular in order to attract listeners, but not too popular for fear of alienating the traditional Radio 4 opt-out listeners. It could not appeal to Radio 4 Scotland listeners and those listeners who normally preferred Radios 1 and 2 or the ILR stations. BBC national policy, particularly since the introduction of the new network radio structure in April 1970, had been to place emphasis on specialised radio networks. However, with only one wavelength, Radio Scotland had to provide a balanced programme output for all listeners in Scotland and seek to serve both majority and minority interests. The result in programming terms was a rapid change of gear between programme items, resulting in what some newspaper articles at the time referred to as culture shock. It was the use of mixed rather than streamed programming which hindered Radio Scotland in cultivating audience identification. The faulty programme mix caused those listeners who preferred a Scottish version of Radio 4 to be dissatisfied. Likewise, popular music was already catered for on Radio 1 and the ILR stations. The BBC's overall financial problems also forced Radio Scotland to carry an increasing number of programmes taken from Radio 4. Nevertheless, the BBC in Scotland had increased its hours of programme output for listeners in Scotland from 3,175 hours during 1977–8, before the new service began, to 6,723 hours for 1979–80.[18] The number of hours of programme output contributed to other radio networks did, however, fall during this period, from 365 hours in 1977–8 to 240 hours in 1979–80.

In 1979, BBC Scotland's new Controller, Pat Ramsay, had to decide what changes at Radio Scotland were required in order to increase audience levels to a respectable level (at least greater than Radio 4, the channel from which it separated in November 1978), and to impress a clearer stamp of identity on the station. Ramsay wanted to create a more distinctive and distinguished network, and to achieve this he wished to place greater emphasis on news and current affairs programmes. An editorial in the *Glasgow Herald* stated:

> Minority interest programmes could have considerable appeal and Radio Scotland, fulfilling both a national and local role, is the right vehicle for this. There is enough going on throughout Scotland to provide material for a lively station and if the BBC recognises this it will find that there is far less need to pad out programmes with nondescript music.[19]

Based on the outcome of a special audience research survey and an internal report, the main points in Pat Ramsay's plan which were endorsed by the BCS and outlined in September 1979 were:[20]

(1) given that Radio Scotland was a national network operating in addition to the four UK networks (i.e. Radios 1, 2, 3 and 4), Radios 1 and 2 should be left to provide the main competition with commercial radio, since this was not a task which Radio Scotland should seek to accomplish;

(2) the major element in Radio Scotland's output should consist of high-quality news and current affairs programmes which would reinforce the station's identity, enable it to compete more effectively with other stations, and encourage listeners to turn to the station for Scottish, UK and international news;

(3) more emphasis should be given to talks and less to 'blether, pop and triviality', hence speech and music would be more clearly defined within any programme;

(4) there would be a greater focus on Scottish music, country music, light

classical music and folk music at the expense of pop music;

(5) there was to be more attention placed on the scheduling of programmes and on programme content, both of which had been identified as the source of so many criticisms;

(6) there was a recognition of the need to transmit specialised programmes which could generate interest among minority audiences.

The direction in which these changes pointed was a less populist and more traditional Radio 4 format for Radio Scotland. BBC Scotland sought within a single service to place programmes into three or four separate categories during the day, associate these with well-known presenters and thereby appeal to different audiences at different times of the day. This would gain the advantages of streamed programming within the overall framework of mixed programming on one wavelength (i.e. Radio Scotland would assume the guise of three or four separate stations during the day).

Within two years, Radio Scotland had begun to recover from the earlier criticism of its programmes and to implement the new guidelines. The station's share of the audience also began to improve. The BCS stated that Radio Scotland had learned to avoid the more drastic gear-changes of style that had originally formed the basis of much of the criticism of the station's programme output.[21] Improvements were taking place at a time when the BBC as a whole was experiencing pressure on financial resources. Radio Scotland broadcast several programmes which were popular with the audience, and these included *Good Morning Scotland* with Neville Garden and Malcolm Wilson, *The Jimmy Mack Show*, *Andy Cameron's Sunday Joint*, and *Sportsound* with Brian Marjoribanks. The BBC did not originally want Radio Scotland to be a Scottish version of Radio 4, yet it moved in this direction after the programme changes were implemented. From 1 to 5 December 1980, just two years after the launch of Radio Scotland, the station combined with BBC television in Scotland to pioneer radiovision (i.e. the simultaneous broadcasting on radio and television of the radio programme *Good Morning Scotland*) to mark fifty years of broadcasting from the BBC's Queen Street studios in Edinburgh.[22] During the week, the BBC invited the public to come and watch some of the programmes broadcast 'live'. This was the first time that cameras had been brought into a morning news programme on radio, and the BBC centrally took note of this development in order to gauge public response to breakfast television, which was introduced on the network just over two years later. By the close of 1980, Radio Scotland had escaped from the turbulent phase of its early development and now looked forward to consolidate the changes which subsequently had been introduced.

BBC *Scotland and the challenges facing public-service broadcasting, 1980–3*

By the early 1980s, the BBC was faced with a number of challenges, some of immediate importance, others of more long-term concern. From late 1979, there was a shift of emphasis from concern about Regional devolution to concern about the implications of the financial pressures facing the BBC as a whole which also had an impact within Scotland. These financial pressures led the BBC in Scotland to recommend the withdrawal of funding from schools' broadcasting and the disbanding of the Scottish Symphony Orchestra, both proposals which generated controversy and threw into sharp focus the role of the BBC in Scotland. BBC Scotland, as one of the BBC's national Regions, was not immune from the various changes affecting the BBC as a whole over this period, and therefore neither could it distance itself from the financial economies sought in 1980 or from the competitive challenges of new broadcasting services. The BCS was, as the Royal Charter stated, subject to such reservations and directions as appeared to the BBC to be necessary from time to time for reasons of finance. It was, however, BBC Scotland's chosen response (endorsed by the BCS) to the immediate financial problems, where it sought disproportionate economies with regard to schools' broadcasting and the SSO, which put into question its adherence to its Charter obligations to pay full regard to the distinctive culture, language, interests and tastes of the people of Scotland. These obligations appeared to some extent to have been abandoned because of the decisions made in 1980 about how the economies should be achieved. The financial pressures were of immediate concern, but, in the long term, the challenges facing the BBC centred on greater competition from a fourth television channel, breakfast television, more ILR stations, cable and satellite services, and the proliferation of video cassette recorders, as well as the demand by independent producers for greater opportunities for transmission of their work on the existing networks. It is therefore both interesting and relevant to consider what the programming and technical implications of these additional sources of competition had and were likely to have for broadcasting in Scotland. The BBC did not wish to be solely at the mercy of these changes. There was some room for expansion, as in Scottish contributions to breakfast television and in the opening of more community radio stations in Scotland. But overall, the new broadcasting environment, which offered the prospect of an expansion in the choice of services for listeners and viewers, also presented a strong challenge for public service broadcasting.

The financial pressures facing the BBC as a whole were evident some time before the start of the 1980s because of lower than expected increases in the licence fee. The licence-fee system established a direct relationship between the BBC and the public which it served, in contrast to either general taxation or the indirect relationship which existed with the funding of commercial broadcasting. The BBC regarded the licence fee as a buttress to its independence from detailed governmental control, but this independence was only relative, given that the setting of the licence fee was a political decision. It was uncertainty over licence-fee increases, particularly during periods of inflation and rising costs, which hindered the task of long-term planning. The licence fee was related to the BBC's public-service role and not its monopoly of broadcasting, because the arrival of Independent Television in 1954, funded by advertising, did not alter the BBC's method of funding via the licence fee. Thereafter, when the BBC changed its attitude and finally recognised Independent Television as a public-service broadcasting system, this questioned the original belief that the licence fee was essential to the BBC and the maintenance of its public-service role. By the 1980s, the financial doctrine which underpinned the BBC-ITV duopoly was not that advertising was incompatible with public-service broadcasting, but that competition for advertising was incompatible.[1] The level of the licence fee and the proportion of that fee which was actually paid to the BBC have varied over the years. With the increasing costs of broadcasting in the postwar period mainly attributable to the expansion of television broadcasting, the combined licence, which was first issued in 1946, was increased at fairly regular intervals thereafter. In addition to the increase in the level of the licence fee, there has also been a spectacular growth in the number of licences purchased. The number of combined licences purchased increased significantly in the 1950s with the extension of television to the Regions, and reached a peak in 1970 when over 15.5 million monochrome licences were in force throughout the United Kingdom.[2] The number of monochrome licences purchased declined thereafter, first slowly up until the mid-1970s, and then more rapidly because of the increasing number of colour licences bought. By 1980, the number of monochrome licences had fallen to just over five million. By contrast, the number of colour licences increased in line with the extension of colour services throughout the country on all networks and with the willingness of the public to switch from monochrome to colour. The latter was mainly dependent upon the falling cost of colour receivers, hire purchase restrictions and the conditions attached to the renting of receivers. It was, however, not until the mid-1980s that the number of colour licences equalled the number of monochrome licences which had been bought in the late 1960s and early 1970s. These trends in the number of licences bought were of immense importance to the BBC in ensuring that it had sufficient income to fund the expansion of its radio and television services.

In the 1950s, costing was regarded as a device for assisting programme planners in making economies and in taking policy decisions, but not as an end in itself. By the 1970s, with the onset of increasing financial problems, costing in the BBC assumed much greater importance. In a lecture to the Royal Institute of Public Administration on 25 November 1957, J.G.L. Francis (Chief Accountant at the BBC) stated that costing must be the servant, not the master, of the programme planners, but by the 1970s the priorities had altered. The licence fee no longer insulated the BBC from financial pressures. With rising costs, inflation and smaller than anticipated increases in the licence fee, the BBC feared that at some stage the licence-fee intervals might be so short as to degenerate into annual grants-in-aid and thus hinder long-term planning. During the 1970s, increases in the sale of colour licences could not prevent the BBC from borrowing on a more continuous basis. The BBC disliked the idea of borrowing, preferring instead for many years to finance development from income rather than from loan capital which would incur interest charges. Perhaps more importantly, the BBC did not wish to engage in deficit financing on a continual basis, for fear that this might encourage Ministers to postpone increases in the licence fee in the knowledge that the Corporation could increase its borrowing to finance expenditure. Likewise, the BBC rejected accepting advertising for fear that this would alter the character of the service provided, would be extended to all BBC services and would reduce pressure on the government to increase the licence fee.

On 25 November 1978, the level of the colour licence fee was increased from £21 to £25 and for monochrome from £9 to £10. The BBC had hoped for a colour licence fee of about £30 in order to take account of increased costs mainly attributable to inflation. The Corporation began the introduction to its Annual Report for 1978–9 by stating: 'For the BBC, the financial year 1978–9 ended in conditions of much uncertainty. The revision of the licence fee proved, as we had feared, inadequate to stem the erosion of inflation, and the maintenance of our programmes at their existing levels saw us going steadily deeper into deficit.'[3] During 1979–80, financial pressures increased, thereby placing constraints on the ability of the BBC to provide a full range of national, Regional and local programme services. On 24 November 1979, the colour licence was increased to £34 and the monochrome licence to £12, and these figures were not expected by the government to be increased for two years. However, the figures were below the BBC's estimate of the income which it needed to sustain a full public-service broadcasting operation. The BBC therefore ended the financial year as at 31 March 1980 with another deficit and so had to divert part of its income to pay interest charges on money borrowed rather than using this money on programmes. In these circumstances, the Corporation planned major economies. The rapid increase in the number of colour licences purchased during the 1970s had cushioned the impact of rising costs, but by 1980 increases in the number of these licences were tailing off. With economies expected in the BBC as a whole, Scotland was expected to make its own contribution to these savings.

On 7 December 1979, shortly after the licence-fee settlement had been announced, the BBC's Director of Finance indicated in broad terms to the BCS the implications of what was regarded as an insufficient licence fee on the funding of programme services. The BBC estimated that overall it would have to save about £132 million over two years, i.e. £40 million from existing services and £92 million from new items of budgeted expenditure. Scotland was expected to contribute £2.6 million over two years (i.e. 6.5 per cent) towards the £40 million cut in existing services throughout the BBC as a whole.[4] This represented a larger figure than BBC Scotland's percentage share of the total budget, which was 4.2 per cent as at 30 September 1979. BBC Scotland's share of these cuts represented seven per cent of its operating budget. This budget as at 31 March 1980 was £15.2 million, of which £5.8 million was attributable to radio and £9.6 million attributable to television. These savings therefore totalled over £1 million for each of the two years, and they were not to be spread across the whole range of BBC services in Scotland. The infrastructure needed to make programmes, such as studios and equipment, was to be subject to only limited cuts in expenditure; most of the planned reductions in expenditure were expected to affect schools' broadcasting and the Scottish Symphony Orchestra (SSO), together with economies in staff costs and other incidental expenses such as travel costs. The most controversial aspects of the proposed economies related to schools' broadcasting and the SSO, which together represented a significant element in the cuts in the operating budget.

Schools' broadcasting was a programme area in which it was expected that the BBC had an effective role to play, not least in reflecting the more distinctive aspects of Scottish education. Indeed, as early as 1929, a Scottish Sub-Council of the Central Council for School Broadcasting was formed in an attempt to prevent schools' broadcasts from becoming predominantly English in influence. This Scottish Sub-Council was, though, not free to develop its own policy. In 1936, it became known as the Scottish Council for School Broadcasting, and since 1947 the BBC has been advised in Scotland by the School Broadcasting Council for Scotland. The Council was responsible for designating areas of the curriculum where broadcasting could contribute useful material, to advise on policy with regard to schools' broadcasts in Scotland, to define the scope and purpose of schools' series and to review the effectiveness of schools' output. The Council kept in touch with schools, colleges and the Scottish Education Department, and also appointed some members to the School Broadcasting Council for the United Kingdom and its programme sub-committees in order to ensure that UK policy took account of the needs of Scotland. The Scottish Council's programme sub-committees sought to ensure that an adequate provision of programmes was made to meet the special needs of Scottish schools, such as the separate Scottish examination system, curricula, age of transfer between schools, and the different school terms. The recommendations of these sub-committees were considered by the executive committee of the School Broadcasting Council for Scotland prior to liaison with the UK Council and discussion with the BBC about the provision of specific schools' series. The BBC had final responsibility for editing scripts and producing the programmes. Radio broadcasts, such as the geography programme *Exploring Scotland*, were popular in primary schools; listening figures in secondary schools were lower because of timetable problems and pressure from examinations. By 1959, when schools' television broadcasts began for Scottish schools with a series entitled *Around Scotland*, more schools had access to a radio than to television. The School Broadcasting Council was thereafter anxious to make greater use of television in Scottish education to take account of the cultural needs of Scottish schoolchildren who had access to UK schools' programme output. After the changes in the Scottish Examination system in 1962, programmes were more closely linked to schools' curricula. By 1964, thirty-six per cent of schools in Scotland were equipped to receive television programmes, double the UK percentage. From then on, an increasing number of schools began to equip themselves with radio and television receivers, tape recorders, and video cassette equipment to record programmes for playback at times which suited school timetables. In general, educational broadcasting was of particular value to Scotland, not least because, with many small schools in isolated and scattered rural communities, it helped to keep pupils and teachers in touch with new ideas, as well as covering the needs of the Gaelic community. It was therefore not surprising that the BBC's plan to withdraw funding from schools' programmes was controversial.

On 28 February 1980, BBC Scotland announced that it was proposing to withdraw funding from radio and television schools' programmes in Scotland and to phase this over a two-year period. The intention was to reduce both the programme allowance and programme staff by twenty-five per cent in the 1980–1 budget, which the BBC expected would only result in a reduction of five per cent in schools' radio output and fifteen per cent in television output because of the greater use of repeat programmes. In the following financial year, the BBC was planning to withdraw the remaining seventy-five per cent in schools' broadcasting. The BBC wanted the Scottish Education Department publicly to fund schools' programmes, but on 25 March the Scottish Office informed the BBC that it would not be willing to provide financial support for schools' programmes. The BBC estimated that this financial support would represent £350,000 each year and stated that it would continue to provide the infrastructure for making programmes, which represented over £800,000. What it did not wish to fund were the staff costs and the programme allowance.

The BBC's proposal to withdraw from schools' broadcasting in Scotland provoked controversy. The Chairman of the School Broadcasting Council for Scotland wrote to the Board of Governors expressing the total opposition of the Council to BBC Scotland's proposed withdrawal of commitment to schools' broadcasting. He stated:

We are aware that this is currently *not* general BBC policy, since a reaffirmation of commitment is contained in the Director-General's letter to staff of 26 February 1980. We cannot accept that BBC Scotland should withdraw unilaterally from a commitment and a provision which has been part of the BBC's public service function for more than 50 years and which has earned a world-wide reputation.[5]

The Council believed that network schools' broadcasting from London would be unable to provide for the needs of Scottish pupils. Furthermore, it stated that BBC Scotland's plans represented a denial of its Charter obligations. The School Broadcasting Council stated that BBC Scotland's proposals represented a harsher discrimination against education than any proposed elsewhere in the BBC, and that economies should have been spread more evenly across programme services rather than concentrated in a few areas such as schools' broadcasting. The Council also regretted that it had not been consulted over the proposals. The cuts in radio and television schools programme allowances represented eleven per cent of total cuts, and the cuts in staff costs for schools' broadcasts represented fifteen per cent. Both therefore represented a disproportionate share of the proposed economies, particularly since staff and programme costs of over £300,000 represented only two per cent of BBC Scotland's operating expenditure of just over £15 million. The Council also emphasised that although Scottish schools' programme output represented a small percentage of total schools' output, greater use was made of Scottish schools' programmes. For example, although Scottish-produced schools' programmes for radio represented only sixteen per cent of all radio output available to secondary schools, its use by Scottish schools was about thirty-one per cent. Similarly, nine per cent of schools' television programmes for primary schools were produced by BBC Scotland, but they represented twenty-one per cent of total viewing time. In a memorandum to the Committee on Scottish Affairs, the Scottish Arts Council stated:

We are concerned not only about the loss of opportunities for professional writers and actors, but also because the service is highly valued by schools throughout Scotland, because it reflects a vitality, breadth and independence of outlook which is refreshing in Scottish education, and because the programmes contain specifically Scottish material which promotes a better understanding of Scotland's cultural heritage and language.[6]

The Association of Broadcasting Staff argued that it was dangerous for the BBC to rely on external funding to support schools' broadcasts in Scotland, thereby implying that this would unduly influence the content of programmes. The BBC's Educational Department did eventually maintain its output for schools, but there were cutbacks. Developments in other areas, such as the opening of further community radio stations, were also halted during 1981 and 1982. The controversy over BBC Scotland's plans for schools' broadcasts was also reflected in its proposal to disband the Scottish Symphony Orchestra.

BBC Scotland proposed as part of its contribution to overall BBC economies to disband the sso. The cost of the sso was about £600,000 annually. However, although BBC Scotland's orchestras represented only 5.5 per cent of annual operating costs, the disbandment of the sso represented thirty-eight per cent of the total economies planned by BBC Scotland. The sso thus appeared to represent an easy target for making valuable savings without seriously disrupting other operational activities. The Scottish Music Advisory Committee stated that the burden of economies within BBC Scotland should have been spread more evenly. However, BBC Scotland did not regard its attachment to the house orchestras as sacrosanct, and therefore felt no special obligation to guarantee security of employment for musicians at the expense of other creative staff. Furthermore, it argued that the demand for work by the sso would fall because Radio 3 was reducing its own musical output as its own contribution to the BBC economies, and that BBC Scotland would continue to fund the Scottish Radio Orchestra. BBC Scotland referred to a passage in the 1977 Annan Report on Broadcasting to lend support to its policy that it need not necessarily feel obliged to fund its orchestras in times of financial stringency. In a section covering the role of broadcasters as patrons of the arts, the report stated:

> The BBC must feel able to make cuts where it judges they will least affect its programmes, not simply in places where they cannot affect musicians. Secondly, even if the BBC is able to maintain or increase its present expenditure on musicians, we do not consider the BBC should necessarily be tied to the existing orchestral structures.[7]

The committee went on to state that it did not wish to see a national orchestra in Scotland or Wales abandoned, although it did want to see the rigid demarcation abolished between the BBC's orchestras and those orchestras assisted by the Arts Council. In other words, it believed that if the government wished to maintain all the BBC orchestras, then it should be prepared to provide extra finance to the Arts Council for the upkeep of these orchestras if necessary. The Scottish Arts Council stated that, given the underfunding of its existing orchestras and the unwillingness of the government to increase its grant to the Council, it could not take on the responsibility for funding the sso. The BBC's plan to disband five of its orchestras throughout the UK generated intense concern within and outwith the BBC. BBC Scotland received many letters complaining about the proposal to disband the sso. These plans were subsequently adjusted and the sso was maintained but reduced in size, and so the proportion of the cuts borne by Scotland was reduced. The Scottish Radio Orchestra was, though, disbanded. These changes ensured that Scotland did not have to accept so disproportionate a share of the financial cuts in comparison with the BBC's other national Regions. BBC Scotland concluded its memorandum (on the BBC cuts in Scotland) to the House of Commons Committee on Scottish Affairs by stating that 'We regret the circumstances that have made economies necessary but we believe that, by making cuts in the way decided, we can preserve the scarce programme making skills and structures necessary to meet the needs of the Scottish audience as a whole'.[8] In an article in the *Scotsman*, Pat Ramsay (Controller of BBC Scotland) argued that the BBC had to be free to make economies where they would least affect programmes, hence the original justification for seeking to disband the SSO. He maintained that, for some time, the BBC had been providing a first-class service for a second-class charge, thus implying that if the public wished to continue to receive a first-class service, then the BBC would have to be adequately funded.[9] In addition to the financial pressures, the BBC was also faced with the prospect of greater competition from a fourth television channel, the prospect of breakfast programmes on ITV, an expansion in commercial local radio, and the prospect of cable and satellite services.

The most immediate challenge facing the BBC at the beginning of the 1980s was the prospect of a fourth television channel. The proposed structure for the fourth television network appeared to offer Scottish-based independent producers an opportunity to cover topics which BBC Scotland could not adequately cover within the resources available, particularly during a period when the BBC was planning economies in its programme services. It was politically safer to fund the new channel from advertising income than to increase the BBC's licence fee to enable the Corporation to cater more fully for minority and Regional needs. In a more pluralistic broadcasting environment, the new channel was expected to guarantee access for the first time to independent producers and so provide an opportunity for more regional programmes to be networked. It was envisaged that programmes on the new channel would also be supplied by the ITV network and by the Regional companies. Jeremy Isaacs, who became the first Chief Executive of the fourth channel, wrote in 1979 that he expected the primary task of a fourth channel to be to extend viewer choice, to cater for minority interests, and to act as an encouragement to independent production. He did not think that it should simply compete with, or be complementary to, the existing ITV channel.[10] On 29 January 1981, 200 independent programme-makers launched a trade association, the Independent Programme Producers' Association (IPPA), to help independent producers to sell their work to Channel 4, the BBC and the ITV companies. The government was anxious for the broadcasters to allocate a quota of airtime for the work of independent producers. There needed to be adequate funds for the commissioning of programmes on Channel 4 from independent producers, given that the new channel was not wholly immune from market pressures and given the need to attract a sufficient audience. The IBA did not want the new channel to engage in competitive advertising with ITV, because this would force the fourth channel to aim at maximising the audience for its programmes. It therefore appeared that the IBA would have to cushion the new channel from financial pressures which might otherwise thwart its mandate to encourage innovation in programme content, a mandate incorporated in section 3 of the Broadcasting Act 1980.[11] Channel 4 was to be funded by the ITV companies, which then sold advertising time on the channel, but the ITV companies naturally wanted Channel 4 to popularise its output in order to attract a larger share of the audience and thereby increase advertising revenue. Channel 4 appeared to offer opportunities for the transmission of Scottish items which might not ordinarily have been broadcast on BBC Scotland or the Scottish ITV companies. This assumed that Commissioning Editors would accept a fair proportion of Scottish productions and that Scottish-based independent producers provided the type of programmes which these Editors believed the public wanted. In practice, after Channel 4 began broadcasting on 2 November 1982, over ninety per cent of independent programme production was London-based.

The prospect of breakfast television on ITV appeared to offer a more competitive challenge to the BBC's audience than Channel 4, given that the purpose of the latter was to provide programmes covering minority interests not already well served on the existing networks. The BBC was anxious that, if there was to be breakfast television, then it should take part in this new venture rather than leave the field to ITV. The BBC stated that 'It seemed to us that if breakfast-time television was to be inaugurated, the public should have a choice then as at all other times under our broadcasting system, and the BBC should be on the air'.[12] The BBC wished to introduce breakfast television before its competitors, and achieved this on 17 January 1983, when *Breakfast Time* was launched two weeks ahead of its rival ITV service provided by TV-am. With the advent of *Breakfast Time*, BBC Scotland was able to take part in this programme by providing inserts of Scottish news and weather reports for viewers in Scotland and by contributing the occasional topical story of interest to the network. A small television studio was constructed at BH Glasgow to provide these Scottish inserts in the daily breakfast programmes. The introduction of these morning television programmes on BBC and ITV did reduce the audience for radio in the early part of the morning, which had traditionally been a period during the day when radio attracted its largest audience. The gradual extension of daytime television programmes and the prospect of daytime programmes via cable and satellite broadcasting systems also threatened to challenge radio throughout the rest of the daytime period outwith the peak listening period from 7am to 9am. The growth in the number of ILR stations in Scotland in the early 1980s presented a challenge for BBC radio in Scotland and also for Radio 1, where reception on medium-wave was no match for the better quality of sound reception provided by the ILR stations which used VHF. Between 1980 and 1982, ILR stations were opened to serve Dundee, Perth, Aberdeen, Ayr and Inverness. But the BBC in Scotland wished to continue with its plans for opening further community radio stations, despite a halt in such development in 1981 and 1982 as a result of financial constraints. In 1983, two new community stations came on air after a three-and-a-half-year gap since Radio nan Eilean had opened in Stornoway on 5 October 1979. The two new stations were Radio Tweed in Selkirk, which covered most of the Borders and began broadcasting on 11 April, and Radio Solway in Dumfries, which served Dumfries and Galloway and came on air on 15 April. Each station was expected to provide one hour of local programme material on weekdays. By 1984, the BCS, which had given full support to the continued development of community radio in Scotland, was more in favour of resources being directed away from community radio stations to a number of self-operated contribution studios in smaller and more remote centres of population, to enable Radio Scotland to draw upon material from a wider geographical area.[13]

In technical matters, the BBC had responded to the challenge of providing UHF television to as many small communities as possible, but there remained gaps in broadcasting coverage in Scotland. Under phase 3 of the UHF plan, attention was focused on serving communities of between 200 and 500 people. During 1980, what appeared to be of most concern, following the government's decision in May of that year that 405-line television services should be phased out over a five-year period commencing in 1982, was that communities of less than 500 people (i.e. those outwith phase 2 of the UHF plan), would each have to cover the cost of providing a small relay transmitter. Phase 3 was therefore designed, as noted, to cover communities as small as 200 people, but this still left many areas unserved. By 1980, most 405-line receivers were obsolete and it was becoming increasingly expensive to maintain 405-line services. In November 1980, the total number of 625-line transmitters in service throughout the UK reached 1,000, giving a total coverage of 98.9 per cent of the population.[14] But most of the unserved areas were located in Scotland. Moreover, in September 1982, the Merriman Committee advised that the 405-line transmitters should be closed by the end of 1984 rather than 1986 in order to clear bands I and III for an expansion in land mobile radio. The government subsequently accepted this recommendation, and the last of the 405-line stations were closed in January 1985. The Home Office licensed self-help schemes for those communities still unable to receive 625-line UHF services when the 405-line services had closed down. By the end of 1983, over 100 self-help schemes were in operation throughout the UK. Despite the closure of all 405-line services in January 1985, the process of closing these services was in fact longer than originally anticipated, because the Television Advisory Council had recommended in 1967 that 405-line services should cease in seven to ten years, by which time 405-line receivers would be obsolescent. Nevertheless, it was estimated in 1983 that when these services closed, about fifty per cent of the number of viewers without UHF coverage were living in Scotland. In radio, there was the need for more relay transmitters to fill gaps in coverage of VHF services in order to extend the benefits of stereo broadcasting. Scotland received stereo services much later than other parts of the country. Indeed, as early as 1958, the BBC had sought to develop a compatible system in which both stereophonic channels broadcast from a single VHF transmitter would not impair monophonic reception for listeners who only had mono receivers. In January 1958, the first BBC experimental stereophonic transmissions took place in London outwith normal programme hours, using VHF and television sound transmitters. In July 1966, a limited stereo service was introduced on both the Third Programme and Music Programme, but these transmissions were confined to South-East England. In the autumn of 1972, stereo was extended to Radio 2, but it did not reach central Scotland until the mid-1970s. It soon became available on Radios 2, 3 and 4 and on Radio Scotland covering central and southern Scotland. To extend stereo on VHF, the BBC used a distribution system based on the use of pulse code modulation (PCM), which prevented any deterioration in the stereo signal over long distances and thus permitted uniformly high technical quality throughout the country. Stereo was extended to the transmitter at Sandale in November 1978, serving Dumfries and Galloway; the transmitters at Meldrum and Rosemarkie operated in stereo from December 1980. However, apart from the gradual extension of VHF stereo services during the 1980s, in order to improve reception of radio and television services and to widen programme choice, attention began to be focused on a more concerted basis in the early 1980s on the prospects for cable and satellite services.

Cable and satellite services both offered the technical means of providing a wider choice of programmes, although on a selective basis in contrast to the universality of the licence fee, whereby a wide range of programmes would be provided to all viewers in all areas for the same fee. It seemed likely that satellite services would pose a greater threat to the BBC in Scotland than cable services, because the cost of providing cable outwith urban areas would be prohibitive. Indeed, a report published in 1980 recognised that, despite technical changes emerging since the publication of the Annan Report three years earlier which suggested the likelihood of a faster development of broadband cable services, these would be located in urban, not rural, areas.[15] For many years, cable had been useful in areas where broadcast signals were weak, or in high-rise accommodation where individual aerials could not be used. However, the new cable systems envisaged were not these narrowband systems, which only carried a few terrestrial channels. The new broadband systems were capable of carrying a multiplicity of channels. On 22 March 1982, the government announced that a committee of inquiry would be established to consider the implications for public-service broadcasting of an expansion of cable systems. There appeared to be no desire to inhibit the development of cable merely because not all individuals had the financial resources to connect to a cable service or were in areas where cable was available. A committee under the chairmanship of Lord Hunt of Tanworth was appointed on 6 April to examine the various issues. The BBC, in its evidence to the Hunt Committee, argued that since it would be uneconomical to provide cable systems for more than fifty to sixty per cent of the country (and even less so in Scotland), then cable operators should not be permitted to have exclusive rights over coverage of major events, because this would deny access to them for many viewers. Some areas were undoubtedly more attractive to cable than others, and thus many areas of Scotland would continue to depend upon off-air services for many years after the extension of cable services. The Hunt Report, which was published on 12 October 1982, indicated that cable television should supplement public-service broadcasting and be responsive to local demand. The report outlined the purposes of cable services:

> Cable television is therefore all about widening the viewer's choice. It should be innovative, experimental and sensitive to local feeling. It cannot be run as though it was another branch of public service broadcasting providing a balanced service for the country as a whole.[16]

On this basis, the committee therefore recommended general oversight of cable services on a local basis rather than detailed regulation on a nationwide basis after franchises had been allocated by the proposed new Cable Authority. In order to safeguard the interests of public-service broadcasting, the committee stated that multi-channel cable systems must carry all four BBC and ITV channels, so that no viewer would be denied access to them simply by deciding to connect to a cable system. The BBC was pleased that cable operators were not to be allowed to gain exclusive rights to major national sporting events, but there was some disappointment that there were to be no obligations on cable systems to provide community programming and local access. However, the Hunt Committee did indicate that there would be a presumption that the latter would be provided and that proposals for such facilities would be taken into account in the award of franchises. In April 1983, the government published its White Paper on the development of cable systems and services. The government indicated that cable development should be market-led (i.e. expansion would be dependent upon the rate at which individual consumers chose to pay on a subscription basis for cable services). The government would merely create the opportunities to enable cable development to take place through private rather than public funding, in the firm belief that a market did exist for the provision of these additional services.[17]

In contrast to cable, programmes beamed by satellite would be instantly available to all viewers who possessed the appropriate dish aerials carefully positioned with an unobstructed line of sight to the satellite, rather than being gradually extended throughout the country. Unlike BBC transmitter development, satellite services would ensure that Scotland would not be underprovided in comparison with other parts of the UK, as had occurred with the gradual extension of the BBC networks. But the ability of Direct Broadcasting by Satellite (DBS) to provide an instant national service did not imply that the nature of that service could be national if reception of the service were limited to a small percentage of the population who were prepared to purchase the special receiving equipment. With DBS, programmes would be beamed from a ground station to a satellite and then retransmitted from this geostationary satellite using super-high frequencies (SHF) into those homes which were equipped with a rooftop dish aerial or were linked to a cable system which obtained its programmes from a satellite. In comparison with terrestrial broadcasting systems, such as that provided by the BBC, DBS was likely to be able to offer uniformity of signal strength in Scotland because the satellite signals were less affected by mountainous terrain or distance. The technical benefits of DBS were, however, accompanied by drawbacks in the area of programme content. The coverage of DBS services was not guaranteed to coincide with national frontiers, given that the satellite beam would cover a wide geographical area. So not only was there less likelihood of providing a national service for viewers in Scotland, but also there was no possibility of regionalising these services within Scotland, a factor noted in the 1977 Annan Report on Broadcasting.[18] Satellite services would therefore be aimed at what Jeremy Isaacs referred to in a Royal Society of Arts lecture in June 1982 as a 'mass undifferentiated audience'.[19] Moreover, the BBC was concerned that the new technological developments would, by widening the number of channels available, also fragment the television audience and thus undermine the licence-fee system upon which the BBC's income depended. It seemed that, apart from the owners and operators of DBS, the main beneficiaries of the new systems would be advertisers, who would be able to expand their markets, and industry, which would develop and market the new receiving equipment.

On 4 March 1982, the Home Secretary stated that the government was in favour of having Britain make an early start with DBS with the intention of providing a workable service by 1986. The BBC was to be permitted to provide the first two of the five DBS channels which had been allocated to the United Kingdom in 1977 at the World Administrative Radio Conference. With the growing importance of developments in cable and DBS technology, the BBC appointed Bill Cotton (Director of Programmes, Television) to a new post of Managing Director, DBS. In November 1982, Christopher Irwin (Head of Radio Scotland) became General Manager, DBS Development. Irwin was succeeded as Head of Radio Scotland by Stan Taylor, who had been Editor of News and Current Affairs in Scotland. The BBC adopted a cautious approach to DBS in the knowledge that development depended upon so many factors, such as the range and popularity of the programmes available, the cost of the receiving equipment and the operating costs. By the mid-1980s, the traditional viewing habits of the audience had altered appreciably since the heyday of the BBC-ITV duopoly, given the growth in ownership of video recorders and the number of households with multiple television receivers. It certainly posed some problems for programme planners with regard to competitive scheduling. The prospect of DBS threatened to intensify that process, yet also to provide viewers with a greatly enhanced range of programmes and the distant opportunity of better picture quality through HDTV.

Conclusion

Public-service broadcasting had experienced immense changes since the early 1920s. The regulated monopoly had been replaced by regulated competition in television in 1954 and in radio in 1972, so that by the early 1980s the BBC was only one broadcasting organisation and no longer addressed a single national audience. In Scotland, the BBC was faced with competition from the ITV companies and the ILR stations. With the prospect of even more radio and television channels, such as via cable and satellite services, the challenge to the BBC's monopoly in the 1950s had by the 1980s turned into a challenge to the duopoly. The history and development of BBC public-service broadcasting in Scotland is essentially the history of one of the BBC's Regions, albeit a national Region, and therefore has to be viewed in relation to developments in broadcasting within the much wider United Kingdom context. For the BBC in Scotland, this has led to a contradictory pull between the desire to be Scottish and having to operate in Scotland as part of a UK institution. The development of BBC broadcasting in Scotland since the 1920s took place within an essentially centralised broadcasting organisation, of which it represented a constituent element.

One of the major themes which has emerged from this study has been the growth of the BBC in Scotland: growth in terms of organisational structure and number of staff, reaching over 1,200 by the early 1980s; the geographical extension of broadcasting services throughout Scotland; the growth in the size of the listening and viewing audience; and an expansion in the range, quality and volume of programme services provided. Another principal theme has been that of the influence of centralisation on the operation of BBC Scotland and on the nature of the programme services provided. The centralised nature of the BBC, and the constraining factors which have inhibited the devolution of greater responsibilities to the Regions and the decentralisation of programme resources within Scotland, have been considered at various points in terms of the BBC's organisational structure, the decision-making process, the allocation of financial resources, transmitter development and the provision of television and radio programme services. A third salient theme has been the influence of competing services, such as ITV and ILR, on BBC programme policy and consequently on the nature of the programmes provided by the BBC in Scotland.

Comparisons have also been drawn between the different organisational structure of the BBC and these competing services, and emphasis has also been placed on the implications of the differing broadcasting structures for the type of programme services provided. In this context, comparisons have also been drawn between the BBC's English Regional structure and the Regional structure in Scotland, and how this has influenced both the networking of programme material and the frequency and availability of Regional opt-outs. The three major themes which therefore emerge from this study of the BBC in Scotland are growth, centralisation and competition.

John Reith, the BBC's first Director-General, had an immense influence on the BBC during the formative years of broadcasting, and with his cultural mission he helped to mould the Corporation into an established institution operating under unified control as a public service serving most parts of the country. Indeed, after the reconstitution of the commercially-founded British Broadcasting Company in the private sector into a Corporation operating in the public sector in 1927, the BBC was to operate as a public service both in constitutional structure, with a Board of Governors acting as trustees in the national interest, and also in programme output. The centralised nature of the BBC was the product of several factors, not least the need to operate on an efficient basis within available technical and financial resources and to sustain high programme standards throughout the UK, thereby investing broadcasting with a social purpose. Given that successive governments did not exercise control over day-to-day administration or programme matters within the BBC, it was thus left to the Corporation to decide on the balance between central control and the devolution of responsibilities to Regions. The unity of the BBC did not, however, entail uniform treatment of all its constituent parts; this is indicated by the different status and power devolved to the national Regions, such as Scotland, in comparison with the English Regions. This special treatment did not prevent criticism in Scotland, both within and outwith the BBC, of remote control from London. BBC Scotland remained part of the BBC and therefore has always been designated as a Region; it was regarded as a national Region because of its special programme responsibilities with regard to the listening and viewing audience in Scotland. A central question was really the extent to which Scotland was treated more as a region than as a nation in broadcasting terms. In crucial matters such as the allocation of expenditure for operating purposes and capital development or for the transmitter development programme, Scotland was essentially regarded as a region; in programme matters, such as the ability to decide on a separate Scottish programme schedule in radio, the BBC in Scotland had greater flexibility to serve national needs, but within the resources made available by the BBC centrally. The closure of the local stations which had operated in Scotland during the 1920s, and their replacement by a Scottish Regional service in the 1930s, brought a moderately wider choice of programmes and better reception to a greater number of listeners in Scotland by extending coverage beyond the range of existing main and relay stations. But this reinforced the belief that Scotland was regarded by the BBC as a single region rather than as a nation of regions. Furthermore, the policy of centralisation appeared to convert Scotland into a regional outpost. Regions were not expected to duplicate material which could be produced to higher standards in London and broadcast on the National Programme. This, together with the lack of staff and facilities, appeared to leave Scotland to concentrate on only the most parochial of subject matter. In 1936, the Report by the Director of Regional Relations examined the extent to which the policy of centralisation had inhibited programme development in the Regions and made recommendations for improvements in Regional programme policy. Scottish Regional broadcasting was subsequently suspended during the war years, but plans were prepared for a stronger Scottish programme service, and so the most significant changes did not materialise until 1945.

In the postwar period, there was a more rapid development of programme services, and this was accompanied by greater complexity in the BBC's organisational structure at both central and Regional levels, and by changes in the relationship between Scotland and the BBC centrally. With the arrival of television and growth in the radio and television services provided, new posts and departments were created within BBC Scotland. Furthermore, new bodies were created with advisory and executive powers over the conduct of broadcasting services provided in Scotland. The Scottish Advisory Council (SAC), a purely advisory body, was formed in 1947, and its recommendations were not binding on the BBC. Its Chairmen served on the BBC's General Advisory Council, and the Chairmen of the various Scottish Advisory Committees were *ex officio* members of the SAC. This advisory structure provided at times a valuable source of advice for the broadcasters in the formulation of policy in Scotland, but the use to which that advice was put was solely the responsibility of BBC Scottish management. The SAC was superseded in 1953 by the Broadcasting Council for Scotland, which was invested with executive powers to control the policy and content of initially radio, and later television, programmes produced within and for Scotland. The Broadcasting Councils for Scotland and Wales, whose formation was recommended by the Beveridge Committee on Broadcasting in 1951, were not overwhelmingly welcomed by the BBC Board of Governors, which feared that these Councils would pursue a policy of expansion and would undermine the unity of the BBC. The introduction of these Councils represented an attempt to permit the maximum degree of devolution consistent with the maintenance of overall central control by the BBC. Indeed, the powers of the Councils were subject to any reservations and directions which the BBC centrally deemed were necessary from time to time for financial reasons or to maintain a coherent administrative structure. There was in fact no written constitution defining the scope of the Councils. Moreover, successive national Governors have had to reconcile their collective responsibility as members of the Board of Governors for UK matters in broadcasting, with the autonomous rights delegated to the Broadcasting Councils of which they were Chairmen. The BCS could act as a useful intermediary with London when Scotland lobbied for more resources, but the usefulness of the Council in safeguarding Scottish interests was dependent on many factors, such as the willingness of Council members to use the power at their disposal, the personality of the national Governor and his/her personal contacts with the BBC Chairman, and the unity of the BCS on various issues. In practice, the BCS was not consistently successful in safeguarding Scottish interests, although the presence of the Council did to some extent ensure that senior staff had to be more careful in formulating and justifying policy decisions affecting broadcasting services in Scotland. It was in the interests of the Council to have a Chairman who had good relations with the BBC Chairman, who might then be persuaded to be more sympathetic towards the interests of Scottish broadcasting. Such a situation prevailed, for example, when Lord Normanbrook was BBC Chairman and Sir David Milne (a former Permanent Under-Secretary of State for Scotland) was National Governor for Scotland; it was less so when Lady Baird succeeded Milne as national Governor in November 1965. The fact that the national Governor was in a minority within the Board of Governors only mattered if it was accepted that there was an anti-Scottish bias within the membership of the Board. The belief that the BCS would owe an allegiance to the Board of Governors was not necessarily true if tension and disagreements existed between Council members and the national Governor. For example, in October 1967, members of the Council were critical of Lady Baird and the Board of Governors for not being consulted about the appointment of Alasdair Milne as the new Controller of BBC Scotland, particularly since the Controller was the most senior adviser to the Council on policy and programme matters in Scotland. Overall, the BCS never had a high public profile, and indeed was prompted in one of its annual reports to emphasise the marked degree of ignorance about its place, function and existence, perhaps a reflection as much of the degree of its effectiveness in safeguarding Scottish interests in broadcasting as of uncertainty as to the precise role of the Council within the BBC's organisational structure.

The provision of programme services in Scotland was principally dependent upon the financial resources made available by the BBC centrally. According to BBC accounting methods, BBC Scotland has consistently operated at a deficit and thus had to be subsidised by London and some of the other Regions. Scotland was not unique in this respect, because most Regions operated at a deficit. Scotland's contribution towards shared costs appeared large, but the BBC centrally argued that it funded the higher-than-average cost of extending the transmitter networks in Scotland. Scotland could generate more resources by recovering the cost of programmes contributed to the radio and television networks, but network Controllers had the power to decide whether or not to accept Scottish-originated material for UK transmission. In practice, Scotland appeared to be more successful in getting radio than television programmes taken by the networks. This was mainly attributable to the lack of specialised television facilities in Scotland in the early years, and to competition in the later years from the large English network production centres to get material networked. Overall, the BBC maintained that an independent Scottish broadcasting corporation could not have existed solely on licence income generated within Scotland, and in any case it was not so certain that the audience would have preferred a greater volume of Scottish-produced material to replace popular network programmes.

The ability to receive programmes in Scotland was dependent upon the extension of the transmitter networks. In general, technical developments tended to be introduced in London and then extended to the Regions. In the absence of any obligation to provide 100 per cent broadcasting coverage, the BBC sought to bring programmes to the largest number of communities possible in the shortest period of time within variable technical and financial resources. Priority was given where possible to the provision of services within the four nations, and thereafter according to density of population. Technical factors determined that it was more costly to serve scattered and remote communities in mountainous areas, many of which were located in Scotland. Indeed, the cost of providing UHF television transmitters to remote areas increased in inverse proportion to the number of people served, and so the law of diminishing returns began to operate. Moreover, transmitter development was never governed to any significant extent by social and cultural factors, such as the need to sustain cultural traditions, to provide entertainment and educational programmes to compensate for a lack of leisure facilities, to attract labour and tourism, or to halt depopulation. In 1974, the Crawford Committee did however draw attention to the social aspects of broadcasting coverage. The lack of radio and television services in some parts of the Highlands and Islands had, though, not been allowed to hold back the provision of new services, such as BBC2, to other parts of the country which already had access to a choice of programme services. Decisions about the planning of the transmitter networks were coordinated by Engineering Division in London for practical reasons. By January 1985, when the remaining 405-line transmitters were closed down, areas not yet covered by 625-line UHF services had to receive their programmes through self-help schemes licensed by the Home Office.

The analysis of the provision of television and radio programme services in Scotland has to be considered in relation to the provision of programme services by the BBC as a whole as well as the influence of competitive services such as ITV and ILR. These factors determined the nature of the programme services provided in Scotland. Television, which was restarted in the London area in 1946, was extended to the Regions in December 1949, reaching Scotland in March 1952. However, with no television studio facilities and the need to confine Scottish programmes for some time to outside broadcasts, this landmark represented the arrival of television from England to Scotland and not strictly speaking the arrival of Scottish television. For many years, Scotland also had to rely on production teams from England to cover Scottish items of interest to a network audience. This reliance on so-called hosted programming diminished during the 1970s, when Scottish production teams originated more of their own material under their own control. Unlike radio, BBC television provided a national service within Scotland, because television could not be regionalised with existing resources. The arrival of ITV in 1955 with its federal structure, which in subsequent years divided the country into geographical units as new programme companies were awarded franchises, can be contrasted with the BBC, which essentially provided a UK service with Regional opt-outs. Only one programme company was appointed in each ITV Region, and the networking arrangements made many programmes local in origin rather than necessarily in appeal. However, most network material was, unlike the BBC, not produced in London, because there were several ITV network companies, not all of which operated from London. Furthermore, the establishment of three small companies in Scotland enabled ITV to cater more fully than the BBC for regional audiences within Scotland. Moreover, it also persuaded BBC Scotland to review its provision of Scottish programme output and to seek, in common with other BBC Regions, to persuade London – who were unhappy about fragmentation of the network – to agree to more opt-out programmes. As regards the networking of more Scottish material, there were physical constraints in achieving this with only one network in existence. The arrival of BBC2 appeared to offer the prospect of broadcasting more regional material, but BBC2 was never planned as a regionalised channel. Most television programmes transmitted in Scotland were taken from the networks, and so Scottish output represented a small percentage of total programme output. Also, the limited resources available within BBC Scotland, together with its dual programme responsibility, prevented it from competing on a stronger basis with London and the specialised English network production centres to get material accepted for network transmission.

In radio, the resumption of Regional broadcasting in 1945 and the consequent introduction of the Scottish Home Service increased the volume of Scottish material within the resources made available by London. The popularity of the SHS in comparison with the other sound networks, and the ability of Scottish producers to export programme material to the other networks, resulted in greater attention being given by the early 1960s to the possible development of localised services to cater for more identifiable communities and so complement national radio in Scotland. However, BBC Scotland was not in favour of the provision of local stations. The BCS argued that Scotland already served more homogeneous communities than the English Regions, and so it believed that there was less need for local radio and a greater need to develop national radio within Scotland. In any case, the Reithian mixed programming philosophy adhered to by BBC Scotland would not easily have permitted local services whose programme content reflected the social and cultural mix of the geographical areas which they served. It was the success of BBC local radio in England since 1967 and the arrival of Independent Local

Radio in Scotland in 1973 which focused attention on the need for BBC Scotland to review the provision of its radio output and consider how best to supplement national radio with localised broadcasting adapted to meet the needs of local communities in Scotland. By the mid-1970s, plans had been prepared for an area radio station in Inverness, i.e. Radio Highland. This was one of several area and community radio stations which were opened between 1976 and 1983, all of which differed from BBC local radio in England because they operated as opt-out and sub-opt-out services from the national service, namely Radio Scotland. In 1978, Radio Scotland itself became a separate, non-generic programme service operating on its own wavelength rather than as an opt-out service from Radio 4 when the latter moved from medium-wave to long-wave. But the problems which accompanied programme policy in the new service emphasised the need to review the role of radio in Scotland, particularly in the absence of BBC local radio stations on the English model, and because of the nature of the competition provided by the BBC's specialised radio networks and the ILR stations. The first question which had to be addressed was whether radio in Scotland should be primarily local or national in character: BBC Scotland opted for national radio with some provision of localised services to meet specific needs such as in Orkney, Shetland, the Western Isles, the Borders and Dumfries and Galloway. A second question was whether radio should seek to bolster Scottish national identity or reflect cultural diversity within Scotland: Scotland sought the former since this was consistent with the resurgence of national consciousness throughout the 1970s, but the diversity of cultural traditions within Scotland was not totally ignored. A third and final question was what balance should be aimed for in programme output with regard to the broadcasting of Scottish and UK material: Scotland did not seek to broadcast too much Scottish material for fear of alienating listeners who preferred network output, yet it had to remain sufficiently Scottish in order to justify its existence as an alternative to Radio 4 and to adhere to its Charter obligations to pay regard to the distinctive culture, language and interests of the people of Scotland.

During the 1970s, there was greater pressure on the BBC to devolve more power to the Regions. The BBC had to be seen to represent the sum of its parts rather than merely as London with Regional outposts. The Board of Governors believed that it was politically sensible to support devolution within the BBC and so lessen pressure for more radical changes. The enrichment of broadcasting both within Scotland and throughout the UK was dependent upon the BBC providing adequate scope for the development of broadcasting in Scotland, including greater latitude over decisions affecting the conduct of Scottish programme services. The progress of mini-devolution within the BBC was hindered to some extent after the failure of wider political devolution to materialise in 1979 and with increasing financial pressures facing the Corporation as a whole by the beginning of the 1980s. By 1980, BBC Scotland remained part of a centralised broadcasting organisation, but since the 1920s it had undergone significant growth in its organisational structure, in the geographical coverage of its transmissions and in the range of programme services which it provided for the varied listening and viewing audience in Scotland. During the early 1980s, BBC Scotland services experienced modest expansion, such as in contributions towards breakfast television and network output and in the further development of community radio. With the advent of more competition both through the creation of Channel 4 and the introduction of more ILR stations in Scotland, and with the prospect of a multiplicity of new channels through cable and satellite services, BBC Scotland faced a more daunting challenge in meeting the needs of the audience in Scotland than it had ever experienced in sixty years of broadcasting in Scotland.

Appendix 1

A CHRONOLOGY OF BROADCASTING, 1922–83

1922

18 Oct.   British Broadcasting Company formed.
 1 Nov.   The first Broadcast Receiving Licence issued.
14 Nov.   Broadcasting began from London (2LO).
14 Dec.   John Reith appointed as General Manager of the British Broadcasting Company.
15 Dec.   British Broadcasting Company registered.

1923

18 Jan.   Licence to broadcast granted by the Postmaster-General to the BBC (Cmd 1822).
 6 Mar.   Glasgow main station (5SC) opened.
24 Apr.   Sykes Committee on Broadcasting appointed.
29 Aug.   Simultaneous broadcasting inaugurated when land lines linked London with provincial stations.
28 Sept.   *Radio Times* first published.
 1 Oct.   Sykes Report on Broadcasting published (Cmd 1951).
10 Oct.   Aberdeen main station (2BD) opened.
14 Nov.   John Reith appointed as Managing Director of the British Broadcasting Company.

1924

 1 May   Edinburgh relay station (2EH) opened.
12 Nov.   Dundee relay station (2DE) opened.

1925

20 July   Crawford Committee on Broadcasting appointed.
27 July   Daventry (5XX) high-power station opened.

1926

 5 Mar.   Crawford Report on Broadcasting published (Cmd 2599).
10 Nov.   British Broadcasting Company agreed on policy of centralisation.
31 Dec.   British Broadcasting Company dissolved.

1927

 1 Jan.   British Broadcasting Corporation constituted under Royal Charter, operational for ten years; Sir John Reith appointed as Director-General, and Earl of Clarendon as first Chairman.
 4 Jan.   First meeting of the BBC Board of Governors.

1928
9 Oct.   Baird Television Company experiment with television.
1 Nov.   Scottish programmes came under the control of a Scottish Regional
            Director which superseded the post of Northern Area Director.

1929
16 Jan.   *The Listener* first published.
20 Aug.   First BBC transmission of experimental 30-line television.
1 Oct.   BBC Regional Scheme began.

1930
9 Mar.   Alternative programmes for London and the Home Counties began under
            the Regional Scheme.
31 Mar.   First transmission of simultaneous sound and television signals.
14 July   BBC headquarters in Scotland transferred from Glasgow to Edinburgh.
29 Nov.   Broadcasting House at Queen Street, Edinburgh, opened.

1932
15 May   Broadcasting House in Portland Place, London, became BBC's head-
            quarters.
12 June   Westerglen high-power Regional transmitter in Scotland opened; Glasgow,
            Edinburgh and Dundee local stations closed.
25 Sept.   Full dual programme service (Regional and national) began from Scottish
            Regional station at Westerglen.

1933
1 Sept.   Melville Dinwiddie became Scottish Regional Director.

1934
14 May   Selsdon Television Committee appointed.

1935
31 Jan.   Selsdon Report on Television published (Cmd 4793).
20 Feb.   First meeting of the BBC's General Advisory Council.
17 Apr.   Ullswater Committee on Broadcasting appointed.

1936
16 Mar.   Ullswater Report on Broadcasting published (Cmd 5091).
29 June   Government White Paper on Broadcasting published (Cmd 5207).
1 Oct.   BBC established a Listener Research Department.
12 Oct.   Burghead transmitting station serving North-East Scotland opened.
2 Nov.   BBC began first regular public television service in the world.

1937
1 Jan.   BBC's second Royal Charter, operational for ten years.
4 Feb.   Marconi-EMI system adopted for television transmissions.

1938
30 June   Sir John Reith resigned as Director-General of the BBC.
9 Sept.   Aberdeen main station (2BD) closed; Redmoss Regional transmitter opened.
1 Oct.   Frederick Ogilvie succeeded Reith as Director-General.
18 Nov.   Broadcasting House at Queen Margaret Drive, Glasgow, opened.
9 Dec.   Broadcasting House at Beechgrove, Aberdeen, opened.

1939
1 Sept.   BBC Television service closed because of the war; the Home Service replaced national and Scottish Regional programmes.

1940
7 Jan.   The Home Service was supplemented by an experimental Forces Programme.
18 Feb.   Forces Programme extended and designated as an alternative to the Home Service.

1942
27 Jan.   Robert Foot and Sir Cecil Graves became joint Directors-General.

1943
6 Sept.   Sir Cecil Graves resigned as Director-General.

1944
27 Feb.   General Forces Programme began.
31 Mar.   William Haley became BBC Director-General.

1945
8 Mar.   Hankey Television Committee Report published.
29 July   Restart of Regional broadcasting: the introduction of the Scottish Home Service and the Light Programme.

1946
1 June   Introduction of a £2 combined (radio and television) licence; sound-only licence increased to £1.
7 June   BBC television restarted (on 405 lines) in the London area.
2 July   Government White Paper on Broadcasting (Cmd 6852).
29 Sept. BBC Third Programme began.

1947
1 Jan.   Scottish and Welsh Regional Advisory Councils formed; BBC's third Royal Charter, operational for five years.
9 June   Lord Simon of Wythenshawe became BBC Chairman.
29 Sept. School Broadcasting Council for Scotland formed.

1949
21 June   Beveridge Committee on Broadcasting appointed.
17 Dec.   Television first extended to the Regions.

1950
15 Mar.   Copenhagen Plan governing the allocation of wavelengths.

1951
18 Jan.   Beveridge Report on Broadcasting published (Cmd 8116).
10 July   Government White Paper on Broadcasting (Cmd 8291).

1952
1 Jan.   BBC's Royal Charter extended to 30 June 1952.
14 Mar.   Kirk O'Shotts transmitter opened, thus bringing BBC television to Scotland.
16 May   Government White Paper on Broadcasting (Cmd 8550).

1 July   BBC's fourth Royal Charter, operational for ten years.
1 Aug.   Sir Alexander Cadogan became BBC Chairman; Lord Clydesmuir appointed
              as first BBC National Governor for Scotland.
17 Aug.   Kirk O'Shotts high-power television transmitter operational.
25 Nov.   Last meeting of the Scottish Advisory Council.
1 Dec.   Sir Ian Jacob became BBC Director-General.

1953
1 Jan.   BBC Broadcasting Councils for Scotland and Wales established.
8 May   First Report of the Television Advisory Committee, 1952.
18 June   National Television Council formed.
2 July   Popular Television Association formed.
13 Nov.   Government White Paper on Broadcasting (Cmd 9005).
16 Dec.   Second Report of the Television Advisory Committee, 1952.

1954
30 July   Television Act, 1954.
4 Aug.   Independent Television Authority (ITA) established.
14 Dec.   Redmoss temporary television station near Aberdeen opened.

1955
1 Jan.   Tom Johnston became BBC National Governor for Scotland.
2 May   First VHF radio station brought into service at Wrotham.
22 Sept.   Start of ITV transmissions, in the London area.
10 Oct.   Colour television test transmissions began by the BBC.
12 Oct.   Meldrum permanent television station replaced the temporary Redmoss
              transmitter near Aberdeen.

1956
29 Mar.   First VHF radio station opened in Scotland at Meldrum.
30 May   Scottish Television (STV) appointed by the ITA as first programme con-
              tractor in Scotland.
1 July   Lord Balfour became BBC National Governor for Scotland.

1957
8 Apr.   BBC announced changes in radio network programmes.
8 July   Andrew Stewart became Controller, BBC Scotland.
12 Aug.   First meeting of ITA's Scottish Committee.
16 Aug.   Rosemarkie television station opened.
30 Aug.   BBC introduced the first Scottish television news bulletin.
31 Aug.   Start of STV transmissions in central Scotland.
30 Sept.   Start of BBC Network Three.
30 Nov.   Kirk O'Shotts VHF radio transmitters brought into service.
1 Dec.   Sir Arthur fforde became BBC Chairman.

1958
13–14 Jan.   BBC began stereophonic test transmissions.
6 Mar.   Kelvingrove by-election, the first covered by BBC Scotland.
12 Oct.   Rosemarkie VHF radio station opened.
15 Dec.   Thrumster and Kirkwall temporary television transmitters opened.
22 Dec.   Orkney temporary television and VHF radio stations opened.

1959
20 Jan.   BBC television outside broadcast base at East Kilbride opened.
22 Dec.   Orkney permanent VHF radio station opened.

1960
1 Jan.   Hugh Carleton Greene became BBC Director-General.
1 Mar.   Thrumster permanent television station opened.
2 May   Orkney permanent television station opened.
1 June   Report of the Television Advisory Committee 1960 published.
13 July   Pilkington Committee on Broadcasting appointed.
30 Nov.   Sir David Milne became BBC National Governor for Scotland.

1961
22 Mar.   First BBC local radio experiment, at Bristol.
1 Sept.   Border Television began transmissions.
30 Sept.   Grampian Television began transmissions.

1962
7 Mar.   First BBC Gaelic television programme.
20–23 Mar.   BBC Scotland local radio experiment at Dumfries.
27 June   Pilkington Report on Broadcasting published (Cmnd 1753).
1 July   BBC's fourth Royal Charter extended to 29 July 1964.
4 July   Government White Paper on Broadcasting (Cmnd 1770).
17 Dec.   Fort William television and VHF radio relay station opened.
18 Dec.   Government White Paper on Broadcasting (Cmnd 1893).

1963
6 Mar.   BBC celebrated forty years of broadcasting in Scotland.
22 June   Oban television and VHF radio station opened.
31 July   Television Act 1963.

1964
17 Feb.   Studio A at BH Glasgow equipped for dual standard operation brought into service.
26 Feb.   Sir James Duff became BBC Chairman.
25 Mar.   Television Act 1964.
28 Mar.   Radio Caroline, the first offshore pirate radio station, began broadcasting.
15 Apr.   Shetland television and VHF radio relay station opened.
20 Apr.   BBC2 began transmissions in the London area.
14 May   Lord Normanbrook became BBC Chairman.
30 July   BBC's fifth Royal Charter, operational for twelve years.
30 Aug.   BBC introduced the Music Programme on the Third Network.

1965
26 Apr.   Melvaig BBC1 and temporary VHF radio station opened.
27 Sept.   Sandale television transmitter brought into service.
29 Sept.   First party political broadcast on radio and television by the SNP.
30 Nov.   Lady Baird became BBC National Governor for Scotland.
31 Dec.   Pirate station Radio Scotland began broadcasting.

1966
3 Mar.   BBC granted permission by the PMG to introduce colour on BBC2 using the PAL system.
4 Mar.   BBC pamphlet published detailing plans for local radio.
14 Mar.   Skriaig television and VHF radio relay station opened.
28 Mar.   Melvaig permanent VHF radio relay station opened.
9 July   BBC2 arrived in central Scotland from the Blackhill station.
30 July   BBC began regular stereo broadcasts in the Music and Third Programmes from Wrotham.
19 Dec.   Kingussie television and VHF radio station, and Girvan television relay station brought into service.
20 Dec.   Government White Paper on Broadcasting (Cmnd 3169).

1967
15 Feb.   Government agreed to duplication of 625 lines UHF on BBC1 and ITV and for colour to be introduced on this line standard.
8 May   Lochgilphead BBC1 relay station opened.
1 July   BBC2 began regular colour transmissions (not in Scotland).
3 July   Ayr BBC1 relay station opened.
29 July   Durris BBC2 station opened.
14 Aug.   Pirate station Radio Scotland ceased broadcasting.
15 Aug.   Marine etc. Broadcasting (Offences) Act 1967 became law.
1 Sept.   Lord Hill became BBC Chairman.
30 Sept. Start of BBC Radio 1; other network services renamed Radios 2, 3 and 4.
30 Oct.   Blackhill and Durris stations radiated BBC2 colour programmes in Scotland.
8 Nov.   BBC Radio Leicester, the first experimental local radio station, began broadcasting.
2 Dec.   BBC2 colour transmissions extended into a full service.
20 Dec.   Glasgow low-power relay station for Radio 2 opened.
21 Dec.   Edinburgh low-power relay station for Radio 2 opened.
30 Dec.   Ballater BBC1 relay station opened.

1968
1 Jan.   Alasdair Milne became Controller, BBC Scotland; supplementary licence fee of £5 introduced for colour television.

1969
1 Apr.   Charles Curran became BBC Director-General.
10 July   BBC pamphlet *Broadcasting in the Seventies* published outlining plans for network radio and non-metropolitan broadcasting.
28 July   Angus BBC2 station opened.
14 Aug.   Government authorised the BBC to develop local radio on a permanent basis.
1 Oct.   Ministry of Posts and Telecommunications took over responsibility for broadcasting from the Post Office.
27 Oct.   Craigkelly BBC2 station opened.
15 Nov.   Colour television extended to BBC1 and ITV.
13 Dec.   Colour television extended to BBC1 and ITV in Scotland.
29 Dec.   New television studio at Broadcasting House, Edinburgh, opened.

1970
4 Apr.   New BBC network radio structure introduced.
11 July   Rosemarkie BBC2 colour transmissions began.

1971
1 Feb.   Radio-only licence abolished.
29 Mar.   Government White Paper on Broadcasting (Cmnd 4636).
1 May   Lady Avonside became BBC National Governor for Scotland.
16 June   Death of Lord Reith, first Director-General of the BBC.
7 Aug.   Craigkelly BBC1 colour transmissions began.
2 Oct.   Angus BBC1 colour transmissions began.

1972
19 Jan.   Restrictions on hours of broadcasting ceased.
12 June   Sound Broadcasting Act 1972.
2 Sept.   Changes in the BBC's medium-frequency radio services.
1 Nov.   BBC's fiftieth anniversary exhibition opened.
30 Nov.   Report of the Television Advisory Committee 1972.

1973
1 Jan.   Sir Michael Swann became BBC Chairman; Robert Coulter became
            Controller, BBC Scotland.
5–10 Mar.   BBC exhibition at Broadcasting House, Glasgow, to mark fifty years of
            broadcasting in Scotland.
3 May   Crawford Committee on Broadcasting Coverage appointed.
23 May   Independent Broadcasting Authority Act 1973.
8 Oct.   London Broadcasting Company (LBC), Britain's first ILR station, began
            broadcasting.
31 Dec.   Radio Clyde, Scotland's first ILR station, began broadcasting.

1974
1 Jan.   BBC Radio 4 Scotland renamed Radio Scotland.
10 Apr.   Annan Committee on Broadcasting appointed.
17 Apr.   Home Office took over responsibility for broadcasting from the Ministry of
            Posts and Telecommunications.
23 May   Independent Broadcasting Authority Act 1974.
21 Nov.   Crawford Report on Broadcasting Coverage published (Cmnd 5774).

1975
22 Jan.   Radio Forth, Edinburgh ILR station, began broadcasting.

1976
1 Jan.   Alastair Hetherington became Controller, BBC Scotland.
25 Mar.   BBC Radio Highland in Inverness began broadcasting.
19 Apr.   BBC Radio Aberdeen began broadcasting.
1 May   Professor Alan Thompson became BBC National Governor for Scotland.
31 July   BBC's Royal Charter extended to 31 July 1979.

1977
24 Mar.   Annan Report on Broadcasting published (Cmnd 6753).
9 May   BBC Radio Orkney and Radio Shetland began broadcasting.
1 Oct.   Ian Trethowan became BBC Director-General.

1978
14 July   Radio and television studio in Dundee opened.
26 July   Government White Paper on Broadcasting (Cmnd 7294).
31 July   Independent Broadcasting Authority Act 1978.
23 Nov.   BBC Radio Scotland as a separate programme service began broadcasting;
             frequency changes affecting radio networks introduced.

1979
9 May   Patrick Ramsay became Controller, BBC Scotland.
31 July   BBC's Royal Charter extended to 31 July 1981.
5 Oct.   BBC Radio nan Eilean in Stornoway began broadcasting.
20 Oct.   Roger Young became BBC National Governor for Scotland.

1980
28 Feb.   BBC Scotland announced plans for financial economies.
1 Aug.   George Howard became BBC Chairman.
17 Oct.   Radio Tay, Dundee/Perth ILR station, began broadcasting to Dundee.
13 Nov.   Broadcasting Act 1980.
14 Nov.   Radio Tay, Dundee/Perth ILR station, began broadcasting to Perth.
30 Nov.   BBC Scotland pioneered radiovision (the forerunner to breakfast television)
             to celebrate fifty years of broadcasting from Broadcasting House, Edin-
             burgh.

1981
27 July   Northsound Radio, Aberdeen ILR station, began broadcasting.
31 July   BBC's sixth Royal Charter, operational to 31 December 1996.
16 Oct.   Westsound Radio, Ayr ILR station, began broadcasting.
30 Oct.   Broadcasting Act 1981.

1982
23 Feb.   Moray Firth Radio, Inverness ILR station, began broadcasting.
4 Mar.   BBC given approval to operate two satellite services in 1986.
6 Apr.   Hunt Committee on cable expansion appointed.
9 July   Advisory Panel on Direct Broadcasting by Satellite appointed.
12 Oct.   Hunt Report on cable expansion published (Cmnd 8679).
2 Nov.   Channel 4 began broadcasting.
5 Nov.   Report of the Advisory Panel on Direct Broadcasting by Satellite (Cmnd
             8751).

1983
17 Jan.   BBC 'Breakfast Time' television transmissions began.
1 Feb.   ITV TV-am breakfast television transmissions began.
11 Apr.   BBC Radio Tweed in Selkirk began broadcasting.
15 Apr.   BBC Radio Solway in Dumfries began broadcasting.
27 Apr.   Government White Paper on cable systems and services (Cmnd 8866).

Appendix 2

BBC ORGANISATIONAL STRUCTURE

Table A2.1

BBC SCOTLAND ORGANISATIONAL LINKS, 1926

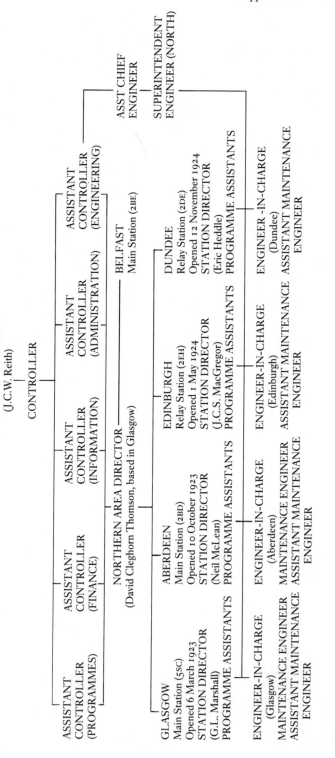

Table A2.2

BBC SCOTLAND ORGANISATIONAL STRUCTURE, 1937

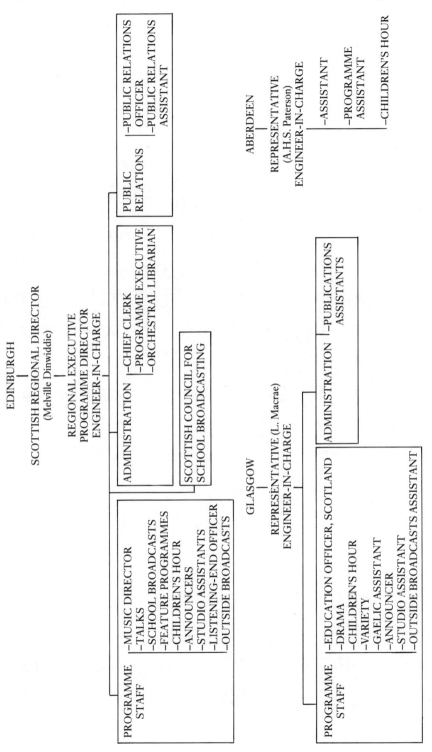

EDINBURGH

SCOTTISH REGIONAL DIRECTOR
(Melville Dinwiddie)

REGIONAL EXECUTIVE
PROGRAMME DIRECTOR
ENGINEER-IN-CHARGE

PROGRAMME STAFF
—MUSIC DIRECTOR
—TALKS
—SCHOOL BROADCASTS
—FEATURE PROGRAMMES
—CHILDREN'S HOUR
—ANNOUNCERS
—STUDIO ASSISTANTS
—LISTENING-END OFFICER
—OUTSIDE BROADCASTS

ADMINISTRATION
—CHIEF CLERK
—PROGRAMME EXECUTIVE
—ORCHESTRAL LIBRARIAN

SCOTTISH COUNCIL FOR SCHOOL BROADCASTING

PUBLIC RELATIONS
—PUBLIC RELATIONS OFFICER
—PUBLIC RELATIONS ASSISTANT

GLASGOW

REPRESENTATIVE (L. Macrae)
ENGINEER-IN-CHARGE

PROGRAMME STAFF
—EDUCATION OFFICER, SCOTLAND
—DRAMA
—CHILDREN'S HOUR
—VARIETY
—GAELIC ASSISTANT
—ANNOUNCER
—STUDIO ASSISTANT
—OUTSIDE BROADCASTS ASSISTANT

ADMINISTRATION
—PUBLICATIONS ASSISTANTS

ABERDEEN

REPRESENTATIVE
(A.H.S. Paterson)
ENGINEER-IN-CHARGE
—ASSISTANT
—PROGRAMME ASSISTANT
—CHILDREN'S HOUR

Table A2.3

BBC SCOTLAND ORGANISATIONAL STRUCTURE, 1942

GLASGOW

SCOTTISH DIRECTOR
(Melville Dinwiddie)

ADMINISTRATIVE OFFICER (SCOTLAND)
ACCOUNTING OFFICER (SCOTLAND)
ASSISTANT PUBLICITY OFFICER (SCOTLAND)

PROGRAMME DIVISION
- SCOTTISH PROGRAMME DIRECTOR
- SCOTTISH MUSIC DIRECTOR
- GAELIC ASSISTANTS
- CHILDREN'S HOUR ORGANISER
- FEATURES AND DRAMA PRODUCERS
- CONDUCTOR
- PROGRAMME ASSISTANT
- PROGRAMME ANNOUNCERS

ENGINEERING DIVISION
- SENIOR ENGINEER, SCOTTISH AREA
- ENGINEER-IN-CHARGE
- ASSISTANT ENGINEER-IN-CHARGE
- LINES ENGINEER
- SENIOR RECORDING ENGINEER-IN-CHARGE
- SENIOR PROGRAMME ENGINEER

EDINBURGH

REPRESENTATIVE AND PUBLICITY OFFICER (SCOTLAND)
(George Burnett)
SECRETARY, SCOTTISH COUNCIL FOR SCHOOL BROADCASTING
EDUCATION OFFICER (SCOTLAND)

HOME DIVISION
- TALKS PRODUCER
- SCHOOL BROADCASTING ASSTS

ENGINEERING DIVISION
- ENGINEER-IN-CHARGE
- ASST ENGINEER-IN-CHARGE

PROGRAMME DIVISION
- FEATURES PRODUCER
- OUTSIDE BROADCASTING ASSISTANT
- PROGRAMME ANNOUNCER

ABERDEEN

REPRESENTATIVE
(A.H.S. Paterson)
- REGISTRY CLERK
- ENGINEER-IN-CHARGE
- ASSISTANT ENGINEER-IN-CHARGE
- PROGRAMME ASSISTANT

Table A2.4

BBC SCOTLAND ORGANISATIONAL STRUCTURE, 1950

GLASGOW
|
CONTROLLER, SCOTLAND
and
SENIOR MANAGEMENT

ENGINEERING DIVISION	–REGIONAL STUDIO ENGINEER, SCOTLAND –ASSISTANT ENGINEER-IN-CHARGE –ASSISTANT TO ENGINEER-IN-CHARGE –AREA LINES ENGINEER –ASSISTANT AREA LINES ENGINEER –SENIOR MAINTENANCE ENGINEER –SENIOR RECORDING ENGINEER-IN-CHARGE
SCHOOL BROADCASTING COUNCIL	|–EDUCATION OFFICER (GLASGOW)

PROGRAMME SERVICES	–HEAD OF SCOTTISH PROGRAMMES –SCOTTISH PROGRAMME EXECUTIVE –HEAD OF SCOTTISH MUSIC –CONDUCTOR –ASSISTANT CONDUCTOR –MUSIC ASSISTANT –DRAMA PRODUCER –FEATURES PRODUCER –GAELIC PRODUCER –GAELIC ASSISTANT –VARIETY PRODUCER –CHILDREN'S HOUR ORGANISER –NEWS EDITOR –NEWS ASSISTANTS –TALKS PRODUCER –OUTSIDE BROADCASTS PRODUCER –RELIGIOUS BROADCASTING ORGANISER –RELIGIOUS BROADCASTING ASSISTANT –ANNOUNCERS –CONDUCTOR (LIGHT ENTERTAINMENT) –RECORDED PROGRAMMES ASSISTANTS –OVERSEAS ASSISTANT –PROGRAMME ASSISTANT –SENIOR PROGRAMME OPERATIONS ASSISTANT

Table A2.4 – *continued*

EDINBURGH

PROGRAMME SERVICES
- ASSISTANT HEAD OF SCOTTISH PROGRAMMES
- FEATURES PRODUCER
- OUTSIDE BROADCASTS PRODUCER
- CHILDREN'S HOUR ASSISTANT
- TALKS PRODUCER
- SCHOOLS ASSISTANTS
- ANNOUNCER
- SENIOR PROGRAMME OPERATIONS ASSISTANT

SCHOOL BROADCASTING COUNCIL
- SECRETARY SBCS AND HEAD OF SCOTTISH SCHOOL BROADCASTING
- ASSISTANT TO SECRETARY (SBCS) AND HEAD OF SCOTTISH SCHOOL BROADCASTING
- ADMINISTRATIVE ASSISTANT
- EDUCATION OFFICER (EDINBURGH)

PUBLICITY
- PUBLICITY OFFICER (SCOTLAND)

ENGINEERING DIVISION
- ENGINEER-IN-CHARGE
- ASSISTANT ENGINEER-IN-CHARGE
- EDUCATION ENGINEER

ABERDEEN

REPRESENTATIVE

PROGRAMME ASSISTANTS

ENGINEERING DIVISION
- ENGINEER-IN-CHARGE
- ASSISTANT ENGINEER-IN-CHARGE

Table A2.5

BBC SCOTLAND ORGANISATIONAL STRUCTURE, 1980

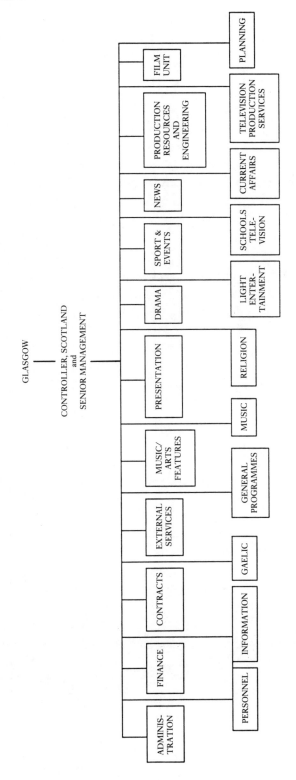

Table A2.5 – *continued*

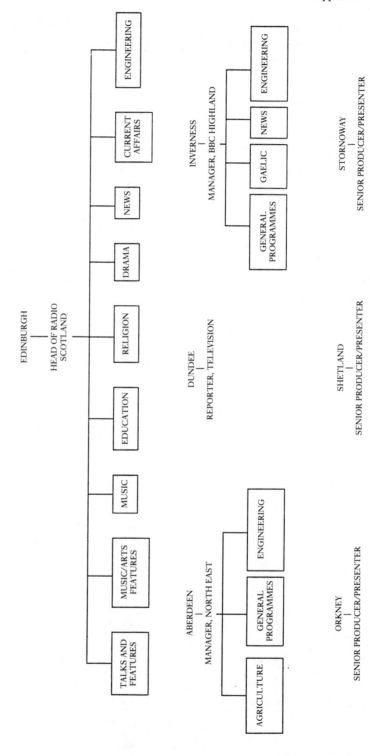

Table A2.6

BBC ORGANISATIONAL LINKS, 1980

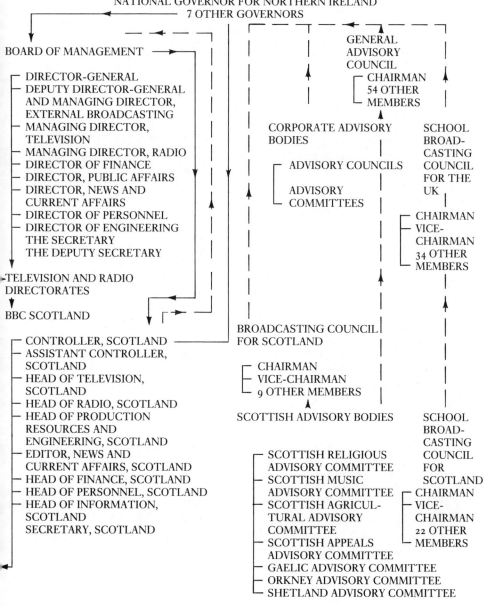

BOARD OF GOVERNORS

CHAIRMAN
VICE-CHAIRMAN
NATIONAL GOVERNOR FOR SCOTLAND
NATIONAL GOVERNOR FOR WALES
NATIONAL GOVERNOR FOR NORTHERN IRELAND
7 OTHER GOVERNORS

BOARD OF MANAGEMENT

- DIRECTOR-GENERAL
- DEPUTY DIRECTOR-GENERAL
  AND MANAGING DIRECTOR,
  EXTERNAL BROADCASTING
- MANAGING DIRECTOR,
  TELEVISION
- MANAGING DIRECTOR, RADIO
- DIRECTOR OF FINANCE
- DIRECTOR, PUBLIC AFFAIRS
- DIRECTOR, NEWS AND
  CURRENT AFFAIRS
- DIRECTOR OF PERSONNEL
- DIRECTOR OF ENGINEERING
  THE SECRETARY
  THE DEPUTY SECRETARY

TELEVISION AND RADIO
DIRECTORATES

BBC SCOTLAND

- CONTROLLER, SCOTLAND
- ASSISTANT CONTROLLER,
  SCOTLAND
- HEAD OF TELEVISION,
  SCOTLAND
- HEAD OF RADIO, SCOTLAND
- HEAD OF PRODUCTION
  RESOURCES AND
  ENGINEERING, SCOTLAND
- EDITOR, NEWS AND
  CURRENT AFFAIRS, SCOTLAND
- HEAD OF FINANCE, SCOTLAND
- HEAD OF PERSONNEL, SCOTLAND
- HEAD OF INFORMATION,
  SCOTLAND
  SECRETARY, SCOTLAND

GENERAL
ADVISORY
COUNCIL
- CHAIRMAN
  54 OTHER
- MEMBERS

CORPORATE ADVISORY
BODIES

- ADVISORY COUNCILS

- ADVISORY
- COMMITTEES

SCHOOL
BROAD-
CASTING
COUNCIL
FOR THE
UK

- CHAIRMAN
- VICE-
  CHAIRMAN
  34 OTHER
- MEMBERS

BROADCASTING COUNCIL
FOR SCOTLAND

- CHAIRMAN
- VICE-CHAIRMAN
- 9 OTHER MEMBERS

SCOTTISH ADVISORY BODIES

- SCOTTISH RELIGIOUS
  ADVISORY COMMITTEE
- SCOTTISH MUSIC
  ADVISORY COMMITTEE
- SCOTTISH AGRICUL-
  TURAL ADVISORY
  COMMITTEE
- SCOTTISH APPEALS
  ADVISORY COMMITTEE
- GAELIC ADVISORY COMMITTEE
- ORKNEY ADVISORY COMMITTEE
- SHETLAND ADVISORY COMMITTEE

SCHOOL
BROAD-
CASTING
COUNCIL
FOR
SCOTLAND
- CHAIRMAN
- VICE-
  CHAIRMAN
  22 OTHER
- MEMBERS

Table A2.7

BBC staff numbers, 1945–84

Year ended 31 March	Full-time Staff	Part-time Staff	Total Staff	Increase or decrease compared to previous year	Percentage change over previous year
1945	10,769	710	11,479	*	*
1946	10,387	540	10,927	−552	−4.8
1947	10,472	619	11,091	164	1.5
1948	10,774	579	11,353	262	2.4
1949	10,963	571	11,534	181	1.6
1950	11,245	603	11,848	314	2.7
1951	11,804	609	12,413	565	4.8
1952	11,912	612	12,524	111	0.9
1953	11,686	591	12,277	−247	−2.0
1954	12,202	632	12,834	557	4.5
1955	12,863	661	13,524	690	5.4
1956	13,810	709	14,519	995	7.4
1957	14,473	769	15,242	723	5.0
1958	14,641	831	15,472	230	1.5
1959	15,236	872	16,108	636	4.1
1960	15,886	1,003	16,889	781	4.8
1961	16,375	1,140	17,515	626	3.7
1962	17,125	887	18,012	497	2.8
1963	17,930	1,010	18,940	928	5.2
1964	19,722	1,114	20,836	1,896	10.0
1965	20,944	1,184	22,128	1,292	6.2
1966	21,539	1,219	22,758	630	2.8
1967	21,653	1,245	22,898	140	0.6
1968	21,680	1,253	22,933	35	0.2
1969	22,493	1,260	23,753	820	3.6
1970	22,641	1,213	23,854	101	0.4
1971	23,671	1,090	24,761	907	3.8
1972	23,863	994	24,857	96	0.4
1973	23,865	1,017	24,882	25	0.1
1974	23,897	1,234	25,131	249	1.0
1975	24,779	1,301	26,080	949	3.8
1976	24,683	1,280	25,963	−117	−0.4
1977	24,453	1,266	25,719	−244	−0.9
1978	24,583	1,305	25,888	169	0.7
1979	25,283	1,350	26,633	745	2.9
1980	26,875	1,098	27,973	1,340	5.0
1981	26,509	1,085	27,594	−379	−1.3
1982	26,846	1,096	27,942	348	1.3
1983	28,002	1,145	29,147	1,205	4.3
1984	28,458	1,214	29,672	525	1.8

Source: BBC Annual Reports and Accounts, 1945–6 to 1983–4.

Notes:

* Staff numbers as at 31 March 1944 were not available, and so absolute and percentage change figures could not be calculated. Figures for staff numbers in Scotland for all years were not available. The total numbers of staff in Scotland as at 31 March 1971 through to 31 March 1990 were as follows: 859 (1971); 883 (1972); 875 (1973); 883 (1974); 937 (1975); 973 (1976); 1,011 (1977); 1,089 (1978); 1,161 (1979); 1,204 (1980); 1,150 (1981); 1,149 (1982); 1,204 (1983); 1,236 (1984); 1,259 (1985); 1,263 (1986); 1,269 (1987); 1,229 (1988); 1,197 (1989); and 1,191 (1990). (Figures for 1971 to 1980: Ian Phillips (BBC Director of Finance) to author, 15 May 1989. Figures for 1981 to 1990: Roger Baxter (BBC Head of Central Finance Services) to author, 14 November 1991.) Some staff figures for Scotland for the period 31 March 1948 to 31 March 1952 were published in the BBC's Annual Report and Accounts for 1951–52 (Cmd 8660). BBC staff lists until about 1966 also included details on staffing levels. However, not all sources include the same categories of BBC staff, and so limitations exist in comparing absolute numbers of staff.

Table A2.8

BBC Scotland: Controllers and National Governors

CONTROLLERS, SCOTLAND

Mr D. Millar Craig was appointed to the post of Assistant Controller, Scotland, in February 1924. This post was replaced by that of Northern Area Director in charge of the Scottish main and relay stations.

David Cleghorn Thomson became Scottish Regional Director on 1 November 1928. This post replaced that of Northern Area Director which Thomson had held since 1926.

Melville Dinwiddie became Scottish Regional Director on 1 September 1933. This post was retitled Controller, Scotland under the administrative reorganisation of 1947. Dinwiddie remained Controller until July 1957.

Andrew Stewart (8 July 1957 to 31 December 1967).

Alasdair Milne (1 January 1968 to 31 December 1972).

Robert Coulter (1 January 1973 to 31 December 1975).

Alastair Hetherington (1 January 1976 to 31 December 1978).

Andrew Todd (temporary Controller) (1 January 1979 to 8 May 1979).

Pat Ramsay (9 May 1979 to April 1983).

Pat Chalmers (April 1983 to January 1992).

NATIONAL GOVERNORS FOR SCOTLAND

Lord Clydesmuir (1 August 1952 to 31 October 1954).

Thomas Johnston (1 January 1955 to 29 June 1956).

Earl of Balfour (1 July 1956 to 26 October 1960).

Sir David Milne (30 November 1960 to 29 November 1965).

Lady Baird (30 November 1965 to 29 November 1970).

Lady Avonside (1 May 1971 to 30 April 1976).

Professor Alan Thompson (1 May 1976 to 31 July 1979).

Dr (later Sir) Roger Young (20 October 1979 to 31 July 1984).

Watson Peat (1 August 1984 to date).

Appendix 3

BBC INCOME AND EXPENDITURE

Table A3.1

Broadcast-receiving licences: Scotland, 1950–85

Year ended 31 March	Radio	Radio and Television combined		Total
		Monochrome	Colour	
1950[1]	1,120,956	12	–	1,120,968
1951[1]	1,119,058	209	–	1,119,267
1952[1]	1,139,927	41,699	–	1,181,626
1953	1,123,583	62,444	–	1,186,027
1954	1,096,079	144,273	–	1,240,352
1955	1,015,709	244,020	–	1,259,729
1956	945,293	348,152	–	1,293,445
1957	842,960	478,432	–	1,321,392
1958	703,475	600,227	–	1,303,702
1959	579,014	750,891	–	1,329,905
1960	462,088	903,111	–	1,365,199
1961	383,379	1,007,716	–	1,391,095
1962	332,583	1,078,247	–	1,410,830
1963	296,340	1,138,270	–	1,434,610
1964	264,923	1,182,176	–	1,447,099
1965	235,183	1,224,696	–	1,459,879
1966	214,799	1,253,122	–	1,467,921
1967	199,300	1,298,500	–	1,497,800
1968	196,468	1,350,056	1,399	1,547,923
1969	183,858	1,376,842	6,104	1,566,804
1970	168,482	1,409,259	13,998	1,591,739
1971	–	1,411,117	35,167	1,446,284
1972	–	1,395,779	95,799	1,491,578
1973	–	1,308,037	221,799	1,529,836
1974	–	1,143,686	433,771	1,577,457
1975	–	961,450	637,046	1,598,496
1976	–	842,602	747,379	1,589,981
1977	–	709,951	915,917	1,625,868
1978	–	599,721	1,030,058	1,629,779
1979	–	509,970	1,136,576	1,646,546
1980	–	434,825	1,206,415	1,641,240
1981	–	392,863	1,279,820	1,672,683
1982	–	343,247	1,305,727	1,648,974
1983	–	299,007	1,335,604	1,634,611
1984	–	255,264	1,391,228	1,646,492
1985	–	227,892	1,417,541	1,645,433

Source: BBC Annual Reports and Accounts 1950–1 to 1965–6 (for licence figures 1950–2 and 1954–66). Post Office (for licence figures 1953). *Scottish Abstract of Statistics* no. 3/1973, table 140, p. 141 (for licence figures 1967). Post Office/National Television Licence Records Office (for licence figures 1968–85).

Notes:

1 Figures for 1950, 1951 and 1952 are as at 31 December.

Figures for 1967 are rounded figures because information on the precise number of licences was not available. Radio-only licences were abolished on 1 February 1971. Combined radio and television licences were also abolished on this date. Thereafter, only television licences were issued. Because of industrial action within the Post Office, the numbers of licences in force as at 31 March 1971 and 31 March 1979 do not reflect the true licensing position at those dates.

Table A3.2

Broadcast-receiving licence fees, 1922–85

	Radio	Radio and Television combined	
		Monochrome	Colour
1 November 1922	10s	–	–
1 June 1946	£1	£2	–
1 June 1954	£1	£3	–
1 August 1957[1]	£1	£4	–
1 October 1963[2]	£1	£4	–
1 August 1965	£1 5s	£5	–
1 January 1968[3]	£1 5s	£5	£10
1 January 1969	£1 5s	£6	£11
1 February 1971[4]	–	£6	£11
1 July 1971	–	£7	£12
1 April 1975[5]	–	£8	£18
29 July 1977	–	£9	£21
25 November 1978	–	£10	£25
24 November 1979	–	£12	£34
1 December 1981	–	£15	£46
1 April 1985	–	£18	£58

Notes:

1 On 1 August 1957, a £1 excise duty was added to the £3 combined licence fee, but this duty was not paid to the BBC. Up until 31 March 1960, the BBC received only a percentage of the licence fee. From 1 April 1961, the BBC received the full proceeds of the licence fee, minus the excise duty.

2 On 1 October 1963, the £1 excise duty was abolished, and so the full £4 combined licence fee was paid to the BBC.

3 A supplementary fee of £5 for colour television receivers was introduced on 1 January 1968 to ensure that the cost of colour programmes would not fall upon all viewers.

4 The Radio-only licence was abolished on 1 February 1971. Combined radio and television licences were also abolished on this date. Thereafter, only television licences were issued.

5 The supplementary fee for colour television receivers was increased to £10 on 1 April 1975, to £12 on 29 July 1977, £15 on 25 November 1978, £22 on 24 November 1979, £31 on 1 December 1981 and to £40 on 1 April 1985.

Table A3.3

BBC Scotland: analysis of income and expenditure, 1955–83

	1955	1960	1965	1970	1975
	£000	£000	£000	£000	£000
INCOME					
1. Receivable from the Postmaster-General/Minister	1,450	2,761	4,848	8,314	12,980
2. Other net income	126	85	102	55	54
3. Total income (1+2)	1,576	2,846	4,950	8,369	13,034
OPERATING EXPENDITURE: RADIO					
4. Gross expenditure in Scotland	601	764	1,004	1,251	1,862
5. Deduct cost of programmes contributed to the networks	59	76	129	174	476
6. Radio expenditure (4–5)	542	688	875	1,077	1,386
7. Scotland's share of network programmes and other costs	609	733	1,041	1,318	3,013
8. Total radio expenditure (6+7)	1,151	1,421	1,916	2,395	4,399
OPERATING EXPENDITURE: TELEVISION					
9. Gross expenditure in Scotland	352	650	1,246	2,082	4,220
10. Deduct cost of programmes contributed to the networks	65	68	146	112	1,338
11. Television expenditure (9–10)	287	582	1,100	1,970	2,882
12. Scotland's share of network programmes and other costs	224	1,109	2,695	4,264	8,860
13. Total television expenditure (11+12)	511	1,691	3,795	6,234	11,742
14. Total operating expenditure (8+13)	1,662	3,112	5,711	8,629	16,141
15. Capital expenditure	331	378	868	986	1,279
16. Total expenditure (14+15)	1,993	3,490	6,579	9,615	17,420
17. Surplus or deficit (−) (3–16)	−417	−644	−1,629	−1,246	−4,386

Table A3.3 – *continued*

	1977	1979	1981	1983
	£m	£m	£m	£m
INCOME				
. Net licence income	20.7	28.6	46.0	61.5
EXPENDITURE				
. The production of Scottish-based programmes for audiences in Scotland....................................	5.8	9.3	14.0	16.7
. Transmission and distribution costs.................	1.8	2.1	3.1	3.7
. Total expenditure (2 + 3)....................................	7.6	11.4	17.1	20.4
. Resources left to pay for capital investment, network programmes and the use of central service departments (1–4)................................	13.1	17.2	28.9	41.1
. If all licensed households contributed equally to these services, the amount required would be	17.3	23.6	38.5	50.9
. Surplus or deficit (−) (5–6)	−4.2	−6.4	−9.6	−9.8

Source: BBC Annual Reports and Accounts, 1954–5 to 1982–3.

Notes:

No BBC Region could support the complete radio and television services it received out of the income arising from the Region, and so each Region is expected to meet the expenditure on its own programme services and to contribute to shared services in accordance with its income receivable from the Postmaster-General/Minister. Income is analysed among the Regions relative to the number of licences in force; capital expenditure is shared in proportion to income.

The format used in the BBC's Annual Accounts for detailing income and expenditure has varied over the years. The format used in the table above has been designed in order to incorporate all the key variables and present these in a consistent format to enable comparisons to be made across the years. A similar analysis, but covering all years from 1951 to 1980, was prepared for my earlier unpublished work on the BBC in Scotland. A modification to the format used in this table has had to be applied to the years 1976–7 to 1982–3 because the BBC's accounts were simplified to a degree which did not permit such direct comparisons with earlier financial years to be made. Ian Phillips, BBC Director of Finance, stated that the changes made in the presentation of statement 6 of the annual accounts in and after 1976–7 were 'intended to provide a simplified and clearer expression of the Regional imbalance between the source of funds and the appropriate sharing of costs in relation to the services available. There were no basic changes in the accounting principles used in sharing costs between the regions, although some of the underlying analysis was also simplified.'

(letter to author, 15 May 1989)

Appendix 4

BBC TRANSMITTING STATIONS AND STUDIO CENTRES

Figure A4.1

Land lines connecting wireless stations, 1927

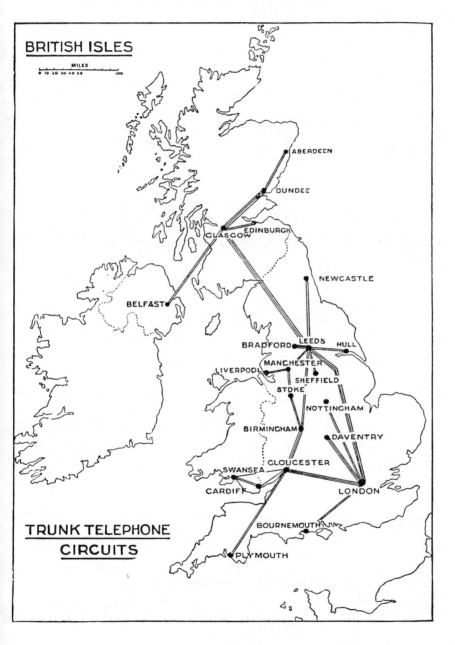

Source: *BBC Handbook 1928*, p. 234.

Figure A4.2

The National Programme Service, 1938

SCOTTISH NATIONAL
MEDIUM-WAVE AUXILIARY
(Westerglen)

NORTH NATIONAL
MEDIUM-WAVE AUXILIARY
(Moorside Edge)

DROITWICH
NATIONAL
LONG-WAVE

LONDON NATIONAL
MEDIUM-WAVE AUXILIARY
Brookmans Park

SCALE OF MILES
0 20 30   100

THE NATIONAL PROGRAMME SERVICE

Source: *BBC Handbook 1939*, p. 108.

Figure A4.3

The Regional Programme Services, 1938

BURGHEAD

ABERDEEN

SCOTTISH
REGIONAL
(Westerglen)

STAGSHAW

NORTHERN
IRELAND
REGIONAL
(Lisnagarvey)

NORTH
REGIONAL
PENMON (Moorside Edge)

MIDLAND
REGIONAL
LONDON
(Droitwich) REGIONAL
(Brookmans Park)

WELSH WEST of ENGLAND
REGIONAL REGIONAL
(Washford)
PLYMOUTH BOURNEMOUTH

SCALE OF MILES
0   40 70 100

START POINT
(under construction)

THE ALTERNATIVE PROGRAMME SERVICE

* Medium-power station in construction at Clevedon, near Bristol.

Source: *BBC Handbook 1939*, p. 109.

Figure A4.4

Long-wave and medium-wave radio transmitting stations, 1984

Source: BBC *Annual Report and Handbook 1985*, p. 228.

Figure A4.5

VHF radio transmitting stations, 1984

Source: BBC *Annual Report and Handbook 1985*, p. 224.

Figure A4.6

Television transmitting stations and Regional boundaries, 1984

Source: BBC *Annual Report and Handbook 1985*, p. 241.

Figure A4.7

BBC Scottish community radio and English local radio services, 1984

Source: BBC *Annual Report and Handbook 1985*, p. 230.

Appendix 5

BBC RADIO AND TELEVISION PROGRAMME OUTPUT

Table A5.1

BBC Scottish programmes: analysis of radio broadcasting output, 1951–83

Year ended 31 March	Scottish Opt-out Programmes (1)	Programmes taken from other networks (2)	Network contributions				Total network contri-butions (7)	Total Scottish Programmes (8)
			Light/ Radios 1/2 (3)	Third/ Radio 3 (4)	Home/ Radio 4 (5)	External Services (6)		
1951	1,493	4,473	88	47	12	253	400	1,893
1952	1,488	4,475	89	58	13	201	361	1,849
1953	1,445	4,525	100	52	14	210	376	1,821
1954	1,490	4,501	114	42	13	198	367	1,857
1955	1,556	4,577	108	51	8	183	350	1,906
1956	1,503	4,565	117	50	14	209	390	1,893
1957	1,436	4,627	105	50	9	215	379	1,815
1958	1,397	4,665	87	48	10	185	330	1,727
1959	1,411	4,722	90	34	7	207	338	1,749
1960	1,446	4,869	138	48	2	243	431	1,877
1961	1,427	4,763	130	66	–	193	389	1,816
1962	1,484	4,725	98	56	–	203	357	1,841
1963	1,511	4,730	111	60	–	193	364	1,875
1964	1,513	4,755	98	56	3	213	370	1,883
1965	1,596	4,866	92	62	11	109	274	1,870
1966	1,597	4,786	136	152	2	107	397	1,994
1967	1,633	4,745	131	143	–	99	373	2,006
1968	1,567	4,829	137	147	–	115	399	1,966
1969	1,574	4,809	146	150	–	132	428	2,002
1970	1,611	4,897	153	175	–	129	457	2,068
1971	1,618	4,786	189	188	–	90	467	2,085
1972	1,600	4,750	129	173	–	88	390	1,990
1973	1,683	–	173	162	67	–	402	2,085
1974	1,750	–	129	201	46	–	376	2,126
1975	2,035	–	92	231	52	–	375	2,410
1976	2,064	–	72	197	48	–	317	2,381
1977	2,539	–	96	130	17	–	243	2,782
1978	3,175	–	146	167	52	–	365	3,540
1979	4,449	–	51	203	59	–	313	4,762
1980	6,723	–	31	176	33	–	240	6,963
1981	6,491	–	7	166	66	–	239	6,730
1982	6,457	–	8	177	71	–	256	6,713
1983	5,452	–	10	181	94	–	285	5,737

Source: BBC Annual Reports and Accounts, 1950–1 to 1982–3.

Notes:
Figures given in the table represent hours of programme output. The Scottish opt-out programmes (column 1) are programmes broadcast only for listeners in Scotland. Figures for hours of programme output taken from other radio networks (column 2) were not available in and after 1972–3. Total hours of output of Scottish programmes (column 8) comprise opt-out programmes (column 1) and network contributions (column 7).

Table A5.2

BBC Scottish programmes: analysis of television broadcasting output, 1953–83

Year ended 31 March	Scottish Opt-out Programmes (1)	Programmes taken from other networks (2)	Network contributions BBC1 (3)	Network contributions BBC2 (4)	Total network contributions (5)	Total Scottish Programmes (6)
1953	–	1,902	28	–	28	28
1954	8	2,031	24	–	24	32
1955	5	2,236	42	–	42	47
1956	11	2,516	58	–	58	69
1957	25	2,647	52	–	52	77
1958	60	2,875	57	–	57	117
1959	148	2,959	61	–	61	209
1960	188	2,991	65	–	65	253
1961	208	3,060	55	–	55	263
1962	193	3,171	64	–	64	257
1963	253	3,154	66	–	66	319
1964	277	3,336	62	–	62	339
1965	359	3,484	1	1	122	481
1966	396	3,582	1	1	107	503
1967	442	3,707	1	1	91	533
1968	444	5,900	1	1	80	524
1969	417	6,110	1	1	77	494
1970	472	6,266	1	1	62	534
1971	422	6,081	1	1	125	547
1972	459	6,541	1	1	63	522
1973	420	–	61	51	112	532
1974	417	–	89	29	118	535
1975	429	–	63	41	104	533
1976	397	–	87	54	141	538
1977	435	–	60	35	95	530
1978	450	–	74	54	128	578
1979	416	–	76	27	103	519
1980	508	–	64	58	122	630
1981	526	–	77	66	143	669
1982	512	–	72	57	129	641
1983	537	–	60	67	127	664

Source: BBC Annual Reports and Accounts, 1952–3 to 1982–3.

Notes:

1 The BBC did not provide a breakdown of Scottish contributions to both television networks until 1972–3; BBC2 did not begin broadcasting until April 1964.

Figures given in the table represent hours of programme output. The Scottish opt-out programmes (column 1) are programmes broadcast only for viewers in Scotland. Figures for hours of output taken from the television networks (column 2) were not available in and after 1972–3. Total hours of output of Scottish programmes (column 6) comprise opt-out programmes (column 1) and network contributions (column 5).

Notes

CHAPTER I

1. 153 HC Deb. ser. 5, col. 1601 (4 May 1922).
2. Ibid.
3. *Wireless Broadcasting Licence* (Cmd 1822; 1923).
4. Board of Directors: Minutes, 21 December 1922, nos 1, 9, BBC Written Archives Centre CO/7/1 (hereafter cited as BBC WAC).
5. *Wireless Broadcasting Licence* (Cmd 1976; 1923), p. 7.
6. Charles Stuart, ed., *The Reith Diaries* (London: Collins, 1975).
7. J.C.W. Reith, *Into the Wind* (London: Hodder and Stoughton, 1949), p. 528.
8. Asa Briggs, 'The BBC's Historian, Asa Briggs, Remembers Lord Reith', *The Listener* vol. 85, no 2204 (24 June 1971), pp. 805–6.
9. J.C.W. Reith, *Broadcast Over Britain* (London: Hodder and Stoughton, 1924), p. 72.
10. *Wireless Broadcasting Licence* (Cmd 1976; 1923), para. 1.
11. 'Daventry Station opened: Future possibilities', *The Times*, 28 July 1925, p. 8.
12. *The Broadcasting Committee: Report* (Cmd 1951; 1923), p. 6.
13. *Report of the Broadcasting Committee, 1925* (Cmd 2599; 1926), pp. 4–5.
14. *Radio Times*, 31 December 1926, p. 5.
15. Asa Briggs, *The History of Broadcasting in the United Kingdom*, vol. 1: *The Birth of Broadcasting* (London: Oxford University Press, 1961), p. 401.

CHAPTER 2

1. A.R. Burrows, *The Story of Broadcasting* (London: Cassell and Company, 1924), p. 155.
2. 'Birthday of 5SC: The first year's work in Glasgow: Developments in the Programmes', *Glasgow Herald*, 6 March 1924, p. 3.
3. 'Scotland: Miss Edwin's Notes', n.d., p. 5, BBC WAC R13/369/1.
4. *Radio Times*, 25 April 1924, p. 205.
5. Board of Governors: Minutes, 16 October 1929, no 68(k), BBC WAC R1/1/1.
6. A.R. Burrows, 'Programme Expenditure', 3 March 1925, p. 1, BBC WAC R3/3/1.
7. Melville Dinwiddie, *The Scot and his Radio: Twenty-Five Years of Scottish Broadcasting* (Edinburgh: BBC, 1948), p. 14.
8. Control Board: Minutes, 17 November 1926, p. 4, BBC WAC R3/3/2.
9. Peter Eckersley, 'Regional Scheme Report', 20 June 1927, BBC WAC R53/207.
10. Control Board: Minutes, 3 July 1928, no 7, BBC WAC R3/3/4.
11. Ibid., 20 November 1928, no 2.
12. Reith to Regional Directors, 25 April 1929, p. 1, BBC WAC R49/571/2.
13. Lord Hill, 'A Labour view of Broadcasting', *The Listener* vol. 92, no 2364 (18 July 1974), pp. 66–7.

14. 216 HC Deb. ser. 5, col. 1327 (30 April 1928).
15. Control Board: Minutes, 14 January 1930, no 8, BBC WAC R3/3/6.

CHAPTER 3

1. 'Broadcasting in Great Britain', *Nature* vol. 117, no 2944 (3 April 1926), pp. 473–4.
2. Sir Oliver Lodge, 'Ten Years of Broadcasting: 1 – The Renaissance of the Twentieth Century', *The Listener* vol. 8, no 201 (16 November 1932), p. 704.
3. Hilda Matheson, *Broadcasting* (London: Thornton Butterworth, 1933), p. 14.
4. J.C.W. Reith, *Into the Wind* (London: Hodder and Stoughton, 1949), p. 99.
5. *BBC Handbook 1928*, p. 34.
6. Reith, *Into the Wind*, p. 101.
7. British Broadcasting Corporation, *BBC 40 Scotland* (Edinburgh: BBC, 1963).
8. Stuart Hood, 'The Corporation', *Encounter* vol. 24, no 4 (April 1965), pp. 76–80.
9. J.C.W. Reith, *Broadcast Over Britain* (London: Hodder and Stoughton, 1924), p. 161.
10. Northern Area Director to Director-General, 31 October 1927, p. 1, BBC WAC R13/369/1.
11. Regional Directors' Meeting: Minutes, 4 March 1937, no 119, BBC WAC R34/735/2.
12. Sir George Barnes, 'Reflections on Television', *BBC Quarterly* vol. 9, no 2 (Summer 1954), pp. 68–9.
13. Controller (Public Relations) to the Scottish National Party, 6 January 1938, BBC WAC R13/369/2.
14. Control Board: Minutes, 18 March 1930, no 1, BBC WAC R3/3/6.
15. Melville Dinwiddie to Director-General, 1 May 1936, BBC WAC R34/731/2.
16. M.G. Farquharson to Mr E. Davies, 20 July 1940, BBC WAC R34/731/3.
17. Melville Dinwiddie to Sir John Reith, 1 August 1933, BBC WAC R13/369/2.
18. Ibid., 1 November 1933, p. 1.
19. Asa Briggs, *The History of Broadcasting in the United Kingdom*, vol. 2: *The Golden Age of Wireless* (London: Oxford University Press, 1965), p. 329.
20. Regional Directors' Meeting: Minutes, 4 May 1934, no 6, BBC WAC R34/735/1.
21. Mark Pegg, *Broadcasting and Society 1918–1939* (London: Croom Helm, 1983), p. 35.
22. Ernest Barker, 'The Constitution of the BBC', *The Listener* vol. 11, no 260 (3 January 1934), p. 13.
23. Regional Programme Directors' Meetings: Minutes, 15 January 1934, no 1, BBC WAC R34/741/1.
24. Paddy Scannell and David Cardiff, 'Serving the Nation: Public Service Broadcasting before the War', in *Popular Culture: Past and Present*, ed. Bernard Waites, Tony Bennett and Graham Martin (London: Croom Helm, 1982), p. 166.
25. 'Report on Regions', January 1936, p. 2, BBC WAC R34/845.
26. *Report of the Broadcasting Committee 1935* (Cmd 5091; 1936), p. 9.
27. 'Decisions on D.R.R.'s Report on the Regions', July 1936, p. 2, BBC WAC R34/845.
28. *Report of the Television Committee* (Cmd 4793; 1935).
29. 297 HC Deb. ser. 5, col. 529 (31 January 1935).
30. *BBC Annual 1936*, p. 149.

CHAPTER 4

1. Asa Briggs, *The History of Broadcasting in the United Kingdom*, vol. 3: *The War of Words* (London: Oxford University Press, 1970), p. 43.
2. *Broadcasting: Agreement between His Majesty's Postmaster-General, the British Broadcasting Corporation, and His Majesty's Minister of Information* (Cmd 6177; 1940).

3. Control Board: Minutes, 27 September 1939, no 787, BBC WAC R3/3/14.
4. Enlarged Control Board: Minutes, 29 September 1939, no 162, BBC WAC R3/5.
5. Home Service Board: Minutes, 17 November 1939, no 86, BBC WAC R3/16/1.
6. Control Board: Minutes, 29 November 1939, no 966, BBC WAC R3/3/14.
7. *Radio Times*, 5 January 1940, p. 5.
8. Home Board: Minutes, 19 July 1940, no 286, BBC WAC R3/16/1.
9. Ibid., 26 July 1940, no 300.
10. 365 HC Deb. ser. 5, *cols 1729–30* (13 November 1940).
11. Special Board Meeting: Minutes, 28 October 1941, no 387, BBC WAC R1/1/9.
12. 'Meeting of Regional Directors to discuss Reorganisation', 22 April 1942, BBC WAC R34/734.
13. P.P. Eckersley, *The Power behind the Microphone* (London: Jonathan Cape, 1941), p. 129.
14. 'Regional Directors' interim proposals for Post-War Development', 18 August 1943, BBC WAC R34/578/2.
15. *BBC Yearbook 1944*, p. 37.
16. *Radio Times*, 25 February 1944, p. 1.
17. Gerald Cock, 'Report on conditions for a Post-War Television Service', 24 January 1944, BBC WAC T16/184.
18. 407 HC Deb. ser. 5, *cols 179–80* (17 January 1945).
19. Regional Directors' Meeting: Minutes, 1 August 1940, no 460, BBC WAC R34/735/3.
20. Ibid., 7 February 1945, no 10 (b)(d), BBC WAC R34/735/4.
21. Board of Governors: Minutes, 22 March 1945, no 58, BBC WAC R1/1/13.
22. Basil Nicolls, 'Post-War Home Programme Set-Up', 23 April 1945, BBC WAC R34/574.

CHAPTER 5

1. Saltire Society, *Broadcasting: A Policy for Future Development in Scotland* (Edinburgh: Saltire Society, 1944).
2. *Radio Times*, 27 July 1945, p. 1.
3. Scottish Director, 'Monthly Report, Scotland', July 1945, no 2, BBC WAC R34/748/2.
4. British Broadcasting Corporation, *This is the Scottish Home Service* (Edinburgh: BBC, 1946).
5. Saltire Society, *Broadcasting: Recommendations of the Saltire Society's Broadcasting Committee, together with comments on the White Paper, and the Reports of Listening Groups on Scottish Broadcast Programmes, January–March 1946* (Edinburgh: Saltire Society, 1946), p. 8.
6. Taped interview with Dr George Bruce, Edinburgh, 11 April 1988.
7. Board of Governors: Paper G.51/46, 4 July 1946, p. 7, BBC WAC R1/3/59.
8. Dyneley Hussey, 'The Third Programme and the Middle-Brow', *BBC Quarterly* vol. 4, no 3 (Autumn 1949), pp. 160–4.
9. 417 HC Deb. ser. 5, col. 1113 (18 December 1945).
10. *Report of the Television Committee 1943* (London: HMSO, 1945), p. 7.
11. *Broadcasting Policy* (Cmd 6852; 1946), p. 21.
12. Gerald Cock to Director-General, 'Report on conditions for a Post-War Television Service', 24 January 1944, p. 5, BBC WAC T16/184.
13. Sir William Haley, 'An Extension of Broadcasting', *BBC Quarterly* vol. 4, no 3 (Autumn 1949), pp. 129–36.
14. Asa Briggs, *The History of Broadcasting in the United Kingdom*, vol. 4: *Sound and Vision* (Oxford: Oxford University Press, 1979), p. 9.

15. Cmd 6852 (1946), p. 6.
16. *Broadcasting: Draft of Royal Charter for the continuance of the British Broadcasting Corporation for which the Postmaster General proposes to apply* (Cmd 6974; 1946), p. 8.
17. Board of Governors: Minutes, 25 July 1946, no 186, BBC WAC R1/1/14.
18. Ibid., 2 October 1946, no 236.
19. Scottish Director to Director-General, 7 September 1946, BBC WAC R6/187.
20. Board of Governors: Minutes, 23 January 1947, no 24, BBC WAC R1/1/15.
21. 'B.B.C. Scottish Advisory Council: Statement by Chairman', c. April 1947, BBC WAC R6/188.
22. Scottish Advisory Council: Minutes, 29 April 1947, no 14, BBC WAC R6/188.
23. *BBC Yearbook 1948*, p. 133.
24. *BBC Staff List*, October 1948, pp. 63–4.
25. 'The Future of Television', *Economist* vol. 157, no 5528 (6 August 1949), p. 288.

CHAPTER 6

1. Board of Management: Minutes, 27 June 1949, no 180(a), BBC WAC R2/1/2.
2. Melville Dinwiddie to W.J. Haley, 25 March 1950, BBC WAC R4/1/3/11.
3. *Report of the Broadcasting Committee, 1949. Appendix H. Memoranda Submitted to the Committee* (Cmd 8117; 1951), p. 156.
4. Ibid., p. 158.
5. Ibid., p. 346.
6. Ibid., p. 441.
7. Ibid., p. 437.
8. Ibid., p. 282.
9. Ibid., p. 365.
10. Ibid., p. 440.
11. Ibid., p. 200.
12. Ibid., p. 364.
13. *Report of the Broadcasting Committee, 1949* (Cmd 8116; 1951), p. 160.
14. Ibid., p. 116.
15. Ibid., p. 84.
16. Ibid., p. 43.
17. Board of Management: Minutes, 22 January 1951, no 19, BBC WAC R2/1/4.
18. 483 HC Deb. ser. 5, cols 119–20 (24 January 1951).
19. Scottish Advisory Council: Minutes, 13 February 1951, no 2, BBC WAC R6/188.
20. Ibid., 12 June 1951, no 6.
21. *Broadcasting: Memorandum on the Report of the Broadcasting Committee, 1949* (Cmd 8291; 1951), p. 4.
22. Ibid., p. 6.
23. 490 HC Deb. ser. 5, col. 1429 (19 July 1951).
24. Ibid., col. 1464.
25. Ibid., col. 1520.
26. Scottish Advisory Council: Minutes, 3 June 1952, p. 3, BBC WAC R6/188.
27. Charles Stuart, ed., *The Reith Diaries* (London: Collins, 1975), p. 484.
28. Lord Beveridge, 'Monopoly and broadcasting', *Political Quarterly* vol. 24, no 4 (October–December 1953), p. 347.

CHAPTER 7

1. 465 HC Deb. ser. 5, col. 1235 (25 May 1949).
2. 467 HC Deb. ser. 5, col. 2951 (30 July 1949).
3. 'Kirk O'Shotts Television Transmitting Station', *Engineering* 171 (29 June 1951), 793.

4. Television Advisory Committee: Minutes, 8 September 1949, no 2(b), BBC WAC T16/208/6.
5. 480 HC Deb. ser. 5, cols 919–20 (8 November 1950).
6. Board of Governors: Paper G.7/52, 11 January 1952, BBC WAC R1/3/96.
7. Board of Governors: Minutes, 20 December 1951, no 255(c), BBC WAC R1/1/19.
8. *Radio Times*, 7 March 1952, p. 5.
9. 'How Television came to Scotland: Promise of 1948 Fulfilled', *Glasgow Herald*, 14 March 1952, p. 4.
10. *British Broadcasting Corporation: Annual Report and Accounts for the Year 1951–52* (Cmd 8660; 1952), p. 37.
11. Scottish Advisory Council: Paper no SAC/5/52, n.d., no 5, BBC WAC R6/188.
12. 'Slow TV sales in Scotland', *Glasgow Herald*, 18 February 1953, p. 4.
13. *British Broadcasting Corporation: Annual Report and Accounts for the Year 1952–53* (Cmd 8928; 1953), p. 26.
14. *BBC Staff List*, April 1952, p. 23.
15. Cmd 8660 (1952), p. 99.
16. Ibid., pp. 102–3.
17. Melville Dinwiddie to Senior Controller, 1 August 1947, BBC WAC R34/731/4.
18. *British Broadcasting Corporation: Annual Report and Accounts for the Year 1950–51* (Cmd 8347; 1951), p. 32.
19. Taped interview with Dr George Bruce, Edinburgh, 11 April 1988.
20. Cmd 8928 (1953), p. 26.
21. Board of Governors: Paper G.93/53, 30 September 1953, para. 5, BBC WAC R1/3/104.
22. *Report of the Broadcasting Committee, 1949. Appendix H. Memoranda Submitted to the Committee* (Cmd 8117; 1951), p. 25.
23. Board of Governors: Minutes, 11 October 1951, no 206(a), BBC WAC R1/1/19.
24. Sir William Haley, 'Home Programme Policy', 15 March 1948, BBC WAC R34/422/1.
25. Board of Governors: Minutes, 25 October 1951, no 211, BBC WAC R1/1/19.
26. Board of Governors: Paper G.84/51, 27 June 1951, p. 8, BBC WAC R1/3/92.
27. 507 HC Deb. ser. 5, *col. 174* (19 November 1952).
28. General Advisory Council: Paper G.A.C. 160, 1 December 1950, p. 3, BBC WAC R6/30/14.
29. 509 HC Deb. ser. 5, cols 39–42 (8 December 1952).
30. 525 HC Deb. ser. 5, *col. 142* (25 March 1954).
31. 514 HC Deb. ser. 5, *col. 100* (29 April 1953).
32. Board of Governors: Minutes, 23 November 1950, no 380, BBC WAC R1/1/18.
33. Sir Edward Appleton, 'The Advantages of V.H.F.', *The Listener* vol. 53, no 1369 (26 May 1955), pp. 925–6.
34. *Second Report of the Television Advisory Committee, 1952* (London: HMSO, 1954), p. 13.
35. 'The Regional Commissions', 15 February 1951, p. 1, BBC WAC R4/1/18.
36. 176 HL Deb. ser. 5, col. 1293 (22 May 1952).
37. Scottish Advisory Council: Paper no SAC/4/52, 3 June 1952, p. 1, BBC WAC R6/188.
38. *Broadcasting: Copy of a New Charter of Incorporation granted to the British Broadcasting Corporation* (Cmd 8605; 1952), p. 9.
39. Ibid., p. 7.
40. Board of Governors: Minutes, 4 September 1952, no 148(b), BBC WAC R1/1/20.
41. Cmd 8605 (1952), p. 10.
42. Controller, Scotland, to Director-General, 2 February 1953, BBC WAC R6/7.

43. Controller, Scotland to Director of Technical Services, 6 November 1953, BBC WAC R6/7.
44. Broadcasting Council for Scotland: Paper no BCS/1/53, 8 January 1953, p. 1, BBC WAC R6/8/1.
45. Cmd 8605 (1952), p. 11.
46. Charles Curran, *A Seamless Robe: Broadcasting – Philosophy and Practice* (London: Collins, 1979), p. 53.
47. Taped interview with John Gray, Edinburgh, 5 April 1988.

CHAPTER 8

1. P.P. Eckersley, *The Power behind the Microphone* (London: Jonathan Cape, 1941).
2. 'The BBC', *Economist* vol. 150, no 5366 (29 June 1946), p. 1036.
3. 'A plan for broadcasting – 1', *Economist* vol. 147, no 5279 (28 October 1944), p. 565.
4. 'A plan for broadcasting – 4', *Economist* vol. 147, no 5282 (18 November 1944), p. 662.
5. R.H. Coase, 'A B.B.C. Enquiry?', *Spectator* vol. 176, no 6149 (3 May 1946), pp. 446–7.
6. *Broadcasting: Draft of Royal Charter for the Continuance of the British Broadcasting Corporation for which the Postmaster General proposes to apply* (Cmd 6974; 1946), p. 3.
7. R.H. Coase, *British Broadcasting: A Study in Monopoly* (London: Longman, 1950), pp. 158–9.
8. John Coatman, 'The Future of the BBC', *Political Quarterly* vol. 21, no 3 (July–September 1950), p. 273.
9. Home Broadcasting Committee: Minutes, 27 September 1949, no 440, BBC WAC R34/414/2.
10. Herbert Morrison, 'Commercial Television: The Argument Examined', *Political Quarterly* vol. 24, no 4 (October–December 1953), p. 342.
11. Ibid., p. 341.
12. Scottish Advisory Council: Minutes, 3 June 1952, p. 4, BBC WAC R6/188.
13. H.H. Wilson, *Pressure Group: The Campaign for Commercial Television* (London: Secker and Warburg, 1961), p. 208.
14. Coase, *British Broadcasting: A Study in Monopoly*, p. 181.
15. J.C.W. Reith and Malcolm Muggeridge, 'Lord Reith in conversation with Malcolm Muggeridge – part two', *The Listener* vol. 78, no 2019 (7 December 1967), p. 744.
16. *Broadcasting: Memorandum on the Report of the Broadcasting Committee, 1949* (Cmd 8550; 1952), p. 3.
17. Board of Governors: Minutes, 13 February 1953, no 40, BBC WAC R1/1/21.
18. 180 HL Deb. ser. 5, *col. 664* (23 February 1953).
19. Briggs, *Sound and Vision*, p. 910.
20. Board of Governors: Minutes, 3 September 1953, no 163, BBC WAC R1/1/21.
21. Board of Governors: Paper G.87/53, 20 August 1953, p. 2, BBC WAC R1/3/104.
22. Board of Management: Minutes, 2 February 1953, no 57, BBC WAC R2/1/7.
23. *Broadcasting: Memorandum on Television Policy* (Cmd 9005; 1953), p. 4.
24. Board of Management: Minutes, 25 January 1954, no 36, BBC WAC R2/1/8.
25. Cmd 9005 (1953), pp. 6–7.
26. Board of Governors: Paper G.6/54, 1 January 1954, p. 2, BBC WAC R1/3/106.
27. D.G.'s Meeting with Regional Controllers: Minutes, 2 December 1953, no 11, BBC WAC R34/733/1.
28. 'Television Aunt', *Economist* vol. 170, no 5768 (13 March 1954), pp. 751–2.
29. *Television Act, 1954* (2 & 3 Eliz. 2, c. 55).

30. *Broadcasting: Copy of the Licence granted on the 6th Day of April 1955, by Her Majesty's Postmaster-General to the Independent Television Authority* (Cmd 9451; 1955), pp. 2–5.
31. Bernard Sendall, *Independent Television in Britain*, vol. 1: *Origin and Foundation, 1946–62* (London: Macmillan Press, 1982), p. 32.
32. Board of Governors: Paper G.10/54, 15 January 1954, p. 2, BBC WAC R1/3/106.
33. Ibid., G.3/55, 23 December 1954, BBC WAC R1/3/111.
34. Hugh Carleton Greene, *The Broadcaster's Responsibility* (London: BBC, 1962), pp. 3–10.
35. Sir Ian Jacob, 'The Tasks before the BBC today', *The Listener* vol. 52, no 1338 (21 October 1954), pp. 661–2.
36. *British Broadcasting Corporation: Annual Report and Accounts for the Year 1954–55* (Cmd 9533; 1955), p. 14.

CHAPTER 9

1. Sir Ian Jacob to Director of Television Broadcasting, 20 September 1955, BBC WAC R34/308/2.
2. 'Cornflour and Cabaret: Commercial TV under way', *Glasgow Herald*, 23 September 1955, p. 7.
3. Board of Governors: Minutes, 29 September 1955, no 195, BBC WAC R1/1/23.
4. Regional Controllers' Meeting: Minutes, 5 October 1955, no 87, BBC WAC R34/733/2.
5. Briggs, *Sound and Vision*, p. 1021.
6. Peter Black, 'A Generation Ago – Peter Black on the rise of Television in the early Fifties', *The Listener* vol. 82, no 2110 (4 September 1969), p. 309.
7. Board of Governors: Minutes, 29 September 1955, no 195, BBC WAC R1/1/23.
8. Ibid., 11 November 1954, no 226, BBC WAC R1/1/22.
9. Grace Wyndham Goldie, *Facing the Nation: Television and Politics 1936–1976* (London: The Bodley Head, 1977), p. 111.
10. Sendall, *Origin and Foundation, 1946–62*, p. 320.
11. Sir Ian Jacob, 'Television Programme Policy', 17 January 1956, BBC WAC T16/435.
12. Lord Thomson of Fleet, *After I was Sixty* (London: Purnell, n.d.), p. 41.
13. Broadcasting Council for Scotland: Minutes, 2 March 1956, no 33, BBC WAC National Broadcasting Council: Scotland, Minutes, 1955–7.
14. Board of Governors: Minutes, 15 March 1956, no 80, BBC WAC R1/1/24.
15. Outside Broadcasts Producer (Television) Glasgow to Head of Scottish Programmes, 22 June 1956, BBC WAC T16/233/2.
16. BBC Scottish Programme Board (Television): Minutes, 6 June 1956, no 168, BBC WAC T16/108/2.
17. Broadcasting Council for Scotland: Minutes, 6 April 1956, no 39(e), BBC WAC National Broadcasting Council: Scotland, Minutes, 1955–7.
18. Ibid., 7 December 1956, no 106(e).
19. Broadcasting Council for Scotland: Paper BCS/24/56, 30 November 1956, BBC WAC National Broadcasting Council: Scotland, Minutes, 1955–7.
20. Ibid., p. 4.
21. 'More Television', *Glasgow Herald*, 31 August 1957, p. 4.
22. *Independent Television Authority: Annual Report and Accounts for the year ended 31st March 1957* (HC 1; 1957), p. 16.
23. Regional Controllers' Meeting: Minutes, 2 September 1959, no 480, BBC WAC R34/733/3.
24. Broadcasting Council for Scotland: Minutes, 4 November 1960, no 115, BBC WAC National Broadcasting Council: Scotland, Minutes, 1960–4.

25. Taped interview with John Gray, Edinburgh, 5 April 1988.
26. *Independent Television Authority: Annual Report and Accounts 1961–62* (HC 3; 1962), p. 2.
27. Hywel Davies, 'The Role of the Regions in British Broadcasting', in BBC *Lunchtime Lectures*, third series, 13 January 1965, p. 7.
28. *British Broadcasting Corporation: Annual Report and Accounts for the Year 1958–59* (Cmnd 834; 1959), p. 29.
29. Gerald Beadle to Director-General, 21 January 1960, p. 2, BBC WAC T16/233/4.
30. 'Control of Television in Scotland and Wales', observations by the Board of Governors, 15 March 1960, para. 12, BBC WAC T16/233/4.
31. *Report of the Broadcasting Committee, 1949* (Cmd 8116; 1951), p. 79.
32. Broadcasting Council for Scotland: Minutes, 28 August 1953, no 54, BBC WAC R6/8/1.
33. British Broadcasting Corporation, VHF. *The BBC's new Sound Broadcasting Service in Scotland* (London: BBC, 1957), p. 5.
34. Broadcasting Council for Scotland: Minutes, 6 December 1957, no 104, BBC WAC National Broadcasting Council: Scotland, Minutes, 1955–7.
35. *British Broadcasting Corporation: Annual Report and Accounts for the Year 1956–57* (Cmnd 267; 1957), p. 24.
36. *British Broadcasting Corporation: Annual Report and Accounts for the Year 1957–58* (Cmnd 533; 1958), p. 28.
37. 570 HC Deb. ser. 5, col. 372 (14 May 1957).
38. E.L.E. Pawley, 'The Technical Problems of Broadcasting. 1. Sharing the Ether', *Engineering* 189 (1 January 1960), 22.
39. Cmd 8347 (1951), p. 32.
40. *British Broadcasting Corporation: Annual Report and Accounts for the Year 1959–60* (Cmnd 1174; 1960), p. 125.
41. Sound Co-ordinating Committee: Minutes, 15 February 1956, p. 2, BBC WAC R34/422/2.
42. 'Sound Broadcasting Future', statement by Director of Sound Broadcasting, 9 April 1957, p. 2, BBC WAC R34/422/3.
43. Regional Controllers' Meeting: Minutes, 5 June 1957, no 195, BBC WAC R34/733/3.
44. Board of Governors: Minutes, 28 March 1957, no 84(b), BBC WAC R1/1/25.
45. Peter Laslett, *The Future of Sound Broadcasting: A Plea for the Third Programme* (Oxford: Basil Blackwell, 1957).
46. Lindsay Wellington, 'Sound Broadcasting Policy and Practice', June 1957, para. 7, BBC WAC R34/1113/3.
47. Cmnd 533 (1958), p. 8.
48. Ibid., p. 27.

CHAPTER 10

1. 'Future of Sound Broadcasting – 1: Will BBC keep its Monopoly?', *The Times*, 4 April 1960, p. 11.
2. *Report of the Committee on Broadcasting, 1960. Volume 1. Appendix E. Memoranda Submitted to the Committee* (Cmnd 1819; 1962), p. 212.
3. *Report of the Committee on Broadcasting, 1960. Volume 2. Appendix E. Memoranda Submitted to the Committee* (Cmnd 1819–1; 1962), p. 1256.
4. Cmnd 1819 (1962), p. 225.
5. Cmnd 1819–1 (1962), p. 938.
6. Broadcasting Council for Scotland, 'The Broadcasting Council for Scotland and Television in Scotland', 10 November 1959, p. 1, BBC WAC T16/233/3.

7. Gerald Beadle to Director-General, 21 January 1960, p. 1, BBC WAC T16/233/4.
8. Broadcasting Council for Scotland: Minutes, 12 May 1961, no 62, BBC WAC National Broadcasting Council: Scotland, Minutes, 1960–4.
9. Cmnd 1819 (1962), p. 322.
10. Basil Nicolls to Director-General, 23 May 1951, no 2(b), BBC WAC R34/422/1.
11. Cmnd 1819–1 (1962), p. 942.
12. Ibid., p. 939.
13. Ibid., p. 934.
14. Ibid., p. 937.
15. Board of Governors: Minutes, 27 June 1962, no 339, BBC WAC R1/1/30.
16. *Report of the Committee on Broadcasting, 1960* (Cmnd 1753; 1962), p. 46.
17. Ibid., p. 66.
18. Ibid., p. 245.
19. Ibid., p. 140.
20. Ibid., p. 139.
21. Ibid., p. 25.
22. Ibid., p. 232.
23. Ibid., p. 225.
24. Ibid., p. 232.
25. Ibid., p. 134–5.
26. Ibid., p. 9.
27. Tom Driberg, 'Pilkington's Purge', *New Statesman* vol. 63, no 1633 (29 June 1962), p. 926.
28. *Broadcasting: Memorandum on the Report of the Committee on Broadcasting, 1960* (Cmnd 1770; 1962), p. 2.
29. Broadcasting Council for Scotland: Minutes, 7 September 1962, no 146(a), BBC WAC National Broadcasting Council: Scotland, Minutes, 1960–4.
30. Cmnd 1770 (1962), pp. 3–4.
31. Ibid., p. 10.
32. *Broadcasting: Further Memorandum on the Report of the Committee on Broadcasting, 1960* (Cmnd 1893; 1962), pp. 4–5.
33. Ibid., p. 10.
34. Asa Briggs, *The BBC: The First Fifty Years* (Oxford: Oxford University Press, 1985), p. 311.

CHAPTER 11

1. *Broadcasting: Copy of Royal Charter for the continuance of the British Broadcasting Corporation* (Cmnd 2385; 1964), p. 10.
2. Broadcasting Council for Scotland: Minutes, 5 October 1962, no 164, BBC WAC National Broadcasting Council: Scotland, Minutes, 1960–4.
3. 'Working Party on Regional contributions to BBC-1', notes of a meeting, 11 December 1962, p. 1, BBC WAC T16/651/1.
4. *British Broadcasting Corporation: Annual Report and Accounts for the Year 1961–62* (Cmnd 1839; 1962), p. 95.
5. Andrew Stewart (Controller, Scotland) to Controller Programme Services, Television, 15 October 1962, p. 2, BBC WAC T16/233/7.
6. 712 HC Deb. ser. 5, col. 813 (13 May 1965).
7. *British Broadcasting Corporation: Annual Report and Accounts for the Year 1963–64* (Cmnd 2503; 1964), p. 130.
8. *British Broadcasting Corporation: Annual Report and Accounts for the Year 1964–65* (Cmnd 2823; 1965), p. 150.
9. *Broadcasting* (Cmnd 3169; 1966), pp. 4–5.

10. *British Broadcasting Corporation: Annual Report and Accounts for the Year 1962–63* (Cmnd 2160; 1963), p. 99.
11. BBC *Staff List*, May 1960, p. 31.
12. BBC *Staff List*, June 1966, pp. 33–34.
13. Board of Governors: Paper G.87/53, 20 August 1953, p. 2, BBC WAC R1/3/104.
14. Board of Management: Minutes, 31 January 1955, no 62, BBC WAC R2/1/10.
15. *British Broadcasting Corporation: Annual Report and Accounts for the Year 1955–56* (Cmd 9803; 1956), p. 8.
16. British Broadcasting Corporation, *The BBC Looks Ahead* (London: BBC, 1958).
17. Sir Ian Jacob, 'Television in the Public Service', *Public Administration* 36 (Winter 1958), 311–18.
18. *Independent Television Authority: Annual Report and Accounts 1960–1961* (HC 52; 1962), p. 6.
19. Cmnd 1770 (1962), p. 6.
20. Broadcasting Council for Scotland: Minutes, 7 September 1962, no 146(c), BBC WAC National Broadcasting Council: Scotland, Minutes, 1960–4.
21. Ibid., 6 July 1962, no 125(b).
22. Ibid., 2 February 1962, no 28.
23. Cmnd 2160 (1963), p. 107.
24. Broadcasting Council for Scotland: Minutes, 6 July 1962, no 126, BBC WAC National Broadcasting Council: Scotland, Minutes, 1960–4.
25. Stuart Hood, 'The Prospect before Us', in BBC *Lunchtime Lectures*, second series, 11 December 1963, p. 7.
26. Cmnd 2160 (1963), pp. 8–9.
27. Michael Peacock (Chief of Programmes, BBC2) to Stuart Hood (Controller Programmes, Television), 7 April 1964, p. 2, BBC WAC T16/315/2.
28. 'Poll shows few BBC2 viewers', *The Times*, 9 June 1964, p. 12.
29. David Attenborough, 'BBC2', in BBC *Lunchtime Lectures*, fourth series, 16 March 1966.
30. *Radio Times*, 7 July 1966, p. 19.
31. Television Advisory Committee: Minutes, 11 February 1954, no 4(a), BBC WAC T16/208/7.
32. *Report of the Television Advisory Committee 1960* (London: HMSO, 1960), p. 13.
33. 632 HC Deb. ser. 5, cols 403–6 (14 December 1960).
34. Cmnd 1819 (1962), p. 122.
35. *Report of the Television Advisory Committee 1967* (London: HMSO, 1968), p. 14.
36. 750 HC Deb. ser. 5, *col. 305* (20 July 1967).

CHAPTER 12

1. Board of Governors: Minutes, 14 January 1960, no 28, BBC WAC R1/1/28.
2. 'Future of Sound Broadcasting – 2: What chance for Local Stations?', *The Times*, 5 April 1960, p. 13.
3. R.D'A. Marriott (Assistant Director of Sound Broadcasting) to Director of Sound Broadcasting, 31 August 1961, p. 3, BBC WAC R34/731/6.
4. Cmnd 1174 (1960), p. 30.
5. 632 HC Deb. ser. 5, cols 406–7 (14 December 1960).
6. Scottish Programme Board: Minutes, 18 December 1961, no 359, BBC WAC T16/108/7.
7. Frank Gillard, 'The Pattern of Regional, Area and Local Broadcasting', 21 August 1961, p. 5, BBC WAC R34/731/6.
8. Cmnd 1839 (1962), p. 24.
9. Hugh Carleton Greene, *The BBC as a Public Service* (London: BBC, 1960), p. 7.

10. Frank Gillard, 'A new dimension of Radio: Local broadcasting', *The Listener* vol. 67, no 1716 (15 February 1962), p. 299.
11. Board of Governors: Minutes, 5 July 1962, no 349, BBC WAC R1/1/30.
12. Cmnd 1893 (1962), p. 10.
13. British Broadcasting Corporation, *Local Radio in the Public Interest: The BBC's Plan* (London: BBC, 1966).
14. *BBC Handbook 1967*, p. 23.
15. *Broadcasting* (Cmnd 3169; 1966), p. 9.
16. Ibid.
17. Cmnd 1770 (1962), p. 4.
18. Cmnd 2823 (1965), p. 30.
19. Ibid., p. 31.
20. Ibid., p. 17.
21. Cmnd 2823 (1965), p. 148.
22. 'Rescuing the BBC', *Economist* vol. 214, no 6343 (20 March 1965), p. 1245.
23. *British Broadcasting Corporation: Annual Report and Accounts for the Year 1965–66* (Cmnd 3122; 1966), p. 12.
24. *Marine, etc., Broadcasting (Offences) Act 1967* (c. 41).
25. Cmnd 3169 (1966), p. 7.
26. *Radio Times*, 28 September 1967, p. 12.
27. Frank Gillard, 'More Music', *The Listener* vol. 78, no 2003 (17 August 1967), p. 194.
28. Benedict Nightingale, 'The Phoney Revolution', *New Society* vol. 10, no 262 (5 October 1967), p. 458.

CHAPTER 13

1. Taped interview with Andrew Stewart, Glasgow, 28 April 1988.
2. Taped interview with John Gray, Edinburgh, 5 April 1988.
3. British Broadcasting Corporation, *This is Local Radio: The BBC Experiment at work* (London: BBC, 1969), p. 4.
4. *Third Report from the Estimates Committee: British Broadcasting Corporation* (HC 387; 1969), p. xxvi.
5. 769 HC Deb. ser. 5, cols 957–8 (25 July 1968).
6. C.J. Curran, *Money, Management and Programmes* (London: BBC, 1970).
7. *British Broadcasting Corporation: Annual Report and Accounts for the Year 1969–70* (Cmnd 4520; 1970), p. 11.
8. HC 387 (1969), p. xii.
9. *BBC Handbook 1969*, p. 184.
10. Richard Hoggart, 'The BBC's duty to society – Part 8', *The Listener* vol. 74, no 1897 (5 August 1965), p. 190.
11. Reith, *Into the Wind*, p. 139.
12. Tom Burns, *The BBC: Public Institution and Private World* (London: Macmillan Press, 1977), p. 106.
13. Ibid., p. 125.
14. Stuart Hood, 'The Prospect before Us', in *BBC Lunchtime Lectures*, second series, 11 December 1963.
15. British Broadcasting Corporation, *Broadcasting in the Seventies: The BBC's Plan for Network Radio and non-Metropolitan Broadcasting* (London: BBC, 1969).
16. Ibid., p. 13.
17. Ibid.
18. *Estimates Committee Sub-Committee D. Minutes of Evidence. Monday, 17 March, 1969: British Broadcasting Corporation* (HC 93-vii; 1969), p. 108.

19. Cmnd 4520 (1970), p. 127.
20. Lord Hill of Luton, *Into the Seventies: Some aspects of Broadcasting in the next decade* (London: BBC, 1969), p. 10.
21. *BBC Handbook 1974*, p. 58.
22. *BBC Handbook 1970*, p. 192.
23. Sendall, *Origin and Foundation, 1946–62*, p. 66.
24. *Independent Television Authority: Annual Report and Accounts 1964–65* (HC 26; 1965), p. 11.
25. Tim Fell, 'The Emasculation of Radio', *New Statesman* vol. 78, no 2022 (12 December 1969), p. 871.
26. John Maddox, 'A Strategy for Broadcasting', *The Listener* vol. 82, no 2124 (11 December 1969), pp. 809–11.
27. 'Policy on Radio Broadcasts: Opposition from staff', *The Times*, 14 February 1970, p. 9.
28. Cmnd 4520 (1970), p. 9.

CHAPTER 14

1. 'Will Radio really be Commercial?', *Economist* vol. 236, no 6631 (26 September 1970), p. 68.
2. Ian Trethowan, 'BBC Radio by the Head of it, Ian Trethowan', *The Listener* vol. 85, no 2180 (7 January 1971), p. 3.
3. 'Local radio: A principle is at stake', *Economist* vol. 237, no 6644 (26 December 1970), p. 16.
4. *An Alternative Service of Radio Broadcasting* (Cmnd 4636; 1971), p. 5.
5. Ibid., p. 7.
6. Frank Gillard, 'The coming of Commercial Radio', *The Listener* vol. 87, no 2241 (9 March 1972), p. 294.
7. *Sound Broadcasting Act 1972* (c. 31).
8. *Independent Broadcasting Authority Act 1973* (c. 19).
9. Hugh Pierce, 'Participatory radio is already here', *The Listener* vol. 88, no 2275 (2 November 1972), p. 584.
10. 'BBC's "arm tied" in competition with local radio', *Glasgow Herald*, 20 September 1972, p. 11.
11. *British Broadcasting Corporation: Annual Report and Accounts for the Year 1971–72* (Cmnd 5111; 1972), p. 109.
12. *Radio Times*, 20/27 December 1973, p. 83.
13. Alasdair Milne, 'Regional devolution and standards of excellence', in *Structures of Broadcasting: A Symposium*, ed. E.G. Wedell (Manchester: Manchester University Press, 1970), pp. 52–60.
14. Alasdair Milne, *DG: The Memoirs of a British Broadcaster* (London: Hodder and Stoughton, 1988), p. 52.
15. Stuart Hood, 'Stern and Wild', *Spectator* vol. 218, no 7238 (17 March 1967), p. 305.
16. *British Broadcasting Corporation: Annual Report and Accounts for the Year 1968–69* (Cmnd 4216; 1969), p. 113.
17. Taped interview with John Gray, Edinburgh, 5 April 1988.
18. System Three (Scotland) Ltd, *Broadcasting in Scotland: A survey of attitudes* (1974).
19. John Caughie, 'Scottish Television: What would it look like?', in *Scotch Reels: Scotland in Cinema and Television*, ed. Colin McArthur (London: British Film Institute, 1982), pp. 112–22.
20. John Gray, 'Broadcasting and Scottish culture', in *A Companion to Scottish Culture*, ed. David Daiches (London: Edward Arnold, 1981), p. 42.

21. Taped interview with Dr Robert McIntyre, Stirling, 7 April 1988.

22. J.G. Kellas, 'Rating Scotland's Television', *Scottish International* (August 1971), p. 17.

23. William H. McDowell, 'The History and Development of BBC Public Service Broadcasting in Scotland, 1952–1980' (PhD thesis, University of Edinburgh, 1990), ch. 3.

24. J.W. Robertson, 'BBC failing in coverage of remote areas', *Glasgow Herald*, 13 March 1970, p. 12.

25. *Television Advisory Committee 1972: Papers of the Technical Sub-Committee* (London: HMSO, 1973), p. 17.

26. Cmnd 4520 (1970), p. 132.

27. Highlands and Islands Development Board: Memorandum to the Committee on Broadcasting Coverage, 1 February 1974, para. 4, Scottish Record Office COM.1/326 (hereafter cited as SRO).

28. *Report of the Committee on Broadcasting Coverage. Chairman: Sir Stewart Crawford* (Cmnd 5774; 1974), p. 15.

29. *Television Advisory Committee 1972: Papers of the Technical Sub-Committee* (London: HMSO, 1973), p. 25.

30. Cmnd 5774 (1974), p. 29.

CHAPTER 15

1. Broadcasting Council for Scotland: Memorandum to the Committee on the Future of Broadcasting, c. June 1975, para. 16, SRO COM.1/101.

2. James Kemp, 'Future of Broadcasting in Scotland', p. 3, SRO COM.1/388.

3. Scottish National Party: Evidence for the Committee on the Future of Broadcasting, n.d., p. 8, SRO COM.1/623.

4. The Labour Party: Scottish Council, 'Evidence to the Annan Commission on Broadcasting', March 1975, p. 2, SRO COM.1/401.

5. Alastair Hetherington: Note for Committee on the Future of Broadcasting, 20 March 1976, p. 6 (of annexe), SRO COM.1/323.

6. Association of Broadcasting Staff (Edinburgh Branch): Submission to Annan Committee, 2 July 1975, p. 2, SRO COM.1/26.

7. Association of Broadcasting Staff: Submission to the Annan Committee on Broadcasting, n.d., para. 22, SRO COM.1/22.

8. Scottish Arts Council: Submission to the Annan Committee on Broadcasting, 21 January 1975, p. 9, SRO COM.1/620.

9. Church of Scotland Committee on Church and Nation, 'Submission to the Annan Commission on Broadcasting', n.d., para. 7, SRO COM.1/167.

10. British Broadcasting Corporation: BBC Memorandum: Choice in Television, February 1975, para. 8, SRO COM.1/87.

11. School Broadcasting Council for Scotland, 'Memorandum of evidence to the Committee on the Future of Broadcasting', n.d., para. 7, SRO COM.1/112.

12. An Comunn Gaidhealach: Submission to the Annan Committee into the Future of Broadcasting, 27 December 1974, para. 12, SRO COM.1/184.

13. Broadcasting Council for Scotland: Memorandum to the Committee on the Future of Broadcasting, c. June 1975, p. 4, SRO COM.1/101.

14. Ibid., p. 5.

15. Scottish National Party: Evidence for the Committee on the Future of Broadcasting, n.d., pp. 7–8, SRO COM.1/623.

16. An Comunn Gaidhealach: Submission to the Annan Committee into the Future of Broadcasting, 27 December 1974, p. 3, SRO COM.1/184.

17. BBC, 'A Summary of Development 1962–1974', n.d., para. 57, SRO COM.1/87.

18. *Report of the Committee on the Future of Broadcasting. Chairman: Lord Annan* (Cmnd 6753; 1977), p. 405.
19. Ibid., p. 406.
20. Ibid., p. 409.
21. Ibid., p. 72.
22. Ibid., p. 405.
23. Ibid., p. 207.
24. Ibid., p. 410.
25. *BBC Handbook 1978*, p. 3.
26. *Broadcasting* (Cmnd 7294; 1978), p. 23.
27. Ibid., p. 13.
28. Ibid., p. 26.

CHAPTER 16

1. 'Report on Regions', January 1936, p. 2, BBC WAC R34/845.
2. *Broadcasting Policy* (Cmd 6852; 1946), p. 6.
3. 'The Regional Commissions', 15 February 1951, p. 1, BBC WAC R4/1/18.
4. *Broadcasting: Memorandum on the Report of the Broadcasting Committee, 1949* (Cmd 8291; 1951), p. 7.
5. *Broadcasting: Copy of a new Charter of Incorporation granted to the British Broadcasting Corporation* (Cmd 8605; 1952), p. 11.
6. Lord Normanbrook, 'The Functions of the BBC's Governors', in *BBC Lunchtime Lectures*, fourth series, 15 December 1965, p. 7.
7. Broadcasting Council for Scotland: Minutes, 7 November 1958, no 119, BBC WAC National Broadcasting Council: Scotland, Minutes, 1958–9.
8. Frank Gillard, 'An Extension of Regional Broadcasting', 28 February 1955, p. 1, BBC WAC R34/731/5.
9. Broadcasting Council for Scotland: Paper BCS/4/54, 18 February 1954, para. 2, BBC WAC R6/8/1.
10. C.J. Curran, *Breaking up the BBC ?* (London: BBC, 1972).
11. *BBC Handbook 1975*, p. 110.
12. Owen Edwards, 'Nation or a Region?', in *BBC Lunchtime Lectures*, eleventh series, 14 December 1976, p. 40.
13. Cmnd 5774 (1974), p. 29.
14. Ibid., p. 36.
15. *BBC Handbook 1977*, p. 17.
16. *Our Changing Democracy: Devolution to Scotland and Wales* (Cmnd 6348; 1975), p. 5.
17. Submission from BBC staff in Aberdeen to the Annan Committee on the Future of Broadcasting, 30 June 1975, p. 1, SRO COM.1/88.
18. Alastair Hetherington: Note for Committee on the Future of Broadcasting, 20 March 1976, p. 1, SRO COM.1/323.
19. Broadcasting Council for Scotland: Memorandum to the Committee on the Future of Broadcasting, c. June 1975, para. 17, SRO COM.1/101.
20. Taped interview with Professor Alastair Hetherington, Stirling, 7 April 1988.
21. *Committee on Scottish Affairs: The BBC cuts in Scotland: Minutes of Evidence Wednesday 2 April 1980* (HC 539; 1980), p. 6.
22. Alastair Hetherington, 'Scotland and the BBC', *New Statesman* vol. 93, no 2412 (10 June 1977), p. 774.
23. *BBC Handbook 1977*, p. 105.
24. Taped interview with Professor Alan Thompson, Edinburgh, 6 May 1988.
25. Scottish Advisory Council: Paper no SAC/8/49, para. 4, BBC WAC R6/188.
26. 'Party Political Broadcasts', 21 July 1958, p. 2, SRO ED.29/5.

27. *British Broadcasting Corporation: Annual Report and Accounts for the Year 1962–63* (Cmnd 2160; 1963), p. 106.
28. *BBC Handbook 1978*, p. 116.
29. *BBC Handbook 1977*, p. 104.
30. *BBC Handbook 1978*, p. 5.
31. Taped interview with Professor Alan Thompson, Edinburgh, 6 May 1988.
32. Taped interview with Professor Alastair Hetherington, Stirling, 7 April 1988.
33. Chris Mullinger, 'London scorn angers Scots BBC Chief', *Scotsman*, 7 September 1978, p. 1.
34. *Broadcasting* (Cmnd 7294; 1978), p. 23.
35. Taped interview with Professor Alan Thompson, Edinburgh, 6 May 1988.

CHAPTER 17

1. *BBC Handbook 1975*, p. 109.
2. Cmnd 5774 (1974), p. 63.
3. Martin MacDonald, 'Gaelic and the Media', *New Edinburgh Review* 33 (1976), 30.
4. *Radio Times*, 1 March 1962, p. 37.
5. Derick S. Thomson, 'Gaelic Scotland', in *Whither Scotland?*, ed. Duncan Glen (London: Victor Gollancz, 1971), p. 148.
6. Cmnd 5774 (1974), p. 36.
7. *Radio Times*, 20–26 March 1976, p. 57.
8. Taped interview with Professor Alastair Hetherington, Stirling, 7 April 1988.
9. *BBC Handbook 1978*, p. 115.
10. Ibid.
11. Taped interview with John Gray, Edinburgh, 5 April 1988.
12. Neal Ascherson, 'Radio Scotland: A frosted window on the world', *Scotsman*, 22 November 1978, p. 13.
13. Taped interview with Professor Alastair Hetherington, Stirling, 7 April 1988.
14. *BBC Handbook 1979*, p. 175.
15. *Radio Times*, 18–24 November 1978, p. 61.
16. John Pickles, 'Radio Scotland: A declaration of faith', *Scotsman*, 8 December 1978, p. 14.
17. Ian Mowatt, 'Why Radio Scotland needs major surgery', *Scotsman*, 16 June 1979, p. 8.
18. *BBC Annual Report and Handbook 1981*, p. 109.
19. 'Problem Station', *Glasgow Herald*, 13 September 1979, p. 6.
20. Patrick Ramsay, 'Radio Scotland: The second blueprint', *Scotsman*, 15 September 1979, p. 8.
21. *BBC Annual Report and Handbook 1981*, p. 78.
22. *Radio Times*, 29 November to 5 December 1980, p. 55.

CHAPTER 18

1. Michael Starks, 'Paying for broadcasting: Public funds for a public service', *Political Quarterly* 56 (October to December 1985), 378.
2. Cmnd 4520 (1970), p. 149.
3. *BBC Handbook 1980*, p. 1.
4. *Committee on Scottish Affairs: The BBC cuts in Scotland: Minutes of Evidence Wednesday 2 April 1980* (HC 539; 1980), p. 13.
5. Ibid., p. 64.
6. Ibid., p. 47.
7. Cmnd 6753 (1977), p. 333.
8. HC 539 (1980), p. 5.

9.   Patrick Ramsay, 'Programme for Survival', *Scotsman*, 8 March 1980, p. 9.
10. Jeremy Isaacs, 'Television in the Eighties', *The Listener* vol. 102, no 2627 (6 September 1979), pp. 298–300.
11. *Broadcasting Act 1980* (c. 64).
12. BBC *Annual Report and Handbook 1984*, p. 2.
13. BBC *Annual Report and Handbook 1985*, p. 97.
14. BBC *Annual Report and Handbook 1982*, p. 64.
15. *Statistics, Technological Developments and Cable Television* (Cmnd 7855; 1980), p. 15.
16. *Report of the Inquiry into Cable Expansion and Broadcasting Policy. Chairman: Lord Hunt of Tanworth* (Cmnd 8679; 1982), p. 3.
17. *The Development of Cable Systems and Services* (Cmnd 8866; 1983), p. 8.
18. Cmnd 6753 (1977), p. 384.
19. Jeremy Isaacs, 'Public Broadcasting in the Eighties', *Journal of the Royal Society of Arts* vol. 131, no 5317 (December 1982), pp. 42–53.

Selected bibliography

The principal source of written archival material for any study on the BBC is to be found at the BBC Written Archives Centre (WAC) at Caversham. The Centre holds thousands of policy and programme files as well as a variety of other useful materials on broadcasting, such as copies of BBC Staff Lists and press cuttings. Some of the files examined for this history of the BBC in Scotland were obtained by the WAC on loan from the BBC Records Centre in London. The unpublished submissions of evidence to the Annan Committee on the Future of Broadcasting can be found at the Scottish Record Office, as can some Scottish Education Department files relating to the BBC in Scotland. The National Library of Scotland holds miscellaneous papers on broadcasting, including papers deposited by the Saltire Society. I have also benefited greatly from the various interviews, some of which were taped, with individuals involved in, or having close connections with, broadcasting in Scotland. This was found to be particularly useful for more recent broadcasting history, where access to unpublished material becomes more difficult. In any case, not all decisions or the reasons for them were put on paper, and so oral history has a part to play in helping to reveal the whole story. A very useful publication which lists a wide range of published material available on broadcasting is *British Broadcasting 1922–1982* by BBC Data Publications (1983). This annotated bibliography contains a number of useful sections covering areas such as the history of broadcasting, Regional and local broadcasting, Government publications and BBC Lunchtime Lectures.

The bibliography in this history of the BBC in Scotland lists all BBC Annual Reports and Accounts, BBC Royal Charters and supplemental Charters, Licences and Agreements, as well as all ITA/IBA Annual Reports and Accounts, Licences and supplemental Licences. In addition to these, there is also a list detailing the reports of all major committees of inquiry into the operation of the domestic broadcasting services, and various other White Papers on broadcasting. There are few reports which are not listed, the main exceptions being some papers relating to the BBC but not directly or indirectly relevant to this study, some papers relating to Independent Broadcasting, and any papers relating to overseas broadcasting. There is also a list of non-parliamentary papers (i.e. papers not presented to Parliament as command papers or House of Commons or House of Lords papers), as well as all Acts of Parliament on the subject of broadcasting. The Annual Reports of the Broadcasting Council for Scotland (BCS) from 1952–3 to 1971–2 can be found in the BBC Annual Reports and Accounts for those years. From 1972–3, these ceased to be published as command papers and were instead incorporated in the *BBC Handbooks* (see below). The Annual Reports of the BCS provide at best a brief overview of policy and programme developments in Scotland, but can be useful as pointers to topics which can be followed up in greater detail using other source material. The BBC's Annual Reports became progressively larger and more detailed over the years, particularly from the early 1950s. As regards House of Commons and House of Lords parliamentary debates, these have been extensively utilised covering the parliamentary sessions since 1920. These official publications also provide an interesting and worthwhile source of additional material on the history of the BBC.

The BBC *Handbooks* are an invaluable source for any study of the BBC, but the format and the range of items covered in these annual publications did, however, vary over the years. This was particularly so with regard to the presentation of statistical data, such as the annual analysis of income and expenditure in Scotland. The BBC *Yearbook 1933* contains a brief summary of broadcasting in Scotland in the early years. The Annual Reports of the BCS from 1972–3 can also be found in the BBC *Handbooks* in and after 1974. Earlier Annual Reports of the BCS were included in the BBC Annual Reports and Accounts which, as noted above, were published as command papers. For programme listings, refer to *Radio Times*.

Although up until now there has been no single standard work on Scottish broadcasting, the books and articles listed in this bibliography contain useful information on both BBC and Independent Broadcasting in general and on Scottish broadcasting. For the UK context of Scottish developments, the best starting point is the four volumes in *The History of Broadcasting in the United Kingdom* by Asa Briggs. These cover the period 1922 to 1955. A fifth volume, covering the years 1955 to 1974, is currently in preparation. The history of Independent Television up to 1980 is covered in four volumes in *Independent Broadcasting in Britain*. Volumes 1 and 2 are written by Bernard Sendall, volumes 3 and 4 by Jeremy Potter. In general, Regional broadcasting is, however, not well covered in books on broadcasting. Some very informative lectures on the practice and philosophy of broadcasting, including some on Regional broadcasting, can be found in the series of BBC *Lunchtime Lectures* covering the period 1962 to 1977. There are also many pamphlets published by the BBC, some on the BBC in Scotland, but these do not provide any detailed analysis of any aspect of Scottish broadcasting.

There are a large number of journals which have published articles on broadcasting. The richest sources for such articles are to be found in *The Listener, Radio Times*, BBC *Quarterly, Broadcast, Economist, New Society, New Statesman, Political Quarterly* and *Public Administration*. Occasionally, an article on Scottish broadcasting can also be found in some Scottish journals such as *Cencrastus, New Edinburgh Review* and *Scottish International*. Several hundred newspaper articles were consulted in the preparation of this history of BBC Scottish broadcasting, although these have not been listed in this bibliography. A condensed list of over seventy newspaper articles was, however, included in my thesis on the history of BBC broadcasting in Scotland (PhD thesis, University of Edinburgh, 1990), on which this present study was to a limited extent based. Newspaper indexes such as the *Glasgow Herald Index, Index to the Times* and the *Scotsman Index* provide a basic guide for locating some relevant articles. Unfortunately, there is no index to *Scotsman* articles prior to 1983. A more comprehensive range of aspects of Scottish broadcasting is covered in newspaper articles than in articles in books and journals, but the quality of these articles does vary very significantly. Those newspapers which were reviewed include the *Scotsman, Glasgow Herald, The Times, Sunday Times* and the *Guardian*.

This bibliography is subdivided into six sections representing different types of primary and secondary source material. Groups 1 to 3 can be classed as primary sources; groups 4 to 6 contain mainly secondary sources with some primary source material. The six broad groups of source material are as follows:

1. Manuscripts and Archival material
2. Official publications
3. Reference sources
4. Books
5. Pamphlets
6. Journal and Periodical articles

I. MANUSCRIPTS AND ARCHIVAL MATERIAL

(A) BBC Written Archives Centre, Caversham Park, Reading, RG4 8TZ

Note: For purposes of simplicity, the list below details in many instances groups of files dealing with a similar subject, rather than individual files. For example, T16/233/1–7 relates to a series of seven consecutive files covering television development in Scotland between 1949 and 1962.

File No	*File Title*
CO/6	British Broadcasting Company: Board of Directors: Correspondence, 1922–9.
CO/7/1–4	British Broadcasting Company: Board of Directors: Minutes, 1922–6.
CO/10	British Broadcasting Company: Experimental and Pioneer Broadcasting, 1922–3.
CO/64	Company Papers: Broadcasting Board: Correspondence, 1923–6.
CO/65	Company Papers: Broadcasting Board: Minutes, 1924.
CO/69	British Broadcasting Company: The Broadcasting Service, 1922–4.
R1/1/1–30	Board of Governors: Minutes, 1927–62.
R1/3/59	Board of Governors: Director-General's Reports and Papers, 1946.
R1/3/81–84	Board of Governors: Director-General's Reports and Papers, 1950.
R1/3/90–92	Board of Governors: Director-General's Reports and Papers, 1951.
R1/3/96	Board of Governors: Director-General's Reports and Papers, 1952.
R1/3/104	Board of Governors: Director-General's Reports and Papers, 1953.
R1/3/106–113	Board of Governors: Director-General's Reports and Papers, 1954–5.
R1/3/117–128	Board of Governors: Director-General's Reports and Papers, 1956–7.
R2/1/2–10	Board of Management: Minutes, 1949–55.
R2/4/2	Board of Management: Papers, 1948.
R3/1	Internal Administrative Committees: Control Board: Correspondence, 1935–41.
R3/3/1–15	Internal Administrative Committees: Control Board: Minutes, 1925–40.
R3/4	Internal Administrative Committees: Control Board (Enlarged Control Board): Correspondence, 1936–49.
R3/5	Internal Administrative Committees: Control Board (Enlarged Control Board): Minutes, 1936–41.
R3/6	Internal Administrative Committees: Control Board (reconstituted Control Board): Minutes, 1941–2.
R3/16/1–2	Internal Administrative Committees: Home Board: Minutes, 1939–41.
R4/1/3/11	Government Committees: Compilation of Evidence – general correspondence. Beveridge Committee, March 1950.
R4/1/10/6	Government Committees: Compilation of Evidence – general correspondence. Beveridge Committee, 1950.
R4/1/18	Government Committees: Beveridge Committee: Recommendations, Governors' comments, February 1951.
R6/7	Advisory Committees: Broadcasting Council for Scotland, 1952–4.
R6/8/1	Advisory Committees: Broadcasting Council for Scotland: Minutes, 1953–4.
*	National Broadcasting Council: Scotland: Minutes, 1955–62. * (three files on loan from BBC Records Centre)
R6/30/14	Advisory Committees: General Advisory Council: Papers, 1949–50.
R6/168	Advisory Committees: School Broadcasting Council for Scotland: Primary Programme Sub-Committee, 1948–54.

R6/169   Advisory Committees: School Broadcasting Council for Scotland:
                  Secondary Programme Sub-Committee, 1948–54.
R6/187   Advisory Committees: Scottish Region: Advisory Council, 1946–52.
R6/188   Advisory Committees: Scottish Region: Advisory Council: Minutes,
                  1947–52.
R13/369/1–3   Departmental: Regions: Scotland, 1926–54.
R13/370   Departmental: Regions: Scotland: Aberdeen, Dundee, Edinburgh,
                  Glasgow, 1924–31.
R34/308/2   Policy: Commercial Television, 1955–9.
R34/402   Policy: The Future of Sound Broadcasting in the domestic services,
                  1957.
R34/403/1–2   Policy: Gaelic Programmes, 1938–47.
R34/414/1–6   Policy: Home Broadcasting Committee: Minutes, 1948–52.
R34/421/1–2   Policy: Home services: General, 1943–59.
R34/422/1–3   Policy: Home Services: Policy, 1948–65.
R34/574   Policy: Post-War Home Programme set-up, 1945.
R34/578/2   Policy: Post-War Planning: general and numbered documents,
                  1943–4.
R34/600/1–13   Policy: Programme Board: Minutes, 1924–45.
R34/730   Policy: Reconstruction, 1942–6.
R34/731/1–6   Policy: Regional Broadcasting, 1923–64.
R34/733/1–4   Policy: Regional Broadcasting: Regional Controllers' Meetings,
                  1948–62.
R34/734   Policy: Regional Directors' Meetings: Correspondence, 1929–47.
R34/735/1–5   Policy: Regional Directors' Meetings: Minutes, 1934–48.
R34/740/1–4   Policy: Regional Programme Directors' Meetings: Correspondence,
                  1936–47.
R34/741/1–5   Policy: Regional Programme Directors' Meetings: Minutes, 1934–47.
R34/748/1–2   Policy: Regions: Monthly Reports, 1943–5.
R34/845   Policy: Report of Director of Regional Relations 1936.
R34/869/1–5   Policy: Scotland: Scottish Programme arrangements, 1933–41.
R34/874/1–4   Policy: Sound Broadcasting, 1926–62.
R34/951/1–2   Policy: Working Party on Sound Broadcasting: Papers, 1956–7.
R34/1020/1–3   Policy: Future of Sound Broadcasting in the domestic services:
                  Programme Planning, 1957.
R34/1021   Policy: Future of Sound Broadcasting in the domestic services: Report,
                  1957.
R34/1113/1–4   Policy: Sound Broadcasting: Reorganisation, 1956–61.
R34/1535   Policy: Scotland: Sound and Television Planning Committee, 1960–2.
R49/571/2   Staff Policy: Regional: Scheme and Centralisation, staff.
R53/207   Technical General: Regional Scheme, 1927–31.
T16/48   Policy: Commercial Television, 1953–60.
T16/83/1–2   Policy: Independent Television, 1953–4.
T16/105/3   Policy: Meetings: Programme Board, 1959.
T16/108/1–7   Policy: Meetings: Scottish Programme Board, Television, 1954–66.
T16/111   Policy: Meetings: Television progress, 1949–52.
T16/184   Policy: Report on conditions for a Post-War Television Service,
                  1944–5.
T16/208/6–7   Policy: Television Advisory Committee: Minutes, 1949–54.
T16/233/1–7   Policy: Television Development: Scotland, 1949–62.
T16/315/1–2   Policy: BBC2, 1958–68.
T16/317   Policy: Broadcasting Councils, 1958–65.

T16/417/1   Policy: Local Radio, 1958–61.
T16/435   Policy: Meetings: Programme Board Papers, 1955–60.
T16/651/1   Policy: Working Party on Regions: Minutes, 1962–7.
T16/652/1   Policy: Working Party on Regions: Papers, 1962–7.

(B) Scottish Record Office, West Register House, Charlotte Square, Edinburgh, EH2

COM.1   Committee on the Future of Broadcasting. Chairman: Lord Annan (several hundred unpublished submissions of evidence to the Committee).
ED.29   Broadcasting, Television and Film files (this series deals generally with radio, television and film policy in Scotland, and schools' broadcasting).

*(C) National Library of Scotland, Department of Manuscripts, George IV Bridge,
Edinburgh,* EH1 1EW

Acc 9393   Saltire Society: Correspondence and papers of, 1936–85.

2. OFFICIAL PUBLICATIONS

(A) Parliamentary Papers

BBC Annual Reports and Accounts

1927 (Cmd 3123; 1928)
1928 (Cmd 3324; 1929)
1929 (Cmd 3599; 1930)
1930 (Cmd 3863; 1931)
1931 (Cmd 4095; 1932)
1932 (Cmd 4277; 1933)
1933 (Cmd 4501; 1934)
1934 (Cmd 4813; 1935)
1935 (Cmd 5088; 1936)
1936 (Cmd 5406; 1937)
1937 (Cmd 5668; 1938)
1938 (Cmd 5951; 1939)
1944–5 (Accounts only) (Cmd 6705; 1945)
1/1/39 to 31/3/44 (Accounts) (Cmd 6758; 1946)
1945–6 (Cmd 6985; 1946)
1946–7 (Cmd 7319; 1948)
1947–8 (Cmd 7506; 1948)
1948–9 (Cmd 7779; 1949)
1949–50 (Cmd 8044; 1950)
1950–1 (Cmd 8347; 1951)
1951–2 (Cmd 8660; 1952)

1952–3 (Cmd 8928; 1953)
1953–4 (Cmd 9269; 1954)
1954–5 (Cmd 9533; 1955)
1955–6 (Cmd 9803; 1956)
1956–7 (Cmnd 267; 1957)
1957–8 (Cmnd 533; 1958)
1958–9 (Cmnd 834; 1959)
1959–60 (Cmnd 1174; 1960)
1960–1 (Cmnd 1503; 1961)
1961–2 (Cmnd 1839; 1962)
1962–3 (Cmnd 2160; 1963)
1963–4 (Cmnd 2503; 1964)
1964–5 (Cmnd 2823; 1965)
1965–6 (Cmnd 3122; 1966)
1966–7 (Cmnd 3425; 1967)
1967–8 (Cmnd 3779; 1968)
1968–9 (Cmnd 4216; 1969)
1969–70 (Cmnd 4520; 1970)
1970–1 (Cmnd 4824; 1971)
1971–2 (Cmnd 5111; 1972)

BBC Royal Charters, including supplemental Charters

Cmd 2756 (1926)
Cmd 5329 (1936)
Cmd 6974 (1946)
Cmd 8416 (1951)
Cmd 8580 (1952)
Cmd 8605 (1952)
Cmnd 1536 (1961)

Cmnd 1724 (1962)
Cmnd 2237 (1963)
Cmnd 2385 (1964)
Cmnd 4096 (1969)
Cmnd 4194 (1969)
Cmnd 5721 (1974)
Cmnd 6469 (1976)

Cmnd 6581 (1976)
Cmnd 7507 (1979)
Cmnd 7568 (1979)
Cmnd 8232 (1981)
Cmnd 8313 (1981)
Cmnd 9013 (1983)

BBC *Licences and Agreements, including supplemental Licences*

Cmd 2756 (1926)	Cmd 8579 (1952)	Cmnd 6468 (1976)
Cmd 5329 (1936)	Cmnd 1537 (1961)	Cmnd 7508 (1979)
Cmd 6975 (1946)	Cmnd 2236 (1963)	Cmnd 8233 (1981)
Cmd 8417 (1951)	Cmnd 4095 (1969)	

ITA *Annual Reports and Accounts*

1954–5 (HC 123; 1955)	1963–4 (HC 316; 1964)
1955–6 (HC 362; 1956)	1964–5 (HC 26; 1965)
1956–7 (HC 1; 1957)	1965–6 (HC 214; 1966)
1957–8 (HC 2; 1958)	1966–7 (HC 120; 1968)
1958–9 (HC 2; 1959)	1967–8 (HC 278; 1969)
1959–60 (HC 1; 1960)	1968–9 (HC 4; 1969)
1960–1 (HC 52; 1962)	1969–70 (HC 177; 1970)
1961–2 (HC 3; 1962)	1970–1 (HC 3; 1971)
1962–3 (HC 276; 1963)	1971–2 (HC 1; 1972)

ITA/IBA *Licences, including supplemental Licences*

Cmd 9106 (1954)	Cmnd 4193 (1969)	Cmnd 7616 (1979)
Cmd 9451 (1955)	Cmnd 5413 (1973)	Cmnd 8467 (1982)
Cmnd 2424 (1964)	Cmnd 6541 (1976)	

Wireless Broadcasting Licence (Cmd 1822; 1923).
The Broadcasting Committee: Report (Cmd 1951; 1923).
Wireless Broadcasting Licence (Cmd 1976; 1923).
Report of the Broadcasting Committee, 1925 (Cmd 2599; 1926).
Wireless Broadcasting Service (Cmd 2755; 1926).
Report of the Television Committee (Cmd 4793; 1935).
Report of the Broadcasting Committee 1935 (Cmd 5091; 1936).
Broadcasting: Memorandum by the Postmaster-General on the Report of the Broadcasting Committee, 1935 (Cmd 5207; 1936).
Broadcasting: Agreement between His Majesty's Postmaster General, the British Broadcasting Corporation, and His Majesty's Minister of Information (Cmd 6177; 1940).
First Report from the Select Committee on Estimates: British Broadcasting Corporation (HC 158; 1946).
Broadcasting Policy (Cmd 6852; 1946).
Report of the Broadcasting Committee, 1949 (Cmd 8116; 1951).
Report of the Broadcasting Committee, 1949. Appendix H. Memoranda submitted to the Committee (Cmd 8117; 1951).
Broadcasting: Memorandum on the Report of the Broadcasting Committee, 1949 (Cmd 8291; 1951).
Broadcasting: Memorandum on the Report of the Broadcasting Committee, 1949 (Cmd 8550; 1952).
Broadcasting: Memorandum on Television Policy (Cmd 9005; 1953).
Broadcasting: Copy of an Agreement dated 28th June 1954, between the Postmaster-General and the British Broadcasting Corporation (Cmd 9196; 1954).
Broadcasting: Copy of an Agreement dated 1st February 1957, between the Postmaster-General and the British Broadcasting Corporation (Cmnd 80; 1957).
Broadcasting: Copy of an Agreement dated 2nd June 1960, between the Postmaster-General and the British Broadcasting Corporation (Cmnd 1066; 1960).
Report of the Committee on Broadcasting, 1960 (Cmnd 1753; 1962).

Broadcasting: Memorandum on the Report of the Committee on Broadcasting, 1960 (Cmnd 1770; 1962).
Report of the Committee on Broadcasting, 1960. Volume 1. Appendix E. Memoranda submitted to the Committee (Cmnd 1819; 1962).
Report of the Committee on Broadcasting, 1960. Volume 2. Appendix E. Memoranda submitted to the Committee (Cmnd 1819–1; 1962).
Broadcasting: Further Memorandum on the Report of the Committee on Broadcasting, 1960 (Cmnd 1893; 1962).
Broadcasting (Cmnd 3169; 1966).
Estimates Committee Sub-Committee D. Minutes of Evidence: 3 to 17 March, 31 March, 5 May, and 11 June 1969: British Broadcasting Corporation (HC 93–v–vii, ix–x, xii; 1969).
Third Report from the Estimates Committee: British Broadcasting Corporation (HC 387; 1969).
An Alternative Service of Radio Broadcasting (Cmnd 4636; 1971).
Second Report from the Select Committee on Nationalised Industries: Independent Broadcasting Authority (HC 465; 1972).
Report of the Committee on Broadcasting Coverage. Chairman: Sir Stewart Crawford (Cmnd 5774; 1974).
Our Changing Democracy: Devolution to Scotland and Wales (Cmnd 6348; 1975).
Report of the Committee on the Future of Broadcasting. Chairman: Lord Annan (Cmnd 6753; 1977).
Broadcasting (Cmnd 7294; 1978).
Statistics, Technological Developments and Cable Television (Cmnd 7855; 1980).
House of Commons Committee on Scottish Affairs: The BBC cuts in Scotland: Minutes of Evidence Wednesday 2 April 1980 (HC 539; 1980).
Independent Review of the Radio Spectrum (30–960 MHz). Interim Report: The Future Use of Television Bands I and III. Chairman: Dr J.H.H. Merriman (Cmnd 8666; 1982).
Report of the Inquiry into Cable expansion and Broadcasting policy. Chairman: Lord Hunt of Tanworth (Cmnd 8679; 1982).
Direct Broadcasting by Satellite: Report of the Advisory Panel on Technical Transmission Standards. Chairman: Sir Anthony Part (Cmnd 8751; 1982).
The Development of Cable Systems and Services (Cmnd 8866; 1983).
Report of the Committee on Financing the BBC. Chairman: Professor Alan Peacock (Cmnd 9824; 1986).

(B) Non-Parliamentary Papers

Report of the Television Committee 1943. London: HMSO, 1945.
First Report of the Television Advisory Committee, 1952. London: HMSO, 1953.
Second Report of the Television Advisory Committee, 1952. London: HMSO, 1954.
Report of the Television Advisory Committee, 1960. London: HMSO, 1960.
Report of the Television Advisory Committee, 1967. London: HMSO, 1968.
Report of the Television Advisory Committee, 1972. London: HMSO, 1972.
Television Advisory Committee 1972: Papers of the Technical Sub-Committee. London: HMSO, 1973.

(C) Parliamentary Debates

House of Commons Debates, sessions 1920 to 1987–8.
House of Lords Debates, sessions 1920 TO 1989–90.

(D) Public General Acts

Wireless Telegraphy Act, 1904 (4 Edw. 7, c. 24).
Wireless Telegraphy Act, 1949 (12 & 13 Geo. 6, c. 54).

Television Act, 1954 (2 & 3 Eliz. 2, c. 55).
Television Act 1963 (c. 50).
Television Act 1964 (c. 21).
Marine, &c., Broadcasting (Offences) Act 1967 (c. 41).
Sound Broadcasting Act 1972 (c. 31).
Independent Broadcasting Authority Act 1973 (c. 19).
Independent Broadcasting Authority Act 1974 (c. 16).
Independent Broadcasting Authority (no 2) Act 1974 (c. 42).
Independent Broadcasting Authority Act 1978 (c. 43).
Independent Broadcasting Authority Act 1979 (c. 35).
Broadcasting Act 1980 (c. 64).
Broadcasting Act 1981 (c. 68).
Cable and Broadcasting Act 1984 (c. 46).

3. REFERENCE SOURCES

BBC *Handbooks 1928 and 1929;* BBC *Yearbooks 1930–1934;* BBC *Annuals 1935–1937;* BBC *Handbooks 1938–1942;* BBC *Yearbooks 1943–1952;* BBC *Handbooks 1955–1980;* and BBC *Annual Reports and Handbooks 1981–1986.* No *Yearbooks* were published for 1953 and 1954. The *Handbooks* for 1974 to 1980 incorporate the Annual Reports and Accounts 1972–3 to 1978–9; the Annual Reports and Accounts prior to 1972–3 were published separately as command papers and are therefore listed in section 2(A) of this bibliography. The *Annual Reports and Handbooks* from 1981 to 1986 incorporate the Annual Reports and Accounts 1979–80 to 1984–5.
Radio Times 1923–83.
BBC *Staff Lists* 1937–9, 1942, 1945–80.
'Broadcast Receiving Licences', 1968–83. (Scottish Regional figures compiled by Post Office/National Television Licence Records Office). Figures for earlier years published in BBC Annual Reports and Accounts.

4. BOOKS

Bakewell, Joan, and Garnham, Nicholas. *The New Priesthood: British Television Today.* London: Allen Lane, 1970.
Baron, Mike. *Independent Radio: The Story of Independent Radio in the United Kingdom.* Lavenham, Suffolk: Terence Dalton, 1975.
BBC. *Scotland 2000: Eight Views on the State of the Nation.* ed. Kenneth Cargill. Glasgow: BBC Scotland, 1987.
Black, Peter. *The Biggest Aspidistra in the World: A Personal Celebration of Fifty Years of the BBC.* London: BBC, 1972.
——. *The Mirror in the Corner: People's Television.* London: Hutchinson, 1972.
Boyle, Andrew. *Only the Wind will Listen: Reith of the BBC.* London: Hutchinson, 1972.
Bridson, D.G. *Prospero and Ariel: The Rise and Fall of Radio: A Personal Recollection.* London: Victor Gollancz, 1971.
Briggs, Asa. *The History of Broadcasting in the United Kingdom.* Vol. 1: *The Birth of Broadcasting.* London: Oxford University Press, 1961.
——. *The History of Broadcasting in the United Kingdom.* Vol. 2: *The Golden Age of Wireless.* London: Oxford University Press, 1965.
——. *The History of Broadcasting in the United Kingdom.* Vol. 3: *The War of Words.* London: Oxford University Press, 1970.

——. *The History of Broadcasting in the United Kingdom.* Vol. 4: *Sound and Vision.* Oxford: Oxford University Press, 1979.

——. *Governing the BBC.* London: BBC, 1979.

——. *The BBC: The First Fifty Years.* Oxford: Oxford University Press, 1985.

Briggs, Susan. *Those Radio Times.* London: Weidenfeld and Nicolson, 1981.

Burnett, George, ed. *Scotland on the Air.* Edinburgh: Moray Press, 1938.

Burns, Tom. *The BBC: Public Institution and Private World.* London: Macmillan Press, 1977.

Burrows, A.R. *The Story of Broadcasting.* London: Cassell and Company, 1924.

Cathcart, Rex. *The Most Contrary Region: The BBC in Northern Ireland 1924–1984.* Belfast: Blackstaff Press, 1984.

Caughie, John. 'Scottish Television: What would it look like?'. In *Scotch Reels: Scotland in Cinema and Television,* ed. Colin McArthur, pp. 112–22. London: British Film Institute, 1982.

Coase, R.H. *British Broadcasting: A Study in Monopoly.* London: Longman, 1950.

Curran, Charles. *A Seamless Robe: Broadcasting – Philosophy and Practice.* London: Collins, 1979.

Eckersley, P.P. *The Power behind the Microphone.* London: Jonathan Cape, 1941.

Falconer, Ronnie. *The Kilt beneath my Cassock.* Edinburgh: Handsel Press, 1978.

Glen, Duncan. 'Nation or Region?' In *Whither Scotland?,* ed. Duncan Glen, pp. 9–24. London: Victor Gollancz, 1971.

Goldie, Grace Wyndham. *Facing the Nation: Television and Politics 1936–1976.* London: The Bodley Head, 1977.

Gorham, Maurice. *Broadcasting and Television since 1900.* London: Andrew Dakers, 1952.

Gray, John. 'Broadcasting and Scottish Culture'. In *A Companion to Scottish Culture,* ed. David Daiches, pp. 38–42. London: Edward Arnold, 1981.

Greene, Sir Hugh. *The Third Floor Front: A View of Broadcasting in the Sixties.* London: Bodley Head, 1969.

Harris, Paul. *Broadcasting from the High Seas: The History of Offshore Radio in Europe 1958–1976.* Edinburgh: Paul Harris Publishing, 1977.

Heller, Caroline. *Broadcasting and Accountability.* London: British Film Institute, 1978.

Hill, Charles. *Behind the Screen: The Broadcasting Memoirs of Lord Hill of Luton.* London: Sidgwick and Jackson, 1974.

Hood, Stuart. *A Survey of Television.* London: Heinemann, 1967.

Hutchison, David. 'Ownership, Finance and Control of the Media'. In *Headlines: The Media in Scotland,* ed. David Hutchison, pp. 78–92. Edinburgh: EUSPB, 1978.

Kellas, James G. *The Scottish Political System.* 2nd ed. Cambridge: Cambridge University Press, 1975.

Kerr, John. 'The Media and Nationalism'. In *Headlines: The Media in Scotland,* ed. David Hutchison, pp. 93–102. Edinburgh: EUSPB, 1978.

Leapman, Michael. *The Last Days of the Beeb.* London: Allen and Unwin, 1986.

Lockerbie, Catherine. 'Radio Scotland: A Short Survey'. In *Scottish Government Yearbook 1987,* ed. David McCrone, pp. 270–82. Edinburgh: Unit for the Study of Government in Scotland, 1987.

Manvell, Roger. *On the Air: A Study of Broadcasting in Sound and Television.* London: Andrew Deutsch, 1953.

Matheson, Hilda. *Broadcasting.* London: Thornton Butterworth, 1933.

Meech, Peter. 'Television in Scotland: A fair day's programming for a fair day's pay?' In *Scottish Government Yearbook 1987,* ed. David McCrone, pp. 257–69. Edinburgh: Unit for the Study of Government in Scotland, 1987.

Milne, Alasdair. 'Regional Devolution and Standards of Excellence'. In *Structures of*

Broadcasting: A Symposium, ed. E.G. Wedell, pp. 52–60. Manchester: Manchester University Press, 1970.

——. *DG: The Memoirs of a British Broadcaster*. London: Hodder and Stoughton, 1988.

Morgan, Janet. 'The BBC and the concept of Public Service Broadcasting'. In *The BBC and Public Service Broadcasting*, ed. Colin MacCabe and Olivia Stewart, pp. 22–31. Manchester: Manchester University Press, 1986.

Negrine, Ralph. 'Great Britain: The end of the Public Service tradition?' In *The Politics of Broadcasting*, ed. Raymond Kuhn, pp. 15–46. London: Croom Helm, 1985.

Pawley, Edward. *BBC Engineering, 1922–1972*. London: BBC, 1972.

Pegg, Mark. *Broadcasting and Society 1918–1939*. London: Croom Helm, 1983.

Potter, Jeremy. *Independent Television in Britain*. Vol. 3: *Politics and Control, 1968–80*. London: Macmillan, 1989.

——. *Independent Television in Britain*. Vol. 4: *Companies and Programmes 1968–80*. Basingstoke: Macmillan, 1990.

Reith, J.C.W. *Broadcast Over Britain*. London: Hodder and Stoughton, 1924.

——. *Into the Wind*. London: Hodder and Stoughton, 1949.

Scannell, Paddy, and Cardiff, David. 'Serving the Nation: Public Service Broadcasting before the War'. In *Popular Culture: Past and Present*, eds Bernard Waites, Tony Bennett and Graham Martin, pp. 161–88. London: Croom Helm, 1982.

——. *A Social History of British Broadcasting*. Vol. 1: 1922–1939: *Serving the Nation*. Oxford: Basil Blackwell, 1991.

Sendall, Bernard. *Independent Television in Britain*. Vol. 1: *Origin and Foundation, 1946–62*. London: Macmillan Press, 1982.

——. *Independent Television in Britain*. Vol. 2: *Expansion and Change, 1958–68*. London: Macmillan, 1983.

Silvey, Robert. *Who's Listening?: The Story of BBC Audience Research*. London: George Allen and Unwin, 1974.

Simon of Wythenshawe, Lord. *The BBC from Within*. London: Victor Gollancz, 1953.

Smith, Anthony, ed. *British Broadcasting*. Newton Abbot: David and Charles, 1974.

——. 'Britain: The Mysteries of a Modus Vivendi'. In *Television and Political Life: Studies in six European Countries*, ed. Anthony Smith, pp. 1–40. London: Macmillan Press, 1979.

Stuart, Charles, ed. *The Reith Diaries*. London: Collins, 1975.

Sturmey, S.G. *The Economic Development of Radio*. London: Gerald Duckworth, 1958.

Thomson, Derick S. 'Gaelic Scotland'. In *Whither Scotland?*, ed. Duncan Glen, pp. 142–9. London: Victor Gollancz, 1971.

Thomson of Fleet, Lord. *After I was Sixty*. London: Purnell, n.d.

Wedell, E.G. *Broadcasting and Public Policy*. London: Michael Joseph, 1968.

Whitehead, Kate. *The Third Programme: A Literary History*. Oxford: Oxford University Press, 1989.

Williams, Bill. 'Broadcasting'. In *Headlines: The Media in Scotland*, ed. David Hutchison, pp. 68–77. Edinburgh: EUSPB, 1978.

Wilson, H.H. *Pressure Group: The Campaign for Commercial Television*. London: Secker and Warburg, 1961.

Windlesham, Lord. *Broadcasting in a Free Society*. Oxford: Basil Blackwell, 1980.

5 . PAMPHLETS

Altman, Wilfred, Thomas, Denis and Sawers, David. *TV: From Monopoly to Competition – and back?* London: Institute of Economic Affairs, 1962.

Attenborough, David. 'BBC2'. in *BBC Lunchtime Lectures*, fourth series, 16 March 1966.

Barton, Michael. 'BBC Radio in the Community'. In BBC *Lunchtime Lectures*, eleventh
   series, 26 October 1976.
Beech, Patrick. 'New Dimensions in Regional Broadcasting'. In BBC *Lunchtime Lectures*,
   eighth series, 19 March 1970.
British Broadcasting Corporation. *Scotland Calling: Notes on forthcoming broadcasts from
   Scottish stations*. London: BBC, 1932.
——. *This is the Scottish Home Service*. Edinburgh: BBC, 1946.
——. *VHF: The BBC's new Sound Broadcasting Service in Scotland*. London: BBC, 1957.
——. *The BBC Looks Ahead*. London: BBC, 1958.
——. *BBC 40 Scotland*. Edinburgh: BBC, 1963.
——. *Local Radio in the Public Interest: The BBC's Plan*. London: BBC, 1966.
——. *This is Local Radio: The BBC experiment at work*. London: BBC, 1969.
——. *Broadcasting in the Seventies: The BBC's plan for Network Radio and Non-Metropolitan
   Broadcasting*. London: BBC, 1969.
——. *Serving Neighbourhood and Nation*. London: BBC, 1977.
——. *Local Radio action stations!* London: BBC, 1979.
BBC Scotland. *Transmitter Development in Scotland*. Glasgow: BBC, 1976.
——. *Broadcasting House Edinburgh 1930–1990*. Edinburgh: BBC, 1990.
Bruce, George. *Notes for a consideration of the ethos and ethics of Broadcasting and of
   British/Scottish Society*. Edinburgh: Nevis Institute, 1977.
Curran, Charles. *Supporting a Public Service*. London: BBC, 1969.
——. *Money, Management and Programmes*. London: BBC, 1970.
——. *Breaking up the BBC?* London: BBC, 1972.
——. *The BBC in the Eighties*. London: BBC, 1972.
Davies, Hywel. 'The Role of the Regions in British Broadcasting'. In BBC *Lunchtime
   Lectures*, third series, 13 January 1965.
Dinwiddie, Melville. *The Scot and his Radio: Twenty-five years of Scottish Broadcasting*.
   Edinburgh: BBC, 1948.
Edwards, Donald. 'Local Radio'. In BBC *Lunchtime Lectures*, sixth series, 24 January
   1968.
Edwards, Owen. 'Nation – or a Region?' In BBC *Lunchtime Lectures*, eleventh series,
   14 December 1976.
Gillard, Frank. 'Sound Radio in the Television Age'. In BBC *Lunchtime Lectures*, second
   series, 11 March 1964.
Greene, Hugh Carleton. *The BBC as a Public Service*. London: BBC, 1960.
——. *The Broadcaster's Responsibility*. London: BBC, 1962.
Haley, Sir William. *The Responsibilities of Broadcasting*. London: BBC, 1948.
Highet, John. *Scotland on the Air: Aspects of Scottish Broadcasting*. Glasgow: University of
   Glasgow, 1949.
Hill of Luton, Lord. *Into the Seventies: Some aspects of Broadcasting in the next decade*.
   London: BBC, 1969.
Hood, Stuart. 'The Prospect before Us'. In BBC *Lunchtime Lectures*, second series,
   11 December 1963.
Laslett, Peter. *The Future of Sound Broadcasting: A Plea for the Third Programme*. Oxford:
   Basil Blackwell, 1957.
Newby, P.H. 'The Third Programme'. In BBC *Lunchtime Lectures*, fourth series,
   20 October 1965.
Normanbrook, Lord. 'The Functions of the BBC's Governors'. In BBC *Lunchtime
   Lectures*, fourth series, 15 December 1965.
Redmond, James. 'Radio and Television Engineering – the next phase'. In BBC
   Lunchtime Lectures, seventh series, 19 March 1969.
Saltire Society. *Broadcasting: A policy for future development in Scotland*. Edinburgh: Saltire
   Society, 1944.

———. *Broadcasting: Recommendations of the Saltire Society's Broadcasting Committee*.
    Edinburgh: Saltire Society, 1946.
Scott, Robin. 'Radio 1 and Radio 2'. In BBC *Lunchtime Lectures*, sixth series, 11 October
    1967.
Sound Broadcasting Society. *Unsound Broadcasting: The case against the BBC's new policy*.
    London: Faber and Faber, 1957.
Swann, Sir Michael. 'The Responsibility of the Governors'. In BBC *Lunchtime Lectures*,
    ninth series, 29 October 1974.
System Three (Scotland) Ltd. *Broadcasting in Scotland: A survey of attitudes*. Gartocharn:
    Fanedram, 1974.
Thorne, Barrie. 'The BBC's finances and cost control'. In BBC *Lunchtime Lectures*, eighth
    series, 22 January 1970.
Trethowan, Ian. 'Radio in the Seventies'. In BBC *Lunchtime Lectures*, eighth series,
    5 March 1970.
Wheldon, Huw. *Competition in Television*. London: BBC, 1971.

6. JOURNAL AND PERIODICAL ARTICLES

'And then came Clyde', *Economist* vol. 250, no 6802 (5 January 1974), p. 26.
Annan, Lord. 'What we were about', *The Listener* vol. 97, no 2507 (5 May 1977), pp.
    585-6.
Appleton, Sir Edward. 'The advantages of VHF', *The Listener* vol. 53, no 1369 (26 May
    1955), pp. 925-6.
'Ariel and Caliban', *Economist* vol. 168, no 5738 (15 August 1953), pp. 431-2.
Barker, Ernest. 'The Constitution of the BBC', *The Listener* vol. 11, no 260 (3 January
    1934), pp. 10-13.
Barnes, Sir George. 'Reflections on Television', *BBC Quarterly* vol. 9, no 2 (Summer
    1954), pp. 65-9.
Barton, Michael. 'Community Radio', *The Listener* vol. 96, no 2482 (4 November 1976),
    pp. 570-1.
'The BBC', *Economist* vol. 150, no 5366 (29 June 1946), pp. 1035-6.
'The BBC scheme for VHF broadcasting', *BBC Quarterly* vol. 6, no 3 (Autumn 1951), pp.
    171-81.
'The BBC's double image', *Economist* vol. 211, no 6295 (18 April 1964), pp. 243-4.
Beveridge, Lord. 'Monopoly and Broadcasting', *Political Quarterly* vol. 24, no 4 (October
    to December 1953), pp. 345-8.
Bishop, H. 'Problems in broadcast engineering', *BBC Quarterly* vol. 6, no 2 (Summer
    1951), pp. 113-21.
Black, Peter. 'A generation ago – Peter Black on the rise of television in the early Fifties',
    The Listener vol. 82, no 2110 (4 September 1969), pp. 306-9.
Briggs, Asa. 'Broadcasting retrospect', *New Society* vol. 1, no 7 (15 November 1962), pp.
    16-17.
———. 'Broadcasting and Society: The social and historical perspective', *The Listener* vol.
    68, no 1756 (22 November 1962), pp. 860-3.
———. 'The BBC's Historian, Asa Briggs, remembers Lord Reith', *The Listener* vol. 85, no
    2204 (24 June 1971), pp. 805-6.
———. 'Problems and possibilities in the writing of broadcasting history', *Media, Culture
    and Society* vol. 2, no 1 (January 1980), pp. 5-13.
'Broadcasting and Television: monopoly or competition?', *Nature* vol. 173, no 4403
    (20 March 1954), pp. 509-12.
'Broadcasting in Great Britain', *Nature* vol. 117, no 2944 (3 April 1926), pp. 473-4.
Coase, R.H. 'A B.B.C. Enquiry?', *Spectator* vol. 176, no 6149 (3 May 1946), pp. 446-7.

Coatman, John. 'The Future of the BBC', *Political Quarterly* vol. 21, no 3 (July to September 1950), pp. 271–9.

——. 'The Constitutional position of the BBC', *Public Administration* vol. 29, no 2 (Summer 1951), pp. 160–72.

Driberg, Tom. 'Pilkington's purge', *New Statesman* vol. 63, no 1633 (29 June 1962), p. 926.

Fell, Tim. 'The emasculation of radio', *New Statesman* vol. 78, no 2022 (12 December 1969), p. 871.

Fraser, Sir Robert. 'Independent Television in Britain', *Public Administration* 36 (Summer 1958), 115–24.

'The Future of Television', *Economist* vol. 157, no 5528 (6 August 1949), pp. 287–8.

Gillard, Frank. 'A new dimension of radio: Local broadcasting', *The Listener* vol. 67, no 1716 (15 February 1962), pp. 299–301.

——. 'More Music', *The Listener* vol. 78, no 2003 (17 August 1967), pp. 193–4.

——. 'The coming of Commercial Radio', *The Listener* vol. 87, no 2241 (9 March 1972), pp. 293–5.

——. 'Green light for Commercial Radio', *The Listener* vol. 87, no 2248 (27 April 1972), pp. 535–6.

Greene, Hugh Carleton. 'Local broadcasting and the local authority', *Public Administration* 39 (Winter 1961), 323–9.

Haley, Sir William. 'An extension of broadcasting', *BBC Quarterly* vol. 4, no 3 (Autumn 1949), pp. 129–36.

Hetherington, Alastair. 'Scotland and the BBC', *New Statesman* vol. 93, no 2412 (10 June 1977), p. 774.

'High-power television in Scotland', *Engineering* 174 (15 August 1952), 204–5.

Hill, Lord. 'A Labour view of broadcasting', *The Listener* vol. 92, no 2364 (18 July 1974), pp. 66–7.

Hoggart, Richard. 'The BBC's duty to society. Part 8', *The Listener* vol. 74, no 1897 (5 August 1965), pp. 189–91.

Hood, Stuart. 'The BBC's second channel', *The Listener* vol. 71, no 1829 (16 April 1964), pp. 611–12.

——. 'The Corporation', *Encounter* vol. 24, no 4 (April 1965), pp. 76–80.

——. 'Stern and Wild', *Spectator* vol. 218, no 7238 (17 March 1967), pp. 304–5.

Hussey, Dyneley. 'The Third programme and the middle-brow', *BBC Quarterly* vol. 4, no 3 (Autumn 1949), pp. 160–4.

Hutchison, David. 'Less Scottish parochialism', *The Listener* vol. 95, no 2445 (19 February 1976), p. 209.

Isaacs, Jeremy. 'Television in the Eighties', *The Listener* vol. 102, no 2627 (6 September 1979), pp. 298–300.

——. 'Public Broadcasting in the Eighties', *Journal of the Royal Society of Arts* vol. 131, no 5317 (December 1982), pp. 42–53.

Jacob, Sir Ian. 'The tasks before the BBC today', *The Listener* vol. 52, no 1338 (21 October 1954), pp. 661–2.

Kellas, J.G. 'Rating Scotland's Television', *Scottish International* (August 1971), pp. 16–17.

'Kirk O'Shotts television transmitting station', *Engineering* 171 (29 June 1951), 793.

'Local Radio: A principle is at stake', *Economist* vol. 237, no 6644 (26 December 1970), p. 16.

Lodge, Sir Oliver. 'Ten years of broadcasting: 1 – The Renaissance of the twentieth century', *The Listener* vol. 8, no 201 (16 November 1932), pp. 703–4.

MacDonald, Martin. 'Gaelic and the Media', *New Edinburgh Review* no 33 (1976), pp. 28–33.

Maddox, John. 'A strategy for broadcasting', *The Listener* vol. 82, no 2124 (11 December 1969), pp. 809–11.

Morrison, Herbert. 'Commercial television: The argument examined', *Political Quarterly* vol. 24, no 4 (October to December 1953), pp. 338–44.

Nightingale, Benedict. 'The Phoney Revolution', *New Society* vol. 10, no 262 (5 October 1967), pp. 458–9.

Pawley, E.L.E. 'The technical problems of broadcasting. 1. Sharing the ether', *Engineering* 189 (1 January 1960), 22–3.

Pierce, Hugh. 'Participatory radio is already here', *The Listener* vol. 88, no 2275 (2 November 1972), pp. 583–4.

'A plan for broadcasting – 1', *Economist* vol. 147, no 5279 (28 October 1944), pp. 564–5.

'A plan for broadcasting – 4', *Economist* vol. 147, no 5282 (18 November 1944), pp. 660–2.

Reith, J.C.W., and Muggeridge, Malcolm. 'Lord Reith in conversation with Malcolm Muggeridge – part two', *The Listener* vol. 78, no 2019 (7 December 1967), pp. 744–7.

'Rescuing the BBC', *Economist* vol. 214, no 6343 (20 March 1965), pp. 1244–5.

'£600,000 expansion for Radio Scotland: 90 jobs to be filled for November air-date', *Broadcast* no 949 (13 February 1978), p. 16.

Smith, Michael Kinchin. 'The BBC: A pioneer public corporation', *Public Administration* 56 (Spring 1978), 25–34.

Starks, Michael. 'Paying for broadcasting: Public funds for a public service', *Political Quarterly* 56 (October to December 1985), 374–85.

Taylor, Doreen. 'Who rules Scotland?', *Broadcast* no 988 (8 January 1979), p. 10.

'Television Aunt', *Economist* vol. 170, no 5768 (13 March 1954), pp. 751–2.

Trethowan, Ian. 'BBC Radio by the Head of it, Ian Trethowan', *The Listener* vol. 85, no 2180 (7 January 1971), p. 3.

——. 'The Future of Radio', *The Listener* vol. 89, no 2301 (3 May 1973), pp. 569–70.

Wharton, W. 'UHF coverage in remote and mountainous areas of the United Kingdom', *BBC Engineering* no 95 (September 1973), pp. 19–23.

Whitehead, Phillip. 'The coming of commercial radio', *The Listener* vol. 84, no 2165 (24 September 1970), pp. 393–5.

'Will radio really be commercial?', *Economist* vol. 236, no 6631 (26 September 1970), pp. 68–9.

Williams, Bill. 'BBC Scotland', *Scottish International* no 6 (April 1969), pp. 56–8.

Index

QUEEN MARGARET COLLEGE
CORSTORPHINE CAMPUS LIBRARY

———

Please return book by date stamped below